For my parents Ruth and Stan Greenblatt, for inviting, tolerating, and eventually fostering my love of the genre.

For my wife and champion Brittany Fraim, who knew I could, before I even tried. Still winning.

Paperback Edition
ISBN-13: 979-8-9995130-0-7
Copyright © 2025 Lowell Greenblatt


Published by Harker Press
**http://HarkerPress.com**
Book Design by Dustin McNeill

# Nightmare AUTOPSIS

## A RETURN TO ELM STREET

**LOWELL GREENBLATT**

# TABLE OF CONTENTS

## DREAM MATTER

## THE FILMS

# INTERVIEWS

# RAISED ON ELM STREET:
## A FOREWORD BY
## NATHAN
## THOMAS
## MILLINER

### FILMMAKER / ARTIST

I started middle school in 1987. My parents had just moved us to the suburbs of Southwest Louisville, Kentucky and, like Jesse Walsh, I was suddenly the new kid at a new school. Being a new kid is always difficult, but sixth grade is a whole other beast.

I had always been a cheerful kid, but as you move into those pre-teen years of life, things change, your peers change, and it can very quickly become "an only the strong survive" existence. I was a quiet, shy, kind-hearted new kid, which meant I was prey. I was artistic (drawing mostly Dungeons and Dragons material), sensitive and soon found myself as an outsider. I fell in with the "headbangers." The long-haired outcasts who wore denim jackets with Iron Maiden back patches and reeked of cigarette smoke. The kids you saw in *The Decline of Western Civilization Part II: The Metal Years*.

And as 1987 moved into 1988, fitting in became problematic. I soon found myself gaining weight, falling into depression and failing in school. I spent many nights crying, asking why people didn't like me. I was a good person. Why can they not see that? I was taken to talk to a therapist and his conclusion was that I was a very serious young man and that I didn't know how to have fun.

I was very unhappy and feeling as if I had no place in the world around me. And when you feel like an outsider, you start searching for where you belong. You start looking for those dark places others won't normally go to. In 1988, those places were heavy metal music, nerd culture, and horror.

My first glimpse of *A Nightmare on Elm Street* and Freddy Krueger was seeing the TV spots on television in 1984. I can still recall the moment Nancy's feet sank into the stairs standing out and staying with me. I was not very versed in scary films at that time. I'd seen *Poltergeist* and *Cujo,* but that was about as far as I'd gone. I wanted no part of *Elm Street* and that weird looking guy with the clawed hand. It didn't help that a year or two later over breakfast, my dad shared with us that he had stayed up late the night before and watched the original *Elm Street* film and relayed us the fact that he dreamt that Freddy stabbed him with said clawed hand through our back screen door!

No thank you, Mr. Craven! You can keep your damn movie away from me.

By 1988, Freddy Krueger was becoming difficult to avoid with the success of the third movie and his growth into the mainstream pop culture world. He appeared on MTV hosting video hours, rocked out in Dokken videos, and killed DJ Jazzy Jeff on a *Fresh Prince* phone call. The boogeyman of Springwood was starting to take a firm grip on me and my imagination. I was curious.

HBO advertised the premiere of *Dream Warriors,* which they were pairing with *Freddy's Revenge* in the Summer of 1988 and I told my mom that I wanted to watch and record them. She said okay and, on that night, a big missing piece of my life was suddenly found.

As I sat there on our couch with my mom, anxious and excited, I saw that school bus picking up students on suburban streets that looked so familiar to me and I saw myself—the outsider boy, Jesse—sitting alone, awkward, and laughed at by the cute girls. I immediately fell under the trap Jack Sholder had unfolded for me. I was hooked! I was quickly becoming a horror fanatic. I didn't realize it just yet, but that evening birthed someone who would grow up to become a fairly well-known horror artist, a horror filmmaker, and commentator. A kid who would grow up to be asked to write a foreword to a book about the *Elm Street* films.

An adolescent Nathan Thomas Milliner rocking a familiar look and a TV listing for the HBO double feature that introduced him to *Elm Street*.

By the time Neil went to bed and the lights inside Kristen's paper mâché 1428 Elm Street house popped on, triggering those first few notes of *Dream Warriors*, I had become a full-blown Fred Head. *The Dream Master* TV spots were airing and I was talking my dad into taking me to see my first Freddy film on the big screen. I wore out the VHS tape that had part two and three on it (along with *Legal Eagles*) and had started drawing Freddy Krueger so often that I'd get into trouble in school, drawing him in class when I should have been learning algebra instead.

I had to draw him from memory or from spare images of him in *Fangoria* most of the time, but I talked my mom into taking me to Waldenbooks at the mall in search of any book on the series they might possibly have in stock. They had nothing, but the guy working there went into their computer and ordered us a copy of a book by Jeffrey Cooper called *The Nightmare on Elm Street Companion*. The book mostly covered the making of the first two films with an overview of the original screenplay for *Dream Warriors*. While it gave me plenty of black and white reference material for drawing everyone's favorite dream stalker, it also laid the seed that would one day lead me to making my ultimate tribute to Wes Craven and the series.

One chapter of Cooper's book was titled *The Life and Death of Freddy Krueger*. Cooper had written the tie-in books for the series and this little piece served as the origin story of the Springwood Slasher. I was completely enthralled by this prequel and certain moments from it stuck with me such as the story of how Freddy killed a boy in an alleyway trying to steal his liquor and the idea of the four bladed glove came to his diseased mind.

While *Freddy's Nightmares* and *Freddy's Dead* gave us prequel material, I never felt they truly did justice not only to Cooper's very sinister short story, but I felt those outings betrayed the character that Wes Craven invented. By 1989 when the TV show came out, the vile, twisted child killer that Craven imagined had been lost to popcorn material where he suddenly had a wife and kid and was, in many ways, the entertaining anti-hero for filmgoers.

My desire to see the Fred Krueger that Craven and Cooper gave me in 1988 is what prompted me to write *The Confession of Fred Krueger*, which sat on a shelf for three years before I finally made it a fan film and my ultimate tribute to them. My goal was to capture the Freddy who had gotten lost through the success of the franchise. Don't get me wrong, I enjoyed all of the Freddy films, but I felt the latter Freddy had made people forget that this character was the villain and not their hero.

I've been fortunate enough to work on many other *Elm Street* projects over the last fifteen years, like illustrating the cover to Thommy Hutson's book *Never Sleep Again*, illustrating several packaging for NECA Freddy action figures and even working with *Elm Street* alumni like Ken Sagoes, Tuesday Knight, Mark Patton and Mick Strawn to name a few. And I'm often asked what was it about *Elm Street* that really resonated with you? I really found the answer which I shared on Mark Patton's wonderful documentary *Scream Queen: My Nightmare on Elm Street*.

In 1988, I was lonely, depressed and bullied, but I found support watching Nancy, Kristen, Taryn, Jesse, Will, Joey, Kincaid, Alice, Rick, and all the other Elm Street children because they showed me how to fight back. Freddy Krueger was the ultimate bully. That's what set him apart from all the other popular horror icons of the era. He preyed on those who were weaker than him. Children. But he gained his power over them out of their fears and insecurities. It was in *Dream Warriors* that Nancy inspired those lost children to dig deep within and find their strength. To find their powers that only they possessed and to use them to overcome the big bully who disappeared when she realized that he was nothing without her fear of him. When she turned her back on her bully and told him he was shit.

When I finally met Robert Englund in 2010, after driving six hours, standing in lines for four hours and running on fumes, having been awake for nearly forty hours straight, I told him what I was doing for a living, working as a horror artist and that I owed it all to him. His wife, Nancy quickly joked that they were sorry about that. Robert was just so wonderful to me as he has been with all of his fans and as I walked away from his booth with my autographed part one glove replica coming full circle, I suddenly became overwhelmed. I felt myself choking up, my breathing unstable, my eyes tearing up and I told my wife, "I need to sit down."

I found a quiet corner in a chair in that hotel lobby in Chicago and allowed myself to be overtaken by the emotions rushing through me. I could have cried my heart out in that moment had I not been in public. The tears, however, did not hold back in 2015 when just a few weeks out from the premiere of my fan film, I got word that Wes Craven had passed away.

I called up my editor, David Bonnell. We had a typical disclaimer at the opening of the film, but I told David with a shaking voice to replace it with a black screen and, using the part one credits font, simply write "For Wes." And then I hung up the phone and that twelve-year old kid in 1988 who stayed up with his mom to fall in love with all things *A Nightmare on Elm Street* allowed himself to truly cry for the great loss that it was. Those tears didn't stop for quite some time. Days even. Wes Craven didn't just make a movie. He told me how to fight. He told me how to face things. He saved my life.


Nathan Thomas Milliner
July 3, 2025

# AWAKENING:
## A WORD
## FROM THE
## AUTHOR

No one chooses their gateway drug. The thing that grabs ahold of them at a formative age and helps to define a major part of their lives. That's why it's a drug. It could be anything. Maybe your jaw hit the floor the first time you saw a home run at a baseball game. Maybe your eyes went wide as you looked at stars through a telescope for the first time. Maybe you heard someone sing and it was so beautiful, you had to follow their voice. Or maybe you saw a movie, like I did. No, it wasn't *Star Wars*. Why is it usually *Star Wars?* Don't bother with the answer. You can find it in countless books, YouTube videos, and fan conventions for the rest of time. There's so much written about how much people love the film series that they love. There's virtually nothing out there about *A Nightmare on Elm Street*.

Ask a horror fan of a certain age, and they'll tell you that the 1980's was the best decade for genre films. It's still a topic of debate today, though many people overlook the fact that a certain style of '80s horror films were still being made in the early '90s. In fact, American pop culture entered the 1990's without changing much, at least until Nirvana unleashed "Smells Like Teen Spirit." There's a sort of "grace period" before grunge, cynicism, and self-referential horror took over. It was in that pop culture no-man's land that I stumbled upon *A Nightmare on Elm Street*. It all started in 1992 with the VHS release of *Freddy's Dead: The Final Nightmare.*

If you're familiar with the *Nightmare on Elm Street* series, I'd bet money you're rolling your eyes. Released in 1991, *Freddy's Dead* was the sixth entry in a series that started out terrifying and slowly became a joke to audiences. But not to me.

It's all Danny Ventura's fault. Danny was a classmate, and until he moved away a few years later, my best friend. He and his brother Rafael came over to my house for a sleepover, and brought the tape, which they rented from Video Encounter, one of several local video stores surviving in the wake of Blockbuster. At six years old, I knew nothing about Freddy Krueger or horror movies. As Danny entered the tape into the VCR, I wondered how one pretends not to be terrified in front of their peers. Should I just smile the whole time? Before I could formulate a plan, the movie started.

But it wasn't scary. It was incredible.

In fact, it lit my imagination on fire. I was drawn in by the humor, danger, special effects, fight scenes, and a Lynchian weirdness I didn't understand, but came to appreciate later when it echoed through Nickelodeon shows of the time. When it was over, a montage of scenes from the series played over the end credits. I ran to get a pen and paper to write down the names of all the previous films with numbers in their titles. Soon after, I went on a journey to see them all, knowing no matter how scary they were purported to be, Freddy *was* dead by the end.

It may seem unfathomable for some, but in an age before streaming, my viewing habits, like many kids my age, were at the mercy of several gods: The availability of tapes at the video store, my parents' (totally understandable) rule of only renting one tape at a time, and TV channels, both local and basic cable, that would rerun films (always censored and edited, but you didn't know and/or care). As a result, I watched the other five entries out of order. If the USA Network cut out the "good stuff," it didn't matter. I was hooked. This was filmmaking, baby! And I wanted to know all about it.

To this day, I remember watching films with my dad and asking him to explain the titles in the opening credits. God love him, he knew "director" and "starring," but I think he made the rest up just for fun. Yes, my father let me watch horror movies before I was out of elementary school, because he knew two very important things: One, I knew it wasn't real, but I was utterly captivated by the idea that people had jobs to make what I was watching on screen. Two, he didn't believe in censorship, but I won't go there because I can hear my mother rolling her eyes. Mom was not happy about my dad's lax viewing rules, but I never had a nightmare, so she couldn't really say anything. Love you, mom.

Yet despite my growing love for these films, I became a fan in a vacuum. There was no internet, no message boards, and even most of the kids at school weren't allowed to watch horror. Sure, we all had the films of Walt Disney, *Power Rangers*, and various other nostalgia hallmarks that are no doubt being rebooted into cash cows as we speak. My inquisitiveness about the behind-the-scenes machinations started a lifetime love of film across many genres, but I always came back to *Nightmare*. It was the seed of my tree of knowledge. I knew a few kids who liked horror movies. Danny also turned me onto *Creepshow 2* (yes, 2), which was also formative for me, but I didn't know anyone who loved the *Nightmare on Elm Street* films like I did. It was a lonely fandom until I got older and connected to others who loved the films, only to discover the fanbase was wildly underserved, yet no less rabid than those of other slasher film franchises.

What are the *Nightmare on Elm Street* films about? Glad you asked, because if you've gotten this far without being familiar, I applaud your patience.

Written and directed by Wes Craven, *A Nightmare on Elm Street* was unleashed in 1984 at the tail end of the slasher craze. The popular horror movies of the time featured silent, masked killers like Michael Myers and Jason Voorhees. Craven made a terrifying film featuring one of the screen's most notorious boogeymen, Freddy Krueger. Portrayed by classically trained actor Robert Englund, Krueger was a child murderer who was arrested but freed on a technicality. A vigilante mob of local parents hunt him down and burn him to death. He returns in the dreams of the remaining children, now teenagers, to finish the job. If he kills you in your dream, you die in real life.

Like the aforementioned cinematic boogeyman, Freddy was defeated at the end of (mostly) every entry, but he always came back, year after year, to take on new casts of teenagers during elaborate set pieces with state-of-the-art practical special effects. His victims weren't faceless cookie cutter-types you'd find in other films, but characters with real problems and afflictions you cared about, which, of course, he would later exploit. Combine that with Englund's consistently iconic performance, and you have a series that changed horror forever. In the pages of this book, I chronicle the first eight films in the series, their highs and lows, the moments that made them, and I even speak to a few people involved. It's time these films had their time in the sun.

To date, the *Nightmare on Elm Street* franchise has yielded nine films and a spinoff television series. This includes six films in the original cycle, a "tribute" film set in a different universe (*New Nightmare*), a team-up film that keeps continuity, but mostly acts as a fun "What if?" (*Freddy vs. Jason*), and a remake from 2010. I will not be covering the remake or the television show for a variety of reasons. Chief among them is the fact that they are not part of a whole. Except for a few episodes, *Freddy's Nightmares* wasn't about Freddy Krueger and wasn't about the Elm Street children. Robert Englund mostly showed up as a "Crypt Keeper" figure to introduce unrelated tales. As for the remake starring Jackie Earle Haley as Freddy, I don't see much value in it. Haley is a fine successor for Englund, but the film seems to exist less to elaborate on the themes that Craven and New Line Cinema birthed, but rather a cash grab featuring actors left to their own devices and taglines lifted wholesale from previous entries. Wes Craven was not consulted, and everyone involved, even those who made it, wish to pretend it didn't happen. I grant them their wish.

On that note, drink your coffee, blast your music, grab your Hypnocil, hug your stuffed animal, or whatever it is you need to do to stay awake. We're going back to Elm Street, so whatever you do... *don't fall asleep*.

Lowell Greenblatt
February 14, 2025

"To surrender dreams — this may be madness."

-Don Quixote


"Being dead wasn't a problem. But being forgotten?
Now that's a bitch."

-Freddy Krueger

A NIGHTMARE ON ELM STREET

The master of horror needed a job. Despite having redefined the genre a decade prior with *The Last House on the Left*, by 1984, Wes Craven was broke. In his desperation, he made a sequel to his other '70s landmark of horror cinema, *The Hills Have Eyes*. Sure, he had a sterling reputation as the thinking man's scaremonger, but it didn't do much good when he made a film where a dog has flashbacks (seriously, *The Hills Have Eyes Part 2* is wild) purely for cash. How did he get here?

Craven was raised in a fundamentalist household, and famously didn't see a film until he was in his twenties. He grew up to be an erudite professor who transitioned to filmmaking, and churned out several horror films, including the aforementioned classics. The inspiration for *A Nightmare on Elm Street* came from an article he read about Southeast Asian refugees who fled to America after the Vietnam War. They had escaped a horrific situation, only to unexpectedly die in their sleep over the course of a few years. As if that wasn't mysterious enough, one teenager stayed up for days, insisting to his parents that he would die if he slept. He even hid a personal coffee pot, just in case. When his father slipped him sleeping pills, they took effect, only for his parents to be alerted to his screaming. The teen died in the midst of a nightmare. No cause was ever determined for these deaths. They were all chalked up to Sudden Arrhythmic Death Syndrome, or "SADS," as if that wasn't morbid enough. As soon as he read about them, Craven's wheels started turning.

A force of evil killing teenagers in their dreams was a great idea that Craven would pepper with experiences from his own life. As a child, he once saw a vagrant outside his home, just staring at him. It was frightening enough for young Wes, but what was worse, was that the man seemed to take pleasure in scaring a little boy. Craven never forgot him, nor a childhood bully named "Freddy." Having taught Humanities at Clarkson University, he took Elm Street from Potsdam, New York, where the college is located. It helped that it was also the name of the infamous street where JFK was shot (well, depending on which conspiracy theorist you're willing to talk to).

According to Joseph Maddrey's book *The Soul of Wes Craven*, this script was the first Craven wrote entirely for himself. "His first true spec script, written on faith in his own abilities." He was rightfully proud of his work, but he had to change the origin of Freddy Krueger from a child molester to a child murderer. While it seems like a nominal change for a film like this, the McMartin Preschool trial was gripping the nation at the time. The day care sexual abuse case was all over the airwaves, which made the would-be origin too real. Personally, it makes more sense for the character who forged his own steel claw to be a child killer, rather than just a pedophile, though he most surely was that, as well. Nevertheless, Craven couldn't sell it for years.

Robert "Bob" Shaye started New Line Cinema in the late 60's as a film distribution company. Money was always tight, but by the mid-80's, they had made enough to dabble in making their own low-budget features. Though a producer, Shaye had his own artistic aspirations, and his sensibilities allowed him to respond well to Craven's imaginative script. Despite the declining popularity of the slasher sub-genre, New Line Cinema agreed to make Wes's script into a feature that would change the game.

Slasher films, once heralded by groundbreaking indies like *Halloween* and copycats like *Friday the 13th* (directed by Craven's colleague Sean S. Cunningham) had reigned supreme for years, but were now falling out of fashion. Remember, 1984 was the same year audiences experienced *Friday the 13th: The Final Chapter*, one of the most regrettable titles in horror, until…well, *Freddy's Dead: The Final Nightmare* (more on that later). Nobody on the cast and crew intentionally set out to redefine the slasher film, but to say that Craven, Shaye, and New Line struck gold would be an understatement.

# DREAM SCENARIO

*A Nightmare on Elm Street* opens with dirty hands in a workshop making… something. The unseen creator (Robert Englund) grabs a glove and some tools and makes a hinge. Then we see it with a knife attached. It's not until he slips his hand inside that we realize it's a glove. Four razors and metal plating, grafted onto fabric for one explicit purpose.

Why not just use a normal edged weapon? Axes and knives are good enough for the established killers of the genre, so who are we dealing with here? What kind of person puts time and effort into making something like this when they can use literally anything?

Craven transitions to an intensely surreal scene, where a teenage girl in a nightgown wanders alone inside a working factory. This motif will repeat throughout the series, but our first glimpse is so off-putting, even the letters in the credits are slightly jagged. She's not a sexy coed being chased, but a vulnerable girl being toyed with, or perhaps lured somewhere.

Tina (Amanda Wyss) first appears walking down a hallway, backlit by an impossibly white light at the end. While it's already inexplicable that she's in an industrial space in a nightgown, she sees a lamb running across her path. Before realizing she essentially IS the lamb, she enters a new, multi-leveled section of the factory. We still hear the lamb's tortured bleating throughout the scene. Cinematographer Jacques Haitkin makes the endless, hissing pipes feel claustrophobic and oppressive, though Tina appears to be the only one there, until we see the silhouette of the mystery man appear right behind her, when…

Tina suddenly bolts upright in her bed. It was all a dream. Tina's mom comes into her room to see if she's okay. They both notice four identical slashes on Tina's nightgown, but before Tina can tell her mom about her dream, or god forbid look for an intruder, her mom's boyfriend calls her back to bed. Her mother seems not to recognize the slashes, but Tina notices a certain reaction in her eyes, however subtle. Still, she writes off what is obviously an attack on her daughter as the result of Tina scratching in her sleep, and leaves her frightened girl alone. We're not even five minutes into the film and already so much has been established. Child predation, parental indifference, and the possibility that dreams can lead to real-world consequences.

The next day, Tina walks to school with her best friend Nancy (Heather Langenkamp), her boyfriend Glen (Johnny Depp with an "Introducing" credit if you can believe it), and Tina's boyfriend Rod (Jsu Garcia, billed as "Nick Corri," because Hollywood hadn't begun to get it's shit together). The teens walk by a group of kids jumping rope and singing a prophetic song we'll come to understand later. They appear in a haze, as if they're not supposed to be there at all, but no one seems to notice.

Tina explains her dream to her friends, who wave off her concerns. Since her mom is heading to Las Vegas for the weekend with her boyfriend, Nancy and Glen sleep over at her house to keep her company. (On a school night? And all their parents are cool with this? Judging by Tina's mom's prior behavior, some of them probably don't even know.)

That night at Tina's, it quickly becomes clear that Nancy, Glen, and Tina are all having similar dreams. It's all but confirmed when Rod shows up, scraping a hand rake outside the house. Instead of getting to the bottom of the mass delusion they appear to be having, Rod and Tina sleep together in her mom's bed while Nancy and Glen roll their eyes and lock the door. The dream man sees Nancy in Tina's bed, pushing his head into the wall above her, which creepily expands like rubber. She doesn't notice, but feels the need to grab the crucifix above the bed. He decides to pursue Tina by luring her to an alleyway outside her house.

The man appears in a dirty red-and-green sweater, with a fedora, and of course, the razor glove. And oh, his arms have extended impossibly out to both sides of the alley, blocking Tina's path. She begs god to help her, only for the dream man to pull the glove to his face, which is horribly burned, and declare "THIS…is god." She runs back to the house, but he's seemingly everywhere. He could strike at any moment, but instead toys with her and even cuts off his own finger just to show that he can't be harmed. But as Tina's nightgown showed us, she can be harmed and soon is.

Tina begins thrashing in bed, having been asleep since having sex with Rod. Long slash marks appear on her body out of nowhere as Tina bleeds out and levitates off the bed, all while calling for Rod to help. He stands there, helplessly frozen and unable to comprehend what he sees. Tina is dragged across the ceiling by an unseen force until she falls onto the bed, splashing a puddle of her own blood onto Rod. Horrifying, surreal, and iconic.

Can you imagine the impact this must have had on audiences in 1984? Aside from the fact that her death is a misdirect in the tradition of Janet Leigh in *Psycho*, (making you think she's the protagonist, only to kill her off, a trick Craven would later re-use in *Scream*.) she perished in one of the bloodiest onscreen deaths up until that time. Nancy and Glen break down the bedroom door, only to see their mutilated friend with Rod nowhere in sight.

Before we can process what happened, we see Lt. Donald Thompson (John Saxon) getting debriefed at the local police station. His number two, Sgt. Parker tells him what we already know, so why repeat the information? Well, it turns out Donald is Nancy's father. He's divorced from his wife, and her mother, Marge (Ronee Blakley). Despite living in the same town as his daughter, he doesn't know Nancy's friends and he needs a coworker to tell him she was staying at Tina's. Let's not even mention the fact that the next morning, he uses Nancy as bait to catch Rod, who he thinks viciously murdered her friend. When she calls him out, his response is "what the hell were you doing going to school today for anyway?" Jesus, Don.

Nancy arrives at school, despite the protests of her mother, but she can barely stay awake through English class. Her teacher (Lin Shaye, sister of Bob and future genre star, herself) is discussing how Hamlet tries to learn the truth about his parents, which is so on the nose for these films that it rivals the discussion of fate in the original *Halloween*. Nancy appears to finally doze off when she sees a vision of Tina in a bloody body bag, the same one she saw earlier on the morning news. Nobody in the room seems to notice, though the student reading *Hamlet* looks directly at her while, quoting the play in a stage whisper:

```
O God, I could be bounded in a
nutshell and count myself a king
of infinite space, were it not
that I have bad dreams...
```

If you're paying attention, the teens of Elm Street, like Hamlet, are haunted by their dreams and the infernal "king of infinite space" they are encountering. This is far from the final literary quote in the series, but it's another of Craven's runners. He immediately follows it with another: the hidden transitions from the "real world" into the dream world. It's meant to always keep the audience off-balance, but here it's quickly obvious Nancy is dreaming. Even the white void at the end of the hallway reappears behind Nancy after she runs into a hall monitor. The monitor is a teenage girl in a red-and-green striped sweater that the film doesn't call attention to at first. The monitor demands to see a hall pass, but having bigger fish to fry, Nancy tells her to "screw her pass." The monitor then taunts her and appears to brandish the same metal glove that killed Tina. But we know she's not the murderer, right? Nancy doesn't stick around to find out. She follows Tina's body into the school's basement, only to realize she's no longer in school. She's in the same industrial space as the first scene: a working boiler room. Whereas Tina's entrance was disorienting, we immediately recognize where Nancy is, and that she's not alone.

The dream man returns, glove raised, to kill Nancy, just like Tina. He even cuts himself in a show of invincibility and scrapes his claws against metal to scare her. Getting into a rhythm, he approaches slowly, savoring the moment. It's possible he's just overconfident after making his first (we assume) kill. He even says his name – "Freddy." It's not until Nancy thrusts her arm onto a scalding pipe that she wakes up in class with a matching burn she couldn't have gotten just from sitting there.

Deeply confused, but very much determined to solve her friend's murder, she visits Rod in the local police lockup. He confirms the details of Tina's death and describes her killer, inching Nancy closer to the truth. It's a nice scene and his line delivery on "he cut her while I watched" always gets me. Rod may pretend to be a badass, but he's only a kid, just like the rest of them.

Later that night, Nancy falls asleep in the tub while singing the rhyme we previously heard sung by the ghostly jump rope girls. As she sleeps, the now-familiar claw steadily reaches up from the tub in Nancy's direction. Yet it disappears when her mother wakes her up, ironically to tell her falling asleep in the bathtub is how a lot of people die. As soon as she leaves, an unseen Freddy yanks her under the water to an aquatic void. Nancy wakes before she can drown, quite shaken, but still she goes to bed. Not surprisingly, she can't sleep. Glen climbs up the rose trellis outside her room to check on her. He believes, like everyone else, that Rod killed Tina, but Nancy isn't so sure. She has an idea, but it's not the one Glen's hoping for.

Structurally, we're still the first act. How much have we seen Freddy? How many dreams have we experienced? How often has Craven blended the worlds of dreams and reality? We still have a long way to go.

Nancy is next seen walking down her street, late at night in her pajamas. Glen is inexplicably watching her from a distance. She ventures all the way to the police station where she sees Rod through the window, asleep in his cell. In the light of the station, Freddy openly walks in unchallenged, phasing right through the bars. It's our first good look at his hideous visage. A layer of soot covers his scorched flesh, and he has a near-constant, lascivious grin. He's enjoying this. Nancy backs away from the window, calling for Glen, when Freddy jumps out of a bush and chases her. In an instant, she's back at her house. When she shuts the front door, the music cuts off. Surely she's safe, right? As Nancy runs up the steps, Freddy breaks the door window and holds up the skin of Tina's face, begging for help in a mocking voice, before revealing his own, as the steps of her comfortable suburban house become quicksand traps that try to keep her in place. She makes it to her room and slams the door.

We're watching a dream as Nancy has fallen asleep to search for answers. She's asked Glen to keep watch and wake her if he sees her thrashing around. It's the first time in the series we see a character fall asleep with intent and also the first time we see someone tasked with the seemingly simple job of watching someone sleep. This scene also delivers a grim reality, that people who don't believe the truth can't protect you. Nancy looks in the mirror on the inside of her door, while repeating "he isn't real," until Freddy bursts through the mirror (and her bubble). They fight on her bed amidst a flurry of feathers after he slices her pillow. It looks as though Nancy is a goner, until her alarm goes off.

Glen, of course, didn't take his task seriously and fell asleep on the job. He wakes long enough to hide from Marge, who runs to Nancy to see what's wrong, but she's oblivious, and well, drunk as hell. Glen has probably climbed up the trellis to see Nancy numerous times without Marge having a clue. Thankfully,

Nancy is more aware of her surroundings, like when she sees a single feather floating in the air, as if from her dream…

Nancy and Glen race to the police station to check on Rod. Donald and the night shift cops shuffle their feet, because who cares? They got their perp, and he's sleeping, which means Freddy is finishing the job. Rod's sheet comes to life like a snake and hangs him in his cell, making it appear like a suicide. Case closed. Except for Nancy, who is galvanized.

At Rod's funeral, Nancy describes Freddy to her parents. They clearly know who she's talking about, but refuse to admit it, even after the violent deaths of two of her friends. Donald is taciturn, but Marge immediately takes Nancy to the Katja Institute, a local sleep clinic. Nancy is hooked up to electrodes and told to fall asleep so they can study her. She knows it's a bad idea, but Marge implores her to "please trust us." This is juxtaposed with the doctor and Marge observing her sleep, when he tells her "we still don't know what [dreams] are or where they come from." But sure, "trust us," Nancy.

In this scene, Craven roots out any scientific explanation for what's going on. Dr. King (Charles Fleischer, later the voice of Roger Rabbit) presents us with the science of sleep through monitors and observation. All of which is immediately invalidated by the impossible spikes in Nancy's charts when she appears to grapple with someone during a nightmare. Dr. King is befuddled, especially when Nancy wakes up with a nasty slash on her arm. If that wasn't enough, she pulls out a hat. HIS hat. It's likely Dr. King immediately retires after this or goes crazy himself, because the bedrock of his understanding of the world has shifted completely.

There's no point in hiding what's happening anymore, but Marge sure does try. Her rampant alcoholism is supercharged when Nancy throws the hat in her face. ("He's after us in our dreams!") There's even a name in the hat: Fred Krueger (which begs the question, if you're going on a murder spree, why put your name in your hat? Is that how he was caught when he was alive? But I digress…). Marge slaps Nancy, which isn't just out of bounds, it's the first real emotional response she's had so far. All because, she says, "Fred Krueger is dead." Nancy can't believe her mother knows who he is, and has been lying to her this entire time. She storms off, while Marge insists "it's only a nightmare." Nancy, taking her life into her own hands replied "that's enough." Is she merely scolding her mother, or pointing out the fact that a nightmare is enough to kill her?

A plan starts to form in Nancy's mind, and she buys a book titled "Booby Traps and Improvised Anti-Personnel Devices." Glen tries to mollify her by talking about the Balinese way of dreaming, where the dreamer becomes lucid and acknowledges their dreams aren't real. What a time for this guy to get philosophical.

She forgets all about it when she comes home and sees that Marge has put bars on all the windows. Their house is now a cage. A trap, without even the rose trellis in place, essentially turning Nancy into Rapunzel. Fairy tales play an important part throughout the films, but it all starts with Wes evoking the Brothers Grimm. Speaking of tales, Marge finally tells Nancy what happened to Fred Krueger, in front of the house's boiler, no less, about how the local parents got together and murdered Freddy. Craven drops another horrifying reveal when Marge, drunk, yet lucid, insists "Mommy killed him. I even took his knives," She proceeds to show her Freddy's glove, in living color, which she had been hiding in their boiler ever since the murder. All through Nancy's childhood, his instruments of death were in her childhood home. Did Marge take it as a trophy? It doesn't matter, because "mommy" took care of it. The implications send chills up our spines when we see that it, and Freddy are very real, indeed.

We're now into the third act. Since Glen lives across the street from Nancy, the two look at each other from their bedroom windows when Nancy calls him. She has a plan to end this once and for all: go to sleep, pull Freddy out like she did with his hat, and have him arrested after Glen subdues him.

Glen's parents don't appear as dysfunctional as hers, but they're still wary of the one person who can save their son's life. When Nancy tries to call Glen, they shut her down and take the phone off the hook (See? Kids couldn't live without their phones, even in 1984). She keeps trying to call, until she hears a familiar metallic screeching over the line. Freddy's tongue protrudes from the receiver, as he utters the famous line: "I'm your boyfriend now, Nancy." The script indicates this was a micro dream, which would only be enough to scare her, not finish her off. Glen, however, is fast asleep, while he's summarily pulled into his bed by Freddy, which then erupts in a geyser of blood.

Between Glen and Tina, *A Nightmare on Elm Street* has two of the most unforgettable deaths in horror. Glen's death is the most emblematic of the early films in the series: it occurs in a safe, "normal" place (his bed), it's surreal, but not fantastical, yet impossible according to real world rules. The human body doesn't contain as much blood as the amount that surges out of the bed, which flows UPWARDS from the hole in the bed when his mom finds him. The character deaths gradually change over time to include the specific fears and anxieties of the victims, and with them, major set pieces. For now, we just see unbridled spectacle, but on a budget.

Even after Glen's fate is sealed and Donald shows up to his house with a squad, Nancy calls her father and STILL wants to arrest Freddy when he comes out of her dream. Donald admits he knows that name, but ever the authority figure, he tells her to get some rest. She is now truly alone.

Several years before they became synonymous with *Home Alone*, Nancy starts setting booby traps around the house. As we'll come to see, handmade traps are a Craven staple. He has characters set traps in most of the films where he directs his own scripts, such as *The Last House on the Left*, *The Hills Have Eyes*, and *The People Under the Stairs*.

In a role reversal, Nancy tucks a once-again drunk Marge into bed. Before she goes to sleep, she tells Nancy in a moment of clarity, "You face things. That's your nature. That's your gift. But sometimes you have to turn away, too." This is Marge's most honest moment in the whole film. She insists Nancy "turns away" just like she tried to do after killing Freddy. Marge's repression and alcoholism obviously didn't work out well for her, but despite her many flaws, she still loves her daughter and doesn't want to see her go down the same path. She doesn't have to worry about that.

Nancy sets the alarm on her watch, says a prayer, and goes to sleep. She walks down to the basement, where she finds the glove is missing. Suddenly, she's in the boiler room and her dream becomes an echo of Tina's. She hears Freddy scrape his claws and taunt her among the pipes. She finds her friend's artifacts (Tina's crucifix, Glen's headphones, and Rod's hand rake), but unlike Tina, she doesn't try to hide. She calls to Freddy, her voice reverberating like his, but louder. ("Come out and show yourself, you bastard!") He obliges and the chase is on. With ten seconds left on her alarm, she grabs him and...wakes up in her bed while siren lights flash outside. No Freddy. Glen is still dead, but maybe it was a dream after all. Then Freddy jumps up next to her bed. Another fake-out. The chase continues.

It's so entertaining to watch him hit every trap Nancy set. He gets the shit kicked out of him, via sledgehammer, a lightbulb filled with gunpowder, and she even sets him on fire (in one of the longest burn takes in cinema history). This is all while SHE's the one taunting HIM and calling out across the street to her father.

Donald finally runs across the street with some cops, and enters just as Freddy apparently kills Marge in her bedroom and disappears. Before we can get our bearings, Donald hugs his daughter, but she dismisses him from the room. She's the authority figure now.

Freddy rises from the bed, as if summoned by Nancy. She doesn't look at him, but not out of fear. She's had enough. It's time to embrace the Balinese way of dreaming Glen mentioned. Before he can go in for the kill, Nancy essentially tells Freddy he's powerless. She knows she's still dreaming after setting the traps. But it's not real, and he can't hurt her because it's only a dream. He strikes her, but fades away, seemingly into oblivion. In a way, her mother was right, "sometimes you have to turn away, too."

Nancy takes one step out of the bedroom and suddenly she's outside. It's morning. Marge is there, and she's sober! Glen, Tina, and Rod pull up in a convertible. All is well. Except it's not. Yes, she's *still* dreaming. It's all a trick by Freddy, who traps the kids in the car, which drives away by itself as Marge is sucked through the small window on the door. The children in white are jumping rope and singing that damn rhyme as we fade out. The end. Freddy wins. Right?

## NIGHTMARE AUTOPSIS

First of all, we have to address the lamb. In 1962, Spanish director Luis Buñuel released *The Exterminating Angel*, a dark comedy about a dinner party full of wealthy guests, who find themselves inexplicably unable to leave the home of their hosts. As the night descends into a Sartrean hell, Buñuel uses dream logic to make his characters confront their vulnerability. This includes a motif of sheep running through the halls. As a reference to this surreal satire of the comfortable class, Craven has a lamb run across Tina's path, which continues to bleat as Freddy moves in to strike.

Who puts a Buñuel tribute in a slasher film? Wes Craven, at your service. The first entry in the *Nightmare on Elm Street* films leaves little to be desired, but a lot to discuss. Like any good movie, we start with Craven's script, perhaps his best. It's tight, scary, and it moves relentlessly while planting information that is paid off. In the 2010 documentary *Never Sleep Again*, Jim Doyle, who did special effects for the film (including acting as Freddy's hand in the tub scene) praised Craven's screenplay as "one of the two scripts I've picked up that I've read straight through."

It's not until Tina finds cuts in her nightgown, that the teens address they're dreaming about the same man. It's obvious something strange is happening, but who would bring it up? We all have bad dreams, but the weather's nice, there are palm trees, and Johnny Depp is always trying to sleep with you. Who cares? In Wes Craven's suburbia, nobody talks. The teens don't talk about their shared nightmares. Donald and Marge won't tell the truth. He won't listen to his daughter, and she hides vodka around the house to try and shield Nancy from her alcoholism. Marge might be the worst offender, as she tells Nancy "it was worse after they caught [Freddy]." When Krueger was first arrested, it was surely a relief to a community in turmoil, but when the law let him go, it reignited a wave of anguish that led to murder, which in turn led to Marge drinking away her tortured conscience. Craven never says why Donald and Marge are divorced, but it's not hard to see their contribution to an angry mob had something to do with it. The repression is so strong, it's no wonder Freddy was able to rise in the town's collective unconscious. Even the film's title card is thematic: A large, red "A NIGHTMARE" envelops and looms over the small, white "on Elm Street," in jagged text like the opening credits. Just slightly off-kilter because of the massive, well, nightmare behind it.

In Heather Langenkamp's documentary *I Am Nancy*, Craven speaks about the philosophy of George Gurdjieff, who had an indelible impact on the film. Gurdjieff talks about how people want to be close to the truth, even if it makes them uncomfortable. The higher the truth, the more uncomfortable they get, so they start looking for an escape. Everyone in the film is in close proximity to a dangerous truth, and most of them exit through a door, which they subconsciously feel will make them safe. Marge's door is alcohol. Glen's door is sleep and food (he might be the most oblivious character in the film, and sleeps more than anyone else). Donald's door is his belief in the rule of law and his job, and both Tina and Rod find their doors in each other and are distracted by their romance, Rod moreso. Nancy is the only one who doesn't try to escape and faces Freddy head on. Craven has previously stated the longest human truth is that you only have control over yourself, and thus, you can only save yourself in the end.

Before we go any further, let's stop to discuss Freddy Krueger. He is pure, cackling evil from the creation of the glove to his descent into nothingness. Robert Englund's performance is indelible. Unlike the masked murderers at the time, Freddy isn't played by a silent stuntman. Englund is a classically-trained actor who used his physicality to craft a full performance with an unforgettable silhouette. He let his shoulder slump ever so slightly like he was a gunslinger, and pranced menacingly like James Cagney. Plus, he SPEAKS. He has few lines, but he spouts them with glee. His threats and gallows humor "seasoning" his victims before going in for the kill. In Mick Strawn's book *Behind the Screams*, the production designer describes how Englund "worked really hard to sell the scenes because they went beyond what he was doing." That's not a man in a mask. That's an actor who understands filmmaking, and his part in it.

Craven always intended Freddy to be a "shape changer," who could be "more than his body," and Englund's constant slithering makes you think he's itching to change form. Freddy doesn't fully transfigure into different characters here, but his elasticity is felt. Recall his arms stretching across the alley when Tina sees him in full. His mouth coming out of Nancy's phone, and the hall monitor with the red and green sweater. His reputation as a trickster starts here, though the concept is taken to its full conclusion in the sequels. He retains his signature look (despite adding green stripes to his sleeves), and his makeup fluctuates flighty with different applicators, though the concept stays the same: He is burnt, nearly beyond human recognition. Makeup artist David Miller was inspired by a pepperoni pizza, of all things. You can see it in the red splotches of Freddy's face.

The film's score by Charles Bernstein is a barrage of synthesizers, piano, and percussion. It sounds like a dead insect being reborn, Bernstein layers in religious overtones and pop tones to play over the dream sequences, but also to haunt us when characters are awake. The nursery rhyme that the jump rope girls sing was always in the script, but Craven didn't know how to set the rhyme to music until Bernstein came along. Perhaps this is why the first time we hear it, it's not as sing-songy. The rhyme, featured in every film in the franchise, is as follows:

```
                CHILDREN (OS)
            (singing)
    One two, Freddie's coming for you...
    Three four better lock your door
    Five six grab your crucifix...
    Seven eight, gonna stay up late!
    Nine ten -- never sleep again!
```

As mentioned by Nancy, this rhyme has been around for years before Tina's first nightmare. Assuming this is Freddy's first killing spree in the dream realm, where did the rhyme come from?

Craven's film just prior to *Nightmare* was 1982's *Swamp Thing*, an adaptation of the DC Comics hero, who was also rooted in horror. When Craven showed it to his daughter Jessica, she reacted strongly during a scene where a character played by Adrienne Barbeau trips while running. Jessica asked her father why women in these films were always clumsy. Wes didn't have an answer, but he was about to provide one with his next script with the help of actress Heather Langenkamp.

Most slasher films have female protagonists, even to this day. The "final girl" is often the last character standing, who must defeat the monster, in order for the film to end. The term was introduced after the slasher boom by Carol J. Clover in her seminal book *Men, Women, and Chainsaws*, but trope had never been given a name before. Laurie Strode in *Halloween*. Sally Hardesty in *The Texas Chain Saw Massacre*, and Alice Hardy in *Friday the 13th* had all withstood the crucibles of their respective films by reacting to the threats they faced before they could be subsumed by seemingly inhuman monsters. Even Sarah Connor from *The Terminator*, released the same year, followed a similar trajectory (which she made up for tenfold in the sequel). Craven told Langenkamp he wanted to get away from "boy heroes," and he did by creating arguably the greatest final girl in cinema history: Nancy Thompson in *A Nightmare on Elm Street*. She sets a template that has been repeated for decades.

Unlike the "final girls" before her, Nancy doesn't stumble upon the bodies of her friends in the third act. She's not a babe in the woods experiencing a well-timed adrenaline boost. Nancy is proactive and vocal. She stands up to her parents from their first scene in the police station, insisting the obvious solution, that Rod killed Tina, is a lie. Her strength only grows from there. As her friends die around her, she makes it her mission to figure out why, driving the story towards the end. Before the internet came along to tarnish the phrase "I do my own research," Nancy buys a book that teaches her to make traps. She sets them up all by herself, as the so-called "authority figures" toil uselessly across the street at Glen's house. She runs towards the darkness, intending to confront it without any help. Then she finally faces Freddy. And she tells him to "fuck off" (No really, that line was filmed, but deleted, probably for its redundancy) Surely this couldn't be the first horror movie heroine to go above and beyond like this, but Craven made it seem fresh, even revolutionary.

Nancy's plan is surprisingly benevolent considering what she's been through. The booby traps are plan B. Plan A involves pulling Freddy out of the dream so Glen can "whack the fucker and we got him." When Glen dies, she sets the traps to subdue him so her father can arrest him.

Yes, arrest him. Put Freddy Krueger behind bars, but in the real world where he can't walk through them. It sounds remarkably naive, but think about it. Is it even possible? The answer is subtle, but a wonderful rejoinder to Marge's tale. In a nice bit of irony, Nancy believes in justice, unlike her parents. She wants him put behind bars, where he was supposed to go before he was freed on a technicality. Unlike Lt. and Mrs. Thompson, who deign to still call themselves authority figures, after their transgressions caused immeasurable damage, Nancy seeks to rectify the trouble her parents have caused, truly surpassing them as the moral pillars of her world, and even the town at large. Yes, "mommy killed him," but Nancy isn't above the law.

As I mentioned in the introduction, several factors caused me to watch these films out of order. When I first watched "part one," after seeing several unique, visually exciting ways Freddy was dispatched (we'll get there, I promise), my six-year-old mind was completely dismayed that an awesome character would do something so...well, stupid. She turns her back on him. Literally. Didn't she know he was Freddy Krueger!? My child logic involved kung fu battles and magic, so I thought it was lame. When I saw the film again in college, it was one of the most startling endings I've ever seen.

Forget the downbeat epilogue for a minute. In truth, it wasn't even what Craven had in mind for his film. Bob Shaye knew he had a hit and wanted a final scare to bring the audience back for a sequel, but Craven never intended to continue the story. To him, good defeats evil. The end. As the producer, Shaye convinced Craven to write the ending we see in the film as a favor to the man who took a chance on producing *Nightmare*. Shaye actually wanted Freddy driving the car, which was shot, but thankfully left on the cutting room floor. Shaye would eventually get the ending he originally wanted from Craven, not here but rather in *A Nightmare on Elm Street* 2, but we'll get there...

Craven's original ending set us up to watch Nancy and Freddy fight to the death, only for her to discover the answer was for her to stop fighting. There's nothing to fight because Freddy is not real. He is able to break through her bedroom mirror because, even though she repeats to herself "It's just a dream, he isn't real," she doesn't truly feel that way. Now she does, and she tells him as such: "You're nothing. You're shit." She doesn't grab a knife, an ax, or any physical weapon. She more powerfully refutes him and he fades away. Absolutely badass. And how is she able to figure out she's still dreaming? When her father comforts her after her mother dies in front of them. Donald showing the least bit of tenderness towards her is what "wakes her up" to the fact that she's still asleep.

### NANCY

```
I take back every
bit of energy I
ever gave you.
```

Langenkamp has mentioned how, watching these films, "you never feel like you're in a slasher movie." She and Englund always took their roles seriously, like they were in a Greek tragedy. In a way, they are perfect opposites. He's big and broad, seemingly everywhere in the dreamscape, whereas Nancy is the girl next door. She's not flashy, she won't be dancing on the hood of a car belonging to a hair metal band (the 80's. Don't ask), but she's pretty and appealing. She's someone you can trust, like a good friend, and importantly, she's not introduced with any fanfare. Nancy is just one of Tina's friends, who listens to her.

John Saxon and Ronee Blakley really lean into their roles as Nancy's parents. Horror movie parents are usually thankless parts, but Craven provides them with pathos and regret. They're real actors, and they lend considerable weight to the film and the very real question of morality: would you have killed the man who killed your child? If you were in their shoes, and you had the chance, would you have done it? The Thompsons are frustrating parents all through the film, but even in learning of their devastating flaws, you still sympathize with them. Saxon and Blakley are attuned to this and they don't disappoint. Like Glen said in the beginning, "morality sucks."

## THE ORIGINAL SCRIPT

An earlier draft can be found online which includes several changes, but deserves to be discussed. Craven wrote it in precise detail, knowing he would be the director, as well. First of all, while the palm trees aren't hidden and there's a line about earthquakes, the finished film is essentially set in "Anytown, USA." The original script sets the film explicitly in California. There's mention of the Santa Ana winds, banana trees, and even an establishing shot of the San Fernando Valley before we get to Tina's dream. There are also title cards sprinkled throughout, marking time (The First Day, The Second Day, etc.), presumably to make us feel how long Nancy's staying awake.

Curiously, Freddy's sweater is red and yellow instead of red and green. Craven mentioned he came up with the combination of red and green from reading they were the two most jarring colors for the eye to see at once, which very well could have been after writing this draft. With the rest of it so fully formed, it's an odd scriptnote, especially when the stripes show up as a motif throughout.

During Tina's death, she spots the "ashen faces" of her neighbors watching Freddy chase her and do nothing. She calls out for Nancy, but Freddy replies "she's still awake, she can't hear you." Maybe Craven didn't trust his audience enough at that point to get what was happening, or maybe it was extra flavor he added to help the script sell. Either way, we don't need it. When Freddy cuts his fingers off to scare her, they originally flop on the ground and retract to his hand. Cool idea, but what we have is enough and it was probably a budget issue.

As Tina is being sliced all over the room, Rod sees a shadow with her. Initially, forced perspective was written in to make Tina appear to be dragged on an endless ceiling. With her dying breath, she rakes 4 fingers on the wall to send a message. When she first meets her friends, she subconsciously rakes them on a tree. Creepy, but we don't need it.

While observing Nancy, Dr. King brings up Buddha and the true story of the Filipino teenagers that Wes based the script on. Dr. King also turns into Freddy at the end of the scene, but he would've looked odd in the doctor's office (don't worry, they recycle this for part 4).

There are literary references that are pure Wes Craven. Nancy is described as having a "Cassandra quality," and instead of entering the boiler room through her basement at the end, she walks to an abandoned building (most likely where Freddy died). Craven writes that "Nancy descends like Orpheus into hell, but without [a] weapon to save her wits." She keeps descending level after level, but I would imagine no boiler room has that many sub-basements.

Donald and Marge are shaded a little more. The script makes a point to say they're divorced and Marge's maiden name is, I'm not kidding, Simson. Could you imagine the lawsuit?

Donald and Marge share a secret cigarette at Rod's funeral, where Donald tells Nancy is "tougher than you think." Marge refers to "10 years ago," implying that's when Freddy died and giving us a timeline the finished film keeps under wraps. There's an extended bit after Nancy pulls the hat out of the dream, when Marge talks to Donald on the phone. She says "we were ALL there." Later, after Glen dies, Glen's dad tells Donald he knows Freddy did it. Donald is still in denial, even after the coroner finds one of Freddy's razor fingers. Once again, a creepy idea, but it flies in the face of continuity.

The backstory of Freddy takes a melodramatic tenor, since it's Marge at her most inebriated. Not only did they light Freddy on fire, he runs out of the boiler room, and while burning, declares he'll come back and kill their kids. So Marge takes a gun and shoots him, dead. Mommy killed him, literally. As if that wasn't dramatic enough, Marge tells her that her friends had siblings. Nancy, too. It's meant to add an extra layer of motivation, but come on, wouldn't they remember siblings who died when they were in elementary school? Even their friends' siblings? It would definitely add to the air of repression, but it's just not believable.

Finally, when Freddy is chasing Nancy throughout the house, Marge appears and jumps in front of Freddy's blades before they can strike her daughter, dying a heroic death. Though since Nancy is still dreaming, it's unclear if that actually happens.

## WHAT DREAMS HAVE COME

No one could have possibly imagined the reaction to A *Nightmare on Elm Street* when it opened in less than 200 theaters on November 9th, 1984. While it didn't initially set the box office on fire, audiences spread the word, leading to lines forming around the block in major cities. The film eventually grossed over $25 million in America, alone. Overseas, it grossed more than double its domestic take. Not bad for a gamble that cost an indie like New Line just over $1 million.

The genie was now out of the bottle and Craven finally had the hit he so desperately needed. With his reputation solidified as a horror maestro, it was on to the next project. Shaye, on the other hand, fulfilled the promise of the controversial epilogue by focusing on a sequel right away.

*A Nightmare on Elm Street* is still one of the best, and most influential horror films of all time. While certain music cues and hairstyles might not stand the test of time (sorry, Mr. Depp), its themes, scares, and message of empowerment still resonate to this day.

# INTERVIEW
# LIN SHAYE

## "Teacher," "Nurse"

 WES CRAVEN'S
NEW NIGHTMARE

**You were already an established actress when it came time to film *A Nightmare on Elm Street*. Did Bob ask you to do the movie for him?**

It was really simple. I think Bob and Wes really hit it off. I still miss [Wes] in a way. The film community was richer with him in it. He was one of the kindest, smartest people I knew. Period. But I think Bob said "Put my sister in your movie." He was very funny about that, because he used to pretend he hated me (laughs). He still does. I was his little sister and he used to make fun of me and introduce me to people "This is my sister, Linda Shaye. She wants to be an actress" (laughs). I changed my name to "Lin," because my dad thought that would be a better stage name.

So Wes had written this part of the teacher and I don't think they had anybody in mind, so they just asked me. I was thrilled to be included. Those were groundbreaking films. The horror genre hadn't bloomed in that big way. Heather was wonderful. She had the hard part because she has that sort of breakdown at the end [of the scene]. It was just one day. With low budget movies, you don't spend very much time on a scene, in general. It's very important for an actor to have their game together for the first take, I think. Everything changes, of course, and you have new information thrown at you at the moment. You might rehearse at home alone, then suddenly you're in a classroom with forty kids and everything shifts. It never goes that same way.

**Bob loved to make cameos in the films. Did you ever help him with them, since you're the actor in the family? Please don't tell him I said that…**

No, Bob kind of wanted to be an actor, and we all acknowledged he was not very good (laughs). Part of what I love about acting is pretending to be other people. I want to know how we're all the same and how we're all different. Bob doesn't want to pretend to be other people. He wants to be him. It just wasn't his expertise. It kind of became a showcase for him. Orson Welles and Alfred Hitchcock would have cameos in their films. I think it was important to Bob to put his stamp on what he was creating. It was a nice touch, actually. It was fun for him.

**And for the audience, too.**

It was fun for me!

**I never figured out your name was "Linda" until I talked to Jack Sholder. It seems so obvious.**

He refuses to call me "Lin." That's a very Jack Sholder thing (laughs). I'm still "Bobby's little sister" to him, but whatever, it's all good.

**Even though you had a small role in the original, people would still recognize you on the street. Did you feel any other effects from the *Nightmare* phenomenon?**

No. Really, I didn't. My focus moves from one thing to another, but I was happy to have that opportunity and I loved Wes. He was such a supportive person. He directed an episode of *The Twilight Zone* and I was asked to come in to audition. I was excited because it was Wes, and I had already done *Nightmare on Elm Street*. Wes was in the room for the audition and the character was a ghost who had a very emotional scene. So I played the scene with the casting director, and I kind of teared up, because I made it as real as I could for myself. At the end, he looked at me and said "Can you do it again? A little less emotional?" I was still in the moment, and I just went [Lin raises her middle finger and we both laugh]. And I forgot Wes was in the back. I was slightly horrified, but I looked over at him. His face was in his hands and he was laughing as hard as he possibly could! He cast me on the spot. That was Wes.

**Let's fast forward to *New Nightmare*. It's ten years later and everyone knows *Nightmare on Elm Street*, Wes has made more films and New Line is a powerhouse. Did it feel different to step back on the set of a *Nightmare* film after all that time?**

Not really. It's always new because there's new people. I'm always nervous, because I want to do a good job and there's a lot to think about. It's just the basics: trying to relax, remembering my lines, and running through the material, because it's always different when you do the scene with someone else, as opposed to, you know, in my living room with my dog. I mean, I'm a nervous wreck every time I work. I absorb it into the character so I don't appear as a "nervous actress" kind-of-thing. But I don't remember anything really different, other than those elements. Again, it was a nice day.

**Did *New Nightmare* still have the indie feel of the first film or did it feel like a major studio production?**

It didn't feel any different, really, because I think Bob kept a pretty small cast and crew around him. It wasn't a big thing. Like, sometimes I do television and it's so vast, it scares the shit out of me. It's different now, because it's more like film. There are lots of locations now, but the studio stuff is tough. But once you crack the back of it, it's fun. It's really pretend and it challenges how well you can pretend and imagine. It's a little like doing theatre, where you pretend a door goes somewhere, but it doesn't. But it was similar to me because my points of focus were the same.

**There's a direct line between *Nightmare on Elm Street* and *Insidious*. Not just for your career but for the horror genre in general. Both films were inflection points for their respective directors. I'm sure you've been asked this before, but how would you compare working with James Wan and Wes Craven?**

I've never been asked that question by anybody. James and Wes have very different sensibilities, but they're both filled with a certain kind of grace, as people. They're both renaissance men, in their own way. James is also a terrific artist, which I gathered from looking at the drawings on *Insidious*. He did all of them. They're both intellectual and very focused on what it is that they've created. There's a specificity in the way they attack their [respective] material. They both give total freedom to their actors. They were both really "you tell *me* how it goes. Here are the tools, show me what it is." It may be different than what they're thinking.

James was hilarious. He used to come in wearing a hoodie and sit in the corner. You couldn't even find him because he would melt into the chair. I know he was really excited about what I did for Elise [her character in *Insidious*], which I didn't ever really think about. I met him and Leigh Whannell when I did their short film, *Doggie Heaven*, which is still on YouTube. Afterwards, he came over and showed me the script for *Insidious*. Elise had pages of monologues, which for an actor is... blech. You have to learn it, and I made it really work. He was thrilled that I took his dialogue and made it "chilling," he said. That sealed my relationship with him. I'm never intimidated by anyone in that world. My focus is always making my character feel as real as possible and finding my backstory. I'm forever grateful for my training.

**Is there anything about the *Nightmare* films that you feel doesn't get talked about enough?**

I think everyone has their favorites. Each one has its own story to tell. I love all of them, but I think my favorite is still the first film. We saw it again at the Egyptian Theater in LA, and I forgot how funny Ronee Blakley was. Heather was just great. I kind of wish they kept Freddy a little more mysterious in the rest of the series. He became a little bit of a joke, which has obviously served him extremely well. I never wanted to see his full face. I wanted him in full shadow until the very end. Robert Englund has, of course, become the "king" of the storyline. I was really glad to see Heather come back in a strong way. She's a wonderful actress and a really terrific person. I'm very grateful to have this be part of my early career. And it's with my brother, Big Bob (laughs).

# INTERVIEW
# MIMI CRAVEN
## "Nurse"

**I've been harping on the fact that there's so much of *A Nightmare on Elm Street* in the horror films of today, but people don't always draw a connection.**

No they don't. It's funny. I used to do those autograph shows. The last one I did was in Indianapolis where I live. Robert was here, along with Heather, Amanda, Ronnee, and Jsu. I had been kept in the loop that Wes was ill… Sorry, I'm gonna cry. I do every time.

**It's okay.**

The day before the show my friend called me and said "He's gone." We all got together, and we were gonna do one of those Q&A sessions where we're all up on a dais. Everyone knew he passed, and they said "Mimi, why don't you make the announcement?" I said okay and I quickly went "You know what? I know what scared Wes Craven."

You could hear a fucking pin drop! "The only thing that scared him was that he would only be remembered as a horror director. He was a filmmaker." When he passed, the royal family made a statement, which he would've loved. He was an amazing filmmaker, but he was so worried he'd be remembered for being "the horror king." He was best friends with Peter Locke and Sean Cunningham, who were the "best men" at our wedding. Peter and [his wife] Karen have been friends of mine forever. They were with Wes from the very beginning, even before *Last House on the Left*, when he was doing the films [whispers] we don't talk about (laughs) just to get into the business. I called Sean "Seannicent" because he called me by my real name, Millicent.

**That's precious. I have to acknowledge how strange it is to be talking to you ten years after Wes's passing, compounded by the fact that you were separated from him since the 80s.**

After all these years, Wes is still the smartest, funniest man I ever met. I was best friends with Sharon Stone for twenty-five years. From "Isn't that the girl from *Total Recall*?" to *Basic Instinct* opening the Cannes Film Festival, where our underwear and lipstick were stolen! Though we were still basically the same people. I've met everyone and done amazing things, met important people and unimportant people. And Wes was still, the smartest, funniest man I ever met. He was almost twenty years older than me. His mother was very Christian and their bedrooms were separated by a sheet. She used to knock on the bathroom door. "What are you doing in there?!" So he had some strange ideas about women and I wasn't old enough to go "Hey, whoa, excuse me…" But had I been a little older, we would've stayed married. He was the love of my life and I wasn't capable, which is not to say it was his fault. It just wasn't right. I was way too young (laughs), but I was married to him at a very important time in his life. When I first met him, he was writing *The People Under the Stairs*.

**He wrote it that far ahead of when it was made?**

Yes, it wasn't finished, but he also wrote an adaptation of *Hansel & Gretel*. Can you imagine Wes Craven's spin on *Hansel & Gretel*?

**That doesn't surprise me since he was so into myths and storytelling, but I would kill to read it.**

I don't know where it went, but it was amazing. He had just started *A Nightmare on Elm Street* when I moved in with him. We lived in Venice, California and he had a studio behind the house, where he would write every day in a bright blue bathrobe and a pith helmet.

**(laughs)**

I have pictures! (laughs) He would slide down in his chair and write on his computer, then at the end of the day, he would print it and we would read it out loud together. We'd act it out, put it on its feet, as they say in the theatre, and talk about it. So I basically helped edit the script. I would be all the characters, then he would be all the characters, and we'd figure out what worked and what didn't. Mostly him, but I always put my two cents in.

**Speaking of the script, I feel like as much as the film is praised, not enough is written about how good it is. There's an earlier draft that's not much different from the finished film.**

Every single penny is up there on screen. The film cost $1.3 million and there's no fluff. It's a genius script. "Tight" is the word I'm looking for. That's who he was. He was very good at what he did and writing was his first love. I still have poetry he wrote for me. Reams and reams of it. I never took off the side strips with the paper holes from those old printers. I couldn't. I wish I knew where that *Hansel & Gretel* script was. I really do (laughs). Do you know who Michel Uslan is?

**Of course. He produced *Swamp Thing* and brought *Batman* to the big screen.**

He put himself and his wife through Indiana University's law school by selling half his comic book collection. For the past eight years, he's come back to IU every year and does an intensive course on how to produce and, you know, survive in Hollywood. I always go down to teach for a day and give my take. We call it our "dog and pony show."

There's something I point out to Michael's classes every single year, and he knows I'm going to do it. The first person that Wes gave *A Nightmare on Elm Street* to, was Michael. He said it was a great script, but he didn't want to spend two years covered in blood and gore. It wasn't his thing, so he turned it down. He says it was the only mistake he's made in his career (laughs).

**You also play a nurse in the Katja Institute scene, which is one of the most important scenes in the film. Do you have any memories of shooting it?**

Yeah, because this was the scene where she brings the hat out of the dream and the audience realizes Freddy's real. I don't remember any other film where something was brought out of a dream.

**Right. Wes has been showing us his imagination for most of the film, and now we, the audience, have to use our own.**

He made me wire [Heather] up by the way. He made me wear that silly little hat and all that stuff (laughs). I didn't want to wear it. I just happened to be there because I was there every day. You always called the director "sir," whether they were male or female. When I worked on HBO's *Dream On*, and Betty Thomas directed, we called her "sir." On *Nightmare*, they all called me either "Mrs. Sir" or "mom." By the end of the film, everyone called me "mom."

In 1992, I went to Cannes for the first time. I was on Harvey Weinstein's yacht and I suddenly heard "Mom!" from across the room, and there's Johnny [Depp] jumping up and down!

**Do you have any stories of young Johnny Depp?**

When Johnny came in and read, he sucked. He was a musician who never acted before. If it wasn't for [Casting Director] Annette Benson, Wes wouldn't have cast him. We were sitting there. I'm sure you've heard this story.

**I believe from the documentary where Wes said his daughter Jessica went "Dad! Johnny Depp…"**

No, no. She didn't say a word. She was in the back of the room with her friend. They were visiting from New York. Annette was sitting next to Wes with his clipboard of names, and Wes brought them in because there would be a lot of cute boys. Johnny came in to read, and when he left, Wes crossed his name off. Annette and I looked at him, then pointed to Jessica and her friend. You know that sound that only dogs can hear? That high-pitched squeal that young girls do when they can't help themselves? They were squealing! Then it became "Oh my god." I think Johnny gives Annette her due, because it was all her. But he was terrible. (laughs)

We hosted the wrap party at our house in Venice. Johnny and his friend were totally shitfaced, and I sat him down and took care of him. Later, I got this postcard from him (laughs) and I still have it. It's just him waxing on about how wonderful it was and how I took care of him, and he said "PS - I'm taking acting lessons."

**That's amazing!**

(laughs) Yes it is! If I was that type of person, could you imagine what it would go for on eBay?

**You have to frame that. That's film history.**

Then he took acting lessons and learned on the set of *21 Jump Street*. TV will always teach you how to get it done, and done fast. I've done enough TV to know they don't do ninety-seven takes.

**Are there any other production memories you have from *Nightmare*?**

I loved Sara Risher. She was, I think, eight months pregnant while doing *A Nightmare on Elm Street*. If it wasn't for her, Bob Shaye would be dead. I would have shot him where he stood. Bob Shaye doesn't talk to people. He yells. He's a name-caller. I did not like the way he talked to Wes. There were several shooting days that ended with us Bob and I screaming at each other. Thank god for Sara. She's the one that did all the work. Sara got that movie made.

I'll tell you a funny story about the one day I wasn't on the set. They built the revolving room to shoot Amanda's death scene. It was a box where they glued everything down and they had a seat and a four-point harness for Wes, the camera guy, and I believe the focus puller. They were strapped in, and when Wes said "rolling," the grips pulled the box with ropes. It was a moving room, like the kind they did with Fred Astaire. They reused it for Johnny's death scene. It had a false bottom, which they filled with the red dye that I have spent so much of my career covered in, which was probably just made illegal. So I'm at home when I get this call. I think it was from one of the ADs. "Hi Mimi, just to start, he's okay…"

**Oh no…**

Uh-huh! "Excuse me?" So they set the room up. Everyone's in their chairs, the grips pull…and they didn't think about centrifugal force. So the liquid goes out and the grips lose the ropes, because the room started spinning and spinning and they lost control. They finally stopped it and everyone got cleaned up, but that phone call…"He's okay!" They got the shot, because that was the important part (laughs). Remember, we had no money, so if they didn't get the shot, we were in so much trouble. That scene was important. Same thing with Ronee Blakely being pulled through the door. We had no money, so it was like "What if we just did this real fast?!" But by the time that scene comes, you're already invested.

That's the thing about Wes's movies. It's such a key to him. At the start of a movie, he asked the question "Hey, wanna go on a ride? Wanna see something? Come here." He knew that people went "Yes, please show me." And once he's got you, he's got you. That's why they're still talking about him. Because they said "Yes, show me." He didn't yell it. My acting coach once told me that if you want someone's attention, don't lean forward. Lean back, so they come to you. That's what Wes did. He made people want to follow him like the pied piper. He looked and spoke like a college professor. If you met him, you would never think he made a living scaring the shit out of you.

# INTERVIEW
# TONY TIMPONE
## FORMER EDITOR-IN-CHIEF
### FANGORIA

**What was the state of the horror genre when you took over as editor of _Fangoria_ magazine in 1985?**

The big slasher boom had kind of slowed down. You were lucky if the big studios put out one horror movie a year, like _Ghost Story_, _The Hunger_, or _The Keep_. They tended to be misguided and not very good, and they weren't connecting with audiences. So horror was in a bit of a lull for a few years until _A Nightmare on Elm Street_ came along and kind of reignited the slasher genre by taking it up to a whole new level.

Part 2 came out a year later and was one of the first big movies I was involved with for the magazine. I think it was intended to be a quick cash-in, but it was successful, too. Then part 3 came along, which completely took off and became bigger than the first two films. It made New Line Cinema want to do more horror films, so they became like the A24 of their day with films like _Critters_ and _Alone in the Dark_. They did a great job of marketing their horror films and connecting with their audience. One of the ways they did that was to canvas me at _Fangoria_, trying to get us to do a lot of coverage and cover stories. They were great. They gave me everything I needed. There was a great publicity executive named Gary Hertz, who was a fan. He knew the importance of _Fangoria_ and helped us out.

When the _Nightmare_ films started taking off, there was a great, fertile period of horror in the 80s. Paramount started pushing their _Friday the 13th_ films again, New Line made a third *Texas Chain Saw Massacre*, and there was *Child's Play*. Then everybody's doing Freddy rip-offs, which weren't very successful. Then you hit a valley again, until *Scream* came along. Then forget it. It was a huge success unlike anything the genre had seen. The slasher genre came back and the studios dove in.

What we have today is an embarrassment of riches. Studios haven't been making as many films since the COVID-19 pandemic, and a lot of their films go straight to streaming. It's left a vacuum for horror, and now every week a new horror movie comes out and they're doing quite well. A movie like *Terrifier* never would have played in theaters, but because studios didn't have the same theatrical output, it created a perfect scenario for *Terrifer 2* to be a big success. Also, the rise of A24 and Neon, who again, are the new "New Lines." They're doing a great job marketing and selling them. Horror is pretty much all you see in theaters, along with comic book movies, but even those have been sputtering the last few years. It's a great time to be a horror fan, because there's so much content, and a lot of it is on the big screen. Sorry for the rambling answer. [laughs]


**No, that's perfect. To my generation, horror in the 80s always seemed like Woodstock. Everyone wanted to be part of it. Do you recall how Freddy Krueger was initially received in such a crowded landscape of boogeymen?**

Yeah, there were faceless, voiceless killing machines like Jason Voorhees and Michael Myers, but Freddy was a character with personality. He was closer to the fun Universal monsters of the 1930's. He also had a compelling backstory and Robert Englund really brought the character to life. In the beginning, *A Nightmare on Elm Street* was really niche. Our audience loved it, but [the films] really became a mainstream success with *Nightmare on Elm Street 3*, which was huge. Every year, New Line would bang out a new one and it became a cultural phenomenon. Rappers put out songs about Freddy and there were all these tie-in products. Records, posters, toys, masks, you name it. The genre really had never seen anything like that, in terms of a character, a killer, becoming a mainstream success. The films got funnier, and the audiences kept growing.

It was something fans would look forward to. When we put Freddy on the cover every year, our sales went through the roof. That's when *Fangoria* really reached the next level in terms of circulation and popularity. Since we championed the films, it led to people picking up *Fangoria* who might not have read it before. It was a very symbiotic relationship.

**From your vantage point, what was it about the third film that made it blow up more than the previous films?**

It was really well-written. A lot of that was Frank Darabont, who went on to work on *The Shawshank Redemption*, *The Green Mile*, and *The Walking Dead*. There was much more imagination put into the elaborate nightmare sequences. Chuck Russell directed that one. They brought it to a new level, visually. It was a real funhouse of horror with a great sense of humor. Freddy had all these great catchphrases that the audience loved. Also, they brought back Heather Langenkamp as Nancy Thompson. There was a lot of effort put into it and it succeeded beyond their wildest dreams.

**I always thought the timing of the original film brought about the second wave of 80's horror. *Friday the 13th: The Final Chapter* came out the same year, and I wonder if the series would've died there if Freddy didn't reinvigorate the genre. Same thing with *Halloween 4: The Return of Michael Myers* years later. Is that a stretch?**

No, I think the success of *A Nightmare on Elm Street* proved there was still a lot of money to be made in the slasher format. It probably pushed Paramount and Moustapha Akkad to re-launch their franchises.

**With all the press coverage *Fangoria* has done over the years, can you recall any pieces about the franchise that stick out to you?**

We had a lot of fun covering the movies. We always wanted to do something different. For example, we had Robert Englund keep a set diary on *Nightmare on Elm Street 3* that we published. New Line did a special photo shoot with Freddy and Heather in eveningwear. Then for *Nightmare 5*, since there were a lot of screenwriters on the movie, we did a big expose on all the different Freddy films that could have been. Since New Line was churning the films out so fast, they'd have different sets of writers working on scenarios for the next film, and they picked the ones they liked best. The article really went into the paths not taken, which was cool. We had a special licensed movie magazine licensed for *Freddy's Dead*, which had 3D pictures since part of the film was in 3D.

**Do you recall when interest in the series started to wane?**

I started losing interest in the series with *Dream Child* and *Freddy's Dead*. They were running out of ideas and the character was overexposed by that point. They didn't need to do that shoddy tv show [*Freddy's Nightmares*] that further diluted the character. I was still happy to put them on the cover. I thought the character was really reinvigorated with *New Nightmare*. It's one of Wes's best films and the best Freddy film after the original and *Dream Warriors*.

**Did you have any issues working with New Line?**

Not with the Freddy movies. The only time I had problems with them was over [1996's infamous] *The Island of Dr. Moreau*. New Line was great, compared to say, the Weinsteins, who were a nightmare to deal with. We were covering the *Scream* films and they wouldn't give us photos or set access. It was a real challenge to cover those movies. It was the same when they took over the *Halloween* franchise [in the '90s]. I wish all the companies back then were as cooperative and easy to deal with as New Line was.

**You've seen franchises come and go. What is it about the *Nightmare on Elm Street* films that's still relevant today?**

They were very innovative for their day. They certainly had a huge impact, and I could see their inspiration in a few seasons of *American Horror Story* and especially in movies that sort of throw everything at you. They operated in a dream world with no rules, and we still see that in movies today. Art [from *Terrifier*] is very Freddy-like. He taunts his victims and has a sense of humor. Also, Longlegs, the Nicolas Cage character. I can see Freddy in that persona. The influence of Freddy is still being felt in today's modern horror films.

**Is there anything else you wish people knew about the franchise?**

Just for me personally, it was a great ride. The series was so successful. We always knew when a new *Nightmare on Elm Street* movie was coming out. We'd cover the latest entry for 4 or 5 issues in a row, really banging the drum for them. Again, it was reciprocal, because we knew it had a fanbase and we were expanding our readership. We couldn't ask for anything better. I loved meeting the people associated with the films. We became friends with Robert Englund, Wes Craven, Heather Langenkamp and we had a lot of fun covering the makeup effects. We got a lot of mileage out of that. It was a great time to be associated with the magazine when the films were becoming popular. We'd also promote them at our conventions. Robert Englund still has hundreds of people lining up to see him and get his autograph, and it never gets old or boring. He's just as entertaining as he was forty years ago. I'd love for him to do one more *Elm Street* movie.

Opposite: A dozen *Nightmare*-related covers from *Fangoria*'s long history.

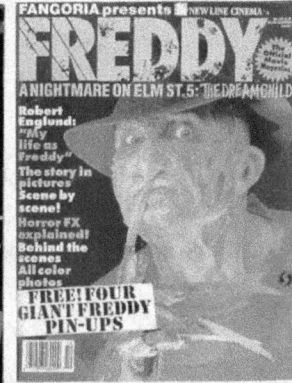

# A Nightmare
## ON ELM STREET 2
### FREDDY'S REVENGE

*A Nightmare on Elm Street* was a massive success, both critically and financially. New ground had been broken in the horror genre and both Wes Craven and New Line Cinema were reaping the benefits. Among the celebrations, Bob Shaye was plotting. He had leveraged New Line Cinema to the hilt in order to make the film, and a not-insignificant portion of the returns was used to refill the coffers. It was then immediately time to go back to Elm Street.

The seeds for a sequel had already been planted in the original film, much to Craven's chagrin. Inspired by the success, if not quality, of other contemporary horror films like *Friday the 13th*, he insisted upon an ending for the first film that scared the audience and made them want to come back for more. Craven had always intended his picture to be a complete story of good's triumph over evil, which was a message he didn't want diluted with compromise. Shaye, to his credit, knew the film would be a smash, and fought Craven tooth and nail over the ending. Given that New Line had essentially rescued his script from obscurity, the director ultimately gave in and filmed Nancy and her friends being whisked away in a Freddy-esque convertible.

Shaye wanted to go so far as to have Freddy driving the car, which was actually shot, but (perhaps wisely) unused. The New Line CEO's friends and family all hated the new ending, including his very own father. Some horror lovers wish it was never included at all, myself included. (Sorry folks, Craven's ending is better and you didn't need a hook to bring Freddy back. Then again, it does set the stage for future films.) So what would the next chapter look like? And who would write it?

David Chaskin was an aspiring screenwriter within New Line, though his day job at the company was working as a film inspector. Known to promote people from within the organization, Shaye gave him the job to write the sequel after submitting a favorable spec treatment. *A Nightmare on Elm Street 2: Freddy's Revenge* was then rushed into production and released less than a year later. Craven did reluctantly give notes on what he felt wasn't a good script, but that train had otherwise left the station with New Line editor Jack Sholder promoted to the helm.

Sholder had slightly loftier expectations for his filmmaking career than directing a horror sequel. He often claimed "I never set out to be Wes Craven. I set out to be Jean Renoir." Though genre films were never his primary interest, he was known for editing the 1981 slasher classic *The Burning* and making his feature debut with New Line's *Alone in the Dark* the following year. Two years after his stay on Elm Street, he released the acclaimed alien noir *The Hidden*, which featured several key crew members from *Freddy's Revenge*. For a filmmaker who claimed to not be of the genre world, he sure was important in the history of New Line Cinema. The suddenly-successful independent film company would now follow up their most profitable project with one of the most controversial horror sequels ever made.

## DREAM SCENARIO

The sequel opens with a school bus dropping teenagers off in an idyllic suburban neighborhood. Nothing seems amiss, aside from the droning score that keeps us uneasy. The only remaining students to be dropped off are two random girls and Jesse Walsh (Mark Patton), a silent, sweaty loner they laugh at.

Before the bus can make its last stop, it speeds down the street, leaving the familiar landscape for the California desert. The driver ignores his passengers' cries of panic as the bus now barrels through the barren land. Then it stops. The teens struggle to leave the bus, but all they can do is watch the sun disappear and the ground gives way to a massive canyon. Soon, the bus is balancing precariously on tall rock pillars within the pit. Just like the first film, we're starting in a nightmare.

The bus driver is revealed to be Freddy, who approaches Jesse and the girls, scraping his razor glove on the metal ceiling and fabric seats. You might think he's oblivious to the bottomless pit beneath them all, but he simply doesn't care. Before Freddy can strike, Jesse wakes up in bed. We never learn the two other girls' names, or if they were even real at all.

It's been five years since Nancy faced Freddy. Jesse, his mom Cheryl (Hope Lange), curmudgeonly father Ken (Clu Gulager), and little sister Angela (Christie Clark), have since moved into the house at 1428 Elm Street where Jesse has taken Nancy's old room. The house is always hot. Jesse's grouch of a father says the air conditioner just needs "a shot of freon."

Jesse's friend Lisa (Kim Myers) comes over so they can carpool to school together. At least I think they're just friends. She obviously has a thing for him, but the line is muddled until the end. We'll get there, but first we have to go to everyone's favorite school class, you guessed it, gym! We meet Lisa's friend Kerry (Sydney Walsh) and Grady (Robert Rusler), who is…well, he's sort of not really Jesse's friend either. They fight during a baseball game, drawing the ire of Coach Schneider (Marshall Bell), a sadist who smokes between classes (oh, the 80s). Grady tells Jesse that "some chick" used to live in his new home and that she allegedly went crazy after her boyfriend was murdered, referencing Nancy and Glen. Leaning into his status as the "new kid," Jesse laughs it off. *Freddy's Revenge* is the only film in the series that focuses on "the new kid at school" trope, so Jesse becomes the audience surrogate in several ways.

That night, the stifling heat keeps Jesse awake. He walks around the house and encounters a strange man in his basement. We don't see his face, just the back of his head, though it's obviously that evil bus driver from earlier. Jesse calls for his father, but Freddy appears in front of him, razors glistening. Instead of trying to kill Jesse, he tells him they're going to be…co-workers. Then Freddy grotesquely peels his scalp back, and delivers the infamous line "You've got the body, I've got the brains."

There are several firsts here. It seems like Freddy has a plan beyond simply killing kids in their sleep, and though he's still the same Freddy, cackling and delighting in self-mutilation, he looks different: darker, more demonic. While Robert Englund's makeup changes slightly throughout the series, it's a testament to the makeup artists for maintaining a sense of continuity when other franchises switch out masks and appearances like a fashion show. Sholder doesn't call attention to it, but eagle-eyed viewers will clock Englund as the bus driver in the opening scene.

The next day, Jesse falls asleep in science class. He wakes up screaming when he feels a snake crawling on him. A nearby Grady laughs at Jesse and he flips him off, seemingly solidifying their bond. It's a bit of weird symbolism that's more of a sledgehammer than Craven's finely-tuned scalpel. Later on, Jesse's dad makes him finish unpacking his moving boxes instead of seeing Lisa. He dances in his room to pass the time (man, we really loved *Risky Business*, didn't we, 1985?) when Lisa shows up to help him, making us feel second-hand embarrassment for Jesse AND Mark Patton. (I can't even watch when Lisa and Cheryl walk in and see him gyrating with a pop gun.)

While cleaning, they find Nancy Thompson's old diary. You know, the one she apparently kept during the original film that we never saw or heard about. It provides much-needed backstory and acts as a totem for the rest of the film. They need it because Jesse still can't sleep that night. It's so hot that the items in his room start to melt. He heads to the basement and finds the razor glove, which he previously saw Freddy remove from the boiler. The slasher himself then appears and tells Jesse to "try it on for size" before asking him to "kill for me." As Freddy makes his request, he places his hand upon a scalding pipe, not even registering that his flesh has begun to sizzle. Frightened and confused, Jesse throws down the glove. Of course, it's just a dream, but things get very real when the family's parakeet goes crazy from the heat. It attacks the Walshes before bursting into flame. Naturally, Ken blames Jesse out of sheer frustration. Alright, enough "real world" nonsense. It's time for our first kill.

Jesse can't sleep AGAIN, so he wanders to a seedy leather bar with punks, new wavers, and Bob Shaye in a leather vest, playing a bartender. Coach Schneider shows up and brings (kidnaps, really) Jesse to the high school gym to make him run laps. He doesn't contact his parents or the police, and he's clearly enjoying it. Scheider is the only victim in the entire franchise we actually root for Freddy to kill and it's downright cathartic when Scheider is assaulted by his own gym equipment, which somehow gains sentience. Racket strings heat up and break, and every ball in his office flies at him, before jump ropes (no kids? Maybe that's for the best) drag him to the shower and strip him naked. Finally, Freddy appears out of the shower's mist and claws him to death. Except it's not Freddy. The mist recedes, revealing Jesse, wearing Freddy's glove, having been in a fugue state, so that Freddy could control him. Freddy's plan starts to take form: when Jesse falls asleep, he takes over his body so he can kill outside of the dream world. Though we didn't see Jesse fall asleep, it's still a terrifying prospect.

When the cops find Jesse wandering by the highway, they bring him home to his befuddled parents. Ken and Cheryl actually want to know what's going on with him, and Cheryl is genuinely one of the most sympathetic parents in the series. Ken is concerned, but Clu Gulager portrays him as wary and pissed off. It's different enough from the Thompsons to stand out, especially with the parents we see later on in the series.

One night, Jesse sees the glove in his drawer, moving slightly, as if to taunt him. Surely killing Schnieder was fun, right? Jesse is drawn to Angela's room, where he has a ghostly vision of her as a jump rope girl from the previous entry. It's the only time we see that "jump rope kids" motif or hear the nursery rhyme in this film. You'll only understand this if you've seen the original, and its inclusion is strange. Later entries are all full of those references, but here we get just a tease.

Jesse confronts his parents about the house's lurid history. The "record" states Marge killed herself in the living room (What was THAT autopsy like?). Ken admits he knew ("How do you think we got it so cheap?"), but Cheryl and Angela are frightened. As if on cue, an unplugged appliance lights on fire.

In a neat bit of worldbuilding, Lisa and Jesse go to the now-empty factory where Freddy worked, killed, AND died, hoping to find some useful information from such a loaded location. They don't find anything, but luckily for the audience, Lisa provides some exposition about Freddy's crimes. The tipping point comes for Jesse later that night when he almost kills his sister in her bed, under Freddy's control. This scene feels like a continuation of the first time Jesse goes to her room, but now we're aware of Freddy's escalation when we hear his voice talking through Jesse. When Jesse realizes he's suddenly wearing the glove, he snaps out of it.

The final act begins the following night at Lisa's pool party. Eschewing the revelry, Jesse is instead brooding in her pool house, so Kerry suggests Lisa comfort him. They start to make out furiously as the party rages outside. Suddenly, Freddy's long, demonic tongue shoots out of his mouth. Lisa's eyes are closed, so she doesn't understand when he runs away (Did he fall asleep while rounding second base? We'll unpack that later.)

Jesse runs to Grady's house and breaks into his room, begging him to watch him sleep. (I said we'll unpack that LATER!) Of course, Grady attended the Johnny Depp school of watching people sleep, and fails to notice when Jesse dozes off. He falls asleep and wakes up just long enough to feel Freddy bursting out of him in the film's best sequence. Freddy "sheds" Jesse like a husk and kills Grady as his parents bang on the door. (Just wondering, how could this happen if Jesse's awake, and why doesn't this kill Jesse?) Let's just get back to the pool.

Lisa is about to leave her own party to find Jesse when returns to her house. He's defeated and mostly resigned to being a meat puppet for a serial killer, but Lisa's not having it. As Jesse sweats and goes into hysterics, she reads from Nancy's diary to help him try to fight Freddy's influence. The struggle is personified by strange happenings around the room. Doors in her house begin to lock on their own. Several lights explode and the pool water starts to boil. Lisa's fish tank explodes, and finally, Freddy emerges once again from Jesse's flesh. Lisa tussles with the slasher, who bites her, which is new, but probably not uncommon for someone as insane as him, I guess. As Freddy goes in for the final blow, Jesse pleads with Lisa to kill him. His voice is coming out of Freddy, proving he still has some measure of control over the body he now shares with the demonic killer. This disturbs Freddy, who needs some air and leaps out through the patio doors.

Ah, the infamous pool party scene, where Freddy kills indiscriminately as panicked teenagers try (and fail) to escape the carnage. Lisa's parents race downstairs to the party and her dad fires a shotgun at Freddy (Hey, more good parents! Gee, I hope this continues in every entry.) He misses, and Freddy, sensing Lisa's influence, disappears in a blaze of fire.

Lisa somehow knows he's retreating to the power plant and follows after. She arrives to find..."hellhounds?" They're junkyard rottweilers with distorted human faces. No explanation, but the dream world is now blending with the real world, so anything is slowly going. Even the factory itself appears to be coming back to life. The pipes are hot and the whole area is lit by red and green lights. It's a live-action version of the boiler room dream. The lack of score makes it all terrifying as Lisa acts as a makeshift Theseus looking for her minotaur. She navigates a demonic cat and an illusion of the walkway giving out, none of which deter her.

When Freddy finally appears, she dodges his glove while tearfully declaring her love for Jesse. She kisses Freddy, which is what Jesse needs to purge the slasher from their shared body in a spectacle of fire and blood like he's Jesse Targaryan. Beauty has conquered the beast. The next day, Jesse joins Lisa and Kerry on the school bus. Everyone seems oddly chill, especially when the bus driver doesn't appear to be Robert Englund. But wait! Freddy's gloved hand bursts from Kerry's chest as the bus speeds off into the desert once again.

## NIGHTMARE AUTOPSIS

A film franchise usually establishes itself with a few similar entries before stagnation and experimentation lead the creative forces behind it to try something wholly new. *A Nightmare on Elm Street 2: Freddy's Revenge* is the series' biggest outlier, and it's not even close. The black sheep of the *Nightmare* franchise arrived earlier than other big-swing horror entries like *Halloween: The Curse of Michael Myers* (cults!), *Jason X* (outer space!) or *Jaws: The Revenge* (don't ask). Maybe we're lucky to have experienced the most divisive entry early on to make way for the established mythology.

The overall consensus is that it's one of the lesser entries. Horror historian and critic Kim Newman called it "possibly the lamest of all the sequels." Celebrated gay horror producer Bryan Fuller wrote in *Fangoria* "'Freddy's Revenge' is less queer horror than it is a straight man's idea of a gay Nightmare. Homoerotic, yes, but also homophobic, exploitational and tone-deaf. It utilizes the type of gags commonly played for laughs in the 'Blue Oyster Bars' of 80s franchise comedies. This time, however, those gags are played for jeers."

To be fair, the film's status has risen over the years. Chad Collins of *Dread Central* claims it "ascends kitsch and quietly emerges as possibly the greatest sequel in the series." Joe Lipsett and Trace Thurman of the Horror Queers podcast have mixed feelings about *Freddy's Revenge*, but they agree on its strengths. Lipsett told *Bloody Disgusting* that it "may just be *the* most queer horror movie ever created." Thurman chimed in "[The film] does what a sequel *should* do: try something different. Freddy's modus operandi is completely different and the overall tone is much darker from the first film, while simultaneously leaning into its camp elements." The spectrum is long with this one.

Despite the denial of the filmmakers, *Freddy's Revenge* has a deep vein of homoeroticism running through it, as evidenced in the numerous times your eyebrow raised reading the synopsis. Chaskin eventually said the gay content of the script was meant to be subtext but it quickly became big, bold, underlined text. A snake crawls on Jesse in class and scares him awake which makes his male friend laugh?

And hey, let's get this out of the way: This film is queer. And I am not. Maybe the latter is news, but the former has been discussed ever since the film was released. There are tons of think pieces online by members of the LGBTQIA+ community both lauding the film for wading into those waters, and others, some from the same community, bashing it as incredibly homophobic and problematic. I'm not trying to invalidate anyone who found a certain kind of meaning in *Freddy's Revenge*, so I urge you to seek out those voices for a deeper discussion. Also, definitely check out *Scream, Queen: My Nightmare on Elm Street*, the documentary on star Mark Patton and how the film impacted his life as a closeted gay man in the 80's. For now, like Jesse with Freddy, you're stuck with me.

Apologies to the film's staunch defenders, but it feels less like a visionary chapter than a company trying to strike while the steel claw is hot. As time goes on, I'm convinced the filmmakers were earnest when they pleaded ignorance about how the film would be received. Anyone who's worked on a film set knows what it's like when you're on a deadline, just trying to just "get it done," and with the film releasing a year later, I believe it.

This isn't to say I wasn't affected by the finished product. While I do rank it lower than some of the other sequels, it's far from a bomb. *Freddy's Revenge* is a fascinating watch. Jacques Haitkin mercifully returns as cinematographer, creating a sense of continuity between films. Charles Bernstein's score isn't referenced, except for the one jump rope scene, but Christopher Young does a good job filling in and making it his own with clanking metallic echoes and whale noises. Young, who continues to have a thriving career, which includes creating the iconic theme from *Hellraiser* called working on the film "a dream come true." The film was lucky to have him.

None of the actors are slacking off, either. Kim Myers oozes compassion and Mark Patton balances mania with sadness without being too cloying. When Jesse escapes Grady's home after his murder, you feel for him even more than Rod from the previous entry. In fact, you truly empathize with Jesse's situation for most of the film, even when he's giving up. It's Kim Myers who inherits the role of final girl towards the end, and it suits her. If Jesse is Freddy's battery, then Lisa is essentially Jesse's. He can't defeat Freddy without her.

Clu Gulager and Hope Lange do what's required as Jesse's misunderstanding parents, but Gulager is more memorable as Ken, the stubborn cheapskate. Perennial character actor Marshall Bell is also welcome in whatever he appears in. Schneider may be a perfect example of a bad authority figure, but he's actually malevolent instead of the typical negligence. There's a moment cut from the script where Cheryl tells Ken to "blow it out [his] ass," which would have gotten a laugh because of how prim and proper she appears to be. Plus, Ken kind of deserves it.

Sydney Walsh's Kerry and Robert Rusler's Grady are fine, but they don't have the depth of other *Nightmare on Elm Street* characters. They feel more like the hapless teens from the *Friday the 13th* series or *Freddy vs. Jason*, (I promise, we'll get there). Also, for a film known for it's gay subtext, nobody seems to clock that Kerry is fulfilling the trope of "the gay best friend." She's not coded as queer, but all her conversations with Lisa are about Jesse. Kerry exists to comfort Lisa and reassure her that the film's star wants to sleep with her, and isn't that great? It's not Walsh's fault, but she at least manages to add a campy flair when we see her. Plus, she has the last great scare of the film.

If, like me, you watched the *Nightmare on Elm Street* films out of order, this will absolutely color your view of *Freddy's Revenge*, as unfair as that may seem. This film is treated like a detour because it doesn't have as much in common with later entries. The truth is that NOBODY knew what the franchise would turn into, at least not immediately. The original theatrical poster doesn't even feature Robert Englund and the DVD cover features Freddy with a decrepit farmhouse in the background. Let that sink in. A house that we never see in this, or any of the films. A FARMHOUSE, which obviously isn't on a suburban street, let alone Elm Street. Most of the gripes you may have with this one can be forgiven with that context.

David Chaskin admits what we already know: he wrote a possession film. *Freddy's Revenge* is closer to mid-80's horror films like 1986's *Trick of Treat* or *Hello Mary Lou: Prom Night 2*, both of which are heavily influenced by the original *Nightmare*. He introduced horror elements that would be at home in possession films like the scenes with the parakeet and the snake. Both moments that find fear in the waking world instead of the dream world, breaking the rules Wes Craven established in the original. However, Chaskin carries over Craven's theme of repression and ups the ante considerably.

When Jesse confronts his parents about the house's history, an unplugged appliance catches on fire. This is Chaskin's thesis: repression represented by the stifling heat is bringing Freddy into our world. Ken might not want to talk about it, but the fire burns anyway. Freddy's will is ever-present.

When "Freddy" kills Schneider, he isn't played by Robert Englund, but rather an extra in obfuscated makeup. The actor is still uncredited to this day, most likely to avoid embarrassment. He moved slowly, like a blind robot. As for his appearance? Thank god for all the steam in the shower that hid his terrible mask and sweater. From our limited view, he looked like he robbed a Spirit Halloween and fell down a staircase on the way out. It's atrocious. Thankfully, dailies helped Sholder convince Shaye to get Robert Englund back in the role, making him the only returning cast member for this sequel. Sholder's contributions also include naming the town "Springwood." It didn't have a name in the first film, but it's since been widely canonized. For all the flack Sholder receives for this divisive entry, Elm Street fans owe the guy a fruit basket (no pun intended).

Englund quickly confirms everyone's priors and once again knocks it out of the park as Fred Krueger. Though he's more talkative than he was in the first film, he's not yet the sadistic jokester he becomes in *Dream Warriors*. Englund also evokes a vulnerability as Jesse tries to answer Lisa's cries. It's a credit to Robert Englund that he's able to subtly channel a teenage boy. During the third act, you can see glimmers of Jesse in his eyes. You simply don't get that with a stuntman in a mask. For reasons unknown, David Miller's makeup designs were thrown out after the original film's creation. My personal guess is that New Line had no intention of bringing Englund back to play Freddy, instead opting for a stuntman like in the *Friday the 13th* and *Halloween* films. Therefore, Freddy's makeup for *A Nightmare on Elm Street 2* had to be reconstructed from scratch by a young upstart named Kevin Yagher.

The sequel's lighting keeps Freddy mostly to the shadows, but when he does appear, he glistens like his skin is about to slough off at any moment. This was another directive from Bob Shaye, who'd originally wanted Freddy to appear more melted in the original film, and here he gets his wish. In fact, Shaye was known to micromanage production on *Freddy's Revenge* to ensure that New Line wouldn't be viewed as a one-hit wonder. Having Freddy drive the bus in the opening scene definitely came from him after fighting with Wes over the ending of the original. Also the script mentions a piece of his flesh falling off in the school bus. We don't see it, but you can easily imagine that happening with this slimy, hook-nosed version of Freddy. Yagher also added demonic contact lenses to make him look even less human. The look continues to change through the series, but *Freddy's Revenge* is one of his best, and definitely the scariest. By the film's end, his traditional razor glove is replaced by a flesh-like glove worthy of David Cronenberg.

Speaking of Cronenberg, New Line hired one of his makeup artists to augment the incredible body horror of Jesse's transformation into Freddy. Mark Shostrom is nothing less than a wizard with practical effects, and here he crafts the centerpiece of the film. While the special effects of the original *Nightmare* are indelible on the whole, Jesse's transformation in *Freddy's Revenge* is a singular moment in practical effects body horror that needs to be seen to be believed. The sequel's other gags may fall short of this high mark (the demon parakeet and "hellhounds" come to mind), but one thing is certain - Shostrom's contributions up the effects game in a way that would show subsequent directors of the franchise just what was possible.

# ORIGINAL SCRIPT

In the film's shooting script by David Chaskin, we don't initially realize Jesse is living in Nancy's old house, whereas in the finished film, we get an establishing shot immediately following the bus scene. The script indicates this would be a shocking reveal to contextualize the opening nightmare, but it's possible the filmmakers just wanted the film to get moving. In another change, 1428 Elm Street was originally written to have a pool in the backyard where an early omitted scene finds the Walsh family discussing the home's previous owners. While the *Nightmare* franchise has never depicted a pool behind the house at 1428 Elm, the actual location just south of Sunset Boulevard has long featured an in-ground pool and guesthouse.

Jesse's second nightmare sequence originally featured a hint of Freddy watching him from a kitchen window just before their basement encounter. As first written, Freddy's brains are already exposed beneath his hat, so there's no flesh ripping. It's a small change, but the rip really makes the scene. Later on, when Jesse finds the glove in the cellar, it looks rusty and worn until Freddy appears and it "activates" to the shiny dream version we know.

There's also a running side-plot about Lisa believing Jesse is sensitive to "essential energy," which helps explain why Freddy can take over his body. It doesn't pan out, but it's a noble attempt to add some rules as it's breaking the ones already established.

Jesse and Lisa's investigative factory visit is also longer in the script and alternately takes place before Coach Schneider's death. In the finished film, Lisa shows Jesse several newspaper articles here detailing Freddy's arrest and mistrial. One *Springwood Gazette* headline mentioned in the script but not shown in the film reads "Justice Done - Krueger Killed by Mob! Springwood Slasher Dies in Hellish Inferno," which is a little surprising given the criminal nature of Freddy's demise. (The character's death by vigilante mob has typically been considered a well-kept secret. In the semi-canon pilot for *Freddy's Nightmares*, the parents all swear to secrecy: "The rest of the town hears nothing, understood?" Apparently, someone leaked to the press.) The couple then make out amid the ruins, but stop when Jesse's face begins to visibly throb. (Freddy just can't let him have a moment.)

**METRO FINAL**

**BLUE STREAK**

# Springwood Gazette

*Serving A Most Progressive Community*

WEATHER TOMORROW
**WARM**
Some high clouds. Light wind from the South.
See Page 22.

Vol. XVII, No. 54    SIX PARTS—PART ONE    WEDNESDAY, MAY 14, 1969    38 PAGES    PRICE 20 CENTS

# Springwood Slasher Arrested

**City Bond Issue Nears**

The facts regarding the situation remain the same, state the authorities. Details concerning the action have been given a preliminary investigation but it is felt that only by a more detailed study will the

Many persons feel at this stage that some legal action is forthcoming but it now becomes common knowledge that there is pressure from the inside which will materially change the aspect of the case.

**Upper House Committee**

---

**METRO FINAL**

**BLUE STREAK**

# Springwood Gazette

*Serving A Most Progressive Community*

WEATHER TOMORROW
**WARM**
Some high clouds. Light wind from the South.
See Page 22.

Vol. XVII, No. 54    SIX PARTS—PART ONE    MONDAY, JUNE 16, 1969    38 PAGES    PRICE 20 CENTS

# Krueger Freed on Technicality

**State Backs Tax Resale In Creek County**

**Traffic Safety Plan Outlined by City Roads Authorities**

The present plan again demonstrates belief that the plan will hold force. That is a plan of practical, common, and cultural construction. It will facilitate the further construction and extension of economic solidarity.

WHERE FLOODS ARE DEVASTATING CHINA.

# D. A. RESIGNS

Many persons feel at this stage that some legal action is forthcoming but it now becomes common knowledge that there is pressure from the in-

Of no less importance was the common recognition shown of the fact that any menace from without to the peace of our continents con-

---

**METRO FINAL**

**BLUE STREAK**

# Springwood Gazette

*Serving A Most Progressive Community*

WEATHER TOMORROW
**WARM**
Some high clouds. Light wind from the South.
See Page 22.

Vol. XVII, No. 54    SIX PARTS—PART ONE    TUESDAY, JUNE 24, 1969    38 PAGES    PRICE 20 CENTS

# JUSTICE DONE - KRUEGER KILLED BY MOB

## Property Owners Fight High-Rise Building Zone

**Meeting at City Hall Held to Protest Against Request for Zone Change**

Many persons feel at this stage that some legal action is forthcoming but it now becomes common knowledge that there is pressure from the inside which will materially change the aspect of the case.

An immediate investigation is assured and indications are that some new light will be shed on the situation in the near future. Available facts seem vague but authorities feel that time will disclose some means of arriving at a solution.

Of no less importance was the common recognition shown of the fact that any menace from without to the peace of our continents concerns all of us and therefore property is a subject for consultation and cooperation. This was reflected in the instruments adopted by the conference.

Of no less importance was the common recognition shown of the fact that any menace from without to the peace of our continents concerns all of us and therefore property is a subject for consultation and cooperation. This was reflected in the instruments adopted by the conference.

A suggestion that public hearings on applications be limited to one every six months was taken under advisement by the commission.

Thus at this conference all our governments found themselves in unanimous agreement regarding this undertaking. Arrangements for dealing with questions and disputes between the republics were properly in a subject for consultation and cooperation. This was reflected in the instruments adopted by the conference.

Residents feel that they have been taken advantage of ever since the tax laws governing their additional land holdings were reviewed and increased.

Future plans will, of necessity, have great bearing on the situation as it now stands. Decisions will have to be made of the actual planning of the project will take considerable time but it is felt that these steps are very important.

**DIPLOMATS FETED AS IMPORTANT ISSUES GO BY THE BOARD**

That at this conference all our governments found themselves unanimous in dealing with questions and disputes of no confidence remain all to ce as the republics were feted by the diplomats.

An immediate investigation is assured and indications are that some new light will be shed on the situation in the near future. Available facts seem vague but authorities feel that time will disclose some means of arriving at a solution.

**Volunteer Committee Is Selected To Help Social Service Group**

**Activities Of Children's Bureau, Other Agencies Will Be Given Study**

Thus at this conference all our governments found themselves in unanimous agreement regarding this undertaking. Arrangements for dealing with questions and disputes between the republics were further improved.

An immediate investigation is assured and indications are that some new light will be shed on the situation in the near future. Available facts seem vague but authorities feel that time will disclose some means of arriving at a solution.

## Springwood Slasher Dies In Hellish Inferno

A suggestion that public hearings on applications be limited to one every six months was taken under advisement by the commission.

Thus at this conference all our governments found themselves in unanimous agreement regarding this undertaking. Arrangements for dealing with questions and disputes between the republics were further improved.

A suggestion that public hearings on applications be limited to one every six months was taken under advisement by the commission. Thus at this conference all our governments found themselves in unanimous agreement regarding this undertaking. Arrangements for dealing with questions and disputes between the republics were further improved.

Many persons feel at this stage that some legal action is forthcoming but it now becomes common knowledge that there is pressure from the inside which will materially change the aspect of the case.

An immediate investigation is assured and indications are that some new light will be shed on the situation in the near future. Available facts seem vague but authorities feel that time will disclose some means of arriving at a solution.

Thus at this conference all our governments found themselves in unanimous agreement regarding this undertaking. Arrangements for dealing with questions and disputes between the republics were further improved.

A suggestion that public hearings on applications be limited to one every six months was taken under advisement by the commission.

**World Betterment Institute to Hold Local Meetings**

**Global Educational Program Theme of New Regime**

It would appear that the preliminary inquiry into this matter has in fact not settled any of the minor differences arising from the situation but rather has aggravated the mood of those petitioning for more local involvement by the council.

An immediate investigation is assured and indications are that some new light will be shed on the situation in the near future. Available facts seem vague but authorities feel that time will disclose some means of arriving at a solution.

Prop newspapers from *Freddy's Revenge*, the last of which
lets slip a fairly major secret with its headline.

When Freddy finally emerges from Jesse's body, he doesn't come out of his stomach as in the finished film. Rather, blood sprays across Grady's room "in a fine, almost powdery mist" before Freddy steps out from the red cloud wearing Jesse's face like a mask. Mark Shostrom and the makeup team did a much different, but improved job.

Finally, Kerry gets short changed a bit in the end as originally written. There's a character named Patty, who has one line telling Lisa to go after Jesse at her party. That's all she does. Kerry has that line in the final film, so it doesn't make sense to give it to a random new character. In the final scene, instead of Freddy's hand bursting through Kerry, Freddy's demonic tongue comes through Lisa as she and Jesse kiss. In the novelization by Jeffrey Cooper, it's Freddy's glove that emerges from Lisa instead of Kerry. I think the tongue coming from Lisa would've been a lot more interesting, but also much more on the nose for a film that basically lives on the nose.

# INTERVIEW
# JACK SHOLDER
## DIRECTOR

A Nightmare ON ELM STREET 2
FREDDY'S REVENGE

**You said you happened to read Wes's script for part one and gave notes. Do you recall what those notes were?**

I had a long association with New Line Cinema. I met Bob Shaye when the company was a year or two old, and they had a couple of people working there. They had like four feature films in 16mm that they were distributing to colleges. Bob asked if I knew anyone who could cut a trailer and I said "Me!" We rented someone's cutting room over a weekend, so we could get it for cheap, and we came out Monday at 5 AM with a trailer. We became good friends, and if they needed editing and I wasn't busy, which was often the case, I would cut trailers or do a title sequence or whatever. We hung out a lot. We'd have dinner a couple times a week. He liked to get other peoples' opinions, but then he'd do whatever the hell he wanted. But he liked to test his opinions, because even though he wanted to always be right, he was smart enough to realize he wasn't always right, and it would be good to hear other opinions.

I read an early script of [*A Nightmare on Elm Street*] about a year before he made it. He was very excited about it. He was convinced it was going to be a hit. Maybe not as big as it became, but he gave me the script to read and I gave him my thoughts. It just so happened that I went out to Los Angeles on the day they shot the scene in the upside-down room. I actually met Jacques Haitkin, who went on to shoot *Elm Street 2*. We didn't get to socialize, because he was strapped into this contraption. During editing, they were getting ready for a test screening, and Bob asked me to cut a temp music track. I had no creative input, but I was certainly familiar with it, which I'm sure is one of the reasons he asked me to take over from Wes.

**So when you got the job, how did you reconcile Bob Shaye's opinions? He always seemed to be more involved than other executives.**

I came on the film in pre-production. Wes bailed six weeks before because he didn't like the script. In his mind, it went against the whole concept of Freddy appearing in dreams. [New Line] called me and asked if I'd like to direct a movie. I said "Honestly, no" (laughs). I saw myself as an auteur, like a young Francois Truffaut. I didn't want to be typecast as a horror film director, and I certainly didn't want to be typecast as a horror sequel director. Of course, [Sholder's last film] *Alone in the Dark* hadn't set the world on fire. It got pretty good reviews, but it didn't make a lot of money. I was being a little choosy. A friend of mine, who became a successful Hollywood producer, said "Jack, don't be an idiot. The movie will make money, which means you'll be working, and you'll have a career as a director." He was right and my life changed. *Elm Street 2* was the number one movie that weekend, it got decent reviews, and that Monday morning Dino De Laurentiis called me from his car!

I didn't have any input on the script. Normally, I insist on having a lot of input, because if the script isn't working, the movie won't be any good, period. In this case, everyone was happy with the script, which they handed to me, and it was like climbing Mt. Everest. There were 100 special effects and I had no idea how to do any of it. Jacques Haitkin gave me a level of confidence, but I was pretty much a nervous wreck during the whole pre-production period. I was just trying to get the movie made.

But I'm sure Bob had a lot of input in the script, which was probably part of why Wes didn't like it. (laughs) Some of Bob's ideas could be very corny. Once the movie starts shooting, besides firing the director, there's not much you can do. Bob kind of left me alone. I've worked for other studios, where people are watching the dailies, they don't like this or that. I never got that with him. The only thing was that they wanted to hire a new makeup guy because they didn't like the makeup in the original. So I basically discovered Kevin Yagher.

**Thank you for that, by the way.**

Everyone loved what he did. He was an artist. The only thing they told me was I had to keep [Freddy] dark and scary. As long as the dailies came out, and they looked good and we were more or less on schedule, they left me alone.

**I can't believe you got all the way through pre-production with a stuntman playing Freddy.**

Let me correct you.

**Please do!**

He wasn't a stuntman. Stuntpeople are often actors. They're rarely any good, but they are professional actors. This guy wasn't an actor. He was an extra. They hired someone who fit the outfit and who they thought they could make up to look like Freddy. That was the criteria. I never met him.

**When did the alarm start to go off that you needed Robert Englund?**

Here's what happened. I got out to LA, I'm sitting in my apartment, and I'm caught up in this tornado. I have this big, complicated movie to direct, which I'm freaking out about, and I said "I assumed you're bringing Robert Englund back." They said, "His agent is asking for more money and we don't want them to take advantage of us, so we'll just get a stuntman to play the part." I said "Gee, I think you should bring him back. He was really good. (laughs) I think he's really important to the success of the film." They said "No, no, no, anybody could play that role."

**Jesus.**

I wasn't thinking about it then, but it occurred to me later that the whole thing was a bluff to make Robert and his agent think they weren't going to bring him back, so they could make a deal. I was there for the casting of the entire movie, but we never brought anyone in to read for Freddy. And he had lines! He was a real character, which was what was so brilliant about the original. Two weeks before shooting, Sara Risher said they were able to make the deal with Robert, but he was booked during [our] first week of shooting. We had to move things around, but the only scene he couldn't do was the shower scene. I hadn't met Robert yet, but I went to see a play with Lin Shaye, and who happened to be in the audience, but Robert? At that point, he was going to be doing the movie, so I introduced myself and just started talking a mile a minute for the whole 15-minute intermission. Afterwards, it was like "See you on set." So this guy who I never met shows up in the Freddy makeup and outfit. He walked out the shower like Frankenstein. He was just awful. I said "Stop! Walk like a man, not a monster." So I had *some* success (laughs). At least stuntmen can take direction. But then Robert came in the next week and he was really good. He would just take a step across the room and you could feel his intensity and power.

The summer before last, I was out in LA and I met Sara for breakfast. I said, "Tell me the truth, because it occurs to me you were just playing hardball to make him think you were going to do the film without him." She said "No, we just thought we could get a guy, put the makeup on him, and he'll be fine." I was dumbstruck. You look at the poster for the first movie and who's missing? Freddy!

**He's not even technically on the poster for *Elm Street 2* either.**

I'll go to these conventions, where there's a panel, usually with Mark or Robert, and they'll say "Here's what happened..." and I'm thinking "That's not what happened. I know what happened because I had a pretty good seat." (laughs)

**Were they just unaware of certain things?**

They knew things that I didn't know. I had no idea Mark [Patton] was gay. The hair and makeup people and the art department knew he was gay. I didn't think about it, nobody brought it up, and it was never questioned.

New Line hired a publicist who was trying to come up with an angle to sell the film, and he read somewhere in a poll that Freddy was the scariest man in America. So he set up a midnight screening in New York, and put the word out that people were coming dressed as Freddy. It was a total lie, but he hired people to come dressed as Freddy. To our great surprise, audience members came dressed as Freddy, anyway! Every time Robert appeared on screen, they'd go nuts. That's when they realized Robert was the franchise.

**Freddy's Revenge is more of a classical horror film, then the other entries. It follows the structure of a possession film. You mentioned you're not much of a genre guy, so where did the inspiration come to craft the film if it wasn't already in your wheelhouse?**

I'm gonna digress again. When we tested the film, Bob said it wasn't scary enough. He felt the audience agreed. As you probably know, I was a very good editor. I had won an Emmy, so I said "Let me work on it." I put in some music, and after another screening he said it still wasn't scary. The way the script was structured, [Coach Schneider's death] was at the end of act two. Bob said if we could move it to the start of act two, it would be scarier. Freddy walks around saying "I'm gonna do this, I'm gonna do that," but he never does anything. I said there's no way to move that up because things happen that don't make any logical sense due the order of events.

I was an avid squash player, and there was this young Hispanic kid who worked [where I played]. He was a huge horror fan, so I invited him to the next screening. When it was over, I asked him how it was and he said "Oh, it was pretty good." I asked "Was it scary?" He said "Eh, not really." I thought "Oh fuck, we have a problem here." I edited a lot of non-scripted stuff, and I still feel like I can make anything work in the editing room. I sat there wondering how I was going to move that scene up. I thought about a line I could put in to cover the problem. There's a shot when Jesse and Lisa are in the car, and they're far enough away that you can't see their lips. I was able to take that scene from the end of act two and put it in the beginning of act two. So Freddy's threats weren't empty.

Now the film might have been a hit anyway. The head of distribution hoped to make 70-80% of what the original film made, and of course, we made more. But I think that [change] made the film scarier. Sorry, what was the question (laughs)?

**I'm curious about your horror influences. I know the scene at the pool party has been criticized, but it's still a scary scene of a maniac murdering teens indiscriminately. It's reminiscent of *Carrie*.**

I really wasn't inspired by anything else, even the original film. Jacques felt he could do a better job with the sequel. You know, Wes was a horror film director. He expressed himself through the medium. I like to say I express myself in spite of the medium.

**Yes, I even remember when you said that. Since you're the latter, what part of you was expressed in *Freddy's Revenge*?**

Everyone sets out to make a good movie. Hopefully nobody says "I'm gonna direct this piece of shit, but I'm getting paid." I never went to film school. My film school was the revival houses and the art houses of New York City. I saw every movie that played, including movies that people I know who teach film studies have never seen. If I picked out what I was gonna watch [beforehand], maybe I wouldn't have seen as many kinds of films I saw, but if it was playing, I went to see it. I had a broad range of influences from most of the Hitchcock films to all the films of Buster Keaton. All sorts of films. New Line wanted a film that was scary and my frame of reference was some of the old classical stuff. I tend to be a classicist. I had a feel for how I wanted [*Freddy's Revenge*] to play.

A lot of it came from Jacques, but I never felt I had a real talent, visually. I think I had a talent for knowing where to put the camera. I had a knack for telling a story, because I was an English major in college and I wanted to be a writer. I read all the great literature, including every play Shakespeare ever wrote. I had a musical background, as well, and I really think film has a lot in common with music. Film works like music. It occurs in time. It has a micro rhythm, which is how the cuts work, and a macro rhythm, like the overall structure in a symphony. A lot of people don't really understand how important that is, because it's not as obvious as, let's say, photography. People don't often notice it. If it's done well, the editing pulls the film along.

I also took a lot from Hitchcock. Of those I've stolen from (laughs), visually I stole a lot from Orson Welles. I subconsciously adopted his deep focus thing, which became my style. I read the Hitchcock/Truffaut book several times and took notes throughout the book. Hitchcock would always have a memorable sequence. One big, special thing like the crop duster sequence [in *North by Northwest.*]. So there are a number of scenes like that, such as the gym scene and the transformation scene. I designed everything and had a shot list for the whole movie before we started shooting. I wouldn't say I shot it just like I planned it. Hopefully you don't, because things change, but I had a very clear plan for what I wanted to do. I was in a state of anxiety for pretty much the entire pre-production. I shot listed the entire thing, and when I walked on set day one, I knew what I was doing. Horror films have that structure, with kill scenes and scare scenes.

**To be honest, I don't have any questions about missing the film's gay subtext, especially in the 80's. I don't believe anyone racing to make an indie horror movie in the 1980's had time to really consider what was being expressed.**

I'm not defensive about it at all. You know Mark [Patton]'s story where his agent saw the film and said he couldn't "play straight?" He wanted to be a movie star, and he was highly motivated. I made the movie so I could have a career, and when Dino called me the next day, I never looked back. *Freddy's Revenge* did exactly what I wanted it to do. It got me my next bunch of movies. My next film was *The Hidden*, which I really wanted to do.

We had a 30th reunion at a convention. Mark, Kim [Myers], and Robert Rusler were there. I think Robert [Englund] was there. All these people I haven't seen since the cast and crew screening. Mark was shooting footage for his documentary, which I think is really good, by the way. Initially I found it amusing that the film had developed a subtextual reading, shall we say. As I got to know more about it and see how the film meant a lot to kids who grew up gay, I thought "Well, I never intended to do it, but it's a great outcome." When people say "Oh, he had no idea he made this gay movie," I wasn't, but I certainly knew what was going on. I'd moved to the West Village when Stonewall happened and I moved out at the end of AIDS. I felt the film was about teen sexual anxiety, which Freddy represented. Robert [Englund] was very well aware of that. The song at the end, "Did You Ever Seen a Dream Walking?" was a well-known gay thing in the 40's.

**Really? I thought it was used just because of the title.**

Yeah, it got in there because Bob grew up listening to the radio, and he can be a little corny and hit things on the nose. He wanted to have that song played over the credits and he was willing to pay for the rights.

**Going back to how you were self-taught, that's even more impressive when you look at your work on the first feature you edited, 1981's *The Burning*. The canoe massacre is the most memorable scene from that film, and editing plays a huge part.**

Like I said, I was a very good editor, but I never cut a feature before. I cut mostly documentary footage, unscripted stuff, and a lot of trailers. You learn a lot from cutting trailers. I used to joke that it was like taking a grandfather clock and turning it into a wristwatch.

**Let's talk about directing Robert Englund. Actors need directors, but it always felt like he had a grasp of the character that never wavered. He seemed like you could wind him up and let him go to a point. Was that your experience?**

You're absolutely correct. First of all, Robert was the expert on the character. In my mind, the movie was all about him, really. We were doing the scene where Freddy and Lisa struggle in the house during the pool party. Robert asked "Would it be okay if I bite her leg?" He was a dream to work with. I understood his role, but he understood it better than anyone. I designed the scene and gave him the blocking, but he knew what to do. I've worked with some very good actors. I did two things with James Earl Jones, may he rest in peace. Incredible actor. Plus, the guys from *Alone in the Dark* [Jack Palance, Donald Pleasance, and Martin Landau].

**The first two *Nightmare* films have a similar look, which I attribute mostly to the late Jacques Haitkin. Do you have memories of working with him?**

Yeah, Jacques was a perfectionist. He was very into the technical side of cinematography. If there was a knock on him, it's that his technical skills outdid his creative skills. Everything looked nice, but he tended to play it a little safe.

Like I said, I wasn't born with a great visual sense, so it was something I had to work on. I would just try to push him. If the camera was nose high, I'd tell him to raise it or lower it, just to do something with it. Jacques had the chops to take it to whatever level he wanted. In a way, Jacques was my film school. [Today], you can go to film school, but there are lots of things you learn by just doing them. *Elm Street* was my second feature. Jacques had way more experience than I did. It's often the case where you have a crew where everyone's an expert at what they do, and you have a first-time director who's doing this very difficult thing they've never done before. (laughs) Jacques also had an appreciation of older, more historical things. He'd say "Let's grind some corn" instead of "Move the camera." Back in the days of silent film, you'd crank the camera like you were grinding corn. I picked up a lot of the expressions he used on set.

He was also very respectful of my position. Because I'd been an editor, I understood what was needed. Bob Shaye used to say somewhat facetiously, that he hired me because he knew I'd get all the pieces. In the early 80's, everyone thought they could make a horror film, but a lot of these people didn't know how to make a movie. I'd be working in a place where they'd have several cutting rooms and see people pulling their hair out because their film's director shot a scene incompetently. You couldn't get from this shot to that shot. I knew how to design a film that would at least have a beginning, a middle, and an end. Jacques respected me on that level. He was very picky. We would screen the dailies and sometimes he would go up the screen and go "It's not sharp!" One day I said, "Jacques, you're the only person who could see that." He said "That's the worst kind!"

**You had a top-notch special effects team at your disposal. What was your experience like working with Kevin Yagher and Mark Shostrom?**

The producers felt we needed to have two makeup teams. There would be the "Freddy team," which was Kevin's primary job. He did some other effects, but his chief responsibility was getting Robert to look like Freddy. Mark Shostrom was more the "blood and guts guy." He did the transformation scene with the second unit. If it were up to me, I would have shot everything. Someone once asked me what's the hardest part of doing an action or horror movie. Horror or action takes care of themselves, but the answer is to create good characters. That was most important to me. If I added something to the value of the film, it was that I got good performances. I was very character-oriented. The second unit would be shooting the transformation scene while I was shooting something else, but on breaks, I'd run over to their part of the set. Shooting special effects is very painstaking and time-consuming. I storyboarded the whole thing, so they had to get a lot of little pieces right. It was like putting together a watch. They were shooting the blades coming out of the fingers, and they thought "Wow, this is a cool effect." I said "It's not a prop, it's the hand of a human being. You have to light the hand and have it react like it's happening to him." That was a very important aspect to me.

There's two kinds of effects: makeup effects and practical, physical effects. The pool boiling and melting objects were practical, and I don't think they ever followed up with that.

**In the later films? Not to the same extent, no.**

The huge, intimidating list of effects I mentioned were practical effects like the wheel coming off the bus. [Line Producers] Joel Soisson and Michael [Murphey] said they found a fantastic guy who was going to be in charge of the physical effects, and his name is Dick Albain. Dick was the head of special effects at 20th Century Fox. He was an old timer who'd been in the business for years. He said "Don't worry kid, I know how to do all of this." I asked of all the films he worked on, what was he most proud of. He thought for a minute and said "My work with the Three Stooges." (laughs) He said he did every episode of *I Dream of Jeannie* and they never had to do an optical effect. All effects were practical.

If you froze a special effects guy from a Boris Karloff movie in the 30's or 40's, and defrosted them in the early 80's, they could've gone right back to work. They were using stuff you could find in a magic store. In the scene where the guy grabs the gate and burns his hand, [we used] this stuff called "AB smoke." You put some on your hand and some on what you touch, and when they come together, it looks like smoke. It was on that level. Obviously, in the last twenty years, things have changed. They were still using mortician's wax for lots of special effects makeup. The next movie we did was *The Hidden*, with Jacques and Kevin Yagher. New Line was more than thrilled to have Kevin back. They just came out with this whole new thing called latex. They could do incredibly fine work, and it revolutionized everything. We were shooting a scene with Bill Boyett, and Kevin had made his head.

**The scene where the alien transfers bodies for the first time?**

Yes. The head was so realistic looking that Bill took one look at it and said "Don't ever show that thing to me again." I've seen stuff so lifelike, I could swear they could get up and walk across the room. There's a lot of nostalgia for 60's horror, and I think a lot of it has this handmade quaintness about it, you know?

# INTERVIEW
# SARA RISHER
### FRANCHISE PRODUCER
## NEW LINE CINEMA

**New Line Cinema started in New York, then moved to California, correct?**

Yes, it started in Bob Shaye's Greenwich Village apartment, then it moved around in New York City until I opened the LA office in 1985. I hired some people and realized I had to live here to make independent movies, so I moved here in 1987.

**Bob Shaye was always credited as the producer, and your name always showed up under different titles like co-producer and executive producer. Can you break those down for people who might not understand?**

[New Line] was a very small company. I was running almost everything, certainly acquisitions and production. We'd only made a couple of movies at that time. The *Nightmare* script had been passed around Hollywood when Bob read it and thought it had great potential. He went to Hollywood to meet with Wes Craven, and when he came back to New York, we realized it needed a lot of work. Bob and I had quite a few meetings with Wes to develop the script. When the script was in shape, Bob was able to raise most of the money. He lost one of the partners as I went out to LA to start pre-production. He got a new partner and came out on day one as we started to shoot. By this time, I was six months pregnant.

**In the middle of production?!**

Yeah, it was during the [1984] Olympics, which was a great time to be around. For some reason, LA was empty. It was a great production. Wes knew exactly what he wanted. He was great with the actors. He knew we had no money and always made his days. He never went over budget, even though we didn't have the money for special effects. Bob gave a lot of input into the special effects, like how to do them in camera.

**Was there ever a moment you knew you had something special, or was it when you saw the film's reception?**

I thought we had something special from the beginning and from watching the dailies, but we didn't know how special. Two things happened. My husband at the time entered it in the Hof Film Festival in Germany, where it was a huge success. They had to schedule three more screenings! He's German, and he called me from there to tell me. It was like the first public screening we had. The other thing was opening weekend. Lines were around the block when we opened in New York, Queens, and Brooklyn. Word of mouth spread really fast. Then on Monday, Bob said "Let's do a sequel. Start working on it now!" So I did. (laughs)

We figured out early that Freddy was the one everybody cared about, so we always knew we'd have Freddy. We asked Wes to do the sequel, but he didn't want to, so we went with David Chaskin's script, which we liked. We also had partners by then, who wanted us to go ahead quickly.

**Part two had been a huge hit, but it always fascinated me that New Line wanted part three to be better. Can you talk about the transition to fan favorite *Dream Warriors*?**

Frank Darabont came up with the script with Chuck Russell, and it was brilliant! We knew right away Chuck would be the right director [for the film]. By then, we had more money and we wanted to make it bigger and better.

**Unlike most studios, I always got the impression that New Line and Bob Shaye really cared about making better films.**

Absolutely. There were some good things about being poor. (laughs) When you don't have a lot of money, you have to come up with innovative ways to do things with the director, the writer, and Bob. A lot of it was very creative, and everyone was onboard, pulling together to make the best movie they could. It was always a team effort. After the first *Nightmare*, we made *Critters*, which did very well, so we were still moving ahead, but the *Nightmare* films really solidified us. Not necessarily in Hollywood, because we were still considered independent. There was an article that called New Line Cinema "The House That Freddy Built."

**You mentioned that you went back to Wes to direct the sequels. Do you recall any conversations about why he turned you down?**

I think he was annoyed that we made [part two] without him, and by then we just moved on. I would periodically ask him if he would do another one, then he came to me about *New Nightmare*. It was a terrific movie and Wes was a really good director.

**It's such a far out idea. Do you recall your reaction when he pitched the idea, especially where you play yourself?**

You know, we really thought *Freddy's Dead* was the end of the franchise, so we were thrilled when Wes wanted to come back with such an innovative idea.

**Let's go back to part four for a second. Were you looking for a director like Renny Harlin to make it so visual and stylized, or did he pitch you on it?**

Someone, maybe his agent, came to us with his previous film *Prison*. [Producer] Rachel Talalay and I thought he would be great, so we met with him and really liked what he had to say. We were convinced almost immediately. Bob Shaye wasn't. You probably heard the story. He said English wasn't his first language and it wasn't a good idea. We had three or four meetings before Bob said "Okay."

After a few meetings, we noticed Renny was wearing the same outfit. He looked dirtier and dirtier. It turns out he was living in his car because he had no money! He told us the first thing he did when he got the deal was go to IHOP with a friend and get a big breakfast. (laughs)

**Do you have any memories of working with Annette Benson, the casting director on most of the films?**

Oh, she was amazing! First of all, she found Nancy, who was the perfect girl next door. Innocent, but ultimately very strong. I was telling somebody this story. Michael Bay was involved in the remake, and he totally cast the wrong person [as Nancy], then made the boyfriend be the hero. He brought Freddy into the [real] world, and conquered him, which is so wrong. Annette didn't cast that one, and it was not a great success. But she found Johnny Depp, Patricia Arquette, and Laurence Fishburne. Annette knew who she wanted, she had access to everyone, and she knew how to get them. She was one of the very important elements.

**After working on the first five films, you aren't credited on *Freddy's Dead*. Were you busy with other projects at New Line?**

I don't have a credit on [*Freddy's Dead*]? I thought I had a credit on all of them. Rachel Talalay, who directed it, is a very good friend of mine. She was previously a producer on the *Nightmare* films and I was one of the champions of the idea of giving her the chance to direct it.

**Is there anything else you'd like people to know about the *Nightmare* films?**

I really feel that on each *Nightmare*, I worked very hard with the writers on the female characters. Except maybe the second film, but certainly on the first film. *Nightmare 5* came about because I had just had my baby and it was about a mother. I was very involved in making sure the women came across well. I would like people to know that.

# A Nightmare ON ELM STREET 3
## DREAM WARRIORS

While *Freddy's Revenge* was a financial hit, New Line Cinema recognized there was a dip in quality between the first and second entries in the series. Bob Shaye and company knew they had to do better with the next installment. But did they? Freddy Krueger was a bonafide moneymaker. The company behind the films could have just gone on autopilot, playing the same old song while the executives collected checks. Not New Line Cinema. They wanted a sequel they could be proud of, so they went back to the man who started it all, Wes Craven.

*A Nightmare on Elm Street 3: Dream Warriors* pivots the franchise in a bold new direction that sets the tone for what's to come. It's an undeniable fan favorite that couldn't have been done without the help of Craven and his co-writer, Bruce Wagner. With their initial script, they conceived the idea of teens coming together to fight Freddy in the dreamscape. The setting switches from a suburban neighborhood to a psychiatric hospital where Freddy's potential victims learn to team up against him. This is where Craven's investigation of Carl Jung's "collective unconscious" theory truly comes into play.

Instead of Craven returning to direct, ambitious first-timer Charles "Chuck" Russell was brought in to make one of the most beloved sequels in horror history. Although New Line had passed on his pitch for a remake of *The Blob*, which Russell would eventually make for Cinema Group Pictures, they did still ask if he was interested in taking the helm of the newest *Nightmare*.

Craven and Wagner's original script had been deemed too dark and technically ambitious, so Russell absconded to a cabin in Big Bear with future filmmaking superstar Frank Darabont where they re-wrote the Craven/Wagner draft in only a week. The final film pivots away from the direction of *Freddy's Revenge*, acting as more of a direct sequel to the original. Success has many fathers, and they were all about to birth the son of 100 maniacs.

## DREAM SCENARIO

*Dream Warriors* is the first film in the franchise to open with an apropos quote in red text, this one by the mad genius Edgar Allan Poe. This is also the only *Elm Street* film that doesn't start with a dream sequence. The opening credits stay in a close up of Kristen Parker (Patricia Arquette) making a model house in her pajamas. Dokken's "Into the Fire" plays on her radio as she chases coffee grounds with soda. (I've seen these films countless times, and my gorge still rises when she does it. Gross.)

Despite her attempts to stay awake, her socialite mother Elaine (Brooke Bundy) bursts into her room to make sure she goes to sleep. Not to wish her goodnight or make her feel better about her recurring nightmares, but to make sure she crashes so that SHE can crash into her bourbon-craving date. Elaine is one of the worst parents in a film series filled with bad ones, but Bundy leaves a big impression.

Despite her soda-and-coffee grounds combo, Kristen falls asleep and, when she "wakes up," she's transported to the lawn of the house she was just building, now at full size. If this isn't your first rodeo, it's easy to clock this house as 1428 Elm Street, former home to Nancy and Jesse, now appearing as an abandoned, decrepit mess. This is how the house will look for the rest of the series, and yes, we'll be seeing it again.

> "Sleep. Those little slices
> of death. How I loathe them."
>
> — Edgar Allan Poe

The scene establishes several links to the original film. Kristen sees the jump rope kids, dressed in white, singing the infamous rhyme. A little girl on a tricycle lures Kristen into the house's basement just as the boiler lights up by itself. Freddy is nearby and Kristen instinctively knows they have to book it. She picks up the girl and runs with her down the basement hallway. Her feet get stuck in goo just as Freddy appears and she narrowly avoids him. It's curious that Freddy's first appearance is enshadowed and that we barely see him coming from behind. He isn't introduced with much fanfare, but consider all the references to the original film that we've just seen. If you're new to the world of *A Nightmare on Elm Street*, Russell is giving you a primer.

After stumbling upon a room of hanging corpses, the little girl she's holding turns into a skeleton. Kristen mercifully wakes up, for real this time. Only, not really (that old chestnut). Freddy strikes again by sprouting his claws from her bathroom sink and slashing her wrists in an attempt to stage her death like a suicide. As verified by another character later on, we've never seen Freddy quite like this. He's just as deadly, but stronger and more capable at stretching the fabric of dreams to kill in fantastical ways. Before he can finish the job, Elaine manages to wake her daughter just in time to see her wrists spurting blood. She immediately passes out in shock. (Wouldn't Freddy consider that a mulligan?)

We now move away from Kristen's home to Westin Hills, Springwood's local mental hospital. Russell introduces Dr. Neil Gordon (Craig Wasson), a young psychiatrist who interacts with some of his teenage patients. There's Taryn (Jennifer Rubin), a former junkie who chose to be committed instead of facing jail time, Jennifer (Penelope Sudrow), an aspiring actress who puts her cigarettes out on her arm, and Kincaid (Ken Sagoes), the series' first Black teen with a speaking role. He's currently confined to "the quiet room," a padded cell for kids to go when they have the kind of outbursts you'll see later.

After joking with orderly Max (Laurence Fishburne in a role so early in his career he's billed as "Larry Fishburne"), Neil starts voicing concerns to his superior, Dr. Simms (Priscilla Pointer) about a new grad student working at the hospital. Neil is one of the most sympathetic adults in the franchise. He truly cares about his patients. Simms takes a sterner approach, but cares just as much.

When they're called in to help with a hysterical patient, they run as fast as they can to a room, where none other than Kristen is having an episode. Her mother is there, but she's more embarrassed than concerned. The orderlies are just trying to sedate her when she grabs a scalpel and cuts Max. Neil tries to reason with her, but she's so exhausted and upset, all she can do is hold the scalpel out like a totem and recite part of the rhyme she heard from the jump rope kids. She fumbles through the last line, "9, 10, never...never..."

## (O.S.)
## Never sleep again.

The rhyme is finished by the very same graduate student Neil was moaning about. She's standing in the doorway: Nancy Thompson, alive, well and here to help. If you've seen the first two films, you might have thought she was dead, or according to Grady, a resident in this very hospital. If, like me, you saw *Dream Warriors* before the original film and had never heard of Nancy Thompson before, then this seemingly random woman showing up to finish the rhyme hit like a lightning bolt.

Soon after, Nancy and Neil talk and develop a quick rapport. He notices a medication bottle falling out of her bag and sees a nun staring at him though nobody else seems to notice her. Weird. Max gives Nancy a tour of Westin Hills and introduces her to a few of the residents. Phillip (Bradley Gregg) is a charming smart-ass who sleepwalks and makes puppets. I've wondered if those were related, as if making puppets was a form of therapy to handle his sleepwalking, but it's never explored. We already met his roommate Kincaid in the quiet room. He's subdued, but still a burly hardass with a chip on his shoulder.

Nancy visits Kristen's house to get her things and get some background from her mother. "Hurricane" Elaine isn't helpful (despite the fact that she surely knew Marge Thompson. More on that later). She finds Kristen's half-finished model house. Her house, now HIS. Meanwhile, Neil looks up the medication Nancy dropped: Hypnocil, a dream suppressant not yet approved by the FDA.

Kristen falls asleep and again sees the familiar tricycle melting in her room from that good ol' fashioned Krueger heat. She backs away, frightened, but the door leads her back to Freddy's house. This time, there's something in the walls, waiting for her. It's Freddy in the form of a giant snake. The terrifying creature almost devours her whole when she calls Nancy for help. It seems impossible, but Nancy somehow hears her cry. Kristen's voice wakes her from a nap, pulling Nancy through her chair and into Kristen's dream! (Jung is cheering in his grave.) She helps Kristen escape as the two adversaries suddenly recognize each other. Nancy realizes Kristen has to get them out of there, which she does just before the Freddy snake can strike. The next day, Nancy tells her she used to live in the house from Kristen's dreams. Kristen then reveals that she can pull people into her dreams. This is all suddenly very real.

Next up is our first group therapy scene. Neil and Simms introduce Nancy to the group of teens we met before, including Will (Ira Heiden), a recent paraplegic after a suicide attempt. Jennfier introduces Joey (Rodney Eastman), a shy teen who debated in high school but has since been rendered mute by psychological anguish. They're all here because of their traumas, which Phillip waxes philosophical on. He's snarky, but likable.

That night, Will, Taryn, and Joey play a *Dungeons and Dragons*-esque game before lights out. Will makes Joey watch him sleep for safety and clearly not for the first time. (Unlike Glen, they understand they're in danger when they go to sleep.) Meanwhile, Neil takes Nancy on a date where she fails to convince him to prescribe Hypnocil for the group. He refuses to do so because he doesn't want to add fuel to their fire, instead believing their common boogeyman to be a shared delusion rather than an actual threat. Yet, he doesn't dismiss Nancy outright. There's clearly a spark between them, and the fact that he listened to her is more than most authority figures do in these films.

It's time for our first death scene, and we're not in the boiler room anymore, Toto. This is the first time we see Freddy use his victim's mind as a means to kill them. First, one of Phillip's marionettes turns into a mini-Freddy, walks over to his bed, grows to life-size, and cuts Phillip's limbs so that his tendons rise like puppet strings. Phillip appears to sleepwalk down the hall, phasing through doors. Thankfully, Joey sees him up in the clocktower and makes noise to wake up all the other kids, who can scream for help. They all yell for him to wake up (except Joey) as a giant Freddy appears above him like a puppet master. Freddy cuts his "strings" and Phillip falls to his death. (Holy shit.)

The kids know they're being hunted and only Nancy understands. The next day in group, they talk around Neil and Simms, who are perplexed. Kincaid, scared and probably blaming himself for catching a glimpse of Phillip "sleepwalking" and not doing anything about it, freaks out and winds back up in the quiet room. Desperate for answers, Neil takes a cue from Nancy and prescribes Hypnocil despite Simms misgivings. If only they got it faster...

That night, a scumbag orderly named Lorenzo offers Taryn pharmaceutical drugs (or "Club Meth," because it's 1987). She spurns his advances, however, as she's trying to stay sober and leave that part of her life behind. When she threatens to tell Max, he laughs, asking "Who would take the word of a crazy junkie chick like you?" Sure, the script is planting the seeds for a sequence later on, but this scene is so sad. Isn't it enough that her dreams are deadly and she's watching her friends die around her? Honestly, it's a miracle none of Freddy's other victims are addicts. They have their vices, sure, but she's the only one fighting on both fronts: struggling to get sober when she's awake and fighting to survive when she's asleep.

We don't know much about Taryn's background, but for Lorenzo to gaslight her into keeping quiet is a new kind of awful for a character in these films, a good thirty years before "Time's Up." He's just another asshole preying on the weak like Coach Schneider in *Freddy's Revenge*, or Freddy himself for that matter. (And sadly, unlike Schneider, Lorenzo never gets his comeuppance.)

Jennifer begs Max to stay up and watch tv in the lounge. It's against the rules, but she's mourning Phillip and he's sympathetic. (Another sympathetic adult in these films? Surely you jest.) Jennifer smokes cigarettes and burns herself to stay awake while watching *The Dick Cavett Show* with special guest Zsa Zsa Gabor (playing themselves in the first celebrity cameos in the series). When Jennifer sees Dick turn into Freddy and attack the cop-slapping sex symbol, the screen suddenly turns to static. She then hears a familiar nursery rhyme as she tentatively approaches the tv. Freddy's head and arms pop out and grab her. He says the famous one-liner "Welcome to Prime Time, Bitch!" and smashes her head into the tv.

We now take a bit of a respite to follow Neil to Jennfier's funeral. He finally meets his not-so-secret admirer, Sister Mary Helena (Nan Martin). The elderly, but intense nun tells Neil "the unquiet spirit must be laid to rest." Before she can elaborate, Nancy approaches Neil and Sister Mary Helena is nowhere to be found. (Not for nothing Sister, but you couldn't show yourself to Nancy, too?)

"Straight talk only" is a rule in the group therapy sessions, so it's time for Nancy to lay it out for the remaining kids. She tells them about Freddy and recounts her experience in the original film. She dubs Kristen, Will, Taryn, Kincaid, and Joey "the last of the Elm Street children," meaning the last remaining descendants of the mob that killed Freddy when he was alive. The sins of the parents are once again coming back to haunt their children. The difference this time around is Kristen. She can bring them together to fight Freddy in the dreamscape. Only it's not just her. Nancy supposes that everyone has abilities and talents in their dreams, but they can use them to fight Freddy. Neil lets her go on, but says she sounds like "Peter Pan." It's an apt metaphor in ways he doesn't even realize yet.

Humoring Nancy, he hypnotizes everyone with a Newton's Cradle, a device that symbolizes how they all need each other, as all pieces of the device work together to perpetuate motion. The hypnosis doesn't seem to work, until the balls of the Newton's Cradle separate and fly in the air.

Impossibly, Will stands up out of his chair and conjures a magic butterfly, delighting Nancy. Kristen does a series of impressive flips, which everyone applauds. Kincaid bends a metal chair with his bare hands, and Taryn dons a punk outfit with dual switchblades (this may seem like a curiously aesthetic-only choice, but later we'll see her skills). The only one who doesn't discover his power is Joey, who was lured by an attractive nurse to a room down the hallway. They start to make out, and surprise, the nurse is actually Freddy in disguise. Before you know it, Joey is suspended over a pit of fire by elongated tongues. Kristen becomes aware of Freddy's presence as the light in the room glows red and the walls start to close in and appear metallic (shades of *Freddy's Revenge* popping up). All seems lost, until Simms enters the therapy room and wakes everyone up. Everyone except for Joey, who's now in a coma. Nancy and Neil are summarily fired.

As Neil walks to his car, he sees Sister Mary Helena beckoning him to a shuttered ward of Westin Hills. There she tells him about a young nun who was accidentally locked inside over the holidays with the most criminally insane inmates. She was raped for days until she was eventually found, later giving birth to the "Bastard Son of 100 Maniacs." As it dawns on Neil that she's talking about Freddy, Sister Mary Helena tells him that Krueger's remains were never found and thus never buried. The only way to kill him is to find his bones and give him a proper burial. They're running out of time, however, since Nancy sees "Come and get him bitch" sliced word-by-word into the chest of a comatose Joey. Now she knows what Rod meant when he said Tina's death was caused by invisible cuts "just happening." (Though I have to ask, is she asleep and watching this? Surely he can't actually be cutting Joey, or else everyone else would see.) Nancy doesn't understand the "nun aspect" (join the club!), so she takes Neil to the one man who can find Freddy's bones: Donald Thompson (John Saxon). No longer the tough-talking cop, he's now a down-and-out security guard who may have inherited his ex-wife's alcoholism. It's implied that he and Nancy haven't seen each other in a while. (He probably doesn't even know Nancy's new address.) Ultimately, he refuses to help them.

Nancy then gets a page (1987, y'all) from Westin Hills. It's not from the nursing staff, but rather from Taryn, begging her to come back right away. Kristen understandably flipped out at Simms for firing Nancy, and she's immediately sedated and put in the quiet room. If they can't get to her before she falls asleep, she's dead, and so are their chances at a team up. Nancy rushes back to Westin Hills, while Neil threatens Don to help him. It took him long enough, but Neil is a massive step up from Glen. There's also a funny bit where he stops off in a church to get holy water using Don's flask.

Nancy returns to Westin Hills and convinces Max to let her say a final goodbye to the kids. He's obviously wary (like I said, it's refreshing that there are adults in this film who are active in their protection of the next generation, whether it's their job or not), but he relents. She holds a final group therapy session where she gives the kids a chance to turn back. No dice. Even though they've just met Kristen, they're ready to save their friend and end their pain.

One more mass hypnosis, and they're in the quiet room with Kristen. Her relief is short-lived as Freddy's blades soon cut through the padded walls all around them. Feathers fly out, blinding everyone and obscuring the action on screen. Kristen seemingly wakes up in her bedroom. All is as it was with Dokken and Diet Coke. Elaine comes back with her bourbon-craving gentleman caller right on cue. *It was all a dream!* At least, it was until Freddy decapitates Elaine for not getting the bourbon fast enough. Elaine's severed head then takes it out on Kristen, belittling her as she screams. Kristen deftly avoids Freddy's blades and jumps through her bedroom window. She tumbles down the staircase of the Elm Street house and calls out for Nancy.

We see feathers flying again as Taryn wanders inside the same Elm Street house. She hears Kristen calling and runs to see her, but she winds up... outside? Taryn is now in a seedy alley that could've easily been behind the bar Jesse visited in *Freddy's Revenge*. A brick wall appears behind her with "Taryn & Freddy" graffiti, blocking her escape. Suddenly, Freddy appears, grinning. He asks if the setting is familiar, as it surely is brick-by-brick, one of the spots Taryn did drugs before winding up in Westin Hills.

Instead of answering, Taryn flips her dual switchblades and beckons him to fight. This is the first time in the series that someone looks Freddy dead in the eyes and says "Let's go" (or rather, "Okay asshole, let's dance"). They spar for a little while, until Freddy transforms both sets of his fingers into syringes full of (presumably) the drugs Taryn used to do. Taryn's arms turn into suckling mouths (still icky to think about today) and Freddy shoves the needles into all of them, sucking out her life force.

Next up, we see Will about the quiet room feathers, perplexed to be in the middle of one of the franchise's many long, dark hallways. At one end, Freddy taunts him. At the other, a deadly-looking wheelchair covered in spikes starts to barrel towards him. Finding his inner strength, Will transforms into "the Wizard Master" from the game he was playing earlier. It's basically just him in a Dracula-esque cape, but he can shoot magic from his fingertips, which he uses to blow the chair to pieces and confuse Freddy. But since he doesn't "believe in fairy tales," he quickly kills Will with his glove.

At the same time, Kristen, Nancy, and Kincaid find each other in the house, and after some choice calling-out by Kincaid, they find a metal door suspended in midair. Now it's Freddy's turn to call them to battle. They enter the floating door and descend into Freddy's boiler room where Joey hangs by a...well, a tongue. Four of them, actually, which start to slip. The trio fight Freddy and free Joey as Nancy stabs their enemy with a metal pole. He mocks them by revealing his chest: burnt, scarred, and covered with the screaming faces of his victims! It's revealed that they give him power (another series runner that becomes important). Just as he's about to kill Kincaid, Freddy mysteriously fades away.

Back in the waking world, Don takes Neil to the junkyard where Krueger's bones were buried long ago. Finding them deep in the stacks of totaled cars, the pair dig a grave. When they disturb the remains, the junked cars start to honk and flash their lights. Freddy's spirit then suddenly animates his own skeleton and fights those who would seek to bury him. Technically, this is the second film in which Freddy appears outside of dreams, even though it's only for a little while. At least long enough to kill a vengeful Don (better late than never, Lieutenant!) and knock Neil unconscious in the grave. Thinking he's won, he roars in victory and returns to the dream world, the bones collapsing in a heap as his spirit departs.

Now it's time for the grand finale. Kincaid, Nancy, Kristen, and Joey enter a hallway full of mirrors. Freddy appears in all of them, and his reflections grab one dream warrior each as they struggle to get free. Only Joey remains safe. But when he sees his friends all pulled inside the mirrors, the selectively mute teenager lets out a SCREAM that shatters the glass. With this, his friends burst from the mirrors, unharmed. Joey finally found his power, and with that, Nancy assumes it's over. (She's mostly right.)

Don materializes in front of them to apologize to Nancy. He tells her he's been killed, and he wants to hug her goodbye. Up to this point, Nancy hasn't experienced much of Freddy's shapeshifting and is caught completely off-guard when she feels his razor glove stabbing into her gut. Freddy locks Kincaid and Joey out as he fights Kristen over a bleeding Nancy. Just as Freddy goes in for the kill, Nancy grabs his gloved arm and shoves the knives into HIS gut. It's one of the great "Hell yes!" moments of the series. He's never had a taste of his own medicine before, but it's not enough.

As Nancy screams, Neil wakes up in the junkyard grave and finds the strength to crawl out and finish the burial. He splashes the holy water on the remains and adds in a crucifix as Freddy writes around in pain. Flashes of light tear through him like paper until he eventually disappears. NOW, it's over for Freddy. And Nancy, too. Joey and Kincaid finally get through the door in time to see our beloved heroine cradled in Kristen's arms. As she dies, Kristen sobs and says she'll dream her into a "beautiful dream." It's a pyrrhic victory.

Kristen, Joey, Kincaid, and Neil later attend Nancy's funeral, where Neil notices Sister Mary Helena's grave, along with her real name: Amanda Krueger. That night after the funeral, it's revealed Neil now sleeps next to Nancy's Malaysian dream doll (seen in her apartment). It's not from Bali like Glen mentions in the original but it's still of Southeast Asian origin (and also featured in *Batman Forever*). Neil has also kept Kristen's unfinished model house of 1428 Elm Street. In the last shot of the film, a light ominously shines through a window in the model…

## NIGHTMARE AUTOPSIS

Making his filmmaking debut in the shadow of Wes Craven, Chuck Russell was in a tough spot. He knew he couldn't make a film as scary as the original *Nightmare*, but he and Frank Darabont still wanted to somehow up their game on *Dream Warriors*. His main focus was balancing out the terror with the more imaginative elements. Story-wise, his plan was to go deeper and expand the mythology, including adding a backstory for Freddy. Whereas Jack Sholder was less enthusiastic about the horror genre, Russell, who would go on to helm blockbusters like *Eraser, The Scorpion King*, and *The Mask*, (New Line's first megahit) dove headfirst into the dreamscape, embracing the horror elements, and changed the course of the franchise in the process.

The budget, the cast, and chiefly the special effects were much bigger than before as New Line kept digging for gold. This resulted in one hell of a production team. Notable returns included Kevin Yagher to handle Freddy's makeup and Mark Shostrom for several featured special effects sequences. *Dream Warriors* also benefited from the brother-and-sister art directing team of C.J. and Mick Strawn, who created striking environments that blended reality with the dream world. Visually, this entry was truly the next level of the *Elm Street* saga.

As the popularity of the films grew, it was inevitable that the series would dovetail with the music scene of the mid-1980's. Hair metal was a then-ubiquitous genre that featured loud guitars, guys in makeup, and elaborate music videos that usually involved fire, chains, and sparks. A collaboration with *Nightmare on Elm Street* was a no-brainer. Enter Dokken, a heavy metal band who wrote "Dream Warriors," their lyrical ode to the titular heroes. Robert Englund and Patricia Arquette even appeared in the music video as Freddy and Kristen, respectively. It was yet another indicator of the rising star power of the *Nightmare* films.

Speaking of star power, Robert Englund was once again back as Freddy, but with a noticeably funnier turn. He's still a sadistic child killer, but Russell and Darabont have him cracking way more jokes. Luckily, Englund was game, going so far as to improvise the famous line "Welcome to prime time, bitch." According to Mick Strawn's *Behind the Screams* book, he first saw the humor in Craven's script for the original film and he exploited it "much to Wes's chagrin." *Dream Warriors* saw Freddy tap into his victims' fears in spectacular ways, which Englund called "the logical conclusion of how Freddy haunts your subconscious." (After all, he can't stay in the boiler room forever.) Here, he spends more time out of the shadows, cementing his status as a horror version of the Joker. Except the residents of Westin Hills know there's no Batman, and thus have to step up and be their own heroes. Russell is an admitted comic book fan, going so far as to meet with Stan Lee before his passing.

Pitting Freddy against a group of teens was always in the cards. In a retrospective interview for the film, Craven pondered "How do you take the existing foundation to the next level? [The original film] had Nancy fight alone, but human beings naturally come together for something bigger than themselves." After two films, audiences might still show up to see how characters are killed off, but *Dream Warriors* makes you want to see what they can do to fight back. The cast is excellent. We don't spend much time with Phillip and Jennifer, but we get a good sense of who they are. Rodney Eastman is able to convey so much with a (mostly) mute performance and Ken Sagoes balances the rage and vulnerability of Kincaid. I love that someone who looks as imposing as him and could beat you into tomorrow is still just as terrified as everyone else when faced with Freddy Krueger. Ira Heiden is terrific as the handicapped nerd who becomes a mage. The teens make up a ragtag "Breakfast Club." They don't appear to fit high school stereotypes, but they clearly come from all different families and backgrounds. They probably wouldn't be friends if they weren't all stuck in Westin Hills together, but they're entirely believable as kids who discover each other during a time of intense trauma.

While Ronee Blakely's Marge was a standout in the first *Nightmare*, the adult characters won't be major highlights of the later films. In *Dream Warriors*, they shine pretty bright for a film centered on teens. Saxon shows a pointed, yet sad, evolution of his character. Pointer and Wasson are convincing as doctors who genuinely want to help. Much has been made of Neil telling the group that Phillip's "suicide" was cowardly, but in 1987, surely it was normal for even well-meaning doctors to say something so ridiculous. Nan Martin is appropriately creepy, especially as she reveals the story of the poor nun who was subjugated to a horrible crime.

We also can't forget Elaine Parker as the mom we love to hate. (She'd have made the best memes on *The Real Housewives of Springwood*.) Brooke Bundy once said in an interview that, as vapid and vain as she appears, Elaine was absolutely in the mob that killed Freddy and that, as a result, she spent her subsequent years in extreme denial and probably excess. I've often wondered if she would have recognized Nancy when she visited her house. Surely she knew Marge, but when Nancy wants to talk about her daughter, Elaine acts like she would rather be anywhere else. I believe it's just that: denial. She knows who Nancy is in that scene, but she can't ever admit it, not least because she'd be admitting to murder. The undercurrent of what she's done is palpable on future rewatches.

Of course, we can't talk about this film without acknowledging returning champion Heather Langenkamp as Nancy. Who else but Wes would be the key to moving the series in a new direction, and who else but the character of Nancy Thompson could come back to lead it there? The pathos she displays while recounting her past to the kids is reason enough to be glad Langenkamp was asked back. Nancy appears in every draft of the script, and interestingly, she also dies in every draft. It's to Russell and Darabont's credit that they carried her over from the earlier Craven/Wagner script, and killed her off, just the same. It's a natural progression for horror sequels, signifying that nobody is safe, which has sort of fallen off in recent years. (I'm looking at you, *Scream 6*.)

In Langenkamp's *I Am Nancy* autobiographical documentary, Wes Craven tells her "Heroes aren't free of fear. They face fear. It's one of the great evolutionary catalysts." Future Oscar winner Patricia Arquette makes her film debut as Kristen, showing a lot of promise as a character who appears completely helpless until Nancy finishes her rhyme, and echoes her pain. Nancy rose to the occasion in the original, preparing in advance to take on Freddy, whereas Kristen became her natural successor in this third installment. But before we move on, I want to focus on the importance of Jennifer Rubin as Taryn.

Yes, she has a crazy outfit and hairstyle. She also has switchblades whereas Freddy has a glove made of razors. She's "beautiful and bad," and she dies mostly offscreen. She's not a "final girl" by the strict definition of the term, but Taryn White fucking rules and she deserves her flowers. She's the first character we've ever seen look Freddy in the eye, flip her switchblades, and beckon him to fight with the quip "Okay asshole, let's dance," another iconic line from the film. It's not the last time someone defies their fear in order to fight him. It's not even the first, but the fury in her eyes when she fights him hand-to-hand is one of the most memorable moments of the film.

Detractors (and even some fans) have noted that the film's message of empowerment is rendered moot by the fact that the "dream warriors" don't succeed. For the first time in the series, Neil, an adult, is the one who saves the day with the help of Don and Sister Mary Helena. This line of thinking is incredibly reductive. Consider the mirror hallway scene. Joey literally finds his voice to save himself and his friends. It's a short-lived victory, but an apt metaphor for the film, and the franchise at large. As Ira Heiden put it in *Never Sleep Again*, "It's important to see what these kids get to do, whether they get killed or not."

In a film series, about wall-to-wall death and the horrors of the dreamscape, the "dream powers" scene is a welcome respite of hope and possibility, previously-unthought of. The kicker is, they're not special. They don't have a grand destiny to unlock magic powers and fight Freddy Krueger. They can do this because they dream and EVERYONE dreams. To be sure, this is a new invention of the series. While it wasn't part of Craven's original lore, it is a natural extension of his ideas. Nobody ever uses the term "dream warrior" in this, or any film in the franchise, but anyone can find their inner dream power. Like Rod said to Tina, "It's not like you have a corner on the market" when it comes to nightmares. Perhaps Freddy knew this and tried to kill the teens before they could discover their inner talents. What abilities could Phillip or Jennifer have unlocked? Or Jesse? Notice how Freddy takes a hostage instead of outright murder. Perhaps he's afraid of the newfound abilities of his would-be victims, and a different strategy is in order.

Later in life, I wondered why I gravitated to these films at such a young age. I think the answer can be found in another property New Line turned into the most successful independent film in history for almost a decade: *Teenage Mutant Ninja Turtles*. Think about it. Isn't the *Elm Street* series just a higher stakes version of the story of teenagers forming a makeshift family to team up, utilizing their exceptional talents to fight a man with razor hands of his own, who wants to destroy them? It's not *that* far of a stretch.

*A Nightmare on Elm Street 3: Dream Warriors* is one of the hallmarks of the series. Russell strikes that potent balance of fear and wonder that would define the rest of the films. In Never Sleep Again: The Elm Street Legacy, Jeff Katz sums up the film perfectly: "It moves the franchise along, adds to the mythology without taking anything away, while maintaining or reintroducing characters we already love, balanced with new characters we come to love just the same." This was almost thirty years before *The Force Awakens* attempted to do the same thing.

## THE CRAVEN/WAGNER DRAFT

The first version of *Dream Warriors* was written by Wes Craven and Bruce Wagner. The pair churned out four drafts of this iteration, the final of which was later heavily rewritten by Chuck Russell and his then-partner (and future Hollywood maverick) Frank Darabont. The core ideas of the final film are in both scripts, but they're ultimately so different that they merit closer examination.

In the Craven/Wagner draft, we open, if you can believe it, on baby Freddy ripping out of a pregnant belly, claws glistening. The camera pulls back, revealing the birth occurred in a ranch house in the woods, then keeps pulling back to OUTER SPACE, before falling back to earth and starting the main titles.

Say it with me: *What...?*

The titles play over a montage of missing child posters all over the country. It's like the opening of *The Lost Boys*, except the kids are all teenagers. Has Freddy gone worldwide? We end on the picture of a redhead we've never seen before, until we dissolve to...

Nancy Thompson as she drives down a deserted road, and back into our lives. She changes the car radio from a station talking about a wave of teen suicides, just as she stops to pick up a hitchhiker: the very same redhead from the photo. The girl looks strange, like a "child of the corn." She doesn't say her name but tells Nancy she's going "down where he fucks you."

Huh. Okay then.

Suddenly, a tire blows. Nancy gets out to look for help, leaving the girl in the car. She wanders in the direction of children singing. She finds the jump rope kids playing in front of the ranch house we briefly saw earlier. The lawn is littered with old tricycles and car parts like the house in *The Texas Chain Saw Massacre*. We are definitely not in Springwood anymore. But where *are* we?

Like Kristen's dream in the final film, we're entering new territory that feels enticing, but still resonates as a *Nightmare* film. We even see wind chimes made out of familiar talons (also a cut detail from the Russell/ Darabont script). Nancy enters a long-abandoned house and finds an elevator, which she feels compelled to enter. The elevator plummets and moves sideways into the earth (how would Craven have shot this?), until the famous hand of Freddy Krueger bursts out of the floor! Nancy avoids it as the elevator stops and she runs into a hallway with a giant tricycle and her father. Yes, Lt. Thompson and Nancy were both primed to show up earlier in the script and have major roles. Also, Nancy's dad is strangely named "John" when Marge clearly calls him "Donald" in the original film. We're going to stick with established continuity and go with "Donald," even though canon is flying out the window.

However, flying *through* the window of Nancy's car is the Freddy snake. The unnamed hitcher is waiting in the passenger seat when it shatters the windshield. Instead of the giant mechanical beast with Freddy's visage, this "snake" is Freddy's arm with his claw as the head. It jumps into her mouth but doesn't kill her. Instead, it drags her up a nearby tree.

Back in the impossible house, Donald reveals it's been five years since the events of the first *Nightmare,* though *Freddy's Revenge* was already five years later and the final *Dream Warriors* will take place one year after that. He's been hunting for Freddy and claims this is the house where he was born. Donald then cuts his eyelid off in front of Nancy, who wakes up alone in her car. It's nighttime, and she's been startled by the flashlight of one Dr. Neil Guiness. (Why the name change?) He invites the stalled motorist to stay in his guest room.

This Neil is pretty much the same character in the final film: a smart, compassionate psychiatrist with a major crush on Nancy. She tells him she's been following her father's trail across several states, though she doesn't know what he's looking for. Later that night, as Neil researches Hypnocil in a medical reference book, Nancy dreams that the hitcher floats into her room and sloughs off her own scalp. The tangle of red hair starts to choke her when Neil bursts through the door. Who knew he could distend his jaw to the point where he tries to swallow Nancy- *oh*, it's Freddy. Got it. He swallows her up to her head, makes a joke, and she attacks his face as the *real* Neil wakes her up. She cries that the pills don't work anymore.

That was Nancy's first dream since she "lived on Elm Street." She asks if Neil's town has an Elm Street and Neil surmises that every town has one. Since her car is missing, presumably towed, he takes her to his job at the local hospital. As soon as he arrives, he walks into Kristen's scalpel freakout, but he already knows her as one of his patients. Nancy is there to pacify her, and while Craven surely would have directed the hell out of it, the set-up feels more effective and startling in the later Russell/Darabont draft.

Unlike in the film, the audience meets this version of the teens at the same time as Nancy. Jennifer, Kincaid and Kristen are the same (though she's named "Kirsten" here. Sure.) Instead of a recovering addict, Taryn is a young Black artist who loves fire. Neil reveals that his patients came to this hospital from all over the country. They have two things in common: severe sleep issues and (alleged) suicide attempts. Neil suggests Nancy work there as an assistant based on her fast and easy rapport with Kristen. (Background check, schmackground check.)

Nancy's car is found totaled above a grain elevator, though nobody knows how it got 200 feet in the air. Or why there are four parallel slashes all over it. Both

Neil and Nancy visit Kristen's parents. Yes, parents, but her dad just wants to play tennis and her mom lost the coin toss to talk to them before they left for the club. When Nancy goes to Kristen's room, there's no model house to be found, but she finds a picture of Kristen with a friend: the hitcher with the red hair. On the way back to Neil's, they pass the ranch house where the cops are recovering the hitcher's body. Neil is apparently friendly enough with the local cops to learn that the girl climbed a tree to hang herself before the crows got to her. Nancy enters the house, but there's no sign of an elevator. However, the living room floor turns to liquid and she falls through the surface.

As Nancy tries to get her bearings in the pool from nowhere, she sees something at the bottom: her father, who is bleeding from his eyes. She gets back to the surface and is drawn upstairs when she hears a baby crying. The "baby" is the infant Freddy from the opening, who grows to full-size right in front of her. The script indicates a lot of forced perspective in this section to make Nancy appear small. He chases her out of the house, but he can't follow for some reason. Maybe it's because, *oh yeah*, Nancy's not asleep! How could this be? They investigate what one of the cops refers to as "the old Krueger house." Nothing seems out of the ordinary. Neil mentions someone claimed the house was alive and wound up in the hospital after trying to burn it down. As they leave, an outline of Freddy pushes out of the window to watch them, much like he did to Tina's wall in the original film. The script indicates that Freddy *is* the house.

Neil takes Nancy back to the hospital to see the arsonist, who is of course, her father and his eyes have been cut out. Donald has been trying to find the house, which he calls "an entrance into Krueger's nightmare for those that have known him." He urges her to finish what he started and burn it down before he gets too powerful.

We then meet two other teenage patients. Joey is described as frail and spasmodic, but he has learned to control his movements enough to make a model house that looks familiar. It's the ranch house, complete with the wind chime. We also meet Wi-er, Laredo. Instead of a paraplegic nerd, we get a long-haired D&D enthusiast who tells Joey about the fantasy world he's created. Orderly Max interrupts him to tell them it's lights out. Laredo is picking up his sculpting clay when he sees the 13-year-old Philip sleepwalking. Instead of puppet strings, Freddy himself is positioned behind Phillip and "walking him" down the hallway.

Like in the finished film, nobody sees Freddy at first, but Laredo sees him going in and out like the static on tv. He wakes up Kincaid and tries to warn him when Freddy walks the boy into the path of a speeding ambulance.

The next day, Nancy sits in on group therapy. Instead of Simms, the skeptical doctor role is Dr. Maddalena (named after Wes's producing partner Marianne Maddalena), a hardass who's much less therapeutic than Neil. Kristen reveals she knows her friend Becky, the hitcher, is dead, and the kids start to freak out. The histrionic scene feels very much like a first draft, but we learn Kristen's parents are checking her out the next day. Nancy protests, because she thinks the kids need to stick together. There's a scene that echoes the original film where Neil and Nancy observe Kristen during a sleep study. Nancy sees her disappear into thin air, but Neil just sees her sleeping in the same spot. The next day, very unlike the final film, Kristen's parents pick her up, despite Nancy's protests.

Jennifer's death scene is missing the famous improv, obviously. There's a neat bit where Freddy's head goes back into the tv and appears on the screen after rising out of the top of the tv while he "batters up" Jennifer, but otherwise, it's the same. At her funeral, the script indicates her coffin is inexpensive, possibly to illustrate these kids are coming together across the socioeconomic spectrum. Neil laments that he feels like the Catcher in the Rye.

Kristen's not out of the film yet. She's back in high school, being bullied by a popular girl for her hospital stay. She falls asleep in class and dreams of ripping off the girl's top in class. When she wakes up, her tormentor is topless. So, her dream power is…revenge?

Nancy attempts to burn the ranch house down, but she's thwarted by a cop who stops there to urinate with his police dog. Luckily, he doesn't see what she's there to do. She then visits her dad, who knowingly tells her she'll need to destroy the house from the inside, with a "dream warrior." Yes, he said the line, but what happened in the last five years to make him "Dream Yoda?"

Kristen sits in her bedroom, trying to call Nancy at the hospital, but she's not there. She's upset that her parents are sending her to Catholic school, so when she has a nightmare, she floats above her bed in a pose to mirror the crucifixion. Stigmata starts to appear on her hands, feet, and stomach (which is funny, since Patricia Arquette would go on to star in the horror film *Stigmata*).

An unseen force floats her out of her second-story window, to the Catholic school in her mom's brochures. The cross out front squirms like a pinned animal as Kristen floats through a hallway filled with lockers that belch steam, to a classroom filled with scary-looking girls dressed in red and green plaid. She lands in a coat room when Freddy appears, exiting the same elevator Nancy encountered. In a creepy bit of self-mutilation, he crosses himself with his glove, leaving a Z-shaped cut that bleeds pus as he laughs. Freddy chases her as she calls for Nancy, who's journaling at Neil's. Her pen and journal fly out of her hand, then she's sucked into her bed, just like Glen, albeit without the blood.

Freddy is so confident about his kill, he says a line from the *next* movie ("You can check into this dream, but you can't check out," a version of which he repeats with the famous roach motel kill, but we'll get there). Nancy falls from seemingly nowhere, right on top of Freddy. She's pissed, but Kristen gets them out by wishing out loud to go back to her bedroom. She wakes up with Nancy right next to her! It's a really cool idea, that one can travel physically through dreams, but it's not an element that carried over to the final film.

Kristen and Nancy go to an all-night coffee place to debrief. Kristen mentions bringing her brother into her dreams, instead of her father. Nancy asks if she could possibly take Freddy out of her dream so that she, not Kristen can face him. They go to Neil's house so Kristen can watch Nancy while she sleeps. (By the way, they snuck out of Kristen's mansion and into Neil's house in what, twelve hours? When did they become cat burglars?)

Anyway, Nancy goes to sleep and appears at the ranch house to resume her plan to burn it down. She notices the welcome mat spells out its greeting in maggots, just as Kristen appears next to her for "backup" (let's hope she does better than Glen did). The police dog appears with red and green-striped fur, and Freddy's face, and my GOD did someone force Craven to re-use that gimmick from *Freddy's Revenge*? I hope it would have looked better here.

The dog chases them through the house as Kristen worries he can smell her fear. They see a vision of Jennifer covered in maggots, then encounter Freddy, who slashes Kristen's arm. She calls in Kincaid, who phases through his chair at the hospital. He lands in the house, confused, but he punches Freddy right in the face. The three of them run, until Nancy slaps Kincaid, waking him and making them appear at the hospital in front of Joey. Max and Dr. Maddalena race in. She fires Nancy on the spot.

Distraught, Nancy asks Neil to take her to the bus station, but instead they go home and make love (the script specifies they climax at the same time for some reason…?). She confesses she's thought of taking her life, but she's afraid Freddy would still find her even in death. It feels like a bold, honest moment for a character who's been through so much. Later, she dreams of blood coming out of the faucets in Neil's bathroom, along with the faces of Phillip, Becky, and Jennifer appearing in his shower curtain. They urge her to kill Freddy as a bloody hand pulls back the shower curtain, making the familiar claw screech, before she wakes up. It's time to visit her father again.

Donald tells her she can't be "neutral" anymore, but when has she ever been? He tells her Kristen is part of the next generation who will fight Freddy, and while she doesn't have her abilities, Nancy must be the one to lead them because she's a "veteran." He hands her the hospital master key, which he swiped from Max. The Thompsons then interrupt a group therapy session that's going poorly. Neil is dumbfounded as Nancy, her father, and the kids hold hands and vanish in front of his eyes.

The gang winds up on a hill above the asylum, looking…different. The script doesn't elaborate too much on what's changed, but they're all clear-eyed and confident. Joey is no longer spasmodic. He's surprised he can talk, though he did in the last scene (it's a first draft, so maybe that was an error?). The script calls Nancy "a diminutive Patton" as she addresses them about how Freddy's been stalking them all in their dreams. They only THINK they're suicidal (weird, but ok…). Donald says what makes them outcasts in the waking world makes them survivors and fighters. But if they can't kill him, they don't die, but rather get trapped in a forever dream (still weird, still ok…). Then the "door to nowhere" appears. Taryn, who will carry over her heart and attitude to the finished film, isn't scared of the scorching inferno within, so she dives right through. Her friends follow when they realize she's okay. Donald says he can't follow, but he dives in anyway. Unlike the kids, he catches fire and winds up running into Neil and Maddalena talking to the cops. With his dying words, he tells Neil to join them in the dream.

Inside the house, Nancy can't make it catch on fire. She gives the kids "gasoline bombs" and plans to take them inside to burn it down from within. As they advance, Taryn is distracted by the voice of her grandmother and separates from the group. Of course, it's Freddy, and he kills her by opening his chest to reveal a tooth-filled maw, which devours her. (Holy *shit*, that would have been cool to see.)

Joey douses an empty room in gasoline, when his high school crush, Beth Dorsett (who is totally *not* Freddy Krueger) materializes in front of him. She frenchs him, but "her" enormous tongue pops out his eyeballs. As if that wasn't enough, Freddy pushes him on a bed, which is a weird form for Freddy to take, until we see the posts of the bed literally rip him apart. (Wow.)

Neil arrives at the house, where the razor wind chimes have turned into human fingers that point the way. He goes inside, and feels strange. To test his theory, he cuts off his fingers with scissors, but reattaches them as if nothing happened. As a doctor, he's actually giddy to discover this is all real. Elsewhere, Nancy encounters Freddy, then runs into Neil. Freddy chases them both through the house, which as expected, is much bigger inside, with impossible hallways and dimensions.

If Laredo is such a Dungeons & Dragons fan, he should know that splitting the party is a bad idea. Still, he enters the basement alone dressed as a pirate (like Will in the next Russell/Darabont draft). He sees a vision of a wet seven-year-old boy in a red and green swimsuit. This is Freddy pretending to be Toby, his little brother who drowned in the family pool. Laredo must have passed his perception check because he kicks the boy in the crotch, fully aware that it's Freddy. This gives Laredo the idea to do some shapeshifting of his own, and they fight as various objects and creatures like a gargoyle, crow, and blob of goo. Then Freddy appears behind Laredo with a gas-powered post-hole digger that turns him into bloody vapor. (A claw would do just fine, but…sure.)

Elsewhere in the house, Laredo's ghostly form appears before Nancy and Neil, scaring them both. The pair soon also find the remains of Joey and Taryn. Luckily, they intercept Kristen and Kincaid. Freddy appears, but Kincaid knocks him across the room. They then hit him with their firebombs, but hey, they're in a *house*, so they need to escape before they all burn to death. Kristen teleports them back to her house, where her parents are hosting a party. Her mother is on the phone with Dr. Maddalena, saying Kristen's escape isn't her problem. Until our heroes appear out of nowhere and Freddy jumps out of the floor like in *Freddy's Revenge*. He doesn't decapitate the insensitive mother, but just slashes her and…eats at her guts like a vulture. (Jesus, Wes.)

The group runs into the den, which is stocked with guns. Kincaid grabs an AR-14 and shoots Freddy, because in the 80's, you just *had* to shoot the bad guy. He recovers (so much for bringing him out of the dream world for an even playing field) and announces Kincaid's asshole belongs to him as he pounces. Kristen whisks them away just in time. They wind up back in the asylum, right in front of Dr. Maddalena. Except Kincaid, who's stuck halfway through Kristen's portal. Freddy is still on the other side…

Look, I'm not saying Freddy shoves his claw up Kincaid's ass, because we don't actually see it, but a claw does exit his mouth right after he screams, "He's going inside me! Oh Godddddddd!" And since Freddy just claimed his… you know what? Let's just focus on Freddy's giant crocodile-shaped mouth, which bites Dr. Maddalena's head off. He then chases the group down the hall and they wind up in the basement of the ranch house, which is currently burning. It's here Neil stops to test a theory. He turns around to tell Freddy to go to hell. This is *his* dream, dammit. Amused, Freddy extends his arm just like he did before killing Tina, but this time he punches Neil like Dhalsim in *Street Fighter*, knocking him out.

Nancy and Kristen jump down a coat chute and wind up in the boiler room. Nancy actually says out loud "Jesus, this isn't the way to kill Freddy!" They then turn their back on him, denying his existence, and he bursts into flames. It's all over. Until Donald shows up to hug his daughter. Just like Laredo, she sees through Freddy's charade and they stab each other at the same time. Kristen pulls "Donald's" skin off, revealing Freddy. As they both die, Nancy assures her that Freddy is no more. Kristen takes his glove and drags an unconscious Neil out of the cellar of the burning house.

The house transforms back to the way we saw it in the beginning. Kristen goes inside and sees a nice home straight out of the 1940's. She finds "Baby Freddy," having just killed his mother, and kills it before it can grow up to make the blades "it will never grow up to make." (No, really, that's right from the script.)

The final scene is mostly the same as in the later Russell/Darabont draft with Kristen and Neil having dinner. It's implied Kristen "saved" Nancy, who now lives in the dream world. We see the model house, as a light shines out of one of the windows and we hear the scraping of steel.

It's important to point out this is a *first* draft, as indicated by the title page. Whatever you think of this script (and there are a *lot* of thoughts it conjures) you can't deny that its ambition makes it absolutely fascinating. While set pieces overflow with imagination (and characters actually *say* "dream warriors"), the majority of the draft just doesn't work on the page. Still, it's entirely possible that Craven and Wagner would have refined it further had Craven been brought on board to direct. It reintroduces Nancy as the protagonist but still struggles with too many characters. Taryn is barely in there at all and almost all of Laredo's dialogue sounds like it's from a fantasy book, though it makes sense for the kid who loves Dungeons & Dragons to have miniatures. And apologies to Wes, but turning your back on your enemy in the heat of battle just doesn't work for a story where the danger is amplified to this degree. I truly don't believe Freddy would become an amateur proctologist in any final version of this film.

Interestingly, Craven and Wagner presented a vision of Freddy's birth a full two years before *The Dream Child*, but it's just a vision, not even an actual dream. There's no fetus eating souls this time around. And don't worry, Freddy's not going to space, despite that opening shot. However, we will be heading back to that mysterious house in the deep, dark woods. 1428 Elm Street is absent, but Craven and Wagner introduce the concept of a dream house as a focal point. The fact that it's a physical structure that allows you to enter Freddy's realm without falling asleep is admittedly problematic. It's almost as much a departure from the source material as *Freddy's Revenge*. Plus, I don't know how Craven could have pulled off killing a baby at the end, even if it was a literal monster.

There are some fantastic moments here that I wish carried over to the final film. The scene with the floor becoming liquid originates here, as well as Hypnocil. The set pieces are scary and violent. Kristen's Catholic school nightmare is a real standout. In the third act, Joey asks if he'll wake up strong after they kill Freddy. Granted, his role is entirely different in the next draft, but it's a fascinating question that could have been asked by another character. It's also a philosophical question that no doubt came directly from Craven himself.

Russell and Darabont were pretty surgical when it came to writing their version, and one can argue they kept most of the best parts of this first draft. The eyelid slicing is only mentioned in the final film, and while the snake is entirely different, though there's still an element of swallowing someone whole. In a time before CGI, I can't help but wonder how they would have achieved some of these effects.

It's surprising that Craven didn't have a fleshed-out origin for Freddy beyond showing the house he was born in. (Fortunately, the creation of Amanda Krueger and the hundred maniacs feels organic to the world he created, even if he didn't create it.) Thankfully, Russell and Darabont decided to keep Nancy and Donald in the script, though in altered capacities that fit better. I'm sorry, but John Saxon as the suddenly wise mentor just doesn't make as much sense as the washed-up security guard drowning his guilt in alcohol. I can applaud the inversion of his character from the original film as a "good" parent seeking redemption, but it's just so out of character in this draft. Making Nancy a graduate student focused on dream therapy is the perfect way for her to be around the patients, but how does Neil give a complete stranger the job of his assistant, especially when Dr. Maddalena is much more of a hardass than Simms? Also, Dr. Maddalena is a thinly drawn authority figure, but as Neil's superior, Dr. Simms is less harsh and more believable as his counterpoint in the hospital. You want her to see the truth, not get decapitated by a Freddy-gator.

Phillip's death scenes are emblematic of the differences between the scripts. Wagner had conceived his version of the scene as Freddy forcibly walking him into an oncoming ambulance. Minimal special effects would be required and the scene, as written, is terrifying. It's also telling that he's barely been established as a character before he's killed. In the final film, Bradley Gregg portrays Philip as a confident, snarky teen. His death is still scary, but it's also the first fantastical Freddy kill in the series. It goes above and beyond to scare you, while also making you marvel at all the different effects you're watching. It purposefully encapsulates Russell's vision for the potential of the franchise.

# THE RUSSELL/DARABONT DRAFT

With Russell as the film's director, this second version of the script is pretty close to the finished film. Westin Hills is described as "isolated and somewhat gothic," which is more akin to the wing that Amanda Krueger was locked in, than the bland, but bright hallways we see later. Neil's last name is now Goldman instead of Guiness and Taryn is now blonde instead of brunette, but those details don't matter so much in the long run.

Other changes include Kincaid singing "I ain't gonna dream no more" when we first see him in the quiet room as opposed to later on when he flips out in group therapy. Also, Will has an electric wheelchair. (Were there budget cuts at Westin Hills?) Just before Kristen and Nancy encounter the über-phallic snake version of Freddy in the Elm Street house, the floor becomes water, which Kristen falls in. Later on, the first group session ends with Kristen urging Nancy to tell the truth, but she instead musters foreboding words of encouragement that act as a dog whistle of hope to the kids, which Simms can't hear.

We learn through the wizard game that the "Wizard Master" was originally the "Dungeon Master," a real role in Dungeons & Dragons. The role of the "DM" sets up the stories and challenges for the party. It also connotes control, which is something these teens have too little of. D&D fans would have picked up on this, but to the general public, "Wizard Master" just sounds more powerful.

After Phillip's death, Jennifer mentions she never knows "when he's going to come." Kristen talks about her love of gymnastics, though she admits she's bad at it. In the film, she just does some solid flips to demonstrate, but her reluctance is a nice bit of narrative scaffolding. This really drives home how special the dream world can be when there's nobody trying to kill you. In Jennifer's dream, it's actress Sally Kellerman on *The Dick Cavette Show* instead of Zsa Zsa Gabor, which probably means Sally was too expensive. Or she just turned it down.

In the "dream powers" scene, Taryn has gravity knives instead of switchblades, which would look a lot cooler on screen, but probably involve more training. Neil tries finding his own dream power, but he winds up picturing Nancy in lingerie instead. It's probably for the best that this didn't make it in, but it's fascinating that his "gift" affects other people instead of him.

Isn't that what a psychiatrist is supposed to do? Just not be a pervert. (There are children present, Dr. Gordon.)

The nurse Freddy impersonates to seduce and attack Joey was originally a teenaged candy striper named Marcie. Neil also sees "Come and get him bitch," scratched into Joey's chest along with Nancy. During the final group session, Nancy wishes they had more time to dig into their powers. I wish this line was included, as it adds to the danger. Plus, she's right to be concerned, They're an untrained army, and almost half of them subsequently die.

There's no "Jake's Bar" in Taryn's dream and, when she dies, her head explodes. This was actually filmed, but the prop head wouldn't explode, so they just moved on. Bummer, but it's still an incredible moment in the script. Also, Will is dressed like a pirate with a sword and torch at the start of his death scene. It would have diluted the power of his eventual transformation into the "Wizard Master," so I'm glad it was excised.

During the boiler showdown, Freddy sits on a throne of kids' bones (presumably left behind by Dokken after shooting their music video). Also, when he reveals the souls of his victims on his chest, they're not random heads, but the faces of the films' previous victims. It's a shame this detail was lost, but in a way, they fixed it in the next film, which we'll get to.

At the junkyard burial, Freddy has a makeshift tire iron headstone. Instead of constant honks when the cars come alive, the radios all play "Sympathy for the Devil" and other music. I doubt New Line could have afforded to use the Rolling Stones at that time or included money to hire a (junkyard) dog to appear and get killed by Freddy, so the absence of these details in the final film make sense.

Another big change happens in the mirror room. Instead of a hallway, it's a sewing room with a three-way mirror that multiplies Freddy, and *dozens* of Freddy clones rush out of the mirror. When Joey screams, they explode into glass, along with the mirror itself. Nancy doesn't stab Freddy with his blades in this early draft, but when he dies, the souls escape his body like they will in the next few films. Nancy's last words are also touching: "I'm so proud of you all. Tell Neil I..." and she's gone. In the last scene, Neil and Kristen are having dinner. The model house looks nice and there's no sequel tag.

# THE COOPER NOVELIZATION

Finally, we should take a look at Jeffrey Cooper's novelization of *Dream Warriors*. Film novelizations usually just adapt the film's script prior to shooting to coincide with its release. However, if there are several drafts, it might contain deleted or alternate material from the finished film. Cooper's novelization combines both drafts while introducing new information about Freddy's backstory.

"Kirsten" opens the film instead of Nancy, and rest assured, her mother is still a shrew. Her father is still alive, but inconsequential, and her brother was the one she previously pulled into her dreams. The girl we're still calling "Kristen" listens to the radio, which reports on teen suicide, like in the Craven/Wagner draft. Kristen enters the nightmare house and sees the razor mobile, which never made it to the screen.

Instead of following the little girl to the basement, she goes deeper into the house and finds a room full of destroyed tricycles. There's also a large bicycle built for two…people to die on, since the seats have spikes and the hand brakes are razors. Freddy is waiting for her. Kristen runs, winding up in a room full of hanging teens. Just as Freddy approaches, she wills herself awake. It's not a trick this time. She really escaped him, but she's so distraught, she breaks her bedroom mirror and slits her wrists with a shard.

Neil's last name is still "Guiness" here, but Westin Hills now straps patients to a metal chair in the quiet room. Blame Dr. Maddalena, the hardass from the Craven/Wagner draft. Nancy is once again a grad student, and she hasn't been this comfortable with a man since she first kissed Glen. He tells her that his patients don't dream.

Kristen's dream, which previously started with a melted tricycle, now starts with her holding a crucifix as the figure on the cross "writhes in pain." When she sees Freddy, he crosses himself just like in the first draft. She falls in the "floor water," and Freddy's glove pulls her under. She escapes and resurfaces, but the giant Freddy snake we all recognize comes out of the water. Kristen calls for Nancy, who's journaling, causing her pen and book to fly across the room like in the first draft. When Nancy enters the house, she scratches the Freddy snake's face to release Kristen. It's just about to eat her when she wishes them "back in [their] own beds," to which they return. (At least they don't have to sneak out of Kristen's house together.) Nancy bemoans the Hypnocil failing and she notices Freddy's torn flesh beneath her fingernails.

The next day when Nancy visits Mrs. Parker (not yet "Elaine"), she's the exact same. Mr. Parker is still itching to play tennis and Nancy still finds the model Elm Street house in Kristen's room. Curiously, there's a sign on it that reads "Hathaway House," a detail that hasn't carried over to any iteration of the film.

The first group therapy session is odd. Kincaid is still himself, Joey is now both mute AND spasmodic, and Taryn is the first draft version of herself, a Black girl who loves fire. Phillip doesn't identify himself beyond mentioning that he sleepwalks, and Laredo is the nerd who only speaks in D&D. Neil tries hypnosis right off the bat as a form of therapy instead of doing it to placate Nancy. What happens is a fascinating precursor to the dream powers introduction. The patients all fight Freddy in their mass hypnosis, but we never see the dream, only Neil's POV as he watches the kids react. Taryn says she'll burn him and Laredo claims he has a golden sword. Kincaid claims he can fly, and Joey SCREAMS before jumping across the room. Neil and Dr. Maddalena wake everyone and try to calm them, but Nancy wishes she could have helped. Later, Kristen surmises that the patients have "gifts," which is why they're still alive. Nancy asks her if she could pull Freddy out of the dream world.

Neil and Nancy go out for coffee (I guess Springwood, Ohio wasn't yet hip enough for Thai food), then go back to his place. She tries to tell him about the model house, but when he doesn't take her seriously, she gets mad and says a line I can't believe Craven didn't write: "There are more things in heaven and earth than are dreamt in your philosophy, Neil Guiness." Laredo and Kincaid once again see Phillip being sleepwalked in front of an ambulance like in the first draft. Dr. Maddalena has already had enough and insists to Neil that they increase their medication to induce dreaming, much to Nancy's chagrin.

Nancy addresses the kids without her bosses present, telling them about her history with Freddy. She asks Kristen to take them to him so they can fight once and for all. Everyone joins hands and sings the nursery rhyme to no avail. Then Joey stands up straight, speaks, does a cartwheel, and lifts Kincaid up with one hand. (Well, that was fast.) The dream continues as we see Taryn breathe fire, and hey, Jennifer's still alive! Her dream power is going incorporeal like

Kitty Pryde from the X-Men. Laredo can cause objects to shapeshift into various objects, and Kincaid can fly. Kristen's power is to unite them in the dream.

So now that we've established an entirely new suite of powers for everyone (with Joey *triple*-dipping), they encounter Freddy in the hallway. A battle royale ensues where they beat Freddy mercilessly. Taryn eventually lights him on fire, setting the fire alarm off, and waking them all up in the therapy room. The end! (Not so much.)

Kristen is sent home, but Jennifer is still having trouble sleeping. Her death scene matches the first draft, only without Freddy's head coming out of the tv. Nancy does research into "Hathaway House," the title of her old home. Max tells her one of the original Hathaway nurses is still alive, so Nancy visits her.

The former nurse, Miss Sapphire, tells her that Hathaway House was a small treatment facility for psychotic women that eventually moved to the building that would become Westin Hills. One of the patients was transferred from another local hospital with a less-than-sterling reputation, nicknamed "the Snakepit." The orderlies were paid five hundred dollars to let her be raped repeatedly by the other patients. After arriving at Hathaway House, she died during an awful childbirth where she knocked over a lamp and burned to death. Her son was burned, but he lived. The woman's name was Amanda Krueger.

Nancy plans to go to sleep and steal Freddy's claw. Kristen is supposed to stand guard, but she joins her like in the first draft. Walking down the dream version of Elm Street, they encounter the "Freddy dog" from that draft and are chased to the Elm Street house. They go to the cellar where Nancy's mother hid the claw, only to find Jennifer being eaten by maggots (also from the first draft). Freddy appears and Kristen calls in her friends one by one. Another battle ensues where Kristen is injured. The kids all use their abilities, and the incredibly strong Joey manages to pull Freddy's glove off as Kristen pulls them out of the dream. They all land in the hospital as Dr. Maddalena comes across the scene. She sends Kristen to the E.R. and fires Nancy before taking the glove and threatening to commit her. Just when she thinks it can't get any worse, she realizes Joey is still in the dream, alone. He walks through the Elm Street house, until he comes across "Beth Dorsett" and dies just like in the first draft.

Neil comforts Nancy and they sleep together at his house. She expresses her previous thoughts of suicide, which the psychiatrist isn't in the mood to discuss. She falls asleep and has the bathroom vision of Phillip and Jennifer. Remember, Becky (with the good hair) didn't make it past the first draft.

The next day, Neil helps Nancy break into the "Dragon Lady's" office to steal the glove back. Instead, she finds Joey's severed head declaring "he got them back." She runs past Neil, who only sees a smear of blood in the safe (could this be a micro nap like the phone scene in the original?). Meanwhile, Dr. Maddalena is leading the latest group therapy session, which goes poorly. When she leaves in frustration, Nancy enters for "the final battle." They join hands just as Neil shows up. She reaches out to him, and while it's at this moment he falls in love with her, he's not ready. He watches as they fall asleep holding hands, then disappear. The gang appears in front of the Elm Street house and heads right in. Taryn's death scene is the same, but instead of getting shoved in a maw, Freddy just slices her face.

Neil goes home and tries falling asleep when he thinks of the Shakespeare quote "For in that sleep of death, what dreams may come..." (which isn't in either draft, but it also screams "Wes Craven") He winds up in the Elm Street house and sees his reflection stretch and distort in a mirror. Elsewhere in the house, Nancy runs into Freddy, who chases her into the arms of Neil. Like the first draft, he's giddy to discover the true dream state. It's short-lived, however, as they run into the remains of Taryn and Joey.

Laredo's death is mostly the same, but he turns into a dragon instead of a gargoyle. Instead of a post-hole digger, his sword flies up and impales him before a hellish pit of fire opens up (the kind Joey would be threatened with in the film) and he's scorched to the bone.

Our final four survivors encounter Freddy in the house's living room before Kristen brings them to her parents' party. Everything happens just as in the first draft with Freddy slicing up some guests along his way. There's no line about Kincaid's ass, so it's possible that wasn't part of his death scene. Also, Dr. Maddalenna is decapitated by Freddy's claws, not his shape-shifting reptile head. The Elm Street house is still on fire, but since there are no gasoline bombs, there's no explanation for it. Freddy takes Neil's form to try and surprise Nancy, but she stabs him first with a steel blade she found on the ground. He stabs her, but she tosses the glove to Kristen, who goes to town on him with his own claw. It's not enough to save Nancy, though. Kristen still pulls Neil out of the flaming dream house. The epilogue is even the same as the first draft, with the sequel tease, and the added detail of Neil having written a paper titled "A Nightmare on Elm Street."

It's clear that Jeffrey Cooper had access to both the Craven/Wagner draft and the Russell/Darabont draft while writing the novelization. However, it remains to be seen where "Mrs. Sapphire" and "Hathaway House" came from. The former is obviously a precursor to Sister Mary Helena, clearly an invention of Russell and Darabont. Also, Freddy and Amanda's stories are different. She's not a nun here but rather burns to death giving birth (that's *dark*), and Mrs. Sapphire implies Freddy was burned, as well. (That can't be right, can it? Did he have burn scars his whole life even before the mob killed him? There is a nice symmetry between his birth and death in fire.) More curious is the story of Amanda's previous hospital, the "snake pit" (Phillip's nickname for Westin Hills in the final film). The orderlies were allegedly paid five hundred dollars so the inmates could have their way with her, but…where'd they get the money? How exactly did one hundred maniacs collect five hundred dollars? No, don't do the math. That's just gross.

Character-wise, Dr. Maddalena joins the ranks of Coach Schneider as a character you actively want to see dispatched by Freddy. Personally, I'm glad her character softened a little. These kids are up against so much that we don't need another antagonist. Will hasn't been written yet, but Laredo is a LOT: In group therapy, when Kincaid says the boy wasn't strong enough, Laredo agrees "he showed his weak side to the Sorcerer, so the Evil One killed him." While he's correct about the tenets of the series, one could see how Russell and Darabont would want to replace him with the more down-to-earth Will. Though it's a nice detail that as soon as Kristen pulls him into the cellar, he accepts that he's in a dream quicker than anyone else. His death is also an improvement over the first draft, because that pole digger would have just looked ridiculous.

Also of note, Jennifer was only turned into an actress in the final film. Max is the one who suggests she watch TV if she can't sleep (another misguided adult leading a teen to her death). Speaking of Jennifer's death, Freddy's head only appears on the tv screen instead of coming out of the set.

Freddy uses the suicide epidemic to cover his crimes, so Kristen and Jennifer attempting to kill themselves doesn't quite fit with the pathology of the final film. Though the image of Jennifer dousing herself in lighter fluid is shocking. Nancy also mentions her father disappeared years ago, but that's all we hear of him. The novelization also has much more action and we see multiple fights where the dream warriors take on Freddy. (Though why does Nancy steal his claws before the ghosts in the shower curtain tell her to?)

One final observation: the "floor water" scene survived every draft, as well as the novelization, but it's not in the final film. Everyone clearly thought it was a good idea, so why the omission? While we might not know for sure where it originated from, I'd wager it came from Craven himself, but that the special effects of the time period couldn't accommodate it. (In 2025, it could most assuredly be done with CGI). This was yet another reason Craven was ahead of the curve.

# INTERVIEW
# CHUCK RUSSELL
## WRITER / DIRECTOR

A Nightmare 3
ON ELM STREET
DREAM WARRIORS

**To begin with, I have to point out that I consider *Dream Warriors* to be the *Aliens* to the original film's *Alien* and I know I'm not alone there.**

Wow, thank you.

**Once you got the job to direct, do you remember how you and Frank Darabont went about rewriting Wes Craven and Bruce Wagner's script?**

I remember it very well. We rented a cabin in Big Bear and rewrote the script in seven days. What would you like to know?

**Well, it's one thing to sequester yourself and write a draft from scratch, but how did you guide an existing template to resemble your final film? For example, are you keeping your budget in mind?**

Interesting question. *Nightmare 3* was my first directing opportunity, but I'd been working in the film industry for years as an assistant director and even budgeting as a production manager. Not to mention getting coffee for stunt teams as a kid. So I had a very good idea what the range was. We never write with a cash register attached, but I have the "fifty-thousand foot view" of what we're doing. I wouldn't write the invasion of Normandy in the middle of a dream. On the other hand, if you're writing something and you don't know how it could be done, that's excellent. It means we haven't seen it before. That's a natural part of how I write.

There are obvious things you don't put in an independent horror film. Even before CGI, there were always interesting ways to create these illusions. All the way through to shadows and sound. The beautiful thing about doing films about dreams, and I've done a couple, including in [the upcoming] *Witchboard*, is that they can be stylized. I encouraged myself and Frank to not have limits when writing. I looked at the 4K transfer last week and I'm still impressed with our visual effects and set pieces. I never held back from what we hadn't seen on film.

The "Snake Freddy" scene was an incredible challenge. It was an extremely large animatronic and looks really cool. There's no CGI in that sequence. That's Patricia Arquette on a set with a full-sized Freddy snake. To this day, I give Kevin Yagher credit for the design and execution. Tony Gardner was always part of these things, and his work is excellent. So the answer to your question is yes and no. There are obvious things not to write in. Huge things, location issues, too many pages, things like that. However, doing things we'd never seen before was the assignment in my mind. I needed to at least live up to [the original], if not outdo it, and I wanted to go deeper into the phantasmagorical world of dreams. That was the fun of it. We brainstormed and structured without limits. Then it's up to me, the director, to storyboard these things and break them down. I can't think of one scene we cut, but there must have been some shots I abandoned, which happens.

There's another scene where Patricia Arquette sees a dinner table where a rotten pig jumps at her. We didn't have thousands of dollars to make an animated, full-sized pig, so I said "Guys, just get a [dead] pig and let it rot." So we cut a hole in the bottom of the table to have it jump. No pigs were harmed. (laughs) This was something you could buy, apparently. My point is, on an independent film, you have a second level of work to do in designing the illusions. That's your final test on budgeting.

**I have a BFA in screenwriting, and I've always been fascinated about the push-and-pull of writing out ideas and thinking how they'll be pulled off, and at what cost.**

I encourage you to do the same. There are some people who will read your script and think "I've never seen that before. We can't do it." That's usually not a good director. (laughs). It depends on whether it's really supporting your overall story or if it's someone who wants to go shoot some racecars or something and it's not worth it.

**To stay on the script for a second, it's a firm blueprint. There's really not a lot that was cut out.**

[Frank and I] worked together, almost like an old school, almost Tin Pan Alley writing team. We'd get together and jam. Frank was more freestyle, but I stressed breaking down structure, very specifically, before writing. By doing that, we could each get up, have coffee, and write in order. I would write scene one, he would write scene two, and we'd switch pages and polish each other. Then at the end of the day, given that I'm directing, I would have kind of a final look at it. (laughs) But it was very effective. We both love horror and the first *Elm Street*, so it was an exciting opportunity.

**You can definitely tell. I just rewatched your remake of *The Blob* and it's like a '50s horror film with three-dimensional characters.**

It's my confidence in using what I call "character-driven humor," which I believe is fair game in a suspense or horror film. The danger is you don't manipulate the story. You have to have something truthful to the character. Some of the funniest lines I've ever heard were being in stressful situations with other people and waiting for something stressful to happen. It's like graveyard humor. There's humor in stress, which is appropriate in my films anyway, but when you start to get silly, forget it. You lose the audience. The point is to be true to the story. I believe a sprinkle of humor helps films in general because it exists in life. It just can't be what you design the whole movie for.

**I take exception to the claim that Freddy became a full-on jokester in *Dream Warriors*. For my money, he's still menacing. You walked that fine line.**

Having just colorized it, I was looking at that because I've been asked about it a lot over the years. The riskiest thing was Freddy coming out of the TV and "Welcome to prime time, bitch." The effect was so unexpected and the result was so violent. In my mind, it wasn't risky at all at the time. I knew if it was shocking and surprising, I might get a laugh, but the point was it was all of the above. Dream stuff needs to be eerie and resonant. It makes you say "I had a dream like that once." They don't totally make sense, but in a film about dreams, they have to make a little more sense that you realize. So I felt very liberated to be wild with the dream sequences.

The only way to go after the original film... I mean, Wes had a telephone lick Heather Langenkamp's face, so he was already there. I wanted to do it on a larger scale and have him show up in a tuxedo, as a nightmare that a child of divorce might have. So I made that [Kristen's] nightmare.

**There are so many different types of special effects that are used, sometimes in the same scene. Animatronics, claymation, mirrors, forced perspectives-**

Also a lot of what we called "backloads." Before CGI, we had to carefully shoot things backwards. Some of those effects were reversed. Characters walking backwards always look a little nightmarish. When the snake Freddy gobbles up Patricia Arquette, the metal mechanism from the animatronic was pinching her, making her uncomfortable. With independent films, you really don't have time to screw around. If we didn't get that effect that day, it would get cut out. So I said, "Tear it out and we'll pull it off of her." It was the last shot of the day. We kept other parts of the animation, but we pulled out that hinge, put it up to her shoulders, and pulled it off her as the mouth went up and down. So she was in a Nerf version of [the snake] and it was a reverse load that looks like it's gobbling her up instead of being pulled off. That's a classic solution for an in-camera effect. And we had a stunt double for when she was slammed down. We were all thrilled with that little set. The snake looked too phallic when it was pink, so we had to make it green on the spot. Maybe I should have kept it flesh-colored. (laughs) It disturbed me that day. I didn't want any unnecessary blowback on that.

**We're not going to go kill-by-kill, but I was always astonished with the first death scene with Phillip. It really throws down the gauntlet in terms of the phantasmagorical. Was that meant to signal to the audience they were in for a new kind of *Nightmare*?**

I wanted to be aggressive. It was a raison d'être, a reason to make this film. There are two of them for me. One is to use the whole Freddy experience as a metaphor for suicide. I wouldn't call it a "kill," but when we see Patricia Arquette transition from a Freddy dream to her mother finding her slashing her wrists, that was a tone I wanted to set. It was important to me.

Prior to writing, I spent a couple of weeks volunteering in a halfway house for suicidal teens in Hollywood. I mopped the floors and was asked to play chess with a couple of the kids, things like that. Just to get the vibe. I didn't tell anyone I was doing films. That's a very good thing as a writer. I was approaching a subject that I wanted to know more about and be confident in. The result was being very bold with that theme in the film, regarding suicide and the bonding amongst the kids. Look, I get it, it's *Elm Street 3*. It's not Shakespeare, as they say. But the truth is it has a long life now and I believe it's because of those elements.

**Absolutely.**

The performances are still touching because of the subject matter. You don't usually dare to go that deep into a subject like suicide. In fact, we were literally going to be banned in England. They thought there was a danger that the film would inspire suicides. I forget who it was with, but I had a phone call with some movie organization that was questioning it. I spontaneously said something that insulted them, but it's true. (laughs) There's a much more dangerous show from this guy William Shakespeare called *Romeo and Juliet*, which romanticizes suicide. I was very careful [with the film] to show that's what you're fighting against. When the Phillip character is up on the edge of that belltower, the kids are screaming for him not to jump. That's the vibe I was going for. You have to band together and become dream warriors to fight the evil instinct that is Freddy. For me, it was a metaphor of suicide, drug use.

**How do you even argue that with a censor?**

I told them exactly what I'm telling you and we weren't banned, as far as I remember. One last thing about the puppet scene, I was fascinated by puppets as a kid, which in a way, was associated with my fascination with film. I made puppets that hung in my room, which is something from my own childhood, as well.

**My wife is terrified of puppets and when we watch *Dream Warriors*, she always covers her eyes until that scene is over.**

What's the difference when you make the puppets? What's the difference between the visualization when you create a maquette versus a voodoo doll? It's all about intention, right? There's something creepy about these little human characters, and there has been across time.

**Let's pivot to the cast for a second. God knows I throw the word "iconic" around a lot, but you really can't imagine these characters played by any other actors. Do you recall anything about the casting process?**

Thank you. I love Annette Benson, but I come from the theatre. I always lead my own casting with different casting directors. I don't sit back and go "Who are we casting?" I think most good directors will tell you the same thing. Johanna Ray cast *The Blob* for me. A lot of times, I have very strong first impressions, then I will be trying to get the performance that I imagine out of that character. That comes from theatre.

I encourage all filmmakers and those who want to be filmmakers to act yourselves. Find a little theatre company, and get on stage in front of twenty people. It'll terrify you if you don't like acting, but you'll learn a hell of a lot more of the process of what you're asking your performers to do for the camera. I did a lot of acting when I was a young man in high school, but I determined I preferred directing because I was writing and directing one-act plays in college. The truth is that you learn from doing. It's true in any career.

I can't help myself with casting. Famously, I stopped the motion on *The Mask* because I was getting pushback on casting Cameron Diaz. She had never acted before, and I knew I would have an entirely different movie without her. Jim Carrey was better in auditions when he was reading with Cameron. He was so much better in the romantic comedy part as Stanley Ipkiss. I knew I had to have that chemistry. So the cast [of *Dream Warriors*] works in part because of the chemistry. I tend to read characters together, two or three at a time, to see what I'm getting. There's a reason the cast bonded together on camera.

I'm not bragging. I'm just saying a lot of filmmakers are too seduced by technology. Yes, the technology is fabulous and you gotta know what you're doing. On the other hand, how are you blocking the scene? How are you casting the scene? What's really happening with the chemistry set that is the combination of your actors?


**Luckily, we had to take a class in college for our BFAs. It was really priceless.**

The problem with the entire filmmaking process is that we're now three or four generations into people who have all been raised on television, at least. We all think we're experts by being observers. You need to get on the floor and get a vibe for what acting is on a molecular level. It doesn't mean you have Royal Academy-trained actors to work with. You might have *Instagram* actors. People who look good and got their start recently, so you have to coach them. The difference between coaching and directing is whether your actor has any experience.


**Some of the characters originated in Wes and Bruce's draft, but you and Frank made them your own in the finished film. Were they modeled after specific anxieties or illnesses?**

Kristen represented a family fear of divorce, honestly. There's a fear of abandonment that comes from being raised in a divorced family. An eerie resonance when a single parent starts dating. It's very difficult for teens, and I'm sure for even younger kids. Each one of them represented a fear. I wasn't busy with the labels, and in fact, I don't trust the labels.

I wanted a metaphor [for each character]. A weakness for Freddy to address. Taryn is an addict, which came up with the iconic image of Freddy with the needle fingers. I've seen it in memes today and I'm very proud that it's out there. I have a phobia of needles. A healthy phobia. (laughs) But I've had friends over the years who I saw disappear because of drugs. We got some nice letters from people who said that scene got them over using the needle. So I thought, even if I scared the right few people, it was helpful.

**There's behind-the-scenes footage that showed Taryn's head was originally going to explode, but I think it's more resonant that we don't see it.**

If something doesn't happen on the set, you have not failed. You do your best, but you don't keep anyone up until 3 AM either. You can do it in the audience's imagination if it's the climax of your scene and you know what they anticipate. You can play it off the other character, which is what we did with Freddy's little orgasmic moment of killing her. It sounds pretty perverted, and it was.

**Since you came from theatre and you're working with the classically trained Robert Englund, is it manna from heaven or did he require wrangling among the many special effects?**

Zero wrangling! I have actors I would never say that about, where their performances are the tip of the iceberg. Robert was really on my side with taking Freddy further. The New Line execs were very worried about putting Freddy in a tuxedo, or even taking him out of his usual wardrobe, let along that fucking tv thing. They wanted me to shoot alternatives, which I didn't have the time to shoot. I think they were worried the fans wouldn't accept it. I don't even know what that means. These are dreams. What the fans won't accept is [being] boring. I think *Nightmare 2* was my argument, where he was playing less of what he did in the original. I wanted him to play more. I don't dislike *Nightmare 2*, it's just entirely different. It's got some great moments and has its own intelligence.

Early on in my career, I was working with Max von Sydow and Christopher Plummer on *Dreamscape*. I was rewriting a scene with them both in my trailer. It was the first movie I ever got into production that I co-wrote and got a producer credit on. I was thrilled. It fell to me to revise that film as a writer in the middle of shooting. When you're working with trained actors, that's the difference between directing, which is a joy, and coaching. I love coaching young actors, but when you're on set, it's different, because you're on the clock, you know? You only have a certain amount of time to finish your shots and be inventive in coaching an actor. Robert was a Christmas present every day with his ideas. If anything, he was pushing further than I was on where you take Freddy. As an actor, he's gotta have the character grow as well. He loved the whole backstory we threw in. Darabont's only issue with me was the day I came up with the line "the bastard son of a hundred maniacs." Frank was sure we would be roasted for that line, but it also comes up as one of the favorite lines. It's weird. (laughs) I have a theory that if I'm not entertaining myself on a script like that, we have real problems. I like to color outside the lines. It's one of the only times I vetoed Frank's editing on my stuff.

**Not only is it a classic line, it's evocative. It's basically an origin story in a nickname. The bastard son of a hundred maniacs isn't going to sell insurance.**

Frankly, it was really the concept that was troubling. I doubt I would do it today as a responsible adult (laughs), instead of when I was younger and wanted to make my mark.

**You and Frank pitched _The Blob_ to New Line before getting the job to direct _Dream Warriors_. How did making _Dream Warriors_ your debut feature affect the decisions you eventually made on your subsequent second feature?**

Primarily, it was a level of confidence because the screenings were so good on _Elm Street 3_. The reactions were better than I was hoping for. But I really got put in my place by the creature itself. I was confident in practical effects, but the blob itself most often didn't work. There were a lot of versions of the blob, and again, I mixed techniques, because even to this day, if you do everything in CGI, the human eye does get used to it. No matter how photoreal it appears to be, there's a gut instinct you get that says "Oh, this is lovely CGI." I think practical effects are scarier. We didn't have that choice back in the day, but I was more confident I could work it out. I guess I eventually did, but I would say three out of four of the set pieces work really well. There's one out of four I would certainly redo, but again, we were an independent film with a good independent budget, not a studio budget. I thought with the R&D time we had in prep that we would solve it and we did not. I had to keep pushing the blob scenes back to the end of the schedule.

All the money in the world doesn't get you an effect that works unless you care about the characters and your head's into the story. When I see Superman crash through too many CGI buildings, I start to lose interest. So it's about the internal logic and your visual image system. Once you have a certain tone to your film, are you consistent? That's the question. Maybe that sounds a little technical but I know what I mean (laughs). My point is I'm thankful to everyone that helped make that picture happen because there were a lot of teams making the blob happen in full scale and in miniature. I really am very proud of the result.

I keep hearing about new *Blob* films in development and I think that's cool. You never know when someone's gonna make an *Aliens* out of your *Alien*, and I encourage it, but it's gonna be tough to make CGI look as gnarly as some of the best shots in *The Blob*, especially Donovan Leitch's death.

Horror is cathartic if you're having tension, fear or paranoia in your life. Sometimes seeing a horror film can blow out your nervous system and be a relief. You can face your fears. A lot of directors have consistent subtext. I think I do, and I try not to have happy endings in my horror films. The price of surviving one of my horror films is not worth it (laughs) for the characters in the imaginary world of the film. But there's a catharsis that you can face your fears. My horror film characters tend to be "everymen." My action films tend to have Dwyane Johnson or Arnold Schwarzenegger, but here we have young people facing their fears.

**I want to talk about Wes Craven, since he and Bruce Wagner wrote the draft that you and Frank transformed. I know you thought you'd get to work with him, and you clearly didn't need him around to make *Dream Warriors*, but what was it about the first film that you wanted to build on?**

It was challenging to do *Nightmare 3*, and while *Nightmare 2* was slightly disappointing, as I fan, I knew why. I wanted to go big in the lore and the internal image system. I wanted to expand on what Wes did. The rules in the first film made a lot of sense to me. I liked that if you die in your dream, you die in real life. I kind of believe it's partially true, because you can imagine yourself to death. People die early of despair, things like that. The flipside is that through the love of another, you gain greater strength. Wes's film showed how, at a certain point, you realize adults can't help you and you have to turn to brotherhood or sisterhood.

I thought I understood [Wes's] dynamic and I didn't know the whole story at the time with New Line. There was apparently conflict I'm unclear on between Wes and New Line over the IP, which was eventually resolved [with *New Nightmare*]. I'm very uncomfortable criticizing that script, but I'll just say that while it had more of Wes's DNA in it, I thought it was less spectacular than it needed to be.

**That's entirely fair. It's a fascinating read, but it's very much a first draft and unfilmable in many ways. It only highlights that what you and Frank did was so incredible.**

Well, that's another thing. On one hand, I wanted to do things I hadn't seen before and challenge myself to work it out in storyboards. On the other hand... I trust my own instincts on what I feel I can do on set, and that starts on the script level. A good story structure and a solid setup and payoff of characters.

**Did you work with Wes at all on the film?**

No, but I wish he was around. I only met him when he came to the cast and crew screening with Tobe Hooper, another one of my horror heroes. They were both surprised they liked it.

**Last question: do you have anything you want to say about the film that you feel isn't discussed enough?**

I will just say I think the public assumes actors are coddled and spoiled. That may be true of certain individuals, but I've seen how hard they work. I know Dwayne Johnson and how hard he works, but they don't understand the leads are working their asses off. The guys and girls that are in a certain shape for superhero movies, I promise you, are working their asses off. They don't like going to the gym any more than you do. My point is this: the fear in a horror film is draining, even for me. I'm a method director, meaning if I want the actors to "go there," part of me is going there with them to that emotional place. So I don't mind if you call these pop movies, but don't assume these were easy to make. Don't assume they were partying. The only film I did where the actors were partying was *Back to School*, which I produced. It was a comedy with Rodney Dangerfield, so that's fine.

TV series have rotating directors, not rotating casts. I did an episode of *Fringe* and those people work together week after week, after week! It's unbelievable the amount of memorization and physical work. Of course, actors have stunt doubles, and yes, we're blessed to be in a business that we love. But my *Elm Street 3* cast worked very hard as young actors. There's a correlation between how hard they worked and how successful it was. The audience senses when the actors are going all the way in a role. I think that's one of the reasons we love Nic Cage, because there's no "halfway" with Nic Cage. (laughs)

The casts in *Elm Street 3*, *The Blob*, and most of my films, when they're running in fear, they're doing it for many takes. It's physically and mentally exhausting at a certain point. So I'm just saying a lot of people think "I want to be an actor because I'm attractive and grandma told me I should act." It's a tough business, but it's demanding day-to-day as well. My thanks goes out to everyone I worked with to make these films.

# INTERVIEW
# JENNIFER RUBIN
## "TARYN WHITE"

**Before you got the role, you were a major model in the 1980's. Was this your first acting role?**

I won International Model of the year in 1982 and I went around the world modeling. Phoebe Cates and her sister were models that made the jump, so I learned from them. I was a model-turned-actress, but I didn't have that stigma. People think "Dream Warriors" is my first film, but it started with a line, and being a must-join in SAG. Ilene Starger was the casting director who gave me my first line: "excuse me you guys." Then I got my SAG card and Marcy and Strath Hamilton gave me my first film role. I remember walking down Sunset Boulevard completely stunned. It was quite romantic.

Everything culminates in that timeframe to the great Annette Benson. She's one of the most important casting directors in decades. All the dream warriors rub elbows if you know what I mean. I don't want to be any one of their characters, and they don't want to be mine. When you're acting, it comes from solidarity and that's where it becomes iconic. Annette cast me perfectly by my essence. I think she did the same for Penelope [Sudrow], Ira [Heiden] and even Laurence [Fishburne].

Pretty is a necessary evil, and we can say that evil is a spirit. I fight two evils: I don't get the claw and there is a distinction because I fight the needle and the necessary evil of the medical profession. I fight both of those things. My father was a pharmacist and those needles scare me to death on a primary fear level, as well as the claw getting you when you're unconscious in your bed.

**Well, you go down fighting.**

I do. But there's a saying "Jackie Chan don't die." When I heard that as a young actress, I was like "Fuck, maybe I shouldn't have died." I would just let everyone who's reading this know, and I've never said this before, but in real life I fought those two evils and I didn't die. It's just the conciseness of storytelling that Chuck Russell and Frank Darabont knew. Part of me wishes I didn't die, but I think I had to sacrifice myself for a storyline so people could identify with the character and they could get over both of those evils. Just being a young bunny. Even when you're born, they start giving you shots. I still fight evil to this day. (laughs)

**You had a very distinct place in a very distinct ensemble. Was there much competing for real estate on screen?**

We're not competing for real estate as an ensemble. We were a team. What I mean by "rubbing elbows" is that we were together, but we all had our sovereignty. For me, acting is spiritual, and each voice in this ensemble was iconic.

**Taryn was iconic, too. You're instantly believable as a recovering addict in a mental institution. I was actually surprised to see you were a model before.**

I was born that way. When you're talking about creating the character in the moment, that has a lot to do with Chuck.

**Was he aware of what you were bringing to the table? Were you planning on bringing that out of you when you were cast?**

He was the lighthouse, right? Out of fifty films, I had a really terrific time collaborating on five of them. Chuck and Frank wrote the costume, then they put it on me. I was in the makeup trailer, and because I was a model, I knew my hair wasn't right for that outfit. One day I went to ask Chuck a question when I was in costume. I saw one of the dolly grips reading an issue of Time magazine that featured someone with a mohawk. I grabbed it and asked Chuck if I could do that hairstyle and he said sure. Annette Benson and Chuck kind of allowed this flow from the makeup trailer and costume to the director and the actor. The communication was fun and collaborative.

**Do you remember the casting process? Were you paired off with anyone?**

Did you hear about when they had us all in the room, sitting together on the floor? I was really in my feels and everything. After we finished, he said 'Jennifer…a little less." [Laughs] And it was like "thank you!" [The character was] in and out of consciousness with drugs and where is that fine line? I still had to be friends and play board games, you know?

**Can we talk about your final scene? I hesitate to just call it a death scene because it's so much more. Taryn stands her ground when Freddy appears and she draws first blood in another first for the series. Did that occur to you when you were filming it?**

Well, I'll tell you something. When I was five or seven years old, a man tried that with me. I actually got him to stop, turn around, and leave. (laughs)

**Oh, wow.**

So I have an innate ability to "Obi Wan Kenobi" bad guys. Like, "these aren't the soldiers you want." It's not me, honey. When I have a confrontation like that, whether in real life or in a movie, I only get scared afterwards. I go "Oh that was a really bad guy who was gonna do something! I'm glad I scared him off. What the fuck?" For me, acting is such a healing thing. You can work out your demons, and move on to other projects. It was a very healing experience for me to work that out in art. I always feel that I can stand up to somebody in the moment. I get that the fanbase loves it, and for me the arts are about telling the truth. There's a practical reason for doing the craft, itself.

**It's a triumphant scene even if your character dies.**

I think Christians say they can't see horror films because they're evil, but all my fanmail says "Thank you. You helped me find the lord." (laughs) It's good stuff.

**Did you already come into the role knowing how to work with the knives, or did you have to practice?**

I had to practice, but it wasn't as hard as you think. Working with the stunt coordinator and doing that whole ballet with [Robert] was pretty quick.

**I have to ask, the original script for *Freddy's Dead* had Taryn, Joey, and Kincaid returning as "dream police." Were you ever approached for that?**

No. (laughs)

**Just a few weeks ago, you won an award for "Best Experimental Feature Film" for your directorial debut *Them Public Romantics*. Congratulations.**

Thank you.

**Would you say you took anything from your experience on *Dream Warriors* that helped you make this film?**

Oh, let me think. It's a good question. I always knew I was gonna do something when I was older. My perspective is you have to wait for your audience to grow up and it's not going to happen on your time. Without every film and every director, every moment good and bad in my life, the flower wouldn't bloom. I was a closed flower, but I knew that about my path. I never got impatient. I didn't want to dance if the audience wasn't there. That's very hard for an artist to do. They want it now, or they want to be extroverted, but that's not what art is. Art is gifts, miracles, and blessings. It's what you came here to do. Thinking you're not going fast enough is a common thing.

All of that added up to the moment I pushed "play" on my camera. It all culminated. I'm at that point in my life where everything I did was right. (laughs) I think when you're a true artist, you really know. You can't be distracted too long or believe what someone else wants from you. Kiss a lot of frogs, right?

**Yes, though I wouldn't consider *Permanent Record* to be a frog. I have to bring it up, not just because it's one of the most underrated films of the 80's, but it also touches on suicide.**

I'm glad you saw it! I got a lot of attention from that film. A little too much, even.

Can I tell you what my father said when we saw it together on the Paramount lot? He talked to Jeff Goldblum all night, then when we left, he said "it's so like you to stop the show." (laughs)

It's not so different from fighting Freddy. It's like when you said I drew first blood. I never thought of that before. Nobody mentioned it to me before. When I stop the show, that's when I talk about Annette Benson. She was like "Who's the girl who's gonna pour the ice water and wake everyone up?"

**Last question. Is there anything you want to bring up about the film or your role in it that doesn't get talked about?**

We're already having a conversation where I'm revealing the biological premise, right? In all of my answers, for the young artist, realizing all of your life experiences add up. If it's a stem of a flower, then it blooms. Like, "Can I be an icon if I didn't go to Juilliard?" You can know technique all day, but there is an energy and purpose behind all experiences. If you focus it in the right way, which I like to do, then I think it's putting evil to good use. We have to fight evil, so we need evil.

I'm really glad the movie meant X, Y and Z to you, even if it's not X, Y, and Z of mine. It's absolutely important to tell me what it meant to you. Now that I've produced people on film myself, I now know that when I show my film, people tell me "This meant so much, that meant so much." I haven't heard two of the same things yet. There's so much to choose from. Then when it gets released, they'll say "Oh it's this." I didn't know then because I was in the picture and it threw me through a loop as a person. But I'm really glad to be part of such an extraordinary experience. Do you know Annette Benson?

**I've corresponded with her a bit, yes.**

She's done so much behind the scenes, but she's a bit modest. She once came to a *Dream Warriors* reunion at a con. When I saw her, I couldn't help but start crying when she walked up to me. My eyes just brimmed with water. I was so touched she showed up. Then I went over to Ira's table and asked "Do you recognize this lady?" Then it slowly dawned on him. We all took a picture together. All the dream warriors and Annette. She's a doll.

# INTERVIEW
# IRA HEIDEN
## "WILL STANTON"

**What do you remember about the casting process?**

I remember going in almost six times for the role of Will Stanton. I originally met Annette Benson, then I came back and she put me on tape for Chuck Russell. Chuck watched the tape, and I met with him twice more after that.

**Was there anything that changed between those two meetings?**

Yes, I took some acting lessons with my cousin, David Schacker, who was an acting coach. I remember when I came back, Chuck said "Wait a minute, you're doing something different from before." So, I went back to how I was originally auditioning the first time.

**Did he pair you up with anyone in the audition process?**

Not in auditions, but I had read for the role of Joey. He paired me up with several nurses, which was beyond epic. It was so much fun. I just had to react.

**Did you audition for any other roles in the film?**

No, my manager Marilyn Sherman always wanted me to read for Will. I played a ton of Dungeons & Dragons in middle school and high school, so I was familiar with "the Wizard Master."

**Were you familiar with the Laredo character?**

The "Laredo" character?

**Yes, Will wasn't the original "wizard master." The original script featured a character named Laredo, who still loved D&D, but he wasn't in a wheelchair and he shapeshifted.**

Interesting.

**Did you conceive any backstory for Will?**

No, I was just in the moment. I thought he was insecure from being in a wheelchair. I just knew tons about D&D. I read Tolkien and Gandalf was one of my favorite characters of all time. I didn't actually have a wheelchair at first. Once I got the job, they let me borrow it for a couple of weeks. I remember traveling through Westwood Village with my best friend, Harold Pruett, just going through different areas to see how people would react to me in a wheelchair. Some people would open the door for me, others would look away and not help. It definitely helped me get more into the character.

**I agree, especially when he gets off the floor to attack Freddy. It's one of the most memorable scenes from the series.**

Well, the fans loved it. I owe it all to you. (laughs)

**Dream Warriors is the fan favorite. The chemistry between the characters is palpable. Did you bond with each other offscreen?**

Yes, we had a reading before filming. We also had brunch together and we started to get to know each other. At auditions, I saw Rodney Eastman, Ken Sagoes, and Jennifer Rubin.

**Do you still play D&D?**

No, I haven't played in so long! It would be fun to get back into it.

**Are you familiar with the D&D-style game that Bruce Seddon made based on *Nightmare 3*?**

I'm aware of it. I hope it comes through. I saw some art online and he put me on the poster, which is cool.

**It's very cool. I actually playtested it as Will.**

Right on!

**Is there anything you wish people talked about more in regards to *Nightmare on Elm Street*?**

Truthfully, I think we should approach mental health awareness more. Our characters were thrown in the psych ward because we were supposedly crazy, but we were actually fighting a demon. It feels like a lot of teenagers are fighting demons right now. There was so much good about that in our movie, that I think that needs to be talked about and dealt with more.

Five years ago, I produced a reading of *Dream Warriors* in Los Angeles, at the Whiskey a Go Go of all places. Everybody read the script. Chuck Russell did the narration. I think Jennifer and Ken were at a convention, so they couldn't make it. Brooke Thiess from *Nightmare 4* read Taryn, Heather Langenkamp read Nancy, Tuesday Knight read Kristen, and Robert read Freddy, which was great.

The whole point of the reading was to raise money for Didi Hirsch, a mental health foundation for suicide prevention. We raised $20,000. We auctioned off a guitar signed by my buddy, Robby Krieger from The Doors for $5,000. It was pretty cool. I wish we could do more readings of *Nightmare 3* for mental health awareness. Who knows? Stay tuned.

## INTERVIEW
# KEN SAGOES
### "ROLAND KINCAID"

A Nightmare ON ELM STREET **3** DREAM WARRIORS

**You've shared your famous audition story, where you came into the room frustrated, and got the job after cursing everyone out. I know Chuck Russell liked to pair people, so were you paired with another actor in the next round?**

Yeah, but just for the record, I didn't curse Chuck Russell out, himself. It was Kincaid cursing and saying what he would have said in that incident. People think I cursed him out, but I probably wouldn't have gotten the job if I had cursed him out (laughs).

Chuck Russell did something that I wished a lot of directors would do. He brought us all together more than once. We had a little party and got to know each other, which was very brilliant, because one of the first things we shot was a scene in group therapy. That helped us, because we had gotten to know each other. We had all invested some emotions and feelings in each other, so it wasn't just actors coming to the set. I had gotten to know Jennifer Rubin, who's still a very dear friend, and Rodney [Eastman] and Ira [Heiden]. We knew each other. It wasn't just "How you doin'? I'm doing this [movie], too." We had invested in each other.

**You can definitely feel the chemistry. The film makes a point of saying you've all been fighting Freddy in your dreams, which is why you're still alive at the beginning. Did you work any of that into a backstory for Kincaid?**

No, because I didn't know what *Nightmare on Elm Street* was. I don't think I had heard of it. The reason I knew about it was because of two incidents. I was on the bus going to the audition in the rain, and there was a lady that was older than I was. I told her what I was going to audition for. I still remember the way her head moved. [Ken does a double take]. "Ooooooh, that's a good one!" (laughs). I also remember telling a friend of mine that I was going to audition for it and he praised it. So, when I went to the set, it was new to me. I had just finished doing a film with Denzel Washington, but I hadn't gotten my check to be able to buy a TV or VCR yet. All I heard was what people said about it. So, when I auditioned, I just went in with my personal life. I didn't even have a car. When Chuck had that gathering, I wasn't going to come, because it was too far. Chuck said, "If you come, I'll send you back in the cab," so I was able to get there. Then, I think it was the second day of the shoot, Patricia Arquette gave me a ride home. We had become friends, but she didn't know me, and I lived in the hood. I think she had a little red or yellow Volkswagen, and it was brave of her to do that. I will never forget that. I haven't seen her since *Nightmare*, but I understand she's doing conventions now, and I look forward to seeing her, to thank her, because that is still something dear to my heart. She's a good person.

**Do you have any memories of working with Annette Benson during the casting process?**

Annette Benson. She was a land angel of casting. I don't think I would be where I am if the likes of her had not believed in me. I didn't want to go to the audition because the character breakdown was not who I was. I felt that it was a waste of my time, and I was tired, and all that, so I had an attitude. She probably saw something in me that I didn't see in myself, and I would always be grateful to her for that. Annette Benson was one of those casting directors that was such a gift to this industry. Even now, when you see her, it's like you just saw her last week. I don't say this because she's not casting anymore, from my understanding, and I'm not trying to get in with her. I'm still acting, and I still haven't run across the likes of her. She just saw what we could do. If there was a gift inside of us and we didn't know it, she believed it. When she reached out to me and told me about you, there was never a question [we would talk].

**That's great to hear.**

She won't steer you wrong.

**You mentioned previously that *Dream Warriors* taught you how to act with special effects.**

The closest I got to special effects was going to see a magician (laughs). Working with special effects taught me how to act. It gave me a chance to use my improv skills. In my early days, I was H.R. Pufnstuf at an amusement park. I wanted to be a clown, so I went to Florida one summer for clown university. I learned how to mime, which I thought wasn't going to help me, but all that training helped on *Dream Warriors*. Chuck said there were going to be effects going around, and you have to pretend you're watching them. For example, when the claws came through the walls [of the quiet room], I was really scared, because I didn't know what it would look like.

**But he told you about it beforehand?**

Yes, he told us, but you know, what if somebody tripped? (laughs). We didn't know exactly when it was coming through, so we were scared, but it was effective. As far as physical acting, which I found out was its own category, I give homage to Laurence Fishburne for helping me with that. He took me to the side and told me, "You don't have to work this hard." He was a brother that talked to me. I think that's why I like giving back. I got a lot of gifts that weren't money. All that was asked in return was to pass it on to those coming up behind me.

**Talking to you now, you seem very different from the character, which is of course, usually the case, but how much of yourself did you infuse into Kincaid?**

I went back to part of my upbringing. I wasn't a part of the streets, but I was on the street sometimes. You had to survive, sometimes with just words, like a game we called "Dozens." You know, "Your mama so ugly, your mama this." I think that's where [Kincaid's] quickness and voice came from. I think that's what helped me with some of the language that Kincaid had, because I remember telling Chuck that a Black guy wouldn't say this. He said, "Well, say it like a Black guy would say it." That's when the cursing came in. You know, we wouldn't say "motherfucker." We'd say "mothafucka" (laughs). I'm not saying Kincaid wasn't scared, but when you pushed him into the corner, he became a lion. He was going to fight his way out. With that, I believe I went back and got some of that inside of me, but that was just life lessons.

I find that because of how I was trained, I would get so involved in the character, that I would allow them to latch onto me, as opposed to me latching onto the character. I think it was Kincaid that latched onto some of the "bullcrap" of Ken Sagoes (laughs).

**To me, like the height of the *Nightmare on Elm Street* popularity was between parts 3 and 4.**

Not to brag, but those were the two I was in!

**I know! Did you experience any of the "Freddymania" firsthand? Were you recognized on the street?**

I was, but I had not embraced it. At the time, I was living in a single room, and it meant that I got a job and I had money in the bank. I could pay my rent for the next couple of months. Then people started recognizing me, and it was wild. But you know, I never wanted to be famous when I got into this business, if you can understand it. I loved the craft, and I was getting experience. I will always go back and be around people who said I was going to make it, because I don't think I made it by myself. I made it by the grace of God, and because people believed in me before I came to Hollywood. I felt that it wasn't just me that had made it. It was a lot of other people that had made it.

It had gotten to the point that one time my agent told me I was going to get a call from Taiwan around 3 AM. I got this call, and I said "Hello," and they spoke Japanese. The operator would translate: "Are you Ken Sagoes?" It turned out that it was a dignitary who wanted me to wish his son a happy birthday. That's when I said "Wow." A month later, I got a drawing of Kincaid from Taiwan. I was recognized all over the world, which was kind of new to me, you know, but I embraced it. I still embrace it. You know, I'm still shocked that people recognize me today. I was just shooting a spinoff of *Snowfall*, which wrapped last night. I was surprised at the amount of behind-the-scenes people who knew me from *Nightmare on Elm Street*. It has been wonderful for me. It has gotten me jobs, you know, and that's why I like to take advantage of anytime people want to talk to me. I feel that I owe something to the people who made me. I hope that answered your question.

**I'm glad you felt that way. I saw these movies at a young age, and, as a white kid from suburbia, you were aspirational.**

I didn't realize that until later. I don't think my mom ever saw the movie, but she enjoyed what she heard about it. Some people told me she got a chance to see it before she made her transition. What surprised me was how many Christians saw the movie. At my church, the pastor was adamant about me [not] doing the movie. There was an elderly lady there that helped me, who told me to do it. I came back a year or so later, when the movie was really big and I was going to give them money to help them fix their roof. She pulled me aside and said, "Don't give them one red penny! They didn't want you to do this movie. They said it was the devil's movie, so the devil's money ain't gonna fix this roof! But you are going to take me out to eat" (laughs).

**That's amazing!**

A lot of wonderful things.

**Did you know you were going to die when you read the script for *Dream Master*?**

They didn't have a script when we did *Nightmare 4*. That was around the time that the writers were on strike. All they had was a treatment. I didn't know if I was coming back, but I believe if Patirica Arquette had returned, then I would have been in there a little longer. Since she did not return, they just wanted to get rid of [us]. The new kids were the freshmen or the sophomores, and they wanted to graduate the seniors so they could get on with the movie. As a writer, I understand that, and I was not resentful. I learned a long time ago that if you're going to get upset about things that don't go your way, then you shouldn't be in this business.

So it didn't bother me as much as most people would think. At the time, I was also doing stand up comedy and one of my biggest lines was, "If you want to see me, go right in and sit down. Don't get no popcorn. Don't get no drinks!" Also, because of the impact I had made in *Nightmare 3*, I worked very little in *Nightmare 4*, but I got paid double what I got in *3*! So hey, I won! (laughs) I once watched an audience watch *Nightmare 4*. I felt so honored, because when I died, the audience was pissed.

**Well, you go out like a dream warrior. You throw the car on him.**

Yeah, I got a chance to do a tiny bit of stunt work. There was a rumor that someone who worked on *Nightmare* told me, but I don't know how true it was: they wanted to find a way to bring Kincaid back.

**I was going to ask about that.**

That was why I said "See you in hell." Supposedly, I was trapped in limbo and I would come back to fight Freddy. I also read a script, which brought the dream warriors back as the "dream patrol" or something. I think it was for part six.

**Yes, that was a draft of *Freddy's Dead*.**

I don't know how true that is, but I would have loved to come back. I know there was big talk about it. I wish it had happened. I also found out there had been some comic books with the dream warriors.

**They pop up as ghosts in *Freddy vs. Jason vs. Ash: The Nightmare Warriors*. It's a whole thing.**

People come up to me at conventions to have me sign it, but probably didn't tell us, because they knew they had gotten our image, but not our permission. But it's still an honor.

**How would you compare working with Chuck Russell and Renny Harlin? They're two very different directors with very different styles.**

You just answered the question. As an actor, you have to be professional enough to adjust to [different] styles, and thank God I had gone through enough that I could. Each one of them was the captain of their ship. I have a reputation that when I'm on the set, I try to do what I'm told to do. If I don't really don't like it, I would speak with the director one-on-one. I didn't have a problem with them. You know, I had been around some of the legends of yesterday. I met Alfred Hitchcock in his last days.

**What!?**

I was a security guard at Universal Studios and I met him in 1979. He didn't know me, but he did take a moment to talk to me. I got a chance to go through the stages and watch directors [on shows like] *Quincy*. I couldn't afford acting workshops or classes, so I learned from watching the greats. I saw the newer directors, like the brilliant Oz Scott, who was directing *Bustin' Loose*. I saw who he was and I learned what to do and what not to do.

**Is there anything else you'd like to say about the *Nightmare* films that isn't talked about enough?**

I made a horror short called *Socrates*, which I patterned after the *Dream Warriors*. It's about a killer bird, who's talons grow when he's angry. In my eyes, he's going to be the new villain in town (laughs). The lead is patterned after Kincaid. I wanted to do something original because some of the horror remakes aren't for me.

Who I am is because of *Nightmare on Elm Street*. In terms of popularity, they are the ones that put me out there. So anytime I can thank them, I want to thank the fans for putting me on top of that mountain, and I don't want to ever fall.

# A Nightmare 4 ON ELM STREET THE DREAM MASTER

To no one's surprise, *Dream Warriors* made a ton of money and the coffers at New Line Cinema were overflowing faster than Glen's bed. Freddy Krueger was now officially a horror icon in a decade chock full of them. It's important to note that 1988 was a landmark year for horror. CGI was still in its infancy, but special effects-laden spectacles were king. Producer Moustapha Akkad had resurrected his boogeyman after seven years away for *Halloween 4: The Return of Michael Myers*. Effects guru John Carl Buechler (who worked on several key scenes for the film covered in this chapter) directed the seventh *Friday the 13th* in eight years. Even Kevin Yagher found the time to physically create Chucky the killer doll for Tom Holland's *Child's Play*. Horror was firing on all cylinders, making a fourth *Elm Street* a foregone conclusion. (Maybe Neil shouldn't have used a flask to store his holy water, but I digress…)

New Line knew they had to not only keep going, but also keep innovating and topping themselves. They also knew there was a looming writers' strike, so filming needed to start yesterday. Bob Shaye was initially skeptical of the man he chose to direct the film: a tall Swede who hung around New Line looking for a chance to direct. This was future action director Renny Harlin, who was then a nobody who smelled badly from living in his car like so many other wannabe Hollywood directors. Shaye's gamble paid off in dividends.

*A Nightmare on Elm Street 4: The Dream Master* was rushed into production at the height of "Freddy Mania," as everyone involved was more or less riding high. It was a time when intense demand met unbridled creativity. Fans were clamoring for more and New Line was racing against the clock to give it to them.

## DREAM SCENARIO

Just as with *Dream Warriors*, *The Dream Master* begins with a quotation, this one biblical, and the creation of a house. The opening credits spin around a child's hands as she draws in the dirt with chalk. We hear "(Running from this) Nightmare" by Tuesday Knight, a dark but catchy pop song as we're wondering what we're looking at. It's soon revealed to be a little girl drawing the familiar Elm Street house in front of the actual rotting Elm Street house that was established in the previous entry. Approaching her from behind is a woman who we might not recognize, but should be familiar with all the same. She walks up to the girl and asks where Freddy is. The child giggles and reveals a chalk drawing of Freddy in a window of the house. It starts to rain and the girl disappears. The derelict house is the only shelter around. As the woman tentatively approaches the spooky house, she sees the jump rope kids on the weed-ridden lawn singing the also familiar nursery rhyme.

Once inside the house, the woman realizes she's trapped. She tries to talk herself down. "Be calm, Kristen," says Kristen Parker, re-cast as Tuesday Knight herself. The opening of *Dream Master* is a slight re-write of the opening of *Dream Warriors*. Kristen is once again dreaming about the house, but now she's anticipating Freddy's appearance. After a powerful gust of wind blows her into the basement, she stands up and realizes it's the infamous boiler room. But it's now empty. No heat, no fire, just rotting pipes and chains hanging from the ceiling. But Kristen soon hears a familiar screech and "calls" out for Kincaid and Joey (once again played by Ken Sagoes and Rodney Eastman, who has more lines, obviously).

"When deep sleep falleth on men, Fear came upon me, and trembling, which made all my bones to shake" - Jon IV 13-14

Kristen's ability to pull people into her dreams has been working overtime lately and it's pissing off her friends. They wind up right next to her in the boiler room, unamused that they're being dragged into another nightmare when the man who tortured them is "dead, buried, and consecrated" according to Kincaid. Joey even makes her feel the cold pipes. There's nothing to worry about anymore, though you can practically hear the audience laughing as they say these lines. All of a sudden, Kincaid's dog, Jason, appears and bites Kristen's arm. (Hey, dogs sleep, too.)

The next morning, Kristen, reacclimated to suburbia from her time in Westin Hills, drives her convertible to pick up her boyfriend Rick (Andras Jones) and his sister, Alice (Lisa Wilcox). Rick and Alice are very close, having bonded after the death of their mother. Their father (Nick Mele) is a belittling drunk. He doesn't greet Kristen, his son's girlfriend, who's giving his children a ride to school, which he isn't deigning to do, though he does take a moment to call out Alice's wardrobe. It would be a cliché for him to think his daughter is wearing something revealing, but Alice is a soft-spoken wallflower who's modestly dressed. (There's no way he would have lifted a finger to kill Freddy Krueger alongside the other parents way back when, that much is certain.) He's such an ass that when the audience first meets Rick, he's climbing out his second-story bedroom to avoid him. He knows his dad is hungover and it's "Avoid-all-contact day!" It's clear from this he's the funny one of the group, which charms Kristen and soothes Alice.

When they arrive at school, they meet up with Debbie (Brooke Thiess), a badass with a studded leather jacket, big hair, and an aversion to homework. Alice sees football player Dan Jordan (Danny Hassel) across the parking lot. She daydreams hitting on him, which is a first. We've never seen someone just daydreaming in these movies before and this is also one of the few moments in the dream realm where nothing bad happens.

Debbie's friend Sheila (Toy Newkirk) arrives on a vespa. She's a Black nerd with asthma and the two of them make a great pair, though an odd couple for the time period. Debbie and Sheila don't interact as much as other characters, but they display a great shorthand before Debbie defends her from a catcall. Her victory is short-lived, however, as she soon recoils when a bug crawls onto her nachos. (I know we have to establish Debbie's fear of bugs, but *nachos* in the morning? Isn't she a bodybuilder?) Moments later, Kincaid and Joey arrive and expect an explanation from Kristen for the earlier dream pull. She insists that Freddy is coming back, but they outright dismiss her claim with Joey suggesting they "all have better things to dream about." No one seems to notice the four peculiar slash marks on Kristen's locker, which admittedly don't make much sense, but it's a memorable visual.

That evening, Rick practices karate in the garage and Alice makes dinner as Mr. Johnson arrives home late from work. He insults the salad he's given, leading Alice to break the plate and unleash a short tirade about his alcoholism, which scares him. But it's only a daydream. (That's two so far and we haven't even seen Freddy yet. Something new is around the corner.)

Later that night, Kincaid falls asleep and "wakes up" in the junkyard from the end of *Dream Warriors*. He sees his dog, Jason, pissing a stream of fire on the ground (yes, I said "pissing a stream of fire"), which opens up a deep crevice in the ground. Kincaid stares into the hole and sees bones piecing themselves together. They start to grow burnt flesh. He lets out a mesmerized "fuckin A" before Freddy's razor glove shoots out of the ground. Since he knows what this means, Kincaid runs away and misses a great hero shot of the resurrected Freddy Krueger.

In a nice bit of continuity, Kincaid maintains his dream power of superhuman strength and drops a car on Freddy. He starts to celebrate, but just like in *Dream Warriors*, most of the cars around him start to blink, honk, and encircle him as he yells for Kristen, but it's no use. Freddy appears out of nowhere and impales him with his glove. (At least Kincaid goes out with a "See you in hell.")

Next up is Joey, whom we find watching MTV on his waterbed. He glances over to a poster of a gorgeous centerfold before nodding off. Suddenly, the blonde is under the surface of his waterbed, naked and beckoning to him. (See? Joey was right when he told Kristen that they all had better things to dream about.) Unfortunately, the fun is soon spoiled when Freddy bursts through the surface of the waterbed, stabbing Joey, and pulling him under as he calls out for Kristen. For my money, this is one of the scariest kills in the series. Not only is it reminiscent of Glen's death, which also occurs in the relative safety of his bed, it's horrifying to think you can drown where you sleep. It gets under my skin, even watching it now.

Rick goes to comfort Alice in the wake of their dad's reprehensible but unsurprising behavior at dinner. He tries to teach her a karate kick to boost her confidence, but they laugh after she accidentally kicks her shoe into her aquarium. He also points out her bedroom mirror, which is covered by photos of her friends, Rick and their mother, to the point where she can't even see her own reflection. It's a potent metaphor for someone who subsumes herself for others and seeks comfort in daydreams. Avoiding reality is usually something that can get you killed in these films, but not with Alice. She's in control of her dreams. There are grander plans at work.

Alice brings up her penchant for daydreaming when she meets Kristen at school the next day. Kristen is chain smoking, lost in thought, but she notices bags under Alice's eyes and says they have "matching luggage." Alice reveals that she handles her nightmares with a rhyme her mother taught her. She also tells Kristen to "dream about someplace fun." She soon faints, however, upon learning that Kincaid and Joey have died. Kristen then dreams that the school nurse is actually Freddy in disguise, (which is obviously Robert Englund in drag) only for the nurse to revert to her normal appearance upon waking. Kristen's worst fears are now realized.

Debbie and Alice work at their afterschool job, a throwback 50's diner (The "Crave Inn," get it? If not, put this book down). Sheila stops by and learns that Debbie intends to set her up with a boy, but Sheila only rolls her eyes. (The dork doesn't want to date? What kind of 80's movie is this?) Rick shows up with a distraught Kristen, who makes them go to 1428 Elm Street along with Dan. The run-down, abandoned house looks just like it does in the dream realm, which is fitting as Kristen describes it as "his home." Dan's the new kid in school, so Rick gives him the exposition dump while claiming not to believe any of it.

As if on cue, Elaine Parker (Brooke Bundy, back again) returns to berate her daughter for standing outside the house where the guy she killed tried to kill her only child. She takes Kristen home for dinner when Kristen starts to get drowsy. It turns out "Hurricane" Elaine learned nothing from *Dream Warriors* or Nancy Reagan and has spiked her daughter's drink with sleeping pills. (This actually harkens back to the original story that inspired Wes Craven where the parents of one of the teenage boys secretly gave them sleeping pills before they died.) As she tells Elaine off, Kristen falls asleep in her room, trying to "dream of someplace fun." She winds up in a location we haven't been before: the beach.

Here's the moment most detractors point to as the decline of the series' narrative, though Fredheads love it. After a *Jaws* reference, Freddy appears and dons sunglasses. Kristen begins to sink into quicksand and winds up on the ceiling in her house, evoking both the sticky floor and dream physics of the original *Nightmare*. She runs right into the boiler room, possibly out of habit, possibly because Freddy has made every room in the house the boiler room. Kristen tries resisting Freddy's taunts to pull someone into her dream, which would provide him another victim, but she eventually does just that – accidentally summoning Alice. The girl is sopping wet and rightly confused. She's in the dream just long enough to watch Freddy throw Kristen into the furnace, killing the last child of the people who burned him in his own boiler room. As Freddy takes her soul, she transfers her "power" to Alice, both represented by a beam of light. Freddy then declares "Now, no one sleeps!" (This begs the question: did he have a plan beyond revenge? Like the giallo says, the killer must kill again, but did her death signify something in a grand scheme? It's not like he had a problem killing Kincaid and Joey.)

Waking from the dream, Alice finds an upsetting postcard of Freddy and Kristen in hell, yet another taunt, and along with Rick, rushes over to the Parker residence. They're too late to save Kristen, however, whom they find consumed by flames in her bed. Later after Kristen's funeral, Alice and Rick mourn together by watching home videos of their friends in one of the film's most touching moments. Rick knows something's wrong with Kristen's death but he can't confirm it. Alice witnessed it, so it's more real to her. She tells him "It's like part of [Kristen] is with me." This becomes all the more evident when she starts to light a cigarette the next day at school, but stops herself.

Sheila runs into Alice just before they take a big test. (Who has a test after three funerals?) The tech wiz has made a bug zapper she plans to give to the roach-phobic Debbie. (Say it with me: 'Awwww.') During class, Alice falls asleep and Sheila's test paper starts rearranging the letters to read "Learning is fun with Freddy!" But Sheila never went to sleep, so why is she experiencing this and why doesn't anyone around her notice? It becomes clear that Alice accidentally "pulled" her in just as Kristen did. Freddy appears and "kisses" Sheila, sucking the air out of the asthmatic teen and mummifying her body. This marks one of the most tragic deaths in all of the films – Sheila never actually fell asleep and probably never even heard of Freddy. It's simply unfair when she has an "asthma attack" in class and dies. Only Alice knows the truth. ("He was *here!*") Devastated, she takes Sheila's bug zapper.

We have another scene of mourning as Rick, Alice, Debbie, and Dan watch Sheila's body being wheeled out of the school. Debbie is pissed and doesn't want to hear Alice warn them about Freddy. Alice comes to the heartbreaking realization that *she* brought Sheila into her dream and then watched her die. She runs away and Rick chases after. Later on, Dan stops by the diner where Alice is working around the clock. She doesn't want to sleep or spend time at home. Dan appears to really care about her, even if he doesn't entirely believe what she says is happening. She explains that Freddy needs her to bring people to him once he killed Kristen.

After sitting out the previous entry, "noted thespian" Bob Shaye cameos as a bored teacher with a fascinating lesson about dreams. He talks about the theory of a positive and a negative gate for dreamers. Someone guards the negative gate (Freddy, obviously), but who guards the positive gate? As Professor Shaye notes, the dream master does. With Nancy and Kristen dead, who will now serve as Freddy's opposite? Alice falls asleep in class before she can realize her teacher is a genius.

Rick's been staying up with Alice when she's home, so he falls asleep, most unfortunately, on the toilet. After seeing a vision of Alice and a dead Kristen, the stall becomes an elevator apparently headed for hell. Before he can get there, he exits the cell into what appears to be a Japanese living room and he's somehow wearing a karate gi. Freddy is nowhere to be seen – literally. He's invisible, mocking Rick and punching him just to keep him unbalanced. Rick fights back, sensing where Freddy is, and high kicks his glove right off. The glove then flies off the ground and kills the poor guy. It's worse when Alice wakes up in class and screams so loud that the classroom windows explode. (Could this be a remnant of Joey's dream power?)

At Rick's funeral, Alice daydreams that he comes out of the coffin, safe and sound. She plans with Debbie and Dan to somehow kill Krueger and quotes the late Sheila's motto "mind over matter." In a private chat with Debbie, Dan mentions having noticed that Alice's personality has changed after every recent death. This is later underscored when Alice begins to fiddle with Rick's nunchucks and even does a complicated karate kata as though she's been training for years. It's an awesome moment, but Alice puts a period on it by fearfully wondering out loud what is happening to her.

Mr. Johnson, still drunk but mourning, tries to prevent Alice from going out to meet her friends. (Does he know about Freddy? He has to, even if he wasn't there to kill him.) There's a funny moment where Dan waits for her at the diner, lamenting "[of] all the towns in America, I had to move to the Bermuda triangle." Hassel is subtly funny as an understated jock who can't believe the situation he's found himself in, but still cares about his friends.

Alice eventually sneaks out in defiance of her dad, wandering down the street to a movie theater showing *Reefer Madness* (the old propaganda film, not the hilarious musical). It doesn't quite make sense how Alice gets waylaid, but when she sits down, she finds herself sucked into the screen in one of the most incredible effects of the series. (Cinematographer Steven Fierberg claims that having Alice turn from a person to a 2D image before our eyes had never been done before, and it's impossible to see how it was done, even today.) Now in the movie world, Alice enters a run-down, decrepit version of the Crave Inn, complete with an elderly version of herself as she previously mentioned her nightmare would be working there forever. (Ah, naivete!)

Freddy slides up next to her and proceeds to eat "soul food," meaning a pizza where the meatballs are the souls within him. It's incredibly ghoulish. He "eats" Rick and asks her more, meaning Debbie. Alice wakes up and runs to the diner to meet Dan and head to Debbie's.

Then Alice runs to the diner to meet Dan and head to Debbie's. (Wait, what?)

Then Alice runs to the diner to meet Dan and head – *hold on a second*. They're both dreaming and Freddy has them trapped in a time loop so they can't help Debbie!

Arguably the most elaborate kill in the entire franchise belongs to Debbie. While she's lifting weights to prepare to fight Freddy, he appears above her in a spotting position. Then her arms fall off and she slowly turns into what she fears the most: a cockroach. (It's enough to make Kafka vomit, but looks incredible. The effects were handled by "Screaming Mad" George, a smiley Japanese effects guru whose name is synonymous with on-screen goop.) Debbie finds herself inside a roach motel, which is promptly crushed by Freddy. I know *A Nightmare on Elm Street 4: the Dream Master* plays a little faster and looser with logic than most of the entries and that's a trade-off we're pretty much willing to live with, but… what does that crime scene look like?

After Debbie dies, Alice crashes Dan's truck into a tree, thanks to Freddy's trickery. Alice is mostly unhurt, but Dan is in bad shape, which doesn't make a lot of sense. She goes with him to the hospital but leaves when she realizes she can't stop the doctors from sedating him. At least her dad is there to see if she's okay. (Baby steps, I guess.)

Alice goes home to prepare for the final fight. She takes sleeping pills and tools up with a classic 1980's montage as she decks herself out with the artifacts she's acquired from fallen loved ones: Rick's bandana, Debbie's leather studded bracelet, and Sheila's bug zapper. Alice doesn't yet know why she'll need them, but when she finally removes the last of the pictures from her mirror, she gets a good look at her new self. She's deadly, confident, and ready to bring the pain to her tormentor much like Nancy, Kristen, and the dream warriors before her. She repeats Kincaid's "Fuckin A." Even though they weren't friends, he's with her now, just like the rest of Freddy's victims.

Back in the hospital, Dan sees a vision of Freddy in physician scrubs. ("It ain't Dr. Seuss.") Alice sees this in her now-functional mirror and jumps right through it into the operating room. Having joined in Dan's dream, they escape into a James Bond-esque tunnel with Freddy at the far end. He rolls the sides of their confine, disorienting the dreamers as they fall through a stained-glass window into a darkened and dilapidated church. Freddy is nowhere to be seen, but Dan starts to fade away. Having been badly cut during their fall into the church, he's begun to bleed profusely in the real world, forcing his doctors to wake him from his surgical anesthesia to save him. This means Alice is now alone against Freddy.

Time for a fight unlike any seen before in the series. Even the jump rope kids show up to sing the nursery rhyme. (This is kind of weird on its face. Are they cheering him on?) Massive doors open to a confident Freddy, who welcomes Alice to "wonderland." There's some choreographed hand-to-claw combat, where she fights with karate and dodges with gymnastics. Eventually, Alice improvises with the bug zapper and some electric wires, blowing a hole right through Freddy's chest. He is unamused. "I've been guarding my gate for a long time, bitch," he sneers before sending her flying across the room.

All seems lost, until the jump rope kids recite the poem that Alice's mom used to tell her before she died, a variation on "Now I Lay Me Down to Sleep" called "The Dream Master." (This is an invention of the film, so don't go looking for it among 18th century literature.) The poem ends with "evil will see itself and it shall die." Hearing this, Alice grabs a shard of stained glass and shows Freddy his own reflection while yelling that last line. Then Freddy starts to quake. The souls within his chest actually tear themselves out in a stunning display of makeup and mechanical effects. Hands and heads shoot out of his body, eventually ripping his head in two. (Apologies to all other entries, but this is the most astonishing of Freddy's many deaths in the series. So much so that it's copied in the next installment.) The freed souls eventually fly out of the dream church and Alice walks out, smiling triumphantly.

The next day, Alice and a healed Dan walk by a fountain. She throws in a coin and sees a vague outline of Freddy's reflection in the ripples. This could be a reference to the next entry (we'll get there), but it most certainly means it's not over.

## NIGHTMARE AUTOPSIS

While not considered the best film in the series (the original) or the most beloved by fans (*Dream Warriors*), *A Nightmare on Elm Street 4: The Dream Master* is the apotheosis of the *Nightmare on Elm Street* films. It's what happens when you push Wes Craven's concepts to the absolute hilt. In a way, this film takes the story back to formula. Freddy doesn't have much of a plan beyond killing teenagers in their dreams and structurally, it feels like a remake of the original. Given that, it's no wonder why Craven himself proclaimed his admiration for it.

Consider further connections to the original. Our final girl is backed into a corner as her friends and family members die around her, this before she can claim her power. It's also the first time we're back in Freddy's boiler room. Not the power plant from *Freddy's Revenge* or the unearthly power center where he held Joey captive in *Dream Warriors*. No, we're back to the hissing pipes and chains of the original film, in full force. There's even a scene where a character jumps through their bedroom mirror as well as a bed-based death scene. Freddy's resurrection via flaming dog piss is an attempt by Harlin to reference the hellhounds of various mythologies. Yes, it's a massive stretch, but Harlin admitted it to James Cameron's face, so you have to appreciate the hubris.

*Dream Master* is what Robert Englund often refers to as "the MTV Nightmare." Chuck Russell nailed the balance of scares and imagination with *Dream Warriors*, and Renny Harlin came along and filled it with cocaine. This film is glossy and well-lit, even at night. And boy, are we moving that camera! Steven Fierberg zooms and spins it from seemingly every angle. We even get a few bird's-eye-view shots and plenty of red and green lighting. There are a ton of quick, music video-style cuts. Harlin took inspiration from German Expressionism, kung fu cinema, and even *A Chinese Ghost Story*, a bombastic horror comedy from the previous year. This is an *Elm Street* film that's so excited just to *be* an *Elm Street* film, and it's glad you're there to watch it.

After three outings, Freddy Krueger was a full-on pop culture phenomenon. The character was in that odd space where he was expected to be a villain, but his popularity was undeniable. Harlin met the moment by making a funnier Freddy who is rarely obscured by darkness as in previous entries. Howard Berger took over the Freddy makeup from Kevin Yagher, but he doesn't look much different than he did in *Dream Warriors*. If anything, he's more expressive because of all the close-ups he gets.

At the time, Englund was beginning to feel the strain of playing this character, in constant makeup for years now at this point. He was happy to become a horror icon, but he was understandably exhausted. Watching the junkyard sequence reportedly invigorated him, and you can see it in his performance (Englund's personal favorite as Freddy). Harlin's pitch was to make him more like James Bond, hence why Freddy is noticeably front and center as much as possible. His dialogue is mostly one-liners, though Harlin doesn't show him until eighteen minutes in. When Freddy finally does appear, he's shot in a way that expects the audience to go ballistic. Even his on-screen resurrection (another series first) is ceremonial. Film Editor Michael Knue recalled watching the "hero shot" of Freddy in the junkyard and recalling, "This is not a man in a monster mask. This is a guy who knows what the fuck he is doing. The whole way he held himself, the way he moved, everything."

You can't make the "MTV *Nightmare*" without a killer soundtrack and this one really delivers. Sure, *Dream Warriors* had Dokken, but *The Dream Master* gives us a full tracklist. They're not just great songs, but they're evocative and compliment the scenes they appear in, like all great soundtracks do. The Divinyls' "Back to the Wall" plays when Kristen drives to the Johnson home, adding a melancholy undercurrent to a simple suburban drive. Billy Idol's "Fatal Charm" plays as Joey watches MTV before he falls asleep, but the song becomes louder and diegetic as he sees the playmate under his bed, lulling him into a false sense of safety while making us wait for the inevitable. A remix of "I Want Your (Hands on Me)" by a pre-fame Sinéad O'Connor (with MC Lyte) plays over the end credits, and acts as a motif in Debbie's death scene. And we can't forget about Tuesday Knight's opening "Nightmare," a song that becomes instantly emblematic of the franchise at that point: mysterious but catchy with a pop sensibility. It's not quite a novelty single like "Are You Ready for Freddy" by Fat Boys, a pop rap song that I'm sure some people consider the ultimate shark-jump moment of all the films. Still, in the '80s, a novelty song was considered a big deal for most properties.

The other major highlight is Dramarama's "Anything, Anything," a freight train of a pop punk hook that plays while Rick practices karate in the garage, and again when Alice uses his nunchucks. That song is so indelibly linked with the film that it led to Andras Jones, a musician in his own right, becoming friends with Dramarama's frontman and songwriter John Easdale. Jones eventually covered the song acoustically and worked it into his set. It's the kind of synergy that would bring a tear to Jack Donaghy's eye. In fact, the film has wall-to-wall music, not just through songs, but with the electronic music of composer Craig Safan. His near-constant score makes you feel like you're in a longform music video. It's always colorful and full of energy, providing a different sound for each scene and character. He also updates Charles Bernstein's original theme a bit, though it sounds straight from the original when Alice tries to keep Dan awake at the hospital.

In the film's press kit, Renny Harlin is quoted saying "a film can have all the special effects, but if the audience doesn't care about the characters, you are lost. Great films need great characters." Well, this fourth installment has some of the best characters in the series, thanks to one of the most unsung heroes of the franchise, whom we have yet to talk about: the brilliant casting director Annette Benson (C.S.A. if you're inclined to be nasty)! Benson played a vital role in the series, casting the first five *Nightmares* and introducing the world to future stars like Johnny Depp, Patricia Arquette, and, of course, Robert Englund. Lisa Wilcox told Benson years after the films were shot, that she "unwittingly cast best friends for life," as an inordinate number of cast members are still close in real life. The chemistry of the characters and the cast members almost go hand-in-hand, especially with this entry.

*The Dream Master* exists in a post-*Breakfast Club* world by including a few archetypal characters but not keeping them defined to cliques. Kristen, the pretty lead, maintains her friendship with Kincaid and Joey, the misfits she survived Freddy with before. Dan, the football player, is sensitive and defends Alice against a jerk in the boys' locker room. He also yells at his doctor to sedate him to help her fight Freddy. ("You gotta put me back under, NOW!") And don't get me started again on the chemistry between Debbie and Sheila. They might be "80's Hollywood" attractive, but they're so likable, they truly do feel like a real group of friends. Harlin had an arsenal of talent at his disposal, not just with a crew that worked wonders, but of young actors who were game.

In retrospect, it's impossible to say how much of this was under Harlin's direction. By most accounts, cameras rolled before the script was complete. Some cast members claimed the actors had to direct themselves since Harlin was busy visualizing with the special effects crew. If the actors were on their own, they showed few signs of struggling. Perhaps Harlin knew they could handle themselves. The scene where Alice and Rick watch the video of Kristen and their friends is an emotional and well-acted respite from the gore effects, where the siblings can just breathe and think, even if things don't make sense. You don't have many scenes like these in franchise horror films, but when you do, they tend to feel hollow. All of this lends itself to the film's lasting impact. Production

Designer Mick Strawn's book *Behind the Screams* chronicles the technical aspects of making *The Dream Master*. He charges that a lot of the reason the film has held up is because of the character of Alice. That a production designer would assign so much credit toward a characterization or performance and not a more visual or technical aspect of the project speaks volumes.

As Alice, Lisa Wilcox has one of the best arcs of the entire series. While there are allusions to *Alice in Wonderland*, there's no direct reference to a fairy tale in the film, though her story certainly feels like one. When we first meet her, she's made herself so small compared to the men around her that she can barely talk to Dan in the diner. She has a mirror covered in photos because she doesn't want to see herself and she daydreams as a means to temporarily escape from a sad life with a dead mother and bad father. It's only once her friends start dying that Alice starts to see her reflection in the mirror and feel their presence. After Rick dies, she finally feels ready to confront and kill Freddy. To portray Alice, Wilcox kept track of who died and what characteristics she would inherit from them. The actress wrote notes in her script to follow her character's strength progression, little by little, so there could truly be a noticeable arc.

In the *I Am Nancy* documentary, Robert Englund talks about the character of Nancy Thompson being part of "the great feminist spine of the [*Elm Street*] films, even the silly ones." Nancy is undeniably one of the best final girls of all time, but she walked so that Alice could run. And jump. And blast Freddy right to hell. Wes Craven wrote Nancy as a girl who was able to fight back after the people around her died. Alice Johnson actually *felt* her friends die. She collected their essences and talents to wield as weapons against Freddy, acting as a kind of living memory of the fallen. She's very much the Rey to Nancy's Luke Skywalker. (For those of you who spend way too much time on social media, that's a compliment.) Rey was "all the Jedi" and Alice was all the Elm Street children. If you know *A Nightmare on Elm Street*, you can recognize it in the *Star Wars* sequel trilogy.

The documentary *Fredheads* is a celebration of everything *Nightmare on Elm Street* from the perspective of the fans, and not just the spectacle of Freddy Krueger. Several of the fans interviewed shed more light on the importance of these characters. Interviewee Bob O' Rourke emphasizes "the kids are drawn more completely [than other horror films]. They were kids I could relate to, that I wanted to relate to and be, or be friends with." Writer/Producer Ashlee Blackwell has previously discussed how she could relate to Sheila and identify with Alice's arc as "the shy kid who liked horror." You just don't get that in most horror films where there is an expectation of a body count, especially four years into its life cycle.

*A Nightmare on Elm Street 4: The Dream Master* moves the franchise further along the trajectory set by *Dream Warriors* and maintains continuity to a T, the recasting of Patricia Arquette notwithstanding. Harlin and his slew of writers maintain the plot point of forcibly pulling people into the dream world, which defines this film and the next, for better or worse.

## THE EVER-CHANGING SCRIPT

The development of *The Dream Master* differed sharply from that of other *Nightmare* movies. No member of the Writer's Guild of America was allowed to officially contribute to its screenplay upon commencement of the union's 1988 strike, which lasted from March to August of that year. Unfortunately for New Line, the strike kicked off before *The Dream Master* script had even reached its second proper draft, resulting in a mad dash to have *something* ready for filming. This is where things start to get a little hairy.

The initial screenplay was written by award-winning novelist William Kotzwinkle, in what was to become his screenwriting debut. The studio found his draft unsatisfactory, however, leading to the onboarding of Brian Helgeland, also making his screenwriting debut. While Helgeland kept certain story beats from Kotzwinkle, his effort was a thorough rewrite of the material. Yet the studio also found his draft lacking, leading them to turn to screenwriting brothers Jim and Ken Wheat, who'd just rewritten Mick Garris's draft of *The Fly II* for 20th Century Fox. The Wheat brothers were only able to complete one draft of their *Dream Master* script before the guild strike began, which led to pre-production forging ahead with their unfinished rewrite. Having only recently been admitted to the WGA, the brothers were fearful of being expelled for working during the strike and therefore did not. This led to Renny Harlin rewriting multiple scenes at length, along with producers Michael De Luca and Rachel Talalay, the latter two of whom would later co-write *Freddy's Dead: The Final Nightmare*.

The trio's revisions went uncredited, however, with the script's byline still listing the Wheats as the sole screenwriters. This greatly concerned the brothers, who requested an advance screening of the sequel to see what all had been changed from their script. Harlin denied their request, leading the Wheats to adopt a pseudonym for the project, "Scott Pierce," which was a combination of their middle names. (Ironically, *The Dream Master* would become the highest grossing script of their careers.)

By April 1988, the script's byline credited its story solely to Helgeland and the screenplay solely to the Wheat brothers. A Writer's Guild arbitration panel would later force Helgeland to split story credit with Kotzwinkle and the Wheat brothers (as Scott Pierce) to split screenplay credit with Helgeland. That same year, Helgeland shared writing duties with Robert Englund on the latter's directorial debut *976-Evil* and went on to become one of the hottest writer/directors in Hollywood. He would win an Oscar for co-writing *L.A. Confidential* only a few years later and would garner a second nomination for adapting *Mystic River*. The Wheat Brothers also continued screenwriting after *The Dream Master*, notably co-writing the script for *Pitch Black* and thus creating the character of Riddick, which kickstarted Vin Diesel's career. William Kotzwinkle would pen one more screenplay a year later, an adaptation of his own book, before returning to writing novels.

So, how much was *The Dream Master* script rewritten? In just the month before filming began, the producers issued no less than *eight* official revisions to department heads, none of which would be the final shooting script. Two of these drafts have since leaked out to the fanbase. Surprisingly, they aren't that much different from the finished product, something made all the more remarkable by the fact that Harlin and DP Steven Fierberg eventually abandoned the script altogether in favor of storyboards.

Perhaps this all could have been avoided if New Line had simply gone with Wes Craven's original *Nightmare 4* pitch. Yes, the father of the franchise had once again pitched New Line on an storyline they didn't pursue. To this day, no one knows if Craven wrote a script or outline, but the pitch is said to have involved using dreams to travel through time. (Sure, it flies in the face of what we've come to know about Freddy and the dream world, but then again, so does pulling people into your dreams. Who's to say he couldn't make it work?) Oddly enough, New Line later returned to Craven with the Kotzwinkle draft in hopes that he and writing partner Bruce Wagner might be willing to rewrite it, but they declined the studio's invitation.

Back to the script drafts we do have from the production. While they're similar to the final film, there are a handful of notable changes. For starters, Debbie's katsaridaphobia is revealed when a roach crawls on her books, not her nachos. It's a small change, but at least we don't have to ask why someone who works out is starting the day with chips (maybe Brooke Thiess was just hungry during filming). We also don't see claw marks on the locker after Kristen talks to Kincaid and Joey. It's one of the more memorable images from the film, but as I mentioned, it doesn't make a lot of sense unless it's part of a dream.

When Kincaid is killed, it's written that Freddy's blades pop out of his back, one-by-one, which we don't really need to see. After Joey dies, Kristen has a dream where she exits her house only to realize her house has been replaced by the Elm Street house. She runs away from it but winds up in the foyer of the Elm Street house anyway. (This was actually filmed, but the footage has sadly never surfaced). In the same dream, Kristen runs down a hallway full of arms with Freddy's claws on them and sees that he's been resurrected. A cigarette burn is what finally wakes her from this nightmare. During the exposition scene in front of the "real" Elm Street house, Dan and Debbie are more involved in the discussion (Debbie wasn't even there to begin with). In Kristen's final dream, she lands a blow against Freddy before calling for Alice. It would have been great to have another action beat and see her use her power one last time like Kincaid, but alas.

Instead of the scene where Alice and Rick watch the home video together, we get a much less effective scene of his friends consoling him. Plus, he's wearing his Japanese bandana the entire time. (Yeesh.) Instead of the karate fight, the elevator floor falls away into a hellish pit with Rick inside. It was meant to be shot, but according to Harlin, they ran out of money before they could capture it. (I'm actually glad we got to see Rick go down fighting, no matter how many people rolled their eyes about it in the *Never Sleep Again* documentary.) Also, when Alice feels Rick die in the classroom, she almost reflexively breaks her own desk with Kincaid's strength.

At Rick's funeral, Alice tells a hysterical Debbie to get ahold of herself, showing her inner strength growing, but it might go a little too far. Instead of Robert Shaye's classroom speech, Debbie and Dan go to visit their hippie teacher Bryson, who tells them about the dream gates. While it would have been great to know more, the scene as scripted just doesn't work, especially at the end when Bryson assumes they're on drugs and tells them to "just say no." (Maybe Shaye saw the pages and thought they were lame, which is understandable.)

When Alice later tries to get past her dad, she says "Get out of my way, you pathetic lush!" (Jesus, First Draft Alice, you're not the only one who lost someone. Take it down a notch.) She grabs her dad's shotgun from the den (Do people really mount shotguns on their walls in suburbia?) but decides not to take it to the fight. She even tells herself and the audience, "Save it for Rambo," which might have been the worst line in the entire franchise had they kept it in. Fortunately, she doesn't need it based on what the script describes when she takes all the pictures off her mirror and sees her reflection.

```
It's Alice alright, but everything's turbo-charged. She's
leaner, meaner, her clothes are tighter, more battle-like.
Everything's accented. The gadget around her neck is now
a super high-tech amulet, the bracelet has spikes instead
of studs and seems to be made of shining titanium.

This is no high school girl. This is no dream warrior.
This is the dream master, ancient guardian of the gate
of good dreams.
```

Alice recites the dream master rhyme with her reflection, then lets out a very well-earned "Fuckin A." (Fans would have loved to see this vision of Alice.) She looks great after the final film's "suiting up" montage, but this scripted version is on another level. While rescuing Dan, Alice hurls the hospital instruments like throwing stars. When she and Dan begin falling down the kaleidoscope hallway, Alice uses Debbie's spiked gauntlet to stop them from sliding onto the church floor. The fight unfolds as usual as does the ending scene, but we now see Kincaid's dog Jason at the fountain. Freddy's demonic tongue suddenly shoots out of the pup's mouth. (Gross, confusing, and unnecessary. Let's move on.)

# INTERVIEW

## STEVEN FIERBERG
### DIRECTOR OF PHOTOGRAPY

*Note: For the uninitiated, the cinematographer (also known as the director of photography, or "DP") works in tandem with the director to craft the look of the film through lighting and camera work.*

**When you were hired as the cinematographer on *Nightmare on Elm Street 4*, were you aware there wasn't a finished script?**

Well, how personal do you want to get?

**Totally up to you. Just don't tell my editor I said that.**

I always had horrible nightmares growing up. I saw *Eyes Without a Face* when I was six years old. My mother left me alone in the theater for two hours and I was freaking out in the lobby. I was traumatized. I did one horror film in New York where a woman's head is smashed with a rock. It was fake and she wasn't hurt, but it looked really real. I was ready to throw up while I was shooting it. So, I always had a thing about horror films. When I got asked to interview for [*Nightmare on Elm Street 4*], my initial thing was to not act interested. But my friend said "Just go to the interview."

So, I went to the interview with Renny [Harlin]. What they did have, and I think this is a very important reason why the film is so good, they had storyboarded a lot of the sequences. The artist who drew the storyboards was David Lowery, one of the greatest storyboard artists of all time, who's still my friend. He went on to do *Jurassic Park* and Spielberg's movies. The storyboards were remarkable, and they came from David working with Renny. I saw them and I thought "This isn't a horror film, it's an art film. So, I'm gonna go to my dark side. I'm not a kid anymore. I can handle this, so I'm gonna think of all the fucked up things that I can." And I can because I had those horrible nightmares. I was thrilled to do it.

The thing about *Nightmare* is that the way it was filmed in those days, and I think even the whole time, was that the first unit would come in and we would stage and set up all the scenes. We'd start to shoot the scenes, but they would require visual effects that would take a long time to do. So, we would walk away and the second unit would come in and finish it. Certain sequences were farmed out to a third unit, like when Freddy's chest opens up and people are inside screaming. This was done using all the old visual effects. We didn't use digital at all. We used every technique they used to do, whether it was rear-screen [projection], reverse-motion, models, miniatures. Anything you could think of.

The way we'd work was we'd have a meeting every day in prep. There'd be a pile of storyboards with one shot on each page, and we'd go "How are we gonna do this shot?" We'd sit there and go "Hmmm, I don't know. Let's go to the next page." By the end of three or four weeks, we could figure out how to do any image! We had a tremendous collaboration. Me, Renny, Rachel, and the art director and visual effects person. There would be drawings put up, and if you could draw it, you could get it. I've always felt that. We had this map of drawings, and at one point Renny said "Forget the script. If you want to know what we're doing, look at the storyboards." That doesn't mean that he and I were locked into the storyboards when we were on the set. We weren't. One reason why it was such a wonderful experience for me was that we would shoot the shot and go "What's the next shot we wanna do?" Then we'd look at each other and intuitively know what it was before we said anything. If he said one thing, I'd say "What about this?" and he'd say "And what about this?" And in thirty seconds, the idea had gone from this to that. So, it was one of those dream cinematographer/ director relationships. I've had wonderful relationships with every director I've ever worked with, but this one stood out on a visual level. If I set up a shot, he liked it. I'd go "Look at this" and he'd say "That's just what we need." Alex Cox is the same [as a director]. When I work with him, we see the shots the same way.

**And you shot on the second unit, too?**

Even with storyboards, the second unit probably gets half the shots correct, not because they're not good, but because they weren't on the set to see what [the first unit] did. They heard what you did, but they couldn't watch the playback in a screening room or on an on-set monitor, like now.

One of the things they did on *Nightmare* was when we finished shooting the first unit, I said "Look, give me a day or two, and I'll shoot all those second unit shots so fast, you won't believe it." I shot thirty to sixty shots in a day, or a day and a half. And I got those second unit shots, which connect and make the sequences work. I could do it in my sleep because I shot and lit the original scene. The second unit guys were brilliant. Do you know who the third DP was?

**No, I don't.**

This is a weird story. They needed a second unit DP, so I suggested my friend and former assistant, Dariusz Wolski.

**What?! You mean Ridley Scott's DP?**

Yeah! They said he hadn't done enough. They didn't think *he* was good enough to do the second unit. He was the DP on *Napoleon*. So, they turned him down, and I said "What about John Schwartzman?" He was Michael Bay's DP on films like *Pearl Harbor* and *Armageddon*. So, I gave them two or three of who would become the greatest DPs in the world. They hired my friend, Chris Tufty, who was great. For the third unit, they hired this unknown guy named Russell Carpenter, who went on to shoot this movie called *Titanic*. I don't know if you've heard of it...

**James Cameron's future cinematographer. After they passed on Ridley Scott's future DP and Michael Bay's future DP. Just incredible.**

It's ridiculous.

**That's another element of the franchise I don't think people realize. Some of the most incredible people got their starts on these films. Can you recall anything that was cut out?**

There was one sequence we really wanted to do, which is only briefly in the movie. When [Rick] gets in the elevator, it's basically the same scene Christopher Nolan did in *Inception*. That's what we wanted to do, though we wanted to stay away from visual effects. Christopher Nolan stays away from visual effects as well. We figured out how to do that, but it would have been too expensive. So, they weren't going to shoot the elevator scene at all, but I said "Look, we need a scene here. I can shoot this in half a day." And they let me. I think Renny was shooting something else, so it was just me. That sequence is freaky. I'm pretty happy with it.

By the way, the film doesn't appear as dark as it was. One thing I had done that I was really proud of, was that nobody was doing cyan, steel blue, that much. I worked for Dean Cundey as an electrician, who had worked with it to some extent, but I decided that the color of *Nightmare* was this bluish green. That's how it was shown. I had a print in my garage that I gave to the Academy. Both transfers to video were done without me present, and because of *Nightmare*, it's now in my contract that you can't do that. What happened was they thought it was looking all green, so they took out the green and it became red. The standard definition transfer is horrific. I can't even watch it. Now everybody does it. I thought this was the first dark, blueish green movie that I know of. It was really disturbing.

**There's a huge leap visually throughout the films, especially between *Dream Warriors* and *The Dream Master*. I love Roy Wagner's work on the third film, but it's clear you were going for something completely different. How did you build on the visual language of the previous entries?**

A couple things. I liked the third film as a drama. It's a good character piece. We were shown some Chinese movies like *A Chinese Ghost Story*. Nobody in America had ever shot a movie like that, with that energetic cutting. New Line had it, so we saw a private screening, and Renny and I were like, "That's what we want to do." Renny is a great visual director, and I really think *Nightmare 4* was the first [American] movie to have that Hong Kong "cut, cut" feel because we were the only ones who'd even seen that and wanted to do it.

There's a couple things that are a shame about *Nightmare 4* the way it exists now. We finished shooting it a month before we had to have 2,000 prints in the theater. There were 3 teams of editors working almost twenty-four hours a day, and they're not necessarily seeing what the other [teams] are doing. We screened the movie a week after it was finished and there was one sequence where Renny went insane with the editing. It was when [Alice] sees her brother in the nightmare pizza. The way it was cut, it took your breath away. Bob Shaye, who'd made many good decisions, thought that was too extreme, so they toned it down. The other regret is that there was another sequence, which was the best sequence, visually, without question.

**I already know it's the sequence where Tuesday Knight exits her house and it switches behind her. That sounded impressive. Why wasn't it in the film?**

You have to realize, the first screening was a week after we finished shooting. You have to lock the cut, do visual effects, and it takes almost a week to make 2,000 prints. So decisions were made like this [he snaps his fingers], especially then. I heard from Renny that someone thought it took too long to get to Lisa Wilcox's character, so Tuesday Knight's character had to die sooner. The decision to tone down the pizza scene was a mistake, in my opinion, but [cutting] this scene was the stupidest decision anybody could make, but whoever decided it, I'm not angry at them at all.

**That sounded like it would be a great in-camera trick.**

It's not just that. It's actually two shots, because you can't do it in one shot. It just feels like one shot. [Kristen] seems to come out of her house, the camera looks down on her, then she turns, and boom, her whole fucking house is the *Nightmare* house. It's incredible, but then it keeps going. She turns to run away from the house. The camera pulls back without cutting, and she's suddenly in this nightmarish tunnel where Freddy is waiting for her. It was fucking scary. It was really the most effective scene of everything being normal, then suddenly you're in a nightmare. It's a tragedy they can't find that scene. I heard they tried to find it for the *Never Sleep Again* documentary. Everyone talked about that sequence. Nobody forgot it, so I thought they'd find it and we'd finally see it.

**Speaking of the documentary, Renny comes across as a director who has a vision, but still listens to ideas. Was that your experience with him?**

Here's the thing. He brings a lot to the table, to begin with, like the whole storyboard thing with David Lowery. He's not just letting everyone else do it. There are directors like that, and you can be a very good director doing that. Then there are directors who are like "This is exactly what we're doing, so do what I want you to do." We figured it out together. What was great about Renny, and for me this is also true of working with Alex Cox, is that he is bringing an idea of what he wants, but if his idea gives you an idea, he listens and goes "And what about *this*?" The idea grows, and that relationship is very special and rare. The experience of working on [*Nightmare 4*] was wonderful because of his openness. I'd say "Let me shoot the next shot," and I would show it to him, and he loved it. He didn't have any ego, like "This is *my* film," but it is his film because he does bring a lot, and he knows what he likes. If you set up a shot that wasn't right for the movie, he'd know it as soon as you started moving the camera. He has a tremendous visual sense, but he's an open, collaborative guy.

**I have to tell you that I don't sit on waterbeds because of the scene in *The Dream Master*.**

Why not? That's a pretty hot girl. (laughs)

**It's a personal rule. There's b-roll footage on YouTube of the filming of the waterbed scene, and everyone on set seems so exhausted, yet determined. You should know you traumatized a lot of people!**

Oh, I'm so happy to have made you unhappy! I'm kidding, but I'm thrilled to hear it worked that way. That movie was so difficult to do. We were working fourteen to sixteen hours a day to make the release date. At one point, Renny and I were so tired, we couldn't go on. They hired another director and cinematographer for two days because we couldn't function anymore. We needed to sleep. That's how hard it was. One night after we shot in the junkyard, I fell asleep driving home during morning rush hour. Nobody got hurt, but I hit two cars at ten miles per hour. It was creatively fulfilling, but unbelievably exhausting.

**Can I ask what the other director and DP shot?**

It was a few shots in the church scene, like Freddy's standing on the seats. The third unit got Russell Carpenter to do it, and I remember thinking "This guy's really good." We're still friends. All the stuff you'd put on a reel was mine. The fight, the chest, the moment of transcendence, we did everything significant.

**Is there anything else you wish people knew about *The Dream Master* that isn't talked about?**

I'm surprised how influential the film is. I was watching *It*, going "These are shots we did." I know those shots. I *feel* them. It's like they studied *Nightmare 4*. And then in *Hereditary*, they have all that stuff with people walking around on the ceiling and the wall. We did that thirty years ago. That's what surprised me, is how much it influenced people in that genre. I'm just finishing a horror movie and I'm trying to get a horror movie made, which I wrote, but my agent says nobody gives a shit that I shot *Nightmare 4*. That it's too old and nobody cares.

**That's completely insane. I'll send her a copy of this book when it's done.**

# INTERVIEW
# MICK STRAWN
## ART DIRECTOR

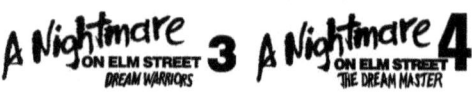 

**How did you get involved with *Nightmare on Elm Street*?**

First of all, Bob [Shaye] wanted ideas. He wanted to go back to Wes Craven for the third film because of the problems with the second film. He said "We're gonna break this chain with the third entry." Robert [Englund] wasn't originally in the second film because he wanted a lot of money, but when it came to the third, Bob said he was gonna use him and let him improvise. I brought the other element. I said we needed to be more expansive with what this world is. We had to get off location and get onto a stage. Ninety percent of *Dream Warriors* was on a stage. As a production designer and an art director, I brought years of construction coordination, and painting, and all that with me.

**The credits for *Dream Warriors* list you and your sister C.J. Strawn as art directors, but would you describe your roles more as production designers?**

I took the sets, buildings, and locations. She took wardrobe, set dressing, and we did the painting together. We had about fifteen to twenty people on the third film, which vastly expanded when we got to the fourth film. People talk about what a great horror film [*Dream Warriors*] was. I always thought if you get beyond the first, and maybe second film, you have to find a reason [for a third film]. My concept for the film was that it was a quest. Something like *Odysseus* or *Aladdin*. I couldn't let go of the idea that the characters were on a journey and that's what made it interesting. There's the circular staircase that goes to the boiler room, the house...

**The door that appears out of nowhere.**

Right! To me it was like *Arabian Nights*. It couldn't have worked out better. *Dream Warriors* was like going to a carnival. You know the kind that shows up in a parking lot? That's how I wanted people to feel watching it. *The Dream Master* felt like going to Disneyland. It was a sophisticated version of that. You'll notice in both 3 and 4 that it's the journey that's interesting.

**The leaps from the second to the third, then from the third to the fourth are all astounding. How did you prepare for those shoots?**

Well, by the fourth film, we had locked down a release date and only had a forty-page outline to start with. Nobody would argue with us about the bits and pieces we brought together to make it because we didn't have writers to argue with. (laughs) It's easier to argue if you're holding a script going "Right *here* it says..." We put it together and Renny would come in and film it. I did it with Peter Chesney, Gerry Olson, and Rachel Talalay. We had so much momentum from the third film, it was... well, I don't want to say "easy." (laughs)

**Well, you were already on a trajectory with the third film, and it made a lot of money, so it primed you for the fourth one, right?**

The old "well-oiled machine." We went to huge lengths to pull in devices that have been used since the early days of film. We did rear projection and forced perspective. *All* kinds of forced perspective, like when you see Freddy's chest up close. While 95% of the junkyard was on location, there was also model work. I would sit in meetings with a rubber mallet, smashing Matchbox cars. (laughs) If you go through any given sequence in that film, you'll see how [the crew] complicated it for ourselves.

The spinning kaleidoscope hallway was in a dream I had, and we shot it three days after I had it. We were shooting the cockroach scene, where Freddy's one big eye was looking into the roach motel. We were doing it all in-camera using rear screen projection. That night, I later dreamed Freddy was looking at me with that big eye, but through a kaleidoscope. You know how you'd polish stones in a tumbler that ran with a motor? Peter Chesney and I put five of those in row. We had two running one way, and three running the other way. Believe me when I tell you it was the most popular ride in the building! (laughs) Those motherfuckers ran that thing from almost the moment it was hooked up, and half the crew was inside that tunnel at any given time. It was a blast! And we could make it go really fast, too.

That last set, the Freddy church, was so interesting. We didn't have anything left. We were out of money. We started shooting in February and the film was out in August.

**That's an insane timeline for a film with extensive special effects. Was that why you didn't come back for *The Dream Child*?**

Well, between the fourth and fifth films, I worked on *Freddy's Nightmares*, the tv show. By the time I was done, I was a crispy critter. (laughs) Also, the director of the fifth film had a new take. He wanted to do more CGI optical stuff, which I thought wasn't quite strong enough.

**It was 1988, so I doubt it was ready.**

Yeah, it wasn't ready. The director would point to me in [preliminary] meetings and go "How was this dealt with in earlier *Nightmare on Elm Street* films?" I'd tell him and he'd respond saying "This is an example of the shit we don't want." (laughs) And he kept asking! He wanted to break down the paradigm. So, I got hired to work on *Leatherface: The Texas Chainsaw Massacre 3*. I was just tired and I wasn't going to argue with him. You can only have so much of that before you become part of the problem.

**That's a great way to look at it.**

Oh yeah, there comes a time when you don't even want to hear yourself, right?

# INTERVIEW
## MICHAEL N. KNUE
### EDITOR / 2ND UNIT DIR.

**Can you tell me how you got the job editing *The Dream Master*? I imagine working on New Line's *The Hidden* was instrumental.**

In a sense, yes, but there were other things that came into play. At the time, I got to know [the people at New Line Cinema]. I wouldn't say they were tight, but they were a small group. I got along well with Bob Shaye and Sara Risher. *Nightmare 4* was my third film for them. After *The Hidden*, I was working on a film that was originally called *Mr. Christmas Dinner* and changed to *Lucky Stiff*. It was directed by Anthony Perkins and written by Pat Proft.

**That sounds like such an unlikely combination.**

It was a bizarre film, because Tony wasn't sure how to make it funny. The direction he went in couldn't have been more different from Pat, who was also the producer. Pat had gags. Anthony's cut was a comedy that had no jokes. We worked and worked, and there were some really bizarre moments, which were essentially takeoffs on Pat's script. His humor was much more adolescent than Anthony's. So, they didn't get along.

**You're telling me Pat Proft, co-writer of *Airplane* and *The Naked Gun* was fond of adolescent humor?**

Well, the thing was they hired Anthony because he wanted to direct a comedy.

Anthony was a beautiful, wonderful man. I loved working with him, but it was not to be. He had a more perverse sense of humor, which didn't sit well with Pat. Anyway, Rachel Talalay and Bob hired Renny to direct the fourth film, but they didn't have an editor. They had Chuck Weiss, who was an extremely good editor who worked on the third film, but I think they wanted someone to work with him.

It's funny, you get these prejudices. At the time, there was a real schism between the union guys and the non-union guys. They flipped each other the bird a lot. I was a union guy and Chuck was not. Since New Line was mostly non-union, they probably saw me more as a "Hollywood guy." He came on and it was convenient to pull me off *Lucky Stiff*.

New Line didn't want to fire me, but Pat had his own editor he wanted to work with. Pat and I got along, but he didn't think I was funny. (laughs) Even Bob Shaye didn't think I was funny, though I told jokes all the time. He felt I was better at horror. So, Rachel came to me and said "If I can work it out, do you want to come onto *Nightmare* with me and Renny?" I said sure and met with Renny.

**By several accounts, the making of *The Dream Master* was chaotic. Chaotic in what way?**

**Mostly as a result of the writer's strike. Though it's all the more impressive considering the final product. Did you get a hint of chaos when working on the film?**

Well, I'm one to say it was chaotic, but that's Renny. It's a good thing! He's not moved by the wackiness on the set. Renny can handle that. When production went nuts on *Die Hard 2*, he got through it and made a decent product out of it.

Billy Weber was a great, A-list editor who eventually directed the film *Josh and S.A.M.* He was once asked if it was natural for an editor to become a director since they're kind of in the same direction. He said "An editor creates order out of chaos. It's the director who creates the chaos." At that point, I was in my early 40's and I was barking up the wrong tree trying to be a director. I'm an editor. I like order and finding and making things out of the pile. I told Billy about this years later. He didn't remember saying it, but I said it stuck with me. It meant something to me. (laughs)

Low-budget films are always chaotic. [Rachel Talalay knows] all about that. She was the nursemaid to the *Nightmare* series. If there's someone who was the heart and soul into *Nightmare on Elm Street*, it was Rachel. If there's someone who put the intelligence into it, it's Rachel.

**I completely agree.**

I'm not a huge horror fan. Did you know *Nightmare on Elm Street 4* was the highest-grossing independent film of all time? Not independent *horror* film, but independent *film* of all time. That says a lot about our film, but it says even more about the series. *Nightmare* goes to an emotional heart in a way most horror films, especially from that time, just don't. They didn't get it the way *Nightmare* did. There's a lot of emotional intelligence. I think the third and fourth films define the series in the way the first film didn't. Prior to working on *The Dream Master*, I watched the first three films in a day and read the script for *4*. I was really wowed by *3* and I loved the script for *4*.

So, Bob Shaye could be grumpy. I remember hearing how Robert [Englund] wanted something. They hadn't made his deal yet, but Bob was thinking about instead having, as they say, "a man in a monkey suit."

**You mean for the second when they thought they could replace Robert?**

No, for *The Dream Master*.

**Really?**

They had Robert in for three *Nightmare*s and Bob was cranking about the fact that [Robert] wanted something and he wasn't rolling over. Now, it wasn't like they didn't get along. The deal wasn't where they wanted it to be, and Rachel was being very cool about, of course, keeping Robert on. If you ask them if Bob made that comment, they would say they didn't remember, but I guarantee he made that comment. It was probably just Bob cranking. But Renny was talking, stylistically, in terms of German Expressionism for this slasher film. Having seen the third film, I completely understood what he meant. Now, do you remember the first time you see Freddy in *Nightmare 4*?

**Yes, you see his shadow as the camera pans up.**

That shadow was *Nosferatu*. When he moves forward, that's Murnau [director of the original *Nosferatu*]. Renny and Robert talked about it. When we saw those dailies, there was an audible reaction. Like "Oh fuck, that's great." Robert was looking at the monitor to make sure the shadow was just right. My thought at the time was "That's not a man in a monkey suit. That's a man who understands his part and the style of Freddy." *Nightmare* is so geared towards the teenage mentality. How did these teens become victims of Freddy? Because their parents murdered him and he's taking revenge on them. It releases the devil inside of him. Do you ever notice that the parents in all these films are hapless? They're completely ineffectual. I guess you can say that about a lot of horror films.

**It's always a factor in this particular series of films.**

That's why I love the third and fourth films. The third one, in particular, because where are the kids? They're doped up in a fucking psychiatric hospital, too afraid to sleep. Their parents and the adults at the hospital are unable to help them.

The original is Wes Craven's point-of-view, and he's more straight-ahead horror. The second is Jack [Sholder] making something different. In the following entries, Freddy is his own entity and separate from that. That's why I said the third one is important to the legacy of the films. The facts are in the first film, but the life is in the third and fourth.

**Before you retired, you edited several episodes of Marvel's Netflix shows, including *Daredevil*, *Iron Fist*, *Jessica Jones*, and *The Defenders*. Is it fair to say your ability to edit fight scenes started with *The Dream Master*? Unless I'm wrong and it started with *Lucky Stiff*…**

(laughs) I don't know. There had never been an action montage in the three previous *Nightmare* films. I cut Rick's "kung fu" montage and I think I found the song ["Anything Anything"]. Maybe I'm wrong? I'll give myself the credit and Rachel can tell me if I'm wrong. Sometimes you get a bunch of songs and they go "We can get the rights to these."

*Nightmare on Elm Street 4* got me the job editing Sylvester Stallone's *Lock Up*. It was produced by Chuck Gordon, who I met on my second feature, *Night of the Creeps*. I guess Stallone knew Renny and had talked to him about the possibility of directing one of his projects, which he eventually did [with *Cliffhanger* and *Driven*]. So, Stallone saw *Nightmare 4*, and asked me to do *Lock Up*. I did two pictures with him and I think it was because of the fight scenes in *Nightmare 4*. I've actually learned a lot from Sly about editing fight scenes, as you can imagine. But Rick's montage was, to me, what was happening in the '80s. That's where action was going after all those years of rules.

There was even a point where I went back to [editing] TV in the early '90s to do an episode of a show called *Civil Wars*. It was produced by Mark Tinker, who I knew from working on *St. Elsewhere*. He asked if I would come in, even though I was a "feature editor." He liked to give me shit about it, and I said sure. So, I'm sitting at the Moviola and I jumped right into someone talking in a scene after a wide, establishing shot. Mark said "You can't do that. This is television." It was typical of the time. My rule of thumb was to cut to the speaker, then cut to the reaction. The idea of cutting all over the place was crazy.

I taught editing at UCLA Extension for sixteen years, and I had just begun teaching at that time. I went to a broadcast film school at the conservatory at the University of Cincinnati, but I didn't have the same kind of training that guys at USC and UCLA had. I learned so much by constantly studying movies. I taught editing theory for ten years, then one year I had to teach "History of Editing" two weeks before it started. It was usually taught by a brilliant documentarian friend of mine who was sick. He sent me his notes: one page on Alfred Hitchcock. I said "Are you kidding me? I need your notes on how you think editing works!" He passed away soon after that. So, I had a sense of how I felt editing had developed. My daughter, my wife, and I watched two to three movies a night for ten weeks at home. We started with Edison, all the way to the modern day. It was a great education.

**Steven Fierberg mentioned that the quick-cut, MTV style of editing in *Nightmare 4* hadn't really been seen in American movies before. Were you looking at Hong Kong films for inspiration?**

I don't know if I'd seen those films already. When I got out to L.A. from Cincinnati in 1975, we had the Nuart Theater. I had a BFA, but that's where I got my film education. I watched a lot of Japanese directors like Kurosawa and Oshima, which I loved. I saw some kung fu, but not much.

**What was the hardest scene to edit on *The Dream Master* and how did you get through it?**

It wasn't so much that it was hard to edit, but the déjà vu sequences. The hard part was, how many times can they go around? We were all there arguing about it. There was an extra loop in there. It was getting boring and Bob said "This is slow. Get rid of it!" But it was a brilliant concept. It goes to the idea of being in a dream. Someone pointed out that things work in threes. You know, jokes work in threes and all that. I think we knocked out the second loop, which was just [Lisa and Danny] looking at each other. For all you know, they just got to a different corner. That took a while to get to.

Jack Tucker was another editor who was brought on, along with Charlie Coleman, who was older than I was and sort of a lifer assistant. He was the easiest guy in the world to work with and I needed him. In the non-union world, people knew a lot about certain subjects, and only so much about others. I promised him I'd get him an editing credit. IMDb doesn't get it right.

**I want to talk about *Freddy's Dead*, where you have a credit as second unit director. Was that the only time you got behind the camera?**

I think I have an additional directing credit for *Leatherface: The Texas Chainsaw Massacre 3*. I'm not sure if I took one for it.

**How did you come back to *Freddy's Dead* after working on *The Dream Master*?**

After *Nightmare 4*, I edited two Stallone pictures and I had been wanting to direct. I just kept asking [New Line] because I liked editing with them. Rachel knew how much I wanted to direct and she said she wouldn't ask me to cut the movie, but would I direct the second unit? She needed someone she could trust, since she was directing and that's how it happened.

**What did you shoot for *Freddy's Dead*?**

Most of the stunts. A lot of the plate shots. In those days, they took a long time to set up. We shot the video game scenes with Breckin Meyer on a trampoline. It was a constant craziness, indoors and outdoors. I learned being a second unit director is like being an editor, but you don't get to change stuff.

We shot in this giant warehouse in Santa Clarita. [Producer] Aron Warner's intention was that Rachel would be working with her crew on one set, then they'd leave and my crew would come into the same set to shoot what we needed. The problem was, since we're on the same stage and they're fifty feet away, our work would have to stop when Rachel was doing a shot. There was the scene where the sleeping kid [Shon Greenblatt] gets sucked through the roof of the van. We made a cardboard roof and rigged the stuntman with a halter. They were gonna weight this crane, let it go, and pitch the stuntman through the roof. We were trying to rig it, and we were ready to go, but then we got word Rachel wanted to look at it first. We would wait and wait, and the stunt coordinator was not a happy camper. He had us take him out just as Rachel came. That was the worst of it, but we had a few of those moments.

**That happens on film and TV sets all the time.**

Needless to say, the second unit worked best when we were on our own, but that's no slam to her. I just knew that if I wanted to direct, it would have to be on my own terms. I got close a couple of times.

**Is there anything you want to bring up about these films that you feel isn't talked about?**

Well, it's a funny thing. Cinephiles roll their eyes when I say this, but not horror cinephiles. I don't think that most people realize how well-made, and more importantly, how intelligent the *Nightmare on Elm Street* films are. They don't see it. That said, *Night of the Creeps* was ahead of its time. I had no idea how funny and spoof-y it was until I saw it again last year. It's a hoot. But when I was working on it as a second-time feature editor, dealing with a first-time director was kind of like being a big brother. Trying to make sure [director] Fred Dekker did well. In many ways, coming to New Line at that point was a lesson for me in how these things worked. Again, I was going to finish *Lucky Stiff* and make it funny, but nobody remembers it. (laughs) I thought that was what I was going to do because I thought I understood comedy better. Bob Shaye didn't think so (laughs). He thought I understood horror better, and maybe he was right.

*Nightmare on Elm Street* is a better series than people realize. It's probably one of the best horror film series ever. I'd put it up there. It's Bob Shaye, it's Wes, but it's also Rachel. There's absolutely no doubt Rachel made the difference. Yes, it's Wes Craven's *Nightmare on Elm Street*, but after the original, it was Rachel Talalay's *Nightmare on Elm Street*.

# RESPECT FOR
# THE DREAM MASTER

Early in *Scream*, Drew Barrymore's Casey describes the *Nightmare* franchise by saying "[Part] one was good, but the rest sucked." It's a cheekily meta moment, which Craven didn't want included, at least partially because of his involvement in parts three and seven. It also undercuts the sequels. Emmy-winning producer and director **Michael Melamedoff** described his admiration for the series, with an emphasis on *The Dream Master* in a way that hasn't often been explored.

"I've always admired the way the original *Elm Street* movies constantly reinvent themselves; they're like a great band that's tinkering with their sound album to album, pushing into new modes. The original *Nightmare* is a gritty fever dream that offers a nihilist response to the vigilante justice films of the 70s and 80s; the second installment is gender bending body horror that feels maybe even more relevant today; the third imbues the series with a fantastical comic book quality... look at the Freddy of *Dream Warriors* and the MCU's Thanos and tell me that Freddy hasn't influenced scores of comic book baddies. This sense of experimentation and play with format continue all the way through the post-modern elements of *New Nightmare*.

Of course, Robert Englund as "Freddy" is the thread that holds the series together, but his performance continues to evolve as well, reaching its apex in *The Dream Master*. That film, with its slapstick infused set pieces, gives rise to a Freddy Krueger no longer constrained to clever one-liners...instead he becomes horror's most gruesome MC and insult comic, fully in control of the room and his victims' psyches.

*The Dream Master* may not be the "best" of the series, but it's a film I have a particular soft spot for; after all, it gave us the version of Freddy that holds firm in the popular imagination."

# RETURN TO

## A Visual Retrospective

# NEW LINE CINEMA

NEW LINE CINEMA, MEDIA HOME ENTERTAINMENT

and

SMART EGG PICTURES

PRESENT

A ROBERT SHAYE PRODUCTION - A WES CRAVEN FILM


## A NIGHTMARE ON ELM STREET

Starring:

| | |
|---|---|
| John Saxon | Lt. Thompson |
| Ronee Blakley | Marge Thompson |
| Heather Langenkamp | Nancy Thompson |
| Amanda Wyss | Tina Grey |
| Nick Corri | Rod Lane |
| Johnny Depp | Glen Lantz |

with:

| | |
|---|---|
| Charles Fleischer | Dr. King |
| Joseph Whipp | Sgt. Parker |
| Lin Shaye | The Teacher |

And

ROBERT ENGLUND

as Fred Krueger


A NIGHTMARE ON ELM STREET is the story of the courage and resourcefulness of one extraordinary girl--a psychological fantasy/thriller that rips apart the barrier between dreams and reality. It will make us all think twice before settling onto our pillows for a night of sweet dreams.

wes Craven

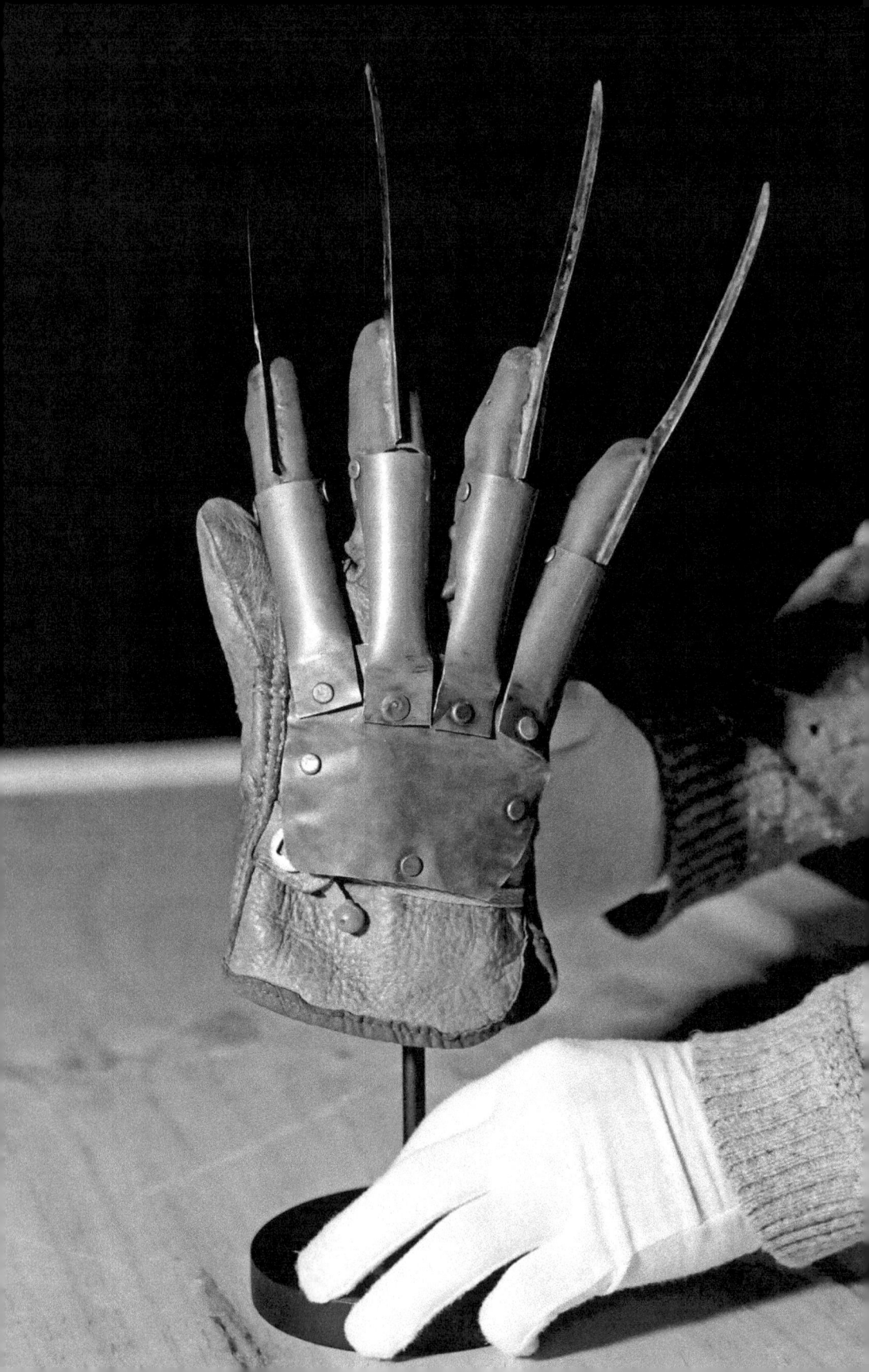

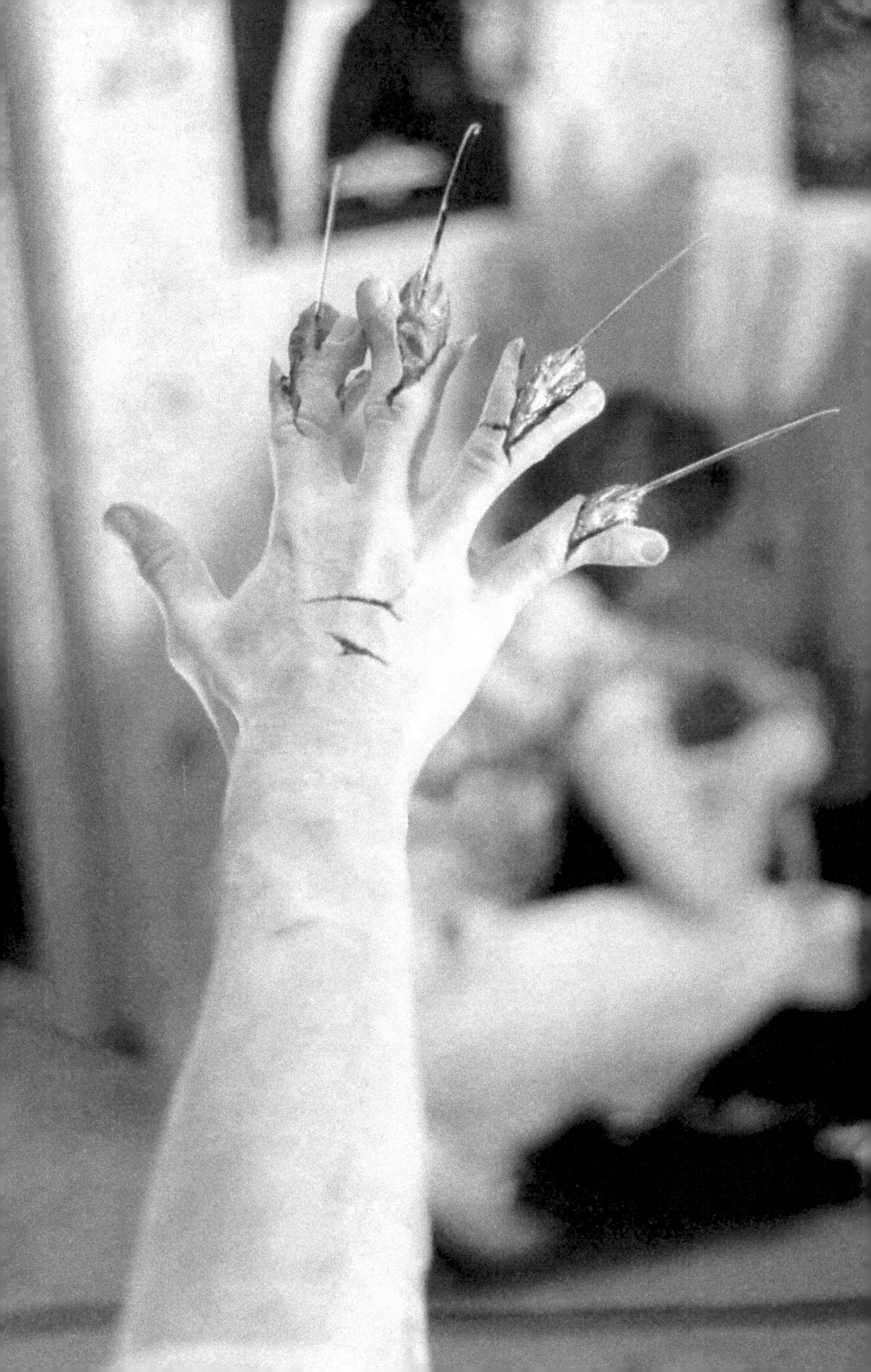

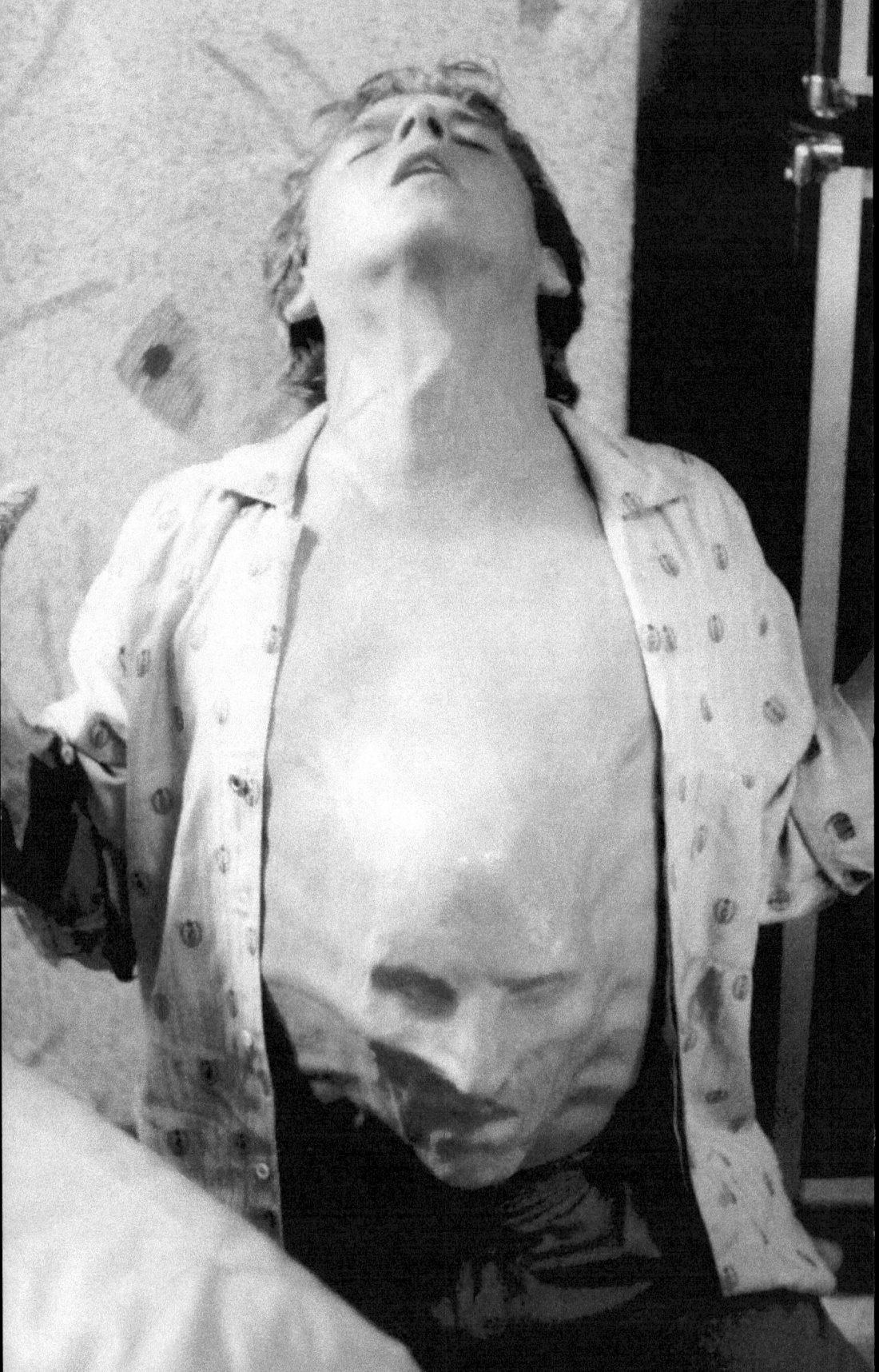

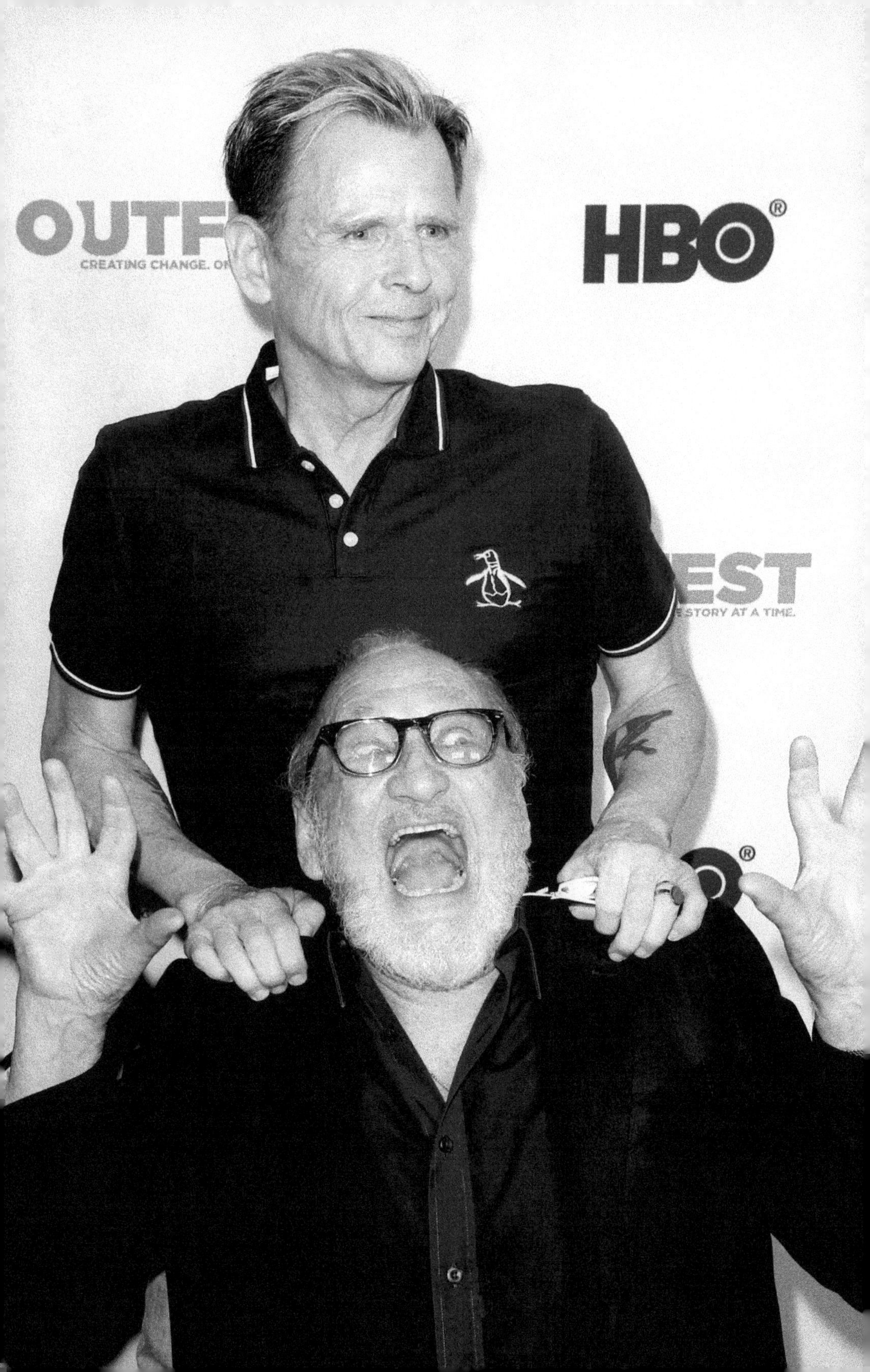
HBO®

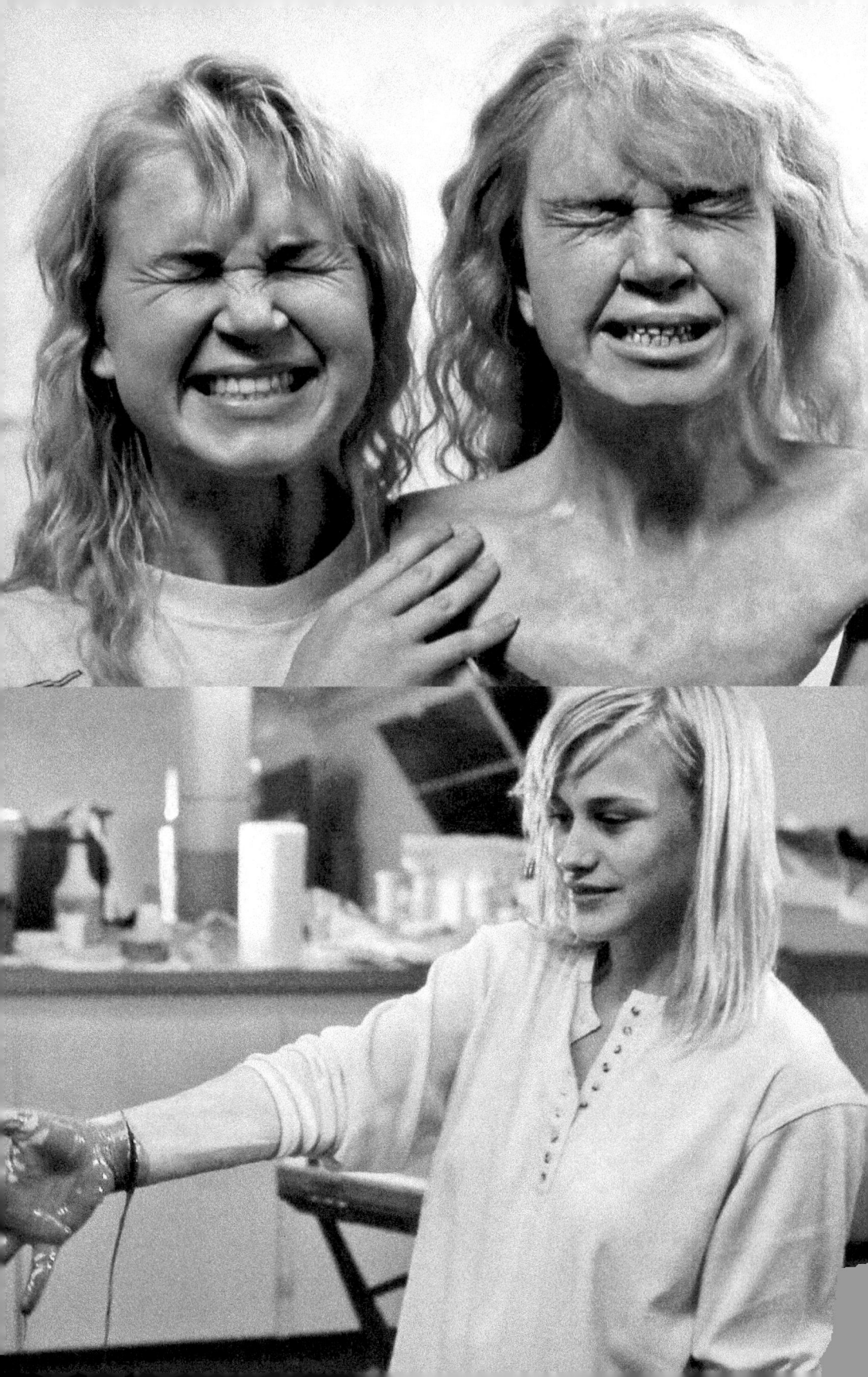

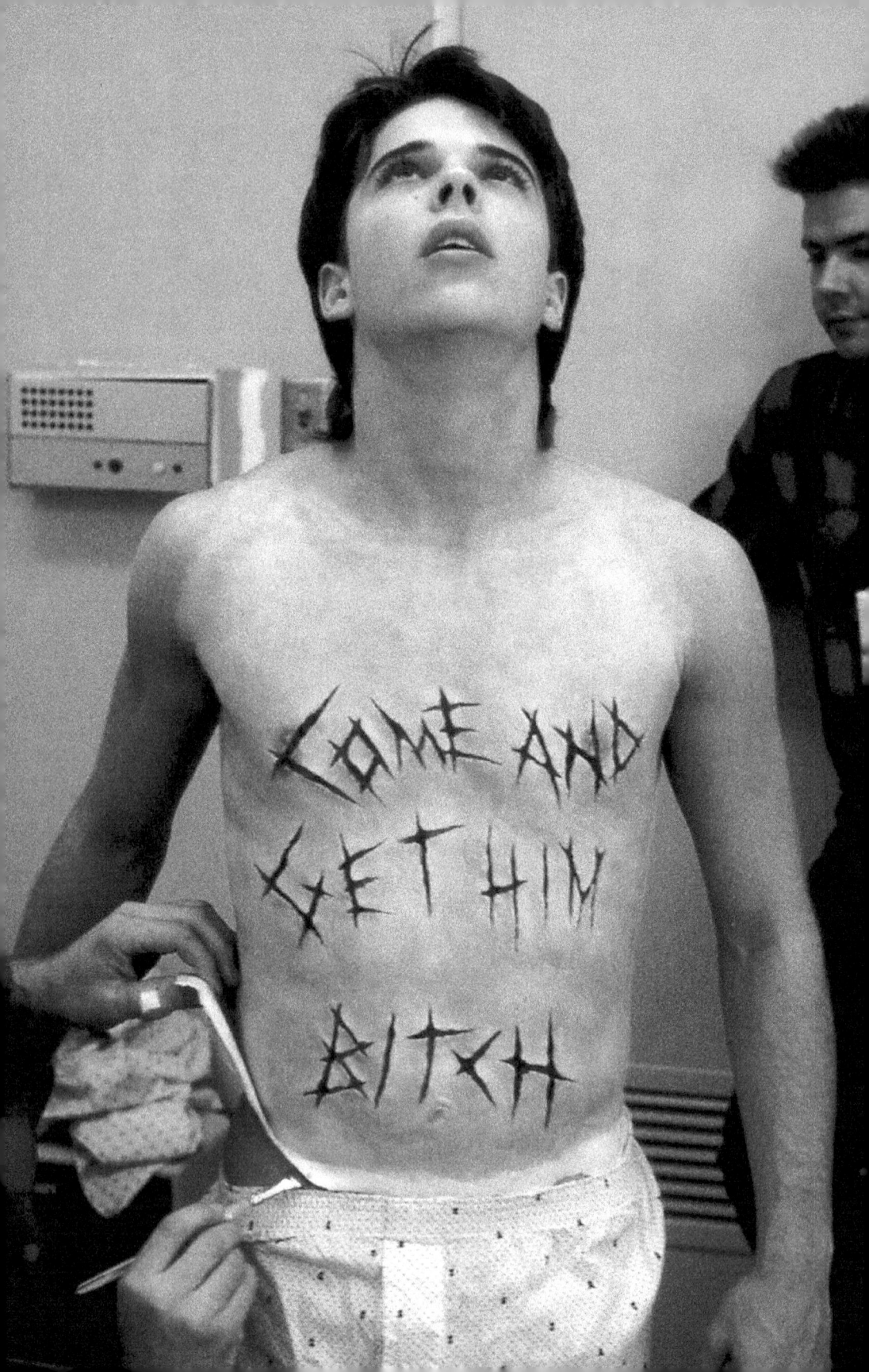

SAM ERIC 4
1 FREDDYS DEAD
FINAL NIGHTMARE R
2 NECESSARY
ROUGHNESS PG
3 THE SUPER
R
4 TERMINATOR 2
R
Sam Eric
FREDDYS DEAD
TERMINATOR 2
1 4
7 10 R
4
THE SUPER
130 345 600
815 1030
R
3
PG
2

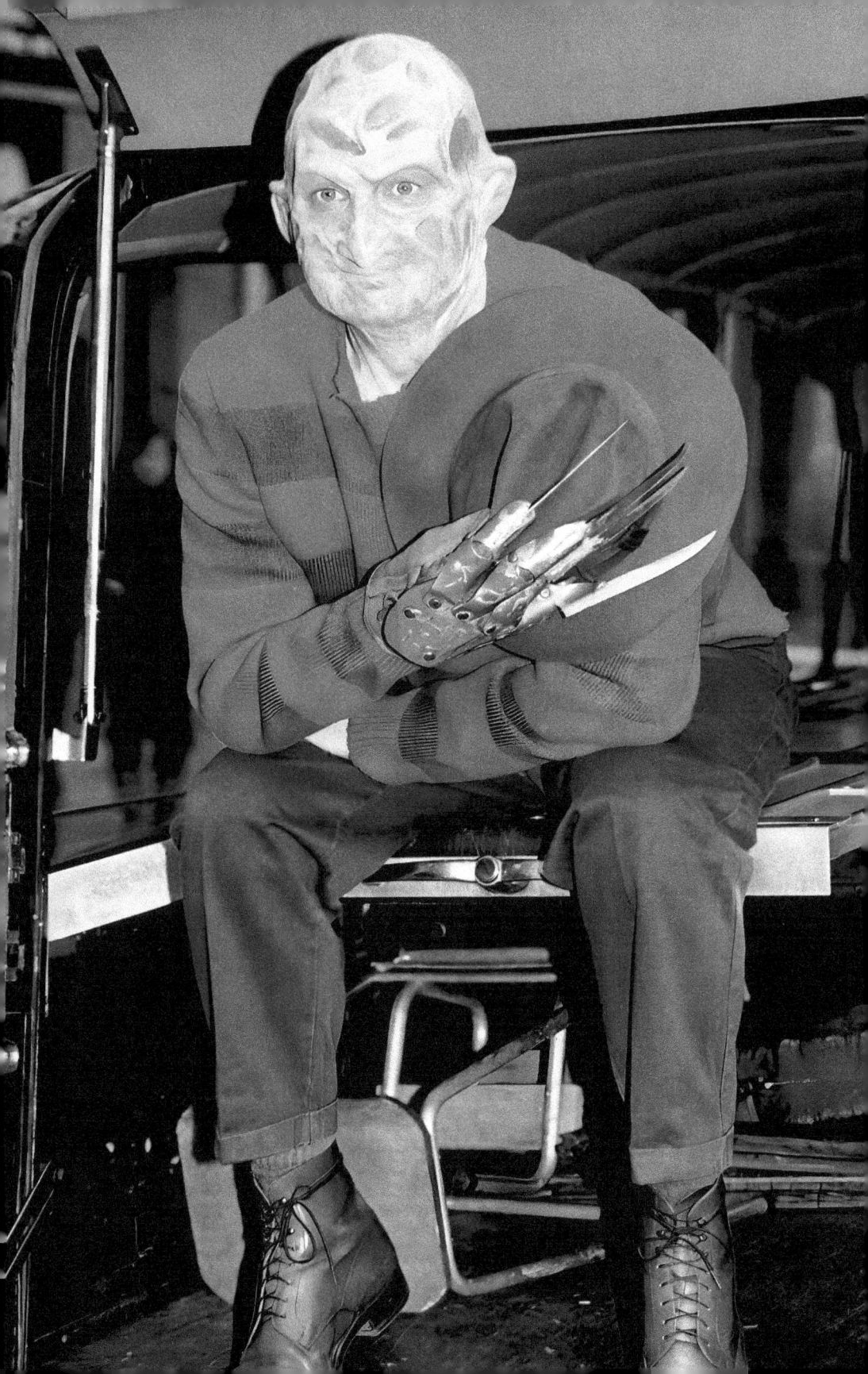

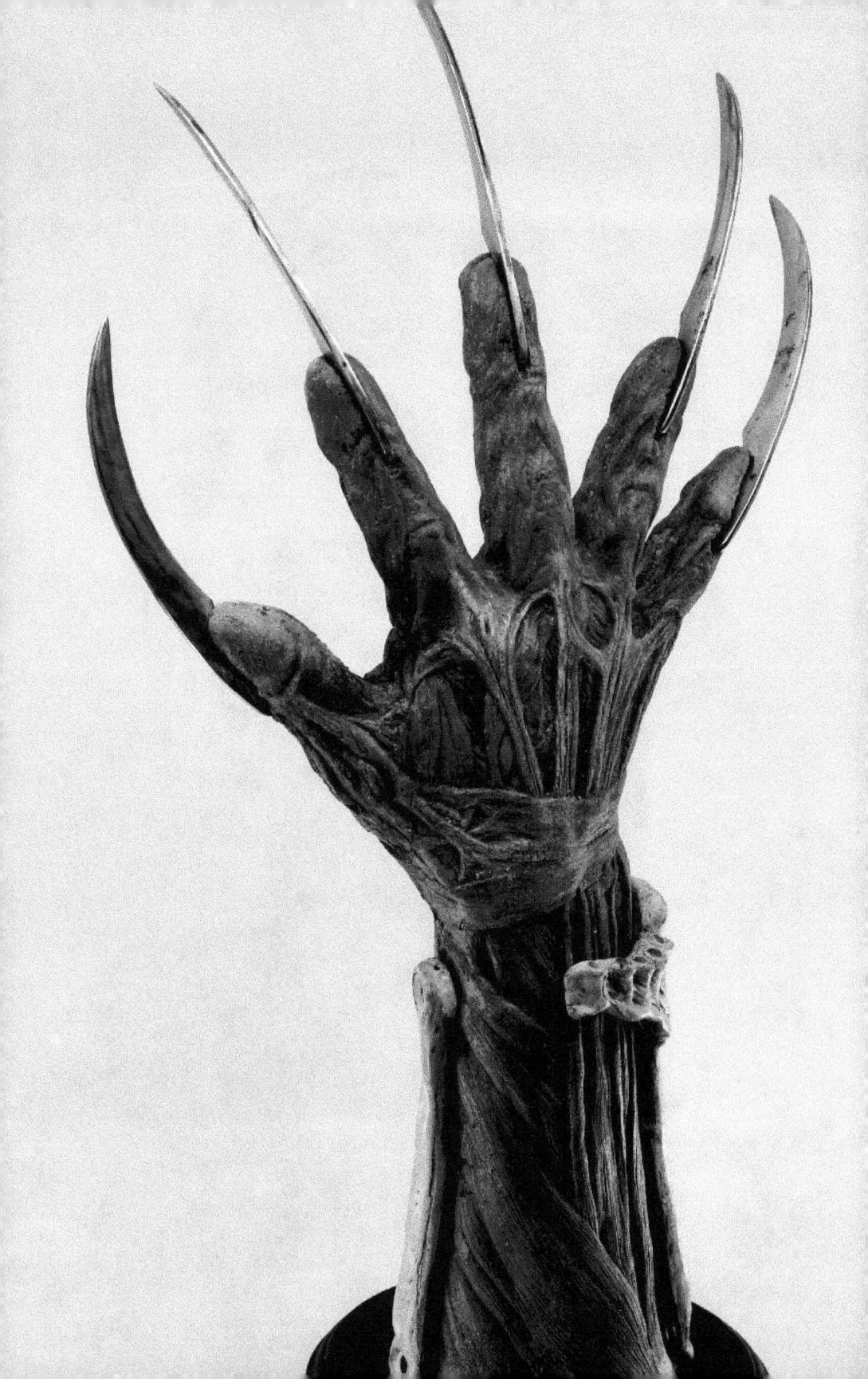

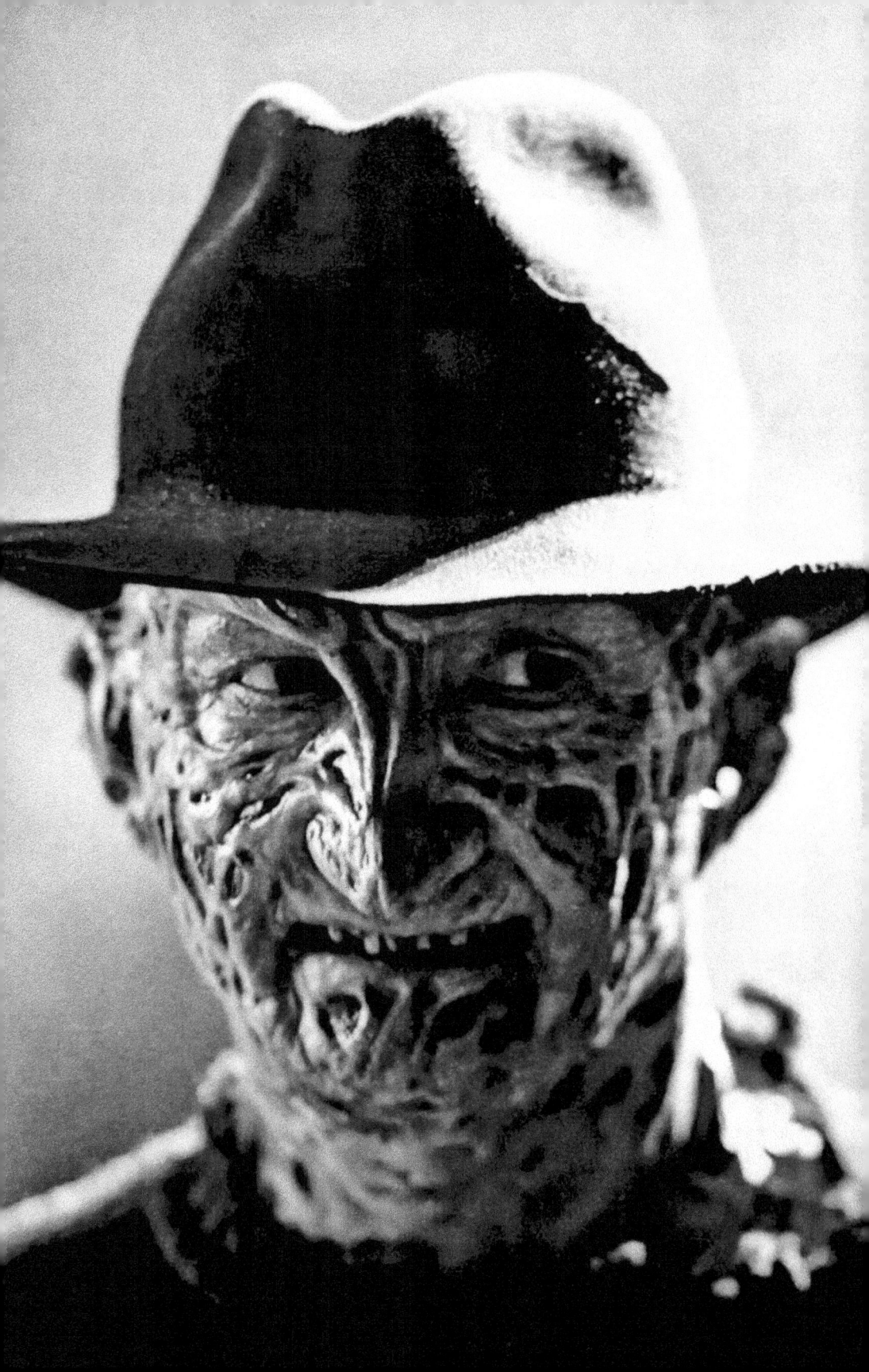

# PHOTO CREDITS

Heather and Amanda (Photo credit: Landmark-Media/ImageCollect)

1428 Elm Street (Photo credit: Tony Hoffarth)

Wes Craven (Photo credit: MGM Television)

Robert and Heather (Photo credit: Historic Hollywood Photographs)

Lin Shaye (Photo credit: s_bukley/ImageCollect)

NOES1 Glove (Photo credit: Andrew Matthews/PA Images/Alamy Stock Photo)

NOES2 Glove Effect (Photo credit: Mark Shostrom)

NOES2 Transformation (Photo credit: Mark Shostrom)

Mark and Robert (Photo credit: AdMedia/ImageCollect)

Robert with Glove (Photo credit: MirrorPix/Alamy Stock Photo)

Robert in Makeup (Photo credit: MediaPunch/Alamy Stock Photo)

Prime Time (Photo credit: Mark Shostrom)

Penelope and Penelope (Photo credit: Mark Shostrom)

Patricia Effects Test (Photo credit: Mark Shostrom)

Rodney Eastman (Photo credit: Mark Shostrom)

Nightmare 3 Marquee (Photo credit: Old Los Angeles Archives)

Nightmare 3 Marquee 2 (Photo credit: Old Los Angeles Archives)

Chest of Souls (Photo credit: Museum of the Moving Image)

Tuesday Knight (Photo credit: Markus Wissmann/Alamy Stock Photo)

Robert in Makeup 2 (Photo credit: MirrorPix/Alamy Stock Photo)

Lisa Wilcox with Lobby Card (Photo credit: ZUMA Press/Alamy Stock Photo)

Freddy's Dead Marquee (Photo credit: Old Images of Philadelphia)

Robert in Makeup 3 (Photo credit: ZUMA Press/Alamy Stock Photo)

Freddy Krueger Day (Photo credit: Sanford of Sherman Heights)

Wes Craven (Photo credit: FeatureFlash/ImageCollect)

Heather Signing Autos (Photo credit: Landmark-Media/ImageCollect)

Stunt Double Mask (Photo credit: Charles Mineo's Ultimate Freddy vs Jason Archive)

New Glove (Photo credit: Charles Mineo's Ultimate Freddy vs Jason Archive)

Ken in Costume (Photo credit: Charles Mineo's Ultimate Freddy vs Jason Archive)

Robert in Makeup 4 (Photo credit: Charles Mineo's Ultimate Freddy vs Jason Archive)

Robert Punches Up (Photo credit: StarMaxWorldwide/ImageCollect)

Robert and Kelly (Photo credit: StarMaxWorldwide/ImageCollect)

Robert and Kelly 2 (Photo credit: StarMaxWorldwide/ImageCollect)

Bob Shaye (Photo credit: AcePixs/ImageCollect)

Monica Keena (Photo credit: StarMaxWorldwide/ImageCollect)

Robert and Heather 2 (Photo credit: WENN/Alamy Stock Photo)

Robert and Heather 3 (Photo credit: David Weiner)

# A Nightmare ON ELM STREET 5
## THE DREAM CHILD

If 1988 was the bacchanal celebrating the second golden age of horror, 1989 was the hangover. The hit horror sequels that of the previous year were followed up with duds like *Halloween 5: The Revenge of Michael Myers* and *Friday the 13th Part VIII: Jason Takes Manhattan*, both considered by many to be the nadir of their respective franchises. (Apologies to those who love them, but you can't deny they strayed far from what made those franchises great.) It was a tough year for the genre. Even Wes Craven's *Shocker*, his attempt at a new Freddy-esque supernatural villain, wasn't greeted that warmly. It would be almost a full decade before he would recalibrate the genre with *Scream*, but the studios were still trying to wring as much money from audiences as possible.

After *The Dream Master*, New Line Cinema was high on their own supply. Freddy Krueger even hosted a syndicated show, loosely (*very* loosely) associated with the films. *Freddy's Nightmares* was *Tales from the Crypt* before *Tales from the Crypt*, with odd horror tales and interstitials with Englund hamming it up, but it didn't set the world on fire. A fifth entry in the *Elm Street* canon was a foregone conclusion. However, with the fear of Freddy's overexposure looming large, there was an edict from New Line to make Freddy dark and scary again. But the genie was out of the bottle at this point. Renny Harlin and Robert Englund had taken turns smashing it to pieces with the humor of the fourth entry, as dark as it was.

Producer Sara Risher had been with the franchise since the beginning and was a new mother at the time. The film that became *A Nightmare on Elm Street 5: The Dream Child* emerged from pitches that responded to her anxieties and fears of being a mother. The opening of Wes Craven and Bruce Wagner's draft for *Dream Warriors* featured a baby version of Freddy, complete with tiny claws, so the idea was already floating around in the ether. British Australian director Stephen Hopkins was hired for a film that needed to hit its release date in six months. With its trademark special effects, some great returning characters, and a new gothic sensibility, *The Dream Child* was rushed into production, much like its predecessor had been. Even so, it still maintained all the wit and imagination needed to call itself a *Nightmare on Elm Street* film.

## DREAM SCENARIO

Foreboding bells sound as *A Nightmare on Elm Street* literally rips into the black screen, followed by *The Dream Child*. There's no number to indicate which numbered sequel we're watching, but I suspect it's by design.

We see the hint of a sex scene as two bodies undulate slowly to childlike ululating and dark, operatic synth breakdowns, with an abundance of organs and bells. Consider it a taste of the mood we'll encounter. The woman rolls out of bed to take a shower. She's revealed to be Alice (Lisa Wilcox, back for more). The shower drain gets clogged, the door locks, and water rushes in at an accelerated pace. Before she can drown, she falls through a membrane of water, landing naked in a deserted industrial hallway. (Dark hallway, take a shot!) But we're not in the boiler room. She tentatively inches down the hall, then appears dressed like a nun with a handy nametag: Amanda Krueger.

Yikes. She finds herself in a room full of men, dirty, drooling, yelling to everyone and no one as a fish-eye lens follows them around the now-closed wing of Westin Hills. If you've seen the earlier films, you know that these are the "hundred maniacs" that Freddy is the "son" of. (Though I'd wager his actual father is the inmate played by Robert Englund, sans makeup.) The orderlies, who are doing a terrible job of counting the inmates, leave and wind up locking her in. The camera spins around her as they encroach, about to do the devil's business. Alice thankfully wakes up next to Dan, but it's not Dan. It's makeup-free Robert Englund! But only for a second, because she does finally wake up. Before she can unpack that, she has to get ready for graduation.

That's right. Springwood High School's class of 1989 is graduating. (Makes you wonder how many moments of silence there were.) After the ceremony, Alice meets up with her friends. (Sure, we need new victims, but it's nice to think the new, post-*Dream Master* Alice went out and made friends confidently instead of adopting most of her brother's circle.) She seems way more open and self-assured this time around. (Plus, Lisa Wilcox keeps her natural blonde hair.)

Her new group includes Yvonne (Kelly Jo Minter), a straight shooter and the series' first Black female character to survive to the end credits. Then there's Mark (Joe Seely), a wannabe comic book artist who openly pines for Greta (Erika Anderson), a knockout with a sense of humor. She doesn't return his affection, but it's clear she cares for him as a friend and he responds in kind. Alice seeks out Dan (Danny Hassel, also returning), now her boyfriend, to share her nightmare with him. It's the first dream where she hasn't been in control since the events of *The Dream Master*. Before they can get into it, his parents whisk him away to talk to a college football coach. Alice bemoans her dad's seeming absence, but Mr. Johnson is revealed to be there, newly sober and dressed for the occasion. He just didn't want to "embarrass her." (Actor Nick Mele also returns, but as a nearly different character here. It's refreshing to see that he's changed, but also to see a parent at this point in the film who isn't a complete drag. Who knew it would be Mr. Johnson, of all people?)

Alice walks across the nearby park to get to her job when she sees the familiar jump rope girls. Curious, she follows them into a field where it's suddenly nighttime. She sees one of the girls, who changes the rhyme ("9, 10 he's back again"), because hey, it's 1989 and we all know it by now. Suddenly, Alice sees the "real" Amanda Krueger (Beatrice Boepple) run inside the previously seen wing of Westin Hills, complete with the bell tower where Philip died in *Dream Warriors*. How is this happening? She clearly didn't fall asleep on the way to work. Alice follows Amanda inside the gothic asylum and sees the "nightmare pram." It's essentially a Freddy-ized version of a baby stroller, which is not at all ominous. Without warning, Alice is back in the nun outfit, being rushed into the operating room on a gurney. She bolts up and we see Alice is now watching

Amanda give birth ("Don't let him do this!") while horrified doctors and a nun look on. The "baby" is a monster with a misshapen head and...well, it looks like Freddy Krueger as a baby. Glistening and horrible, it runs out of the suddenly empty delivery suite. Alice follows it to the next room, which turns out to be the church where she killed Freddy in *Dream Master*. His clothes and razor glove sit, unused. The church is now dark and decrepit, a stark contrast to the colorful vibrancy we saw in the previous entry.

Much to her dismay, the "baby" enters Freddy's discarded clothes and "grows" into them. The church begins to break apart and the altar rises high off the ground. Now full-sized, Krueger is back to declare "It's a boy!" as he holds his distended arms up in a mockery of the crucifixion. Quips and blasphemy: perfect for this kind of resurrection. He appears behind a frightened Alice and rubs her belly as Amanda shows up outside the church doors. Freddy is clearly not pleased. He disappears, but not before making the door slam on her. When Alice runs through the exit, she...winds up back at the Crave Inn? Her co-worker complains she's several hours late, which doesn't make sense.

Anyway, let's have a pool party. But indoors this time, and without a bloodthirsty maniac. Yvonne, a practiced diver, has opened the pool where she practices to the graduating class for a party. Dan, Mark, and Greta are hanging out, complaining about their overbearing parents. We never see Yvonne's parents, but she tells her friends they should tell their parents to back off. Easier said than done, since Greta's mother Racine (Pat Sturges) is driving her to be a model, Dan's parents are pushing him to be a college football star, and Mark's dad wants him to work in the family warehouse. Mark sketches the "Phantom Prowler," a comic book character with a long black duster, a mask, and dueling pistols, presumably his own creation. He mentions Melicertes, a character from Greek myth who "killed his kids because they didn't like the way he was running his kingdom."

Dan gets a call from Alice, who tells him that Freddy's back. He hops in his truck (new and blue since Alice wrecked it in the last film) and races to the diner. Along the way, he listens to talk radio and hears his mom insulting him and Alice, followed by Freddy's voice, happily agreeing. The seatbelts come alive and restrain Dan as Freddy appears, riding shotgun and swigging the champagne Dan got for Alice. Though she's probably better off, since it melts his dashboard. Freddy pours it on his shoulder, which allows his arm to melt off, only for him to use it as a makeshift seatbelt.

Dan crashes the car, but he flies through the office window of the pool he was just at with his friends. Everyone's gone and his clothes are torn, but he seems to be otherwise okay. He doesn't have the keys to his normal-looking truck, so he steals a motorcycle before realizing he's still dreaming. The realization comes hard, when he sees that Freddy *is* the bike. He/it merges with Dan into a machine-man hybrid, reminiscent of H.R. Giger or *Tetsuo: The Iron Man*. Pipes and wires painfully fuse to Dan's body. The bike goes so fast, his skin and hair fly off! He would look like a cool dream warrior if this wasn't intended to kill him, and boy, does it.

Alice has a vision of Dan's soul calling for him as he falls down a large, Freddy-styled umbilical tunnel. At the same time in reality, he crashes his truck in a fiery explosion outside the diner. Alice rushes outside to see Dan's body. He pops up and leers at her with a strange quip ("Hey Alice, wanna make babies?") and she faints. Later that night, Alice wakes up in the hospital surrounded by her dad and Yvonne (who works there as a candy striper). Dan's parents wait outside, too despondent to come in. Alice goes right into blaming Freddy, but she's ignored. There are more pressing issues at hand. For example, she's pregnant with Dan's child.

That night, Alice is recovering from an incredibly shocking evening when a little boy wanders into her room. A pale, wan child who looks anywhere from eight to ten named Jacob (Whitby Hertford). He apologizes to her about Dan, then leaves, presumably to go back to the children's ward. Except Yvonne tells Alice there is no children's ward. Also, how did he know about Dan? Spooky, but at least nobody's getting fired. Meanwhile, Greta is crying over Dan in her room, which is adorned with porcelain dolls. Her mother calls to her from behind her bedroom door and tells her to go to sleep. She has to look nice for her upcoming dinner party. (Priorities, dear!)

When Alice goes home, she invites her friends over to share the big news. Not about her pregnancy, like they expect, but about Freddy Krueger, who's back, though she doesn't know how. The discomfort in this scene is palpable as Greta and Yvonne share concerned looks and Mark sketches on a pad. It makes sense that they'd be grieving. One of their own is dead and they'd much rather talk about the only good thing that might come from this, the baby. They don't believe Alice about Freddy, but they insist they're here for her.

Alice later finds herself crying in the kitchen when her dad shows up with groceries. Their relationship has healed to the point where she asks him if he's ashamed of her. He says no and hopes she has a boy because of Rick. It's a nice moment you would never imagine happening in the last film, but it shows tremendous growth. Alice won't involve her dad in going after Freddy, but he shows he's changed and is there for her. (Unlike Greta's mother…)

Meanwhile, Greta is suffering through a garish dinner party thrown by Racine as an attempt to get her into modeling. Greta is exhausted. She's still mourning Dan and couldn't care less about the long table full of "industry types," who are most certainly not Racine's friends. She closes her eyes for a moment just as she's served by a waiter (also Robert Englund out of makeup). As Greta tells off her mother in a scene that could only take place in her dream, Chef Krueger appears to trap her in a highchair and force feed her until her cheeks are impossibly distended. It's equally horrifying and disgusting. Plus, Freddy makes the obnoxious dinner guests appear in her nightmare and cheer him on. At the same time, Alice sees Greta pop out of her fridge after the food inside rots (courtesy of some nasty claymation effects). Greta's mom and her guests witness Greta choke and die at the table.

Needless to say, Mark is pissed. Yvonne and Alice visit him in his dad's warehouse. Yvonne still doesn't believe in Freddy, but Mark is at least willing to listen. Yvonne leaves, but Alice and Mark stay up late in his bedroom/studio, which is adorned with even more Phantom Prowler drawings. (Do Mark and his father live in the warehouse? That can't be up to code.) Alice goes to get coffee, but when she comes back, she sees a sketch of the Elm Street house in Mark's notebook. A crudely animated Mark walks inside the house to his almost-certain doom. Thinking fast, Alice draws a stick figure of herself on the drawing and closes her eyes. Opening them, she is now in front of the house. Alice runs inside and sees Mark about to fall through the floor into the "Freddy tunnel" she saw Dan fall through before. Luckily, she pulls Mark out, and only his hands are cut from the lip of the hole. Since he previously indicated that he hates the sight of blood, he lets out a hilarious "Oh shit…" and faints. Like Nancy falling through her chair in *Dream Warriors*, he vanishes as soon as he hits the floor. At least he's now awake and safe. Before she leaves, Alice sees Jacob once again. He looks more haggard and pale as he now apologizes for Greta. But who is he and how does he know about her dead friends? Jacob says his mom doesn't want him and gets momentarily mad at Alice. But he runs away when his "friend with the funny hand" summons him. Thus ends the film's one and only scene in the Elm Street house.

Upon waking, Alice concludes that, somehow, Jacob is her unborn child. Mark finally believes her and springs into action, doing research on Freddy. Alice asks Yvonne to take her to an ultrasound, even though it's too early for one. She learns that unborn babies sleep for seventy percent of the day and starts putting the pieces together. If there's enough consciousness in her womb, and her ability to bring people into dreams can be inherited, then no one is safe.

Alice then sees a vision of Freddy's face inside her body. If that wasn't icky enough, she sees him "feeding" the fetus with the souls of Dan and Greta via the "Freddy tunnel" we've seen before, which means she was seeing inside her own body! Alice correctly surmises Freddy is using Jacob's dreams to kill her friends and make the baby like him. Understandably concerned, the doctor calls Dan's parents. Back at Alice's house, Yvonne still won't believe what she's hearing. Mark shows up with files of research and bandages on his hands ("He invited me to his house last night" always makes me laugh). After two of her friends dying and the other two sounding insane, Yvonne storms out. Mark tentatively asks her if she'll have an abortion. He knows it's a sensitive topic, but she hasn't even considered it until then. It's part of her and Dan, after all. (Though don't mistake this for a pro-life message for reasons I'll explore later.)

What follows is a scene you don't see in films like this. Dan's parents show up at the house to report that Alice's doctor called them, saying Alice was hysterical. They want sole custody of the child. Not only is he the last part of their son, but Alice is still just a teenager. It's implied she and her friends are eighteen since they're high school graduates, but they're still very much teenagers at heart, rebelling from their parents. Alice shuts them down, despite Mrs. Jordan's tears. Mark hangs back, not wanting to get involved, but silently supporting her friends. Mr. Johnson stands the tallest yet in the series by telling them to fuck off. It's actually touching.

Mark fills in Alice on Amanda Krueger's history. She was committed after she had Freddy, and lived long enough to see him go to trial. When he was freed, she killed herself. The headstone we saw in *Dream Warriors* was a lie enacted by the church. This is why she presented as a ghost to Neil. Her soul is trapped, so they have to find where she died and set her free. Alice falls asleep in an attempt to find her in the dream asylum while Mark sits on watch.

There's a quick scene of Yvonne in the pool's locker room, just taking a moment to cry. Yvonne has been painted as the disbelieving scold up until this point, but if you really stop to consider her point of view, like this film does, the past few days have been relentless. It's a testament to Kelly Jo Minter's acting, and a refreshing detail to have moments where the characters just breathe. You get the sense that the pool is therapeutic for her, which I'm sure isn't a piece of information that will be exploited momentarily. Alone at the pool, Yvonne falls asleep in the hot tub, which is dangerous enough, but then she goes up to the high dive. The diving board transforms into massive claws (through even more claymation) and she jumps into the pool to escape.

Meanwhile, Freddy lures Alice to a demonic hot tub in the asylum with metal walls and chains hanging from the ceiling. (It's this film's first boiler room-esque scene, but we never actually go to the boiler room in *The Dream Child*.) Freddy yanks a terrified Yvonne out of the water before Alice stabs him in the throat with a pool cleaner. She and Yvonne escape, but Freddy won't pursue them because he senses the spirit of his mother. At least Yvonne is finally a believer...

Back in the real world, Mark reads comics to pass the time. He finds a new one in his collection titled *Nightmare from Hell*, which is an artist's rendering of the events of the film so far. He eventually sees a panel of himself reading the comic, which causes him to be animated in white light and sucked into the book's pages like something out of the "Take on Me" music video.

Mark winds up in a nightmare version of the factory where everything appears in black-and-white except for him. A monochromatic Freddy appears and chases after him on a bladed skateboard. Just as he's about to strike, he vanishes and reappears on a platform above Mark. With him is Greta, kind of. This must be a facsimile of her soul, much like Rick's head appearing as a meatball on the pizza in *The Dream Master*. Here, she appears as a life-sized doll with a bloody stomach, that Freddy gleefully scoops out and licks. (This harkens back to the original version of Greta's death, where it's revealed that Freddy was feeding her pieces of herself the whole time. Take a second to vomit, I totally understand). Greta pleads for Mark's help, but Freddy pushes her over the ledge and she breaks at his feet. Not that there was anything he could do, but it's still a sadistic insult.

Freddy jumps down behind Mark, ready to kill, when Mark screams and whirls around, now dressed as the Phantom Prowler! (We have a new dream warrior, people. This is not a drill!) Mark, as the Prowler, unloads his pistols into Freddy, which is cool, but when Freddy takes a dive, he's not fooling anybody. Up from the ground jumps Super Freddy! No really, it's a superhero version of Freddy Krueger. Bigger, beefier, and with a lightning bolt on his chest. (This is one of the few times Robert Englund doesn't portray Freddy. For this effect, he's played by Michael Bailey Smith, later of the *Hills Have Eyes* remake and its sequel, to name a few films from an impressive career.) Mark fires at him to no avail, until Freddy slashes him and turns back into the Englund Freddy we all know. Mark has also transformed into a life-sized paper cartoon of himself with a big slash coming out of his side. The color bleeds out of him as Freddy cuts the paper Mark to confetti. In the real factory, scaffolding collapses on him and he dies.

The warehouse is now a crime scene. Just as a cop says nothing inside was up to code (told ya!), Yvonne arrives. Alice breaks the news to her about Mark and tells her to find Amanda in the asylum while she goes back to sleep to find Freddy. Just like the final stretch of *Dream Warriors*, the film's focus splits into two. Alice goes back to the dream asylum while Yvonne heads to the crumbling structure, which is still standing. The film crosscuts between the same place in the dream world and our reality. Neither place looks like anywhere you'd want to spend time.

Alice goes to sleep and "wakes up" back in the asylum corridor. She taunts Freddy to come out, and when he shows himself, Alice impales him with the nightmare pram. She runs him right into the room where he was conceived, still flush with the madness of his many fathers, who tear him limb from limb. Alice exits the room, only to see Freddy standing next to Jacob, reassembled. The room they're standing in is a pastiche of the locations we've seen before with inverted gravity. It's an M.C. Escher-esque nightmare space with staircases going everywhere and hallway lamps swinging upwards from the floor. It's as if pieces of all the sets were glued together to make this impossible combination of boiler room, asylum, and even the Elm Street house. Jacob realizes he's in danger upon seeing his mom and Freddy in the same place. She urges him to run away, which he does. He runs up, down, and across the impossible stairs to escape Freddy. Dan shows up in front of the Crave Inn doors and calls to his son, but as we and Alice know, it's just Freddy masquerading as his dead dad.

Alice and Jacob finally reach each other, but where's Freddy? Jacob says he's "inside you where he hides. He says it's easy because he knows you so well," which is enough to make you squirm in your seat. It's established that Freddy knows all of us so well that he uses our hopes and fears against us, but to hear a child phrase it like that is beyond monstrous. Speaking of monstrousness, Freddy starts emerging from Alice's body. Literally. First, he pulls himself out of her face, then appears stuck in her torso. (This is another instance where Freddy is temporarily played by someone other than Englund. The late Noble Craig was a character actor who lost his legs in Vietnam, and here he's credited as "Merging Freddy." To his and the crew's credit, you can't really tell it's someone other than Englund, which is a nice bit of movie magic.) Alice should be dead after such physical trauma, but Freddy needs her and Jacob alive to continue killing. Consider this just more sadism on his part.

Back in our world, Yvonne adds "urban exploration" to her resumé, just below diving phenom and hospital volunteer. (What college did she get into, anyway?) She finds Amanda's ghostly form, finally freeing her from her earthly prison. Yet, ever the servant of the Lord, she makes a pit stop to save the day, appearing before her son and his prey. She implores Jacob to save Alice by giving back what Freddy gave him. Jacob's face suddenly looks scarred, like a mini-version of Freddy. The boy tells Freddy to leave Alice alone because he'd rather hang out with him, the child molester with magic powers. Was this what Amanda had in mind?

Freddy considers having a pupil for a second when Jacob exclaims "School's out, Krueger" and promptly earns his diploma by returning what Freddy had given him, literally vomiting up the souls of Dan, Greta, and Mark. (At least they weren't digested.) They latch onto Freddy and drag him on the ground until baby Freddy is ripped out of his body, similar to his death in the previous film. Jacob has also reverted to a baby and, in a flash of light, he's reabsorbed into Alice. Amanda has a harder time reclaiming her cursed fetus, however. She tells Alice to run as Freddy's glove bursts out of her stomach and several doors slam behind her, each one breaking down, until finally, a door that's finally strong enough closes on Freddy and his mother.

Months later, Yvonne, Alice, and her dad are at the park with baby Jacob. All is well, until we pull back to see a jump rope moving a little more slowly than it should, and we hear a familiar nursery rhyme being hummed by a child.

## NIGHTMARE AUTOPSIS

As uneven, strange, and downright vomit-inducing as *The Dream Child* may be, you have to respect the fact that it is a real attempt to make Freddy dark and scary again. How do you achieve such a reset when the established iconography and one-liners of Freddy Krueger are priced in? It's a commendable challenge, especially after the massive box office of *The Dream Master*. Stephen Hopkins had his work cut out for him.

*The Dream Child* is by no means a reboot, but there are several moments that remind us of the original film. There isn't even a "5" on the opening title card, though that number is on every piece of promotional material out there. When Freddy comes back, he hides in the shadows of the church and scratches his claws on metal before actually appearing. There's even an attempt to obscure him a bit more with smoke and shadows. Freddy also brings back his trademark self-mutilation with the acid champagne in Dan's truck. You could also argue that Alice becomes as relentless as Nancy was by the end.

And talk about relentless, this movie is *grim*. Not only is it full of dark passages and gothic architecture, it's nearly as sadistic as Freddy himself. There are only three death scenes, but they all feel protracted and painful. It's no wonder the MPAA cracked down on Dan and Greta's deaths. The body horror involved is impressive, but a bit much, at least by the standards of the time. This is nowhere near a defense of the puritanical "watchdogs" of the MPAA, who have neutered more movies than can be imagined. If anything, it shows that the effects crew hadn't slowed down, even after four fantastical entries.

However, attached to that darkness is something few horror film series strive for, let alone achieve: maturity. The graduates of Springwood High School are straddling the worlds of high school and the dreaded "after." There's barely a mention of college, and none of our young characters appear to know what they want out of life. Take Freddy out of it, and you still have a scary situation to find yourself in when you're with child, but without a partner. From the second she's pronounced pregnant, Alice is constantly viewed as "hysterical" by her peers, her doctor, and her would-be in-laws. She's hardly the first character in the series whose warnings are ignored, but in this entry there's an air of condescension amongst those who question her. For a while, they walk on eggshells. "Oh, the poor thing lost her boyfriend and the hormones are kicking in" can be read on the faces of her peers at various points. But who is on her side from the beginning? Who doesn't even want the Jordans in his house? Alice's father, Mr. Johnson. This papa doesn't preach. He stands by his daughter, no matter what. It's a hard pivot away from the parents who failed Nancy Thompson once upon a time. Say what you will about this film, it believes in growth.

Bodily autonomy is also a major topic that's perpetually broached. Alice sees Freddy's face *inside* her body, as perhaps the ultimate violation. Jacob later says Freddy hides "inside" her. Even David Cronenberg would gag at something so hideous. The topic of abortion is only brought up once from Mark, but it clearly never crossed Alice's mind until then. This isn't a pro-life statement, either. Not even close. If anything, he's absolutely right. Terminating the pregnancy will stop Freddy in his tracks, but Alice refuses, knowing she could lose what she loves in the process. There has to be another way. Mark accepts this, knowing he could die and, eventually, he does. He and Alice both make that choice in an instant, because this film is pro-choice all the way.

There's also a subtle point about American mental institutions. Alice's nightmare of being locked in with the "hundred maniacs" is exaggerated, but *how* exaggerated is it? Surely mental health facilities weren't regulated in the early twentieth century. It's entirely possible that some unscrupulous doctors kept those patients deemed "too far gone" in a room to wither away. Things got worse in 1981 when then-president Ronald Regan shut down institutions all over the country, leading to a homelessness epidemic that's still felt today. Freddy Krueger has always been treated like suburbia's dirty little secret, but his origin is a tale of institutional neglect and malfeasance. The tombstone that Neil finds in *Dream Warriors* was erected to sweep the church's dirty secret under the rug. Same as it ever was.

For possibly the first time in the series, we get a look at problematic elders across the socioeconomic spectrum. It's implied that Greta is affluent, not least because of her mom's bougie dinner party. She doesn't mention college, though she could most certainly afford it. Racine has bigger plans for her, just like Mark's dad has smaller plans for him. The sign on the warehouse says "Gray & Son." He seemingly expects Mark to run the family's blue collar business, presumably instead of going to college. While we're unsure of the status of Dan's parents, they believe excelling at sports is the key to his future. It's odd that the parents are focused on their kids so much *after* graduation. I've always wondered why Dan needed to speak to a major football coach at the ceremony. Didn't he already get into college? Though it's possible he was deferred due to his hospital stay in *Nightmare 4*, which would also explain why his parents aren't warm towards Alice, but I'm also a huge nerd and this is all conjecture. Still, notice that none of Freddy's victims in this film stand up to their respective parents. Greta only does so in her dream and Dan's parents only receive pushback from Alice. Springwood has never felt so stifling, and the film's cinematic language backs it up at almost every turn.

Stephen Hopkins came in with a new visual style unique to the series. Along with Peter Levy, his longtime cinematographer, Hopkins makes every frame feel dim. There's a bluish tint on many scenes, which make the film feel like it's always a chilly autumn instead of May or June. Even the vibrant high school graduation feels like it's filmed at a distance. The streamers, the crowd, and even the purple graduation robes add a claustrophobic feel to what is supposed to be an exciting day. Much like how the birth of a child is supposed to be exciting for all involved.

This film also marks the first time since *Freddy's Revenge* that Freddy has an overarching plan beyond just killing in dreams. He intended to "feed" Jacob souls and use his dreams to kill. It's not clear what his endgame is, but he eventually won't need Jacob once he's back on his feet. Hopkins also showcases a lot of religious imagery throughout. Of course, this has to do with having a nun as an important character, but there's also a major plot point about suicide leading to purgatory. Like in *Dream Warriors*, a soul has to be put to rest, but instead of Freddy, it's Amanda. Once she's out of her earthly prison, she pulls off half of a deus ex machina with Jacob.

The cast is also above par. The trend of post-*Breakfast Club* friend groups continues from the last film, though the tropes are more pronounced this time. You have "the jock" (Dan), "the outcast" (Mark), "the overachiever" (Yvonne), "the princess" (Greta), and "the rebel" (Alice, as it turns out). It's not explicit, but their characters walk the line. In most Hollywood movies, Mark, the artsy nerd, wouldn't be such good friends with the beautiful future model, Greta. He has an open crush on her, much like Duckie in *Pretty in Pink*, but it's clear that their friendship comes first. This is a difficult dynamic to pull off with making Mark seem creepy or stalkerish. Anderson and Seely play their characters like they have genuine affection for each other. Dan is friends not only with Mark, but overachiever Yvonne. Alice shows no signs of jealousy towards Greta, though she and Dan would probably be the Springwood High "power couple" in a lesser film. These people feel like real friends, through and through.

Young Whit Hertford is also excellent as Jacob, the manipulated child of Dan and Alice. However, the "Jacob" of it all doesn't make much sense. It's too early in Alice's pregnancy for a decent ultrasound, much less a personality to form. I'm aware this is a deep, dark hole to go down in a film series about a man who kills you in your dreams, but follow me here for a second. There's a famous quote that "deciding to have a child is to forever have your heart go walking around outside your body." It's a nice metaphor, but maybe *The Dream Child* is taking it further. When Alice meets Jacob, she tells him she always liked that name. Freddy is eventually killed when Jacob unleashes the souls he took, similarly to how he was vanquished in *The Dream Master*. Does this make Jacob a manifestation of Alice's wants? Is it possible that she is the one who manages to kill Freddy at the end and take back a part of herself that was violated?

Finally, we have a film *starring* Lisa Wilcox as Alice, as her credit expressly shows. Audiences may line up to see what Freddy's up to, but this is Alice's film. She's in almost every scene, spouting exposition and running the emotional gamut like no other heroine in the series. Talk about raising the stakes. Are the abilities of the Dream Master worth a damn when Freddy's target is her unborn child? She's more Cassandra than Cassandra, which would make

Wes Craven proud. Plus, Craven envisioned a happy ending for his characters, but Alice and Jacob Johnson actually got it.

The film still boasts incredible practical effects, despite what was cut by the censors. We also get to see Freddy's second on-screen resurrection of the series. Special effects legend Todd Masters worked on Greta's death, which is still considered a highlight today. The Freddy makeup just isn't as good as it's been previously, despite the return of original makeup artist David Miller. It was allegedly supposed to make Freddy look aged and weathered, but also easier to deal with. Freddy has long, skeletal arms, for his resurrection scene, but it's never explained why.

As mentioned up front, 1989 wasn't exactly a banner year for horror. Though compared to its franchise brethren, *A Nightmare on Elm Street 5: The Dream Child* is best of the lot. It has aged remarkably well, and despite its flaws, shows pangs of maturity unseen for a film this far into a pop horror franchise. When Freddy appears as Dan at the end, he utters the line "Kids. Always a disappointment." We'll see in the next chapter just how prophetic that proved to be.

## THE BOHEM DRAFT

By the late 1980's the literary subgenre of Splatterpunk had entered the zeitgeist. Splatterpunk books portrayed intense graphic violence and New Line Cinema wanted to use some of its black magic to make Freddy scary again. There was no WGA strike to contend with this time, but there were still many rewrites of the script. The writing team of John Skipp and Craig Spector turned in a draft, which was largely thrown out, except for the line "It's a boy!" They would receive a "story by" credit along with Leslie Bohem (*Dante's Peak*), who extensively rewrote their draft and had originally pitched this sequel without success back in the wake of *Dream Warriors*. New Line would eventually bring in Splatterpunk author David J. Schow and William Wisher (*Terminator 2*) to improve the dialogue, but the screenplay we'll look at first is the one in Bohem's name. There's also a British sensibility throughout, which indicates input from director Stephen Hopkins.

In this version, Dan gives a short speech at graduation instead of saying "Let's blow this pop stand!" In its place is... ugh... an ill-advised rap that Alice, Greta, and Yvonne recite. Attributed to Bohem, it's a relief that it was never filmed. As in the final film, Mark's dad barely appears in the story, though he does show up at graduation to subtly lament that his son isn't as macho as he'd like. He tells Mark he thought he'd be "hanging out with the guys." Just an observation: it's interesting to make a film interrogating parenthood when none of the parents who killed Freddy are anywhere to be seen. Mark is also more pervy in this draft. He's a little *too* excited about going to a pool party. So, Alice, Greta, and Yvonne throw him in the fountain at graduation.

The script never says "Westin Hills," instead referring to the Bethlem Royal Hospital, aka "Bedlam," a notorious British mental hospital from the 16th century. When Alice roams the halls, she sees a sheep (another reference to the original *Nightmare*), but it's eating a snake. Later on when Freddy reforms, he looks "more grotesque than usual. Misshapen. Like the Crooked Man." The Crooked Man is, of course, a known British horror legend, most definitely a Hopkins note.

Yvonne's diving nightmare sequence is slightly different. There's no locker room scene where she cries for her friends. When Alice rescues Yvonne, Freddy flips the room up to make them roll down on the wall in yet another throwback to the first *Nightmare*. (It would have been great to see the rotating room again.) The girls also learn about Mark's death in the dream world. When Freddy appears as Dan, he sprouts bone claws (*years* before Wolverine did it). Finally, adding to the religious overtones, Amanda tells baby Freddy she forgives him before putting him back inside her.

## THE SKIPP/SPECTOR DRAFT

While the Bohem draft closely resembled the final film, the Skipp/Spector draft is an entirely different beast. Keeping with the tradition of the previous two entries, this version opens with a quote in blood-red letters:

> **"Even a child is known by his doings."**
> **--Old Testament, Proverbs, xx, 11.**

We see water dripping in the bathroom sink as Freddy's face rises up slowly, then cuts to Alice, asleep in "the dream pool," a dark body of water meant to symbolize a womb (not quite the flooded shower of the final film). She's then thrown out of the pool into an asylum hallway where she witnesses Amanda Krueger get subsumed by the inmates. She wakes up next to Dan, who tries to sooth her, then turns into the face of one of the maniacs. Then she wakes up *again*.

So far, so similar to the film we got... until we visit the Elm Street house. The *real* Elm Street house, which is being demolished to make room for a mall. (Uh, didn't Nancy and Jesse have neighbors?) Jen Valdez, a Hispanic artist draws a charcoal portrait outside as it's torn down in front of her. Dan and Alice arrive to pick her up so they can head to graduation. They're joined by Ginger, a bulimic Marilyn Monroe wannabe. They arrive alongside Dean, a Black teen on a dirtbike who's new to Springwood. Dean is disappointed that his father never showed up, and probably not too happy about moving to a new town in his senior year. Alice tells Dan she "can't believe people could treat their kids like that." (Um...)

The graduation afterparty is at Dan's house. There's a pool and a keg, which his parents are apparently fine with. Alice has been pensive all day and she gets scared when she thinks she sees Freddy's shadow. Ginger is revealed to have a "manager" and Alice makes a joke about Ginger starring in a *Friday the 13th* sequel. Dean starts to give a toast, but since he's already buzzed, he becomes teary and laments the fact that the graduates might turn into their parents. He implores everyone to hang onto their dreams and not "murder" them like so many others.

Later, Alice tells Dan she's "late." Since he's going to college and she's staying in Springwood, it could be a problem, but Dan's committed to her. That night she dreams of a fetus growing inside of her, which morphs into "Baby Freddy," complete with metal claws. He stabs the wall of the womb and she wakes up. Or does she? Alice is suddenly in the hospital, watching Amanda Krueger run away as four blood spots spread on her nun's tunic.

Alice runs after her, winding up in a laboratory filled with jars and books. One jar contains the top of Freddy's head (a remnant from *The Dream Master*). Alice turns around and sees Amanda giving birth, surrounded by nuns, who all flee when the full-sized Freddy Krueger slices out of his mother's stomach and reattaches the missing section of his head. "It's a boy," indeed. As Alice runs away, the liquid in the other jars now contain "screaming bloody fetuses!" (Holy *shit*.) Freddy reiterates his line to her from *Nightmare 4*: "I am eternal." He touches her belly with his claw, indicating she *is* pregnant. Alice then wakes up in Dan's house, just as he brings home pregnancy tests. It's positives all the way down.

Alice visits Jen and Ginger at the loft they share. (Wait, aren't they supposed to be high schoolers? At least put in a line about how they're emancipated.) Ginger brings up abortion, but Alice is against it, having experienced too much loss in her life. As a nice character beat, Jen understands, but Ginger's disappointed. Alice is all business, suggesting they take part in the series tradition of sleeping in shifts so that one person is always awake and watching out for their friends.

Meanwhile, Dan and Dean are riding dirt bikes outside of town. Dan's concerned about Alice's pregnancy, unsure of what to do about his football scholarship. Dean might not have the best perspective, but he tells Dan it doesn't matter if they're in love. Dan's parents aren't too happy, but they don't say anything when he searches for beer in their fridge. (Kind of a weird time to be worried about his judgment, no?) At Alice's house, she longs for her mom to help her when Freddy appears in her mirror and attempts to pull up her skirt after making a rape joke. Thankfully, she wakes up to a phone call from Dan. He's all-in.

Dan's death is different here, though it hits similar beats. The gearshift in his truck sprouts Freddy's claws and literally forces Dan's hand to crash the truck. Since his dirt bike is intact in the flatbed, he jumps on it to warn Alice, The Freddy bike is less involved than in the finished film, not fusing his body with the cycle but turning into parts of Freddy. He crashes in front of a chasm (the local bridge is out), and Freddy finishes him off by impaling him on a steel beam. Alice sees it in a puddle of spilled water and feels him die, then sees Freddy laughing in a puddle at the crime scene.

At Dan's funeral, Alice is ignored by his family while her friends all worry about her. She goes to the fountain from the last scene in *Nightmare 4* and makes a wish, where she encounters "J.J." He's a little boy who says he's "a distant relative" of Dan. When Alice goes home, her dad is about to take a drink to cope, when he breaks down and apologizes to Alice. She then has a nightmare where she sees a white bassinet in the middle of Elm Street. When she approaches it, Freddy's hand shoots out, then all the windows on the block explode, expelling the residents onto their lawns to splatter on impact. A Sam Raimi-esque zoom shot comes upon her when she wakes up.

At the girls' loft, Jen and Dean talk about what to do while Ginger gets ready to go out with her scumbag "manager" Buddy. He drives her to an "audition" at a motel for two "producers." (Honestly, how many more words need to be in quotations before this high school graduate figures it out?) Elsewhere, Alice goes to the library to do research and runs into J.J. again. He says he's also having bad dreams and shows her a book about the dream pool, a place where "all dreams past, present, and future, mingle as one." J.J. is one precocious kid, and he theorizes that she can see Freddy's dreams in the pool.

Alice sees a picture of young Amanda Krueger in the paper followed by a vision of her handing over her baby to stern-looking nuns. Freddy somehow transports her to the boiler room. Instead of killing her, he gives her one of Dan's arms ("You're eating for two now, you know"). Alice runs away, ending up in the Elm Street house where Freddy shows her a vision of Jen nodding off in her room. Alice wakes up in the library and leaves to warn her friend. Again.

Though Dean is hanging out in the loft, Freddy locks Jen's door as she dreams of the art in her room coming to life. The drawing of the Elm Street house shimmers as an animated Freddy emerges, killing an animated dog, who's real head comes flying out. A hunk of clay then transforms into "Claymation Freddy" while her metal sculpture turns into "Metal Freddy." She tries to fight back with an acetylene torch, but her room winds up exploding. Dean escapes the burning apartment, only to run into his future self, then back to Freddy, who stabs his eyes out.

Ginger's big break is never coming, despite how satisfied Buddy and his clients were. She falls asleep when they leave, dreaming about being a featured guest on Club MTV. (Basically, MTV's *American Bandstand*. Downtown Julie Brown is written in as a cameo.) Freddy shows up and force feeds her desserts as the crowd cheers. She starts to transform into a pig and when she forces herself to throw up, she pukes a geyser of blood. Ginger "wakes up" back in the motel, but it's just another trick by Freddy, who viciously kills her just as Buddy comes back. In a bit of karmic justice, Freddy drops a razor on the ground for the cops to find along with Ginger's blood soaked manager.

As Freddy kills Alice's friends, he sends their souls to her fetus, which supernaturally expedites its growth to the point where it appears she's five months along. Alice winds up in an ambulance where she sees Freddy touching her stomach. At the hospital, Dr. Pickman (a Lovecraft reference, I'd wager) reveals her sonogram is showing twins: her baby and a "pulsing, bloated monstrosity." A sickly J.J. shows up saying they have to stick together, but since she was sedated, she's slipping into the dream pool. Alice's bed turns to liquid and she sinks down as J.J. also passes out.

Alice surfaces in a puddle on the floor of an orphanage. She sees Amanda and runs to her asking what happened to her baby. The nun shows her the intervening years of Freddy growing up in the orphanage, being abused and exhibiting homicidal tendencies before burning the building down. We then see an older Freddy making the glove, using it to kill (offscreen, thankfully), briefly appearing in court, and finally being burned by the parents. Amanda tells her Freddy wants to do the same thing to Alice that he did to her, but Alice calls her out: if she knew he was evil, why not abort him? Why hand him over to the nuns who sealed his fate? Amanda can't answer.

Freddy brings Alice back to the boiler room as he's replacing the blade he left behind after slaughtering Ginger. He shows her a vision of a dead world where he's presumably killed the entire human race. He shoves his hand in her stomach, "feeding himself to her." Alice's stomach swells to full-term, causing the hospital staff to prep her for delivery.

Just as it looks like all is lost, Amanda shows up. She shoots out an umbilical cord from her stomach, which pulls him to her, so he can be reabsorbed by his mother (Freud could write so many papers on this one.) The boiler room explodes and crumbles around them as Alice wakes up and gives birth to *one* baby.

Later on, after some time has passed, Alice tends to her crying infant: Jason Johnson. The book about the "dream pool" shows the author's picture: an older "J.J." in 2013. When Alice comforts him, she sees a vision of Mother Superior, who abused Freddy, saying her child is an abomination. She disappears and Alice tells the baby she loves him as we try to figure out what's behind his eyes.

## SCRIPT AUTOPSIS

Production on *The Dream Child* began so soon after *The Dream Master's* release that it's possible Skipp and Spector were only shown a print of that sequel just prior to starting their work. As such, there's an abundance of continuity maintained with the preceding sequel in their draft. Alice doesn't just keep her red hair, she keeps her old personality as a meek observer, eschewing the self-assured badass she'd become by the end of that film. Also, Freddy shows Alice that Jen is his next victim just like he did with Debbie. Dean appears in old age makeup like the Ghost of Springwood Future just as Alice did at the Crave Inn, and Dan jokes about his truck being totaled *again*. Basically, the Skipp/Spector draft is *Nightmare 4.5*.

To those familiar with *A Nightmare on Elm Street 5: The Dream Child*, it's abundantly clear how much groundwork Skipp and Spector laid. The asylum opening is less involved than the finished film, but it still shows Amanda getting overrun and Dan turning into an inmate when Alice "wakes up." Freddy is re-born in this draft, but this scene is much more extreme. Emerging from Amanda's stomach as the Freddy we know and love might have been too much for audiences to handle, but it's gnarly and inspired.

Abortion is brought up much earlier, most likely to get ahead of the audience. However, it's refreshing the way Alice defeats Freddy by asking Amanda why she didn't abort him if she knew he was evil right away. Once again, this script is pro-choice all the way. Dan actually finds out about the baby before he dies, feels conflicted about college, and decides to stay with Alice. Credit goes to Skipp and Spector, two writers who made names for themselves writing stories with extreme gore and violence, for allowing space in their script for the drama of an unplanned pregnancy. Though they more than make up for it with the gore that's written.

Character wise, there's a direct line between Ginger and Greta as they're both beautiful, soon-to-be stars. Ginger has food issues and pressures herself internally whereas Greta doesn't seem to care about being a model in the first place. Freddy force-feeds both of them in every iteration, but Ginger's death is more explicitly brutal. Jen and Mark are both artists who die in environmental "accidents," which are easy for Freddy to cover up. Aside from the fact that they're both Black, Dean is an entirely different character than Yvonne. Dean is more of an attempt to foreground the theme of not wanting to turn into your parents. Also, has Freddy killed two characters at the same time before? (We're not counting the swimming pool scene, where the victims are little more than extras.) Here, he gets a two-for-one special with Jen and Dean.

In addition to returning to the boiler room for several scenes, the Skipp/Spector script examines Freddy's birth and subsequent childhood several years before *Freddy's Dead* would traverse the same territory. It's suggested he's born evil, but his wrath is augmented by the abuse he experienced from the nuns at the orphanage. Speaking in the *Never Sleep Again* doc, John Skipp said, "We were really gonna figure out how Freddy works. He was basically raised by mean nuns, who made him the monster he is. That's how he got twisted at the root."

The screenwriters use water as an agent to view dreams in an interesting touch. The "dream pool" is a fascinating idea, but might've been too big for audiences to wrap their heads around. Ginger's death would have also been a big ask in a pre-*Terrifer* world. Not only does Freddy gut the poor girl, but he slits her throat in a fashion that…well here's the script:

**Her head tips back from the raw meat canyon of her severed neck, held by a hinge of skin.**

As graphic as that sounds, it's not an unusual passage for a splatterpunk novel like the kind Skipp and Spector wrote. Further reminiscing in *Never Sleep Again*, John Skipp discusses the reaction to their draft: "This is the thing with Hollywood. They'll say 'Make it scary, no holds barred. Give us your ultimate thing.' Then you give them your 'ultimate thing' and they shit themselves." One can't help but wonder what the filmed version of this script could have been.

# INTERVIEW

# STEPHEN HOPKINS
## DIRECTOR

A Nightmare 5
ON ELM STREET
THE DREAM CHILD

**By the time you directed *The Dream Child*, you were already a seasoned vet in the music video world with only one indie feature. Do you recall what enticed New Line to hire you?**

I started doing rock videos in England, then I made a whole bunch in New York, where I went from a designer to a director. Then I went to Australia to do some Elton John videos where I stayed for four or five years. While I was there, I did hundreds of videos, commercials, and theatre, but I also directed the second unit on Russell Mulcahy's *Highlander*. He's a great friend and mentor, and I'm actually going to speak to him right after this. So I did my first little film in Australia [*Dangerous Game*]. It went to Cannes and was seen by Paramount, Joel Silver, and New Line, who all liked it.

In February of that year, I got a call to come meet everyone [at New Line]. There was a writer's strike, but I was given three or four scripts to read, which all revolved around the concept of how Freddy was born. I was told [New Line] wanted to make it a little less funny than the previous entry, because Freddy had gotten too silly, I think. Being British, I just went all gothic on it.

I storyboarded all my own stuff because I came from drawing comics, so on the plane from Sydney to LA, I was drawing things that I thought would fit into the film from the different scripts. I was in the back of the plane, sort of annoying everyone. I got off the plane and went straight to New Line, where I met Bob Shaye and a whole bunch of really great people. We talked for a few hours, where I showed the storyboards I had drawn on the plane. My girlfriend was working in Miami, so one of my actor friends drove me to the airport so I could visit her there. I was still there for Valentine's Day, when I got the call saying "Hey, let's do it," so I flew back to LA. I had eighty dollars to my name. It was in 4,000 cinemas that August.

**So, you had a release date in six months and you'd just been hired?**

Yes. I was shooting during and after the sound mix. I even shot until a few days before the release date, actually. (laughs) It was a non-union film we shot in an old shoe factory in Culver City. There were no digital effects in those days, nor were there any on my next film, *Predator 2*. It was all film opticals. My DP, Peter Levy, came over from Australia, but it was otherwise new people. Bob, Peter and I appear as three of the "hundred maniacs" in the mental asylum in the beginning, I think. (laughs) I spotted us when I was color-timing the film the other day.

My great find was Alan Munro, the effects supervisor who later worked on *The Addams Family*. He was an expert in stop motion who worked with Tim Burton a lot and had lots of fun, cartoony ideas. I think I spoke to [credited screenwriter] Les Bohem at one point because the strike was finishing, but I wasn't really allowed to. I'm not sure what it was, but I scanned them all, and grabbed bits from different scripts and storyboarded them. Since I'm a big comic buff, I put that Super Freddy bit in, along with the character of Mark.

**New Line just let you go for it?**

New Line was hands-off. You were just sort of let loose. They took Freddy seriously, because between him and the Ninja Turtles, that gave them the money and the "oompf" to do all these big things. I think we made it for six million dollars or something. We shot what we could. In those days, it took a really long time to make that many copies to go out all over America. Then we had a lot of run-ins with the MPAA, who kept giving it an "X" rating. It became a bigger issue on *Predator 2* because they were determined to take it out on a big film. We just kept cutting and cutting here and there. That's the overall view of it.

**That sounds like an insane amount of work, even by today's standards.**

It would certainly be easier to do it today in many ways. You wouldn't have to shoot practical effects and it wouldn't take as long. A lot of the sequences are purely animated and we didn't have time to finish it, so this time when I was color-timing the film, I tried to finish the nastier bits of the visual effects. (laughs) But it was very bold and bonkers. I don't think it was well-received at the time.

**So, the gothic feel came more from you than New Line?**

Yeah, it's like Bob said to me, "All you Europeans put gargoyles everywhere." (laughs) But it was a gothic story, too. A nun gets raped in a mental asylum, leading to the birth of Freddy Krueger. You don't get more gothic than that, in terms of a storyline. We were building giant womb sets. And shooting scenes inside a fertilized womb. That might be a first, I think! (laughs) It was also about figuring out how to keep another film going in a great series. I remember seeing the first *Nightmare* in Australia with my girlfriend and we were both ducking in our seats, because it was so terrifying. Each subsequent film had a new director and a style. Some were funnier, some were more action-based, in a way. I liked a few of them. But [*The Dream Child*] might have been one of the first to carry over characters from the previous film.

**How do you express yourself through the medium when you're making the fifth film in an established franchise?**

I think I always try to put the film first. I've done many different types of genres throughout my career. Dramas, thrillers, comedies, but I don't think I was particularly good with horror. I think great directors actually get out of the way of the film. Those are the ones I'm fans of. It's not to call out how clever I am. (laughs) I tried to do what [New Line] wanted, because it wasn't like I had to make a *Nightmare* film before I died. It was just a fantastic opportunity. They were great. It was my first Hollywood movie, so I was thrilled to get a chance to do it, but I never set out to do "Oh, what do I think is cool?" I try to base it on the story. I know New Line wanted it to be poppy, colorful, "80's." Freddy's makeup was redesigned for the film by David Miller, which was easier to apply, so Robert Englund was pleased. The little boy [Whitby Hertford] who played Jacob was great. We needed a good actor for that role. You have to be quite a good actor to be in those films, otherwise it appears phony.

**Aside from the characters who came over from part four, were there any other mandates from New Line?**

(pause) Long time ago. (laughs) I remember watching the others, but I can't remember any great, pithy comments. The scripts were always about Freddy entering the dreams of Alice's unborn son. That was a given. Since it was the 80's and I worked on music videos, they also wanted us to have MTV-style music, which wasn't too expensive.

It all came together in a rush. I was shooting six days a week, sometimes two to three parts of the shoe factory on the same day. We hardly shot anywhere else. Maybe UCLA a few times. We'd shoot a few things on stages and sets, while the effects and stop motion were shooting at the same time. Peter and I were involved in the biggest stuff, like the church sequence where Freddy's resurrected on an altar. While they were setting up for that, I'd be shooting a dialogue scene. You're rushing around, editing on film, which is complex. A lot of the post-production crew worked on the other *Nightmare* films, so they knew what was what. Alan Munro was really the guy I had fun with. We worked to combine shots so they didn't feel like they were from entirely different films.

**You might be the only director in the series who brought your own DP, Peter Levy, along for the job. Was he your "number two" on set?**

I met him in Australia when I was working on Elton John's music videos. He had gotten married to a woman, which was shocking to us, so I was delayed there, and I fell in love with Sydney and a girl. I had already directed music videos in London and New York. I was supposed to go back to Europe to do Duran Duran videos, but I was asked to stay and do Elton's videos. That's where I met Peter. He was an ex-documentary cameraman and an assistant to the great DP Dean Semler for a long time. We sort of put a style together. Australian

DPs are some of the best in the world. They were often asked to shoot these incredible landscapes, but they weren't as good with interior photography. Peter was good at everything. We still work together now. In fact, he's moving from LA to France, which is closer to me.

**Do you recall the other script that you took from besides Les Bohem's? I know there's the Skipp and Spector draft.**

There might have been four scripts, but no, I don't remember. I basically storyboarded the whole film from the bits I took. We didn't have a finished script because of the strike. Strangely, my next film, *Predator 2,* was also during a writer's strike, so I thought "Oh this is how they make films in Hollywood: without fully finished scripts." That was more finished, but I wasn't allowed to chat with the poor Thomas brothers [creators of the Predator and screenwriters of *Predator* and *Predator 2*]. It was a pain in the ass. You can't make a great film without a great script.

**Joe Seely said when he auditioned for "Mark," they used his abilities as a skater for the character. Was that part of the casting process?**

No, I was involved with casting, but if someone brings in a skill, of course you're going to try to put that in the character. I think it's silly not to. [Joe and I] thought his character should have been more goth, but for some reason New Line thought it would be a cliché. They wanted to keep it fun and pop arty.

**How much of yourself is in the movie?**

Not much (laughs), except the love of comics and the joy of fun, creepy filmmaking. It's really hard to make a good, creepy film. I rarely see one that affects me. I think *Hereditary* was the last really scary movie I saw. In those days, there were slasher films, but there weren't many thematic horror films. Now there's so many movies like *Smile,* which rely on fantasy rather than the mundane. Back then, Freddy was one of the only really fantastical horror ones. I thought comics were such an important part of that, especially because comics weren't that big then. In the '90s, I tried to make *Spider-Man* with Jim Cameron producing. I had met Stan Lee many times to try and make *Dr. Strange*. They both would have cost an unbelievable amount of money. Everyone thought "Marvel movies" would be stupid, but I had collected comics since I was a kid. I learned to read by reading comics. When I was re-watching the film, you see all these Marvel and DC comics on Mark's floor. I thought "Fuck, you wouldn't be able to do that now." (laughs) Comics were becoming cooler. You had Frank Miller, Neil Gaiman, and Alan Moore.

**What was your most difficult day on set and how'd you get through it?**

I came up with this idea for a sort-of M.C. Escher world. People were running up and down stairs at different angles. Me, Peter, and Alan were holding onto our heads trying to figure out each one of those shots and where the eyelines matched. It wasn't hard where I wished I wasn't doing it. It was like rewiring our brains to imagine a three-dimensional, upside-down, sideways world, where everyone's communicating with each other. Then some characters aren't who they seem and they use a different voice. It was mind boggling. That wacky ending, too, was pretty complicated to shoot. There were days where you're going "We literally can't figure it out."

**That scene begins among a creative pastiche of several sets. Was it always the intention to combine sets that way or was it devised in the moment?**

There were story points that had to be made, so we had to have some of those sets, but I'm a big Escher fan. I also loved *The Name of the Rose*, which had these moving stairways. You want to do stuff that's impossible to do, like the "dream pram" coming down the steps and water pouring upwards. It probably would have been fun in 3D.

**You've gone on to have an expansive career after *The Dream Child*. Most of your films have a running theme about parental conflicts or at least a mentor/ mentee relationship. Did that become your focus after this film?**

I think a lot of American films feel comfortable to base themselves on that, but this film was more about younger people finding community with like-minded peers. It's always a frightening part of being a teenager: distancing themselves from their parents, who are sometimes fucked up. You sometimes wind up taking care of them instead of the other way around. Nicholas Mele, who played Alice's father, is terrific. He brought a lot to the role without hardly doing anything. You need that in the film, or else you're stuck with absolute loonies like Greta's mother. She was so over-the-top. (laughs)

**I noticed there's a reference to Bethlem Royal Hospital in the script, an infamous UK asylum. I can't imagine that it came from an American writer. Do you recall adding it?**

Well, I actually worked in a mental asylum for a few years as a teenager. It was the largest one in Britain with about 3,000 patients, but they maintained the original asylum from centuries ago. It was just one long stone building. You'd walk down the hall, and there'd be cells on your right, which were just metal bars with chains. Underneath the cells was a pit with running water, so they used to chain people in there, feed them, and let them piss and shit through the bars. It was kept as a reminder, and it was a scary place as a young man. I went to a school where you were supposed to do army things two days a week, which I refused. The alternative was to work in a mental asylum, which I grew to love, but it left a mark on me. There was one guy I saw every week. One week he said he was a violinist in ancient Rome, the next week he was the world snooker champion. I used to read to people in padded cells who thought they were Edward II.

In Britain, you also grew up with a lot more gothic horror than in America. A lot of British films in the 40's, 50's and 60's, like Amicus anthologies. They had films about asylums, but they were all wacky and creepy. In the old days, people believed they were possessed. America had more realistic films about mental institutions like *One Flew Over the Cuckoo's Nest*. It's cultural. I think if an American director had done part five, there'd be less organ music. (laughs)

**What lessons, if any, did you learn on this film that you carried with you throughout your career? Besides "Always shoot with a finished script" and "Fuck the MPAA," of course.**

Well, I started prepping *Predator 2* before I finished this film. It was a much bigger film, and I have to say I hadn't seen *Predator* at that point. I didn't have much time to stop and think about it. Then while I was working on *Predator 2*, Fox asked me to do *Alien 3*.

**Oh, wow.**

And it was during another writer's strike, so there was no finished script! I had to apologize, because *Alien* was one of my favorite horror films. Given the choice between those three films, I would have gone with *Alien 3*. The first film changed everything, and Jim did an amazing sequel, which is rare. I couldn't do three of those kinds of films in a row, especially when the script wasn't finished.

I took a break after *Predator 2* because I wanted to do something different, that wasn't reliant on visual effects. You're in that system where everything is expensive and filled with anxiety. *Predator 2* was jammed with visual effects. We shot them on 70 mm and there were no digital effects. I wanted to try something scarier, and more human in a way. The nice thing about those movies is that you're scared, but you know it's not real.

**Is there anything about these films that you feel isn't talked about enough?**

I think the *Nightmare* films were unique because they were about teenage fears. Fear of not being accepted or having strange ideas and being told to conform. They also came at a time when the world was going a bit crazy. Money and status were such a big deal [in the 80's], and often kids were rebelling against that. Rebellion against the status quo was built into the storyline. It's also hard to find someone who doesn't know who Freddy Krueger is. More people probably know who he is than Predator, because it was a truly original idea from Wes Craven. There have been plenty of films made before about bad dreams and spiritualism, but nothing where the dream comes alive. Apart from maybe Hitchcock's *Spellbound* where Dali did the sets, but it's not the same. The *Nightmare* films were unique to each character, where their fears were trying to eat them alive. There's a monster we're all afraid of, and sometimes it rears its head like it does now in some parts of the world. It's come to use its fear against you.

# INTERVIEW
## LISA WILCOX
### "ALICE JOHNSON"

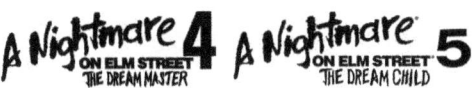

**You joined the franchise at a time when it was gaining a ton of momentum. What was it like to jump on that train?**

It was absolutely amazing! I've always been a horror fan since I was little. [I loved] *Dracula, Frankenstein,* and all that good stuff. So, to be a part of *Nightmare on Elm Street* was a dream come true.

**According to franchise lore, *The Dream Master* and *The Dream Child* had chaotic productions. How did you navigate them?**

I felt it was very organized chaos, honestly. You do a lot of filming, sometimes with another crew on another stage for the special effects. So, you do a lot of revolving from set to set, but I never felt I was unsafe or like I didn't know where I was going. Most times, it wasn't chaotic at all. I think the hardest part for me was that they asked to dye my hair red. I was a natural platinum blonde and I asked them if they could put a rinse on it instead. The rinse had to be put on every morning, and you can't just towel-dry your hair. I had two blow dryers going every day. (laughs) Sometimes Renny [Harlin] would want a quick rehearsal and I would leave the makeup trailer with my hair still dripping.

When we filmed the scene where Kristen dies and I meet Freddy, I'm wearing this white nightgown and I'm kind of wet. Renny says "Cut! What is that all over you?" Well, the rinse came out of my hair and stained the nightgown.

So, we had to stop filming and they had to wash my hair to get the rinse out! I needed a new nightgown before we could proceed with the scene.

**So is Robert Englund just laughing at you this entire time and saying "You have *no* idea?"**

(laughs) Exactly.

**Did you spend time with him while you were in the makeup chair?**

Oh yeah, we spent a lot of time talking in the trailer while I got my makeup done and he got his elaborate makeup done. They actually experimented with my old-age makeup throughout the course of filming, until we filmed the "Old Alice" scene. They tried two or three different ways to see how they wanted me to look, so Robert and I had time to chat a lot. It was interesting, because he's being turned into this monster while we're talking about the colors of the grout he's using to remodel his bathroom!

**Of course, we love Robert Englund, but the casts of these films are truly unsung. There isn't really any merchandise celebrating the other characters, aside from the mini nunchucks you sell at conventions. When did you first notice Alice made an impact?**

I first noticed when I would meet fans at my table at conventions, and they would tell me about how Alice's strength got them through hard times. I heard so many personal stories, through tears, about how much Alice Johnson meant to them. It's an incredibly huge compliment. One of the joys of being an actress is the impact you can have on a person's life and their choices. I love film, and certain performances have had an impact on my life, as well. It's wonderful to hear and to know that it made a difference.

**She's certainly celebrated among fans of the series. Alice is one of the rare characters to survive both of her films. Tell me the story behind the "Alice Lives" shirts you made.**

It's interesting, because there was a period of time where I was like "Hey, I never got my death scene." Then one day a lightbulb went off, and I totally pivoted on the ending of part five. "Alice *Lives*." The monster never gets her through two films. She's a true heroine! For me, "Alice Lives" means you can have anyone's name there for anyone who's gone through personal strife. You live through it.

**Was there anything cut from the *Dream Master* script that you missed?**

There was a scene where I'm sleepwalking and I go into the kitchen, open the refrigerator, and blood spews out all over me. And I'm wearing a white nightgown. (laughs) It was very *Carrie*-esque. Believe me, seeing yourself in a white nightgown covered in blood is very memorable. (laughs) It's a memory that sticks with you.

**Did you and Robert have to learn fight choreography for the final battle?**

We definitely had a stunt coordinator, no question. In the beginning of the fight, we were on a platform a few feet above the ground. We had people around us in case we fell off, but being in that elevated space definitely helped us add tension. They also sent me to karate school and I had excellent stunt doubles. We all know the scene when Alice is looking in her mirror and she's using the nunchaku. When you see my face, that's me using the nunchaku, but when you see the shot from behind with my stunt double, you see the terrible wig. So sorry, Hair and Makeup. The fans and I kind of laugh about that, but my stunt double made me look good, man! And she was like four inches taller than me, which was funny, but she was definitely a pro.

**One of the other unique aspects of part four is how close the cast is, even to this day. What do you think led to that bonding experience and how do you maintain your friendships today?**

Annette Benson was the casting director for the first five entries. I met her years after the films and I told her "You know, you unwittingly cast best friends for life." Particularly with part four since we all lived in Los Angeles. We all bonded and it shows in the film. Brooke Thiess's [Debbie] son and my eldest son were the same age, so we'd do things like go bowling with the boys. Toy Newkirk [Sheila] moved to New York for about ten years, and we maintained a friendship, so when she came back to LA, she lived with me for a year. Tuesday Knight and I had a business, Toe Brights, for almost ten years. It's very, very rare for those kinds of relationships to be maintained. Typically, once a project is done, you don't see those people again.

**When you were shooting part four, did you have any inkling that you'd be asked to come back for part five?**

None. After the film came out in August, they approached me about doing five. Since part four was a huge box office success, they decided to continue the story of Alice.

**It seems like you were in a unique position, because you were introduced in an ensemble, and you came back for the next film in a starring role. You're in almost every scene.**

(laughs) Yeah, it was a big responsibility.

**How did you handle that?**

It was fine. I'm a trained actor and I started in theater. You're up on that stage for two hours. I've developed a great brain muscle. Not so much anymore. (laughs)

**You mentioned in Mick Strawn's book that you made notes in the script while you were shooting part four. Did you continue to do that with part five?**

Not so much for part five. The reason I had my very specific notes for part four is that of course, we don't shoot in order. In the morning, you might be shooting scene thirty-three, and in the afternoon, you're shooting scene eight, you know? So, I had to keep track of my level to make Alice's character arc and her strength believable. I would mark in the script who died in each scene so I could gauge how strong or how meek I was. I probably wrote some notes for part five, but not as much for part four.

**There's a lot of character growth between parts four and five that I love. Alice is still the Dream Master, but she's in sort of a hostage situation where she suddenly has to protect her baby. How did you keep continuity as an actress in part five?**

The continuity of part four was much more difficult. Again, there were different levels for Alice throughout her growth. In part five, I'm pretty much steady throughout the whole film. She's strong, fighting for her baby's life against Freddy, against Dan's parents who want to adopt him, and having to contemplate being a single mother. Would I have an abortion? I call *Nightmare 5* a brave little film for 1989 because of the stigma of so many topics that we were dealing with at the time. We talk about these things at the dinner table in 2024, but in 1989, sex before marriage and teen pregnancy were really heavy. Then we have Alice's dad, who's a recovered alcoholic, which is a good thing. There's a lot going on in part five.

**I've heard you talk about how It's aged remarkably well in a lot of ways. We meet the characters after the major milestone of graduating high school.**

Yeah, we're all eighteen and ready to take on the world. Danny and I were off to Paris!

**And the fact that Dan dies before he finds out about the baby adds an extra layer of darkness. I want to talk about the scene where Dan's parents come to Alice's house and basically threaten an adoption. A lesser film would have diluted it to one line from Yvonne: "They'll take your baby away."**

Yeah. (laughs)

**But it's a great piece of grounded drama in the midst of this fantastical horror film. Can you recall shooting it?**

I love that scene, and I love the fact that a father is standing up for his daughter. He's a great role model, especially for what [his character] became after *Nightmare 4*.

**The two of you switched gears for part five, especially Nick Mele as Mr. Johnson. Did you work with him on the changes?**

Well, the script is our skin. It's what's giving us the information on our characters as we're paying attention to the story. I also love the scene in the kitchen. There was something there that didn't quite work. I'm waiting for the microwave to go off, I'm crying and I'm looking at my watch. I made a choice there that my watch was something Dan had given me. I don't think it reads when I watch it, but that was my intention. Then her dad comes in and it's such a sweet, tender scene. That intimacy between a father and daughter is sprinkled all throughout part five. It's just a great story.

**Did you view the film any differently when you became a mother yourself?**

That's an interesting question. I think I did. It was like "Yay, Alice had the baby!" Eighteen years old or not, she's a fighter.

**Do you ever think about where Alice and Jacob are today?**

Oh my goodness, I do! I think Alice might have become an attorney who defends the innocent. She would have gone to law school or to become a nurse or a doctor. Once she broke out of her shell, she could do anything she set her mind to. I think she would have gotten remarried, and she and Jacob would've had a fabulous family life.

**I wonder if their version of "the talk" was Jacob asking "Mom, did we kill a guy when I was a baby?"**

(laughs) He would say "I have this recurring dream where we killed this monster guy." And I think Alice would've told him the truth. Then he'd go "mom, what kind of drugs were you on back then?"

**Are there any aspects of the *Nightmare on Elm Street* films that you wished people brought up more often?**

I love them, but what I think is the most significant about parts four and five is that there are some amazing role models. I do conventions where I meet people all the time, and they come up to my table crying saying "You have no idea how you've inspired me." To get through high school or whatever personal thing is going on with their parents. Alcoholism, drug use with their mother, sister, brother, or dad. And bullying! Alice is fighting the biggest bully. *Nightmare* gave them joy and inspiration to know [they] can get through it. You can stay strong and get stronger.

*Note: Most of the* Nightmare 4 *portion of this interview originates from a conversation the author had with Lisa for Macabre Daily in 2023. The* Nightmare 5 *portion was conducted over Zoom in 2024.*

# INTERVIEW
# WHITBY HERTFORD
## "JACOB JOHNSON"

A Nightmare ON ELM STREET 5
THE DREAM CHILD

**You're one of the few child actors in the series. Is it weird to have to remember making this film when you were a kid?**

Yes, it is weird, but these memories are still at the forefront. These were pivotal, really sort of landmark memories of my life, so I can recount them, but yeah, it's still weird for strangers to be like "Let me interrogate you about when you were ten." (laughs)

**How much did the adults in your life explain to you about what was happening in the movie?**

They were very rudimentary. "This is your mom, and [Freddy] is trying to attack your mom." That kind of thing. I don't even remember them being like "You're unborn" or anything. I think I caught on to that, but they just made it matter of fact. "This is your mom, you're in the hospital, etc."

**Do you have any memories of working with Stephen Hopkins?**

Yeah, he was great and he really took me under his wing. We shot on my birthday and he bought me a skateboard. Really nice guy.

**It wasn't the one used in the movie, was it?**

No, it was a nice one. It was a Steve Caballero, which is like a quality skateboard.

**Have you been doing conventions for a while?**

Well, I started going to conventions late. I've been doing mostly theater, but I've been doing conventions for like two and a half years or something like that. I love it.

**Is there anything you want fans of the franchise to know that's not discussed that often?**

The idea of like, why there [haven't been more films in the franchise] is a big question. I was talking to Lisa Wilcox about it, and I said there absolutely could be a spin-off where it's *Son of Krueger*, you know? Freddy could kind of pass the torch to me, and I could be sort of an antagonistic character within that, and have it be like a streaming miniseries. That's an idea I think the fans would really like because [the story] just sort of ends at part five. The only people that survived are Alice and I.

# INTERVIEW
## KELLY JO MINTER
### "YVONNE"

A Nightmare 5
ON ELM STREET
THE DREAM CHILD

**Most actors come into the *Nightmare* series with minimal screen experience, but by the time you joined part five, you had already worked with heavyweights like Peter Bogdanovich, Carl Reiner, and Joel Schumacher. Were you reluctant to join the fifth film in a franchise?**

I was at first. I knew who Freddy was, but I'd never seen a *Nightmare on Elm Street* film. My neighbor, who was a friend of mine, said "You need to do this!" After I met Stephen Hopkins, who was young and fresh, I thought it would be cool. I'm so happy I did the movie. I've met so many interesting people. The fans are super loyal. People come to me for other things, but I didn't know this genre was that big and impactful. I was definitely glad to be a part of it. When I heard they were doing part six, I didn't know why Lisa [Wilcox] and I weren't in it, because we survived.

**Joe Seely mentioned that when he was cast, they asked him what he liked to do for fun and when he said he skated, they made his character a skater. Did they ask you the same thing?**

No, I don't recall anything like that. I wouldn't have been a candy striper. I was just an around-the-way girl. I was your friend and I'm gonna tell you the truth. I believe the role transcended that.

**Definitely. I love the *Horror Noire* documentary you appear in, but I had one problem with it. When they illustrate the trope of the "sassy black friend" who is only meant to help the white characters, they show a clip of Yvonne. It's an important stereotype to call out, but I didn't think Yvonne fit that mold. She had her own agency.**

Thank you. It's like, the black experience is different. Black people aren't gonna go down the hallway to "check it out." They're gonna get the hell out of there. It's different how you're raised, and where you're raised. It's funny, but it's true.

**The thing is, you eventually do "go down the hallway" to save everyone. Yvonne is the non-believer for most of the film, but when she realizes Freddy is real, she breaks into an abandoned asylum to find a ghost. I'm aware of how insane that sounds, but she became the cavalry just like in *The People Under the Stairs*.**

(laughs) That was an interesting film to do, too. I had so much respect for Wes Craven. But working with Stephen and that whole crew wasn't really work. I'm still friends with those people. I worked on movies I thought would turn out one way, and they turned out another. I was never a trained actor. You're pretending and you just have to make it as believable as possible.

**You were a mother yourself at this point, correct?**

Yeah, I had a little boy. That was a trip, too. I was working on the tv show *A Different World*. When they found out I had a baby, it didn't go well.

**Why not?**

Lisa Bonet had left and they didn't want an unwed mother on the show. I didn't find that out until ten years later from someone who worked on the show and had power. It is what it is. And there weren't a lot of roles out there, but I worked back-to-back, so I do believe I paved the way for a lot of people who weren't previously working.

**Oh my god. As if I needed another reason to hate Bill Cosby.**

Things happen, that's all I can say. People are not kind in this business. Everybody's desperate. I'm grateful for the career I've had, but I'm just a different person, man. My outlook is different because I grew up very fast. I was in the system, and things that most people want to do, I've already "been there, done that" a couple of times. Everyone's hanging out, but I gotta go home. I have a real house note, you know? I've worked with many actors, but I'm still that same person. At that time, the coke was free-flowing and people thought they could just talk mess. You don't have to agree with me, but you're not gonna disrespect me, no matter how famous you are. People know that, and I've gotten jobs because I've spoken up for myself. You can't always go looking for someone else's validation. It's how I live my life.

**Did you ever get a sense of many changes happening during production?**

My thing is, I come to work prepared. Of course, they're trying to shoot a certain amount of pages every day. We had an excellent DP. It wasn't crazy for me. There was one time when I got food poisoning and I thought I was gonna die. (laughs) That wasn't me jumping off the diving board, but I still had to swim. A day later, they shut down the set for five days because everyone got sick. But I'm gangster like that. I still do that shit. There's a lot of people who don't even have jobs, so don't complain. If you're that sensitive, and you can't roll with it, maybe you should've be in this business, you know? If stuff changes, it changes. You're not the first person on the call sheet. Just do your thing and get up on out of there. That's how I look at it.

I didn't interact much with Robert, which was good, because our scene felt real. I didn't meet him until then and he was in full makeup. It wasn't contrived in that way. It was a great experience, though. I'd do another horror movie, but you never know how they're gonna turn out. I've turned down some stuff and it was like "Wow, this thing went on to do how many sequels?" But it can't be about the money.

**The cast of *The Dream Child* has a chemistry you can't fake. From meeting you all, it seems like you genuinely liked each other.**

You know, I've worked with difficult people, and I could always get my check and go home, but everybody [on part five] was super-cool. I didn't have any issues and we all had a good time.

**Is there anything else you'd like to bring up about *The Dream Child* that people don't really talk about?**

Oh my gosh, I think I've talked about it so much. I'm just so appreciative that people still love these films. I've had three generations of families come to conventions and it's a part of their life. That's amazing to me. Vulnerable individuals say "Oh if it wasn't for me seeing you at this point in my life…" You don't think you have that kind of impact, but you do. I'm grateful for that. It's movie history, you know?

# INTERVIEW
## JOE SEELY
### "MARK"

***The Dream Child* was your big breakthrough, but where did you go after?**

I discovered theater and my agent quit the business. I was like "Okay, I love theater, so I'll do that for a while, and I'll just jump in later." But I never did, so that's why you haven't seen me much. I've done some low budget stuff for my friends. I love my friends, but those movies didn't turn out as great. But I've done a lot of theater and performance art. I build puppets and masks. I have a lot of fun, and I was doing that even before *Nightmare on Elm Street*. That's one of the reasons they thought playing Mark would be a good fit for me. I was already drawing a comic and all that stuff.

People ask me about Mark being a skater, and they asked me at the audition what I was doing that [upcoming] weekend. I told them I was skating downtown and they said "Okay, Mark's a skater now." And there it was.

**You mentioned having a different vision for Mark. Can you talk about that?**

Well, everything was happening fast. They asked me "What do you wanna do? What do you like to wear?" I said "Well, I see him in skulls." I was thinking he was more goth, which was new back then, but they put a lot of color in [my outfit] because they were gonna do the black and white sequence later. They needed to see a change. I saw him as this sort of dark character, who drew all the time. I wanted dark hair with blue highlights, but they gave me blonde highlights. (laughs)

**You still definitely see him as an outsider character, and a fan favorite.**

Thank you, that's nice to hear. I definitely was [an outsider] and I still am. It's kind of me, too. I've always been this guy who is on the outside, doing weird stuff like performance art. I've toured around. For one show, I was wearing a monkey suit for a performance art piece about identity. I played a half-lizard half lizard demigod in another show. That's the kind of stuff I've been doing.

**Did you design the suits?**

I did actually design the masks and then co-designed the bodies. They were cool. I still have the monkey suit.

**You've previously mentioned the constant script changes, but can you recall any of those changes?**

Everything changed! It was a big blur of change. I was being dutiful, doing my thing, and then...whammo. New pages, new pages, new pages. It got so consistent that I just stopped memorizing my lines, because they only got in the way.

**When did you realize Mark was a popular character?**

I think about fifteen years ago. (laughs) I was just a wild kid and I didn't change my hairstyle after that. I just let the blonde stuff grow out. People would go "Hey, I love your show!" Then that went away and I was just me doing me, making masks and puppets and doing wild theater performances and stuff like that.

I think it was Thommy Hutson who brought me in for the documentary [*Never Sleep Again*], then the first con I went to was Monster Mania in Cherry Hill, New Jersey. People really came out. I think just recently people are starting to appreciate that character and part five more, because I think it's really cool.

I wasn't sure what I thought about it early on because it was such a blur, but as time is going on, I see it as really prescient. They were dealing with some really interesting stuff, like women's power and autonomy. I have a great appreciation for that because I'm a feminist. I want women to have control over their own destinies.

**I just have to ask about your "Phantom Prowler" costume. Were there different designs before the one we saw on film?**

It happened really fast, man. When it was first drawn, he had a big, flat cowboy hat. The costume designer [Sara Markowitz] was great. I showed up and they put me in this old duster from Australia and strapped the leather around my head. (laughs) I was a skinny dude and I said "Give me a prosthetic neck. I need a superhero neck." They're like "Nah, we don't have time for that nonsense." But it was fun. The guns were attached to these metal elbows that would almost break all the time. The special effects for guys were like "Don't move the guns too much!" I was like "I'm gonna move the gun!" I also got my favorite line: "Time to die, you scar-faced limp dick." It's silly and it's funny like Freddy is funny. I got to throw my own zinger back at him.

**You said you were surprised you didn't film your own death scene. Do you remember, was it just going to be a shot of you under the debris?**

It's even more interesting than that. I didn't even know that I was dead. I showed up on set to find Lisa [Wilcox] and Kelly Jo [Minter] crying. I asked them why, and they said "You're dead." That was the first I heard of it. They had dressed someone up in my costume and stuck them under the bookshelf. That wasn't even me! We were shooting at such a rapid pace back then, that I had no idea what the next day was going to bring. Everything was changing all the time. I assumed that I would be killed a few days later as the Phantom Prowler, but I had no idea what was coming.

**Talk about how you bonded with your castmates. It's hard to pull off the dynamic of openly pining for a friend without being creepy or intolerable. It happens all the time, but it's not often portrayed like you and Erika Anderson as Greta.**

Well, we were all young actors living in LA, so we had a lot in common. It was easy to find common ground. I would have enjoyed Erika's company regardless of her appearance. She's a really nice person and fun to hang out with. Secondly, she's gorgeous, so being appreciative of her appearance wasn't difficult at all. It was all about letting both things be true while being a gentleman.

A production used cut-out of Mark's animated death from *The Dream Child*.

# INTERVIEW
## ERIKA ANDERSON
### "GRETA"

A Nightmare 5
ON ELM STREET
THE DREAM CHILD

**Do you have any Todd Masters stories?**

I love Todd Masters so much. We had a blast doing what we were doing. The best part of it for me was the makeup test. Once he put the makeup on, you had to do a series of exercises to see what angles and movements look good [on camera]. You move your jaw and all that. He videotaped the whole thing, so we can see it. It was really interesting to me, because I had never done prosthetics before and it's very involved. It took a couple of hours at the studio to do the casts. He had a cast of my stomach and my lower face.

The makeup itself was like three hours every day. Everybody got to go home at the end of the day and I still had to stick around and get all that stuff off. That's a lot of time. I think things have gotten better now. They snap things on and off, which makes it easier. I spent a lot of time with Todd and we're still friends, so I'm happy about that. I haven't seen him in a long time because he doesn't live near me.

**When you get the script and it reads "Greta is what God creates on a good day," do you think "I've got this," or do you become self-conscious?**

I don't. How do I say this? I ignore stuff like that because it just gets in the way. I am who I am, and if it requires makeup or wardrobe for me to change, it's physical and on the outside. I just think about internal stuff more.

**You mentioned in *Never Sleep Again* that part of why you got the role was because a lot of girls weren't willing to get ugly, and you were. Did you know the extent of it?**

I was excited to do it, but I didn't know how grotesque it was going to be. (laughs) I'd never done a horror film before, even though I loved them. Every movie is different, so you don't really know what to expect. It's the surprises that are the best part, really.

**Even for three hours a day? That must have taken some adjusting.**

Well again, that was fine. [Todd's] whole team was great. They let me listen to the music I wanted to listen to. It was fun.

**I've always considered these films to be about friendship, and how your peers might be there for you when your parents won't. The chemistry feels real for the whole cast. Can you talk about how that came about and how you developed a rapport with Joe [Seely]?**

I think from the script, it was pretty obvious that Joe and I were close. I like to try and develop similar relationships when I make films, which are kind of based in reality. So, I hung around with him a lot, but the surprise of that is that he's such an amazing person, that we actually did become really good friends. I think whenever you're doing a movie and there is a real relationship that's being captured, it's palpable. You can feel that. You can see it on the screen, and all of it helps.

**Joe's character pines after Greta, but she has a real friendship with him. That's a difficult balancing act to pull off, but I thought you both did.**

It's funny, because I am still really good friends with someone that I met in third grade. We talk almost every day, and he is very different from me, but we've maintained our friendship over the years and I kind of based [Greta's] relationship with Mark in the film on the relationship that I have with my friend Ronnie. That's what you try to do, but part of it is chemistry. When the chemistry is there, you always can tell.

# FREDDY'S DEAD
## THE FINAL NIGHTMARE

New Line Cinema had garnered the reputation of being "The House That Freddy Built," and now they wanted to close shop and move on. *The Dream Child* was a financial success, but not to the same degree as *The Dream Master*. There was still a hunger for these films, but behind the scenes, everyone was just tired. Even a script by nascent genre director Peter Jackson couldn't get off the ground (though it started a relationship with New Line, which eventually led him to direct *The Lord of the Rings*, so thanks again, Freddy!) Plus, the continuity of the earlier films had painted the series into a corner. If Alice and Jacob Johnson weren't around, who would "feed" Freddy his victims? The answer was to start fresh in order to end strong. Who better to wrap things up than the "Zelig" of the *Elm Street* films, Rachel Talalay?

Talalay (pronounced Tah-LUH-lay. Get it right. She deserves it.) had been working her way up the ranks of New Line Cinema since the 80s, from being a production assistant to the assistant production manager on the original *Nightmare on Elm Street*. In fact, she's worked on every *Nightmare on Elm Street* film up to this point, except part five, since she was producing John Waters' *Cry Baby* for New Line. Bob Shaye had asked her to produce part six after she was successful with part four, but she instead asked to direct. It was her time to shine as the first (and at this time only) female director of a *Nightmare on Elm Street* film, and as one of the few recognizable female horror directors. (Though thankfully, not the last.) Let's begin at the end with *Freddy's Dead: The Final Nightmare*. I want to tell you to stop laughing, but that's not what the filmmakers had in mind...

## DREAM SCENARIO

Main titles begin over an ominous guitar melody. We get another pre-credit quote, this one by Nietzsche. It's spooky... until the melody takes a sharp turn into the 90s grunge as we see another quote, this one by Freddy. You're either rolling your eyes through the rest of the Goo Goo Dolls' "I'm Awake Now," or smiling as you anticipate the ride that's coming. If you've gone to a screening of the film at Alamo Drafthouse, you might be cheering, but either way, viewers have a good sense of the kind of movie we're getting.

We're treated to the series' first and only information crawl on a digital map of the US. It highlights the plight of Springwood, Ohio via MS DOS-like text. "10 years from now, all the teenagers are dead. Adults are experiencing mass psychosis." It's a shocking turn of events, but one teenager has survived, and we meet him during a turbulent plane ride. We never learn his name, but he's given the moniker "John Doe," so let's stick with that. John (Shon Greenblatt, no relation) is afraid of heights and really wants to change his seat. Lightning strikes the night sky outside the plane. A little girl with pigtails (Cassandra Friel) seems unbothered. She's also the only one on the plane who's looking him in the eyes. "He's going to make you help him," she tells him, "because you're the last."

"Do you know the terror of he who falls asleep?
To the very toes he is terrified,
Because the ground gives way under him,
And the dream begins..."
— Friedrich Nietzsche

"Welcome to Prime Time, bitch."
— Freddy Krueger

The salty woman sitting next to him is suddenly sucked out of the plane through the ceiling, but only John seems to notice. He yells "It's not fair, I was almost out!" (We're definitely in a dream.) John proceeds to fall out of the plane and wake up in his bed. All is well, until he realizes his house is falling through space. Why isn't he dead? Maybe Freddy can answer that when he shows up a moment later. Riding a broomstick and sporting a witch hat straight out of *The Wizard of Oz*, this is our introduction to the hammiest Englund has ever been. He's half-Beetlejuice at this point. The house crashes, propelling John out the window, yet he's unharmed for some reason. He stumbles over to the next house, which he's shocked to see is 1428 Elm Street in all its decrepit glory. So much for that plane ride.

He runs away from the house (some self-awareness in the years before *Scream*), and tumbles down a steep hill. He winds up at a deserted bus stop, which is really just a lone ticket booth occupied by a creepy ticket taker (Bob Shaye, natch). John stumbles into the road and is immediately hit by a coach bus driven by Freddy. (An acting role *and* Freddy's driving a bus? It's a great day for Shaye!). For reasons unexplained, John is still alive. Freddy literally knocks him through a tear in reality shaped like a human cutout. Strangely, it's daylight on the other side. Freddy exits the bus and approaches the tear with curiosity. It promptly seals up as soon as he touches it, keeping him in the night realm. Did he expect this?

John isn't dead, after all, but he wakes up, having hit his head on a rock. Checking his pockets, he finds an old newspaper clipping from a town called Springwood, which reads "Krueger Woman Still Missing." Krueger "woman?" That sounds like some vital exposition, but unfortunately for everyone, John has amnesia. There doesn't seem to be anything around for miles, except a city in the distance, which is where he heads. At this point, it's clear Freddy has another plan that involves keeping his would-be prey alive like in *Freddy's Revenge* and *The Dream Child*. Those are historically the least-appreciated entries up until this point, but let's see where this goes.

The city John enters contains a youth shelter, which contains most of our cast. Dr. Maggie Burroughs (Lisa Zane) is one the on-site therapists who tries to reach the kids who come through her doors. This includes Spencer (Breckin Meyer in an early role), the son of a conceited yuppie whose cars he gladly sets on fire. Spencer would rather play a handheld Tiger Electronics game than talk to his dad (and those games *sucked*, even back then). Maggie tells him one day he'll have to face his father. Suddenly, the police chase the unruly Tracy (Lezlie Deane) into the main room. She apparently assaulted someone who was hitting on her. Maggie tells the cops she doesn't like to be touched, which doesn't excuse her, but we're already getting hints that the local police couldn't care less.

We see Tracy working out her anger issues on the heavy bag in the shelter's gym. Her friend Carlos (Ricky Dean Logan) eggs her on and then takes out his hearing aid to mock her. The sound drops out when his hearing aid comes off, implying he'd be functionally deaf without it. Spencer appears and puts it back in his ear. The trio are planning to steal a van from the shelter and run away to California. They all have their reasons, mostly involving their awful parents.

Time to check in with the other shelter therapist, "Doc" (Yaphet Kotto). Maggie comes to his office to lament about Tracy. Doc specializes in dreams, and wouldn't you know it, Maggie has a recurring dream she doesn't understand. Instead of seeking peer review, she's drawn to a poster on Doc's wall. It features three mythical dream demons who, legend has it, seek out evil people and give them immense power. (Who ever could that be?)

When a pair of cops find John wandering the streets, they bring him to the shelter instead of creating more paperwork for themselves. Upon meeting him, Maggies recognizes his newspaper clipping from her recurring dream. They've both seen the little girl with the pigtails. In fact, they dream of her again that night. Maggie dreams of the woman shown in the clippings. Their link isn't clear, but she says "I won't tell" and screams before Maggie wakes up. John can't stay awake in the shelter dorms. The little girl shows up and he realizes he's in the Elm Street house. He finds a padded room where he sees a vision of himself in a straight jacket, who yells "Free me you idiot, I'm your fucking memory!" Naturally, John flips out.

Despite the glaring evidence, Maggie doesn't want to believe her recurring dream is linked to this mysterious new kid. (Come on Maggie, be a Neil, not a Simms!) Doc is insistent that she bring John to Springwood for answers, so they head out in one of the shelter's vans. John falls asleep on the way there, but once they cross the town border, he dreams of the little girl in the middle of the road, imploring them to turn around. He wakes up and grabs the wheel from Maggie, while the force of the van's spin forces stowaways Carlos, Spencer, and Tracy out of the back. (Maybe the shelter just has one van? Cutbacks affect everyone.)

A furious Maggie insists they find a phone to call the shelter. They find one at the eerie town carnival, where there's not a child in sight, but there are a bunch of adults acting out. Spencer finds the phone isn't working, just as the kids encounter a strange local couple played by Roseanne and Tom Arnold (who wanted to cameo). The couple have strange southern accents for an Ohio town. They talk about losing their children to "him," and the trio bolts to the van. Oddly, they can't seem to leave the town. Tracy doesn't realize Carlos dozed off when she asks him for the map. He dreams that the map keeps unfolding out to an impossible size, until it finally reads in big red letters: "You're fucked!" They get fed up and decide to sleep in one of the many abandoned houses they find. The affluent Spencer is taken aback, but Carlos and Tracy have obviously been in worse conditions. As soon as they enter, the house physically bursts and transforms into good ol' 1428 Elm Street. We know where this is headed, but lest we forget, they're *awake*. How is this happening?

John and Maggie look for answers at the local high school, which is as empty as the rest of the town. (We're a long way from a concerned Lin Shaye teaching *Hamlet*.) They find a classroom with a crazed teacher instructing a class with no students. Newspaper clippings featuring missing children adorn the classroom, including the very paper that John's article came from. In his ramblings, he mentions "They took [Freddy's] child!" Child? It's unheard of to imagine Freddy Krueger as a father (*The Dream Child* notwithstanding), but John gets the idea that it's him. Why else wouldn't Freddy kill him right away?

Carlos, Tracy, and Spencer enter the run-down house, and Carlos immediately passes out on an unmade bed. He dreams of hearing Tracy call him from the hallway, which has turned from a run-down house to a tenement apartment building complete with bustling neighbors. His abusive mom appears before him with the longest cotton swab known to man. She threatens to "clean out" his ears (most certainly what caused his hearing damage in the first place) and he begs her not to. But of course, Carlos's mother turns into Freddy, who shoves the Q-Tip in his ear in a scene that makes me, and so many others, squeal. Freddy slices off his ear, causing the sound to drop out, except for Carlos's heartbeat and ragged breathing. He laughs at the young man, then tosses him through a brick wall and into the boiler room. (We missed you, old friend.) Neither Carlos nor the audience can hear Freddy as he whoops and hollers around him just for fun. Eventually, Freddy gives Carlos back his ear, as if he could just reattach it... until he reattaches it and latches onto his head like a parasite. Now the smallest sound hurts him physically. Carlos hears a leaky faucet that pounds like an anvil. He races to turn off and Freddy drops a pin, which he hears falling like a bomb. He catches it, but of course, Freddy has more than he can catch at once. The chuckling sadist finally takes out a chalkboard, which impossibly elongates like a Warner Brothers cartoon, vamping the whole time like he's doing a trick. Freddy's claws scrape all over the board, making a cacophony that eventually causes Carlos' head to explode. Back in the waking world, Tracy finds Carlos's bed inexplicably empty. Freddy always leaves a body, so where is he?

Since John doesn't remember his parents, he and Maggie take a trip to the local orphanage. Like the school classroom, it's empty except for one woman addressing several children who aren't there. Though unlike the nutty professor, this woman recognizes both John *and* Maggie from when they were children. It would be great if she could provide more information, but two of the "kids" are fighting. They find a child's drawing of a family standing in front of a house. The father has a familiar red and green sweater, and the house is 1428 Elm Street, looking like it's the most livable since *Freddy's Revenge*. The picture is signed "K. Krueger," who must be the lone child in the drawing. Is this just more of Freddy's manipulation? Isn't this drawing supposed to be old? They leave the orphanage and run into Tracy, who's looking for Carlos.

It's a credit to screenwriters Talalay and Michael DeLuca for drawing out a mystery we haven't seen in these films in a long time. DeLuca would later hone his ability to write about creepy small towns a few years later by penning the script for John Carpenter's Lovecraftian odyssey *In the Mouth of Madness*. His screenwriting career would end as he would transition to the executive level at New Line Cinema and Warner Brothers.

Back at the house, Spencer gets stoned on the couch and is mystified by an old, busted television. He's not quite asleep, but the weed is working its magic.

Suddenly, the tv works, showing zombified teens milling about and looking at him through the screen. Carlos, looking totally normal, head and all, pushes his way through Freddy's collected souls. Spencer's happy to see his friend, who tries to warn him, just like when Rick and the "soul pizza" scene from part 4. It's no use, as Spencer dreams of an anti-drug PSA starring the world famous Oprah Noodlemantra! (Okay, it's actually an uncredited Johnny Depp, but that was the name he used to keep the cameo under wraps, and it's absolutely worth repeating. This doesn't appear to be the return of Glen, but rather a sight gag that repeats the then-popular ad where an egg is fried and the narrator reveals it to be "your brain on drugs.") Freddy shows up and hits Mr. Noodlemantra with a frying pan, making Spencer laugh. Freddy gets down to business by sucking the unwitting Spencer into the tv as he's surrounded by fun, psychedelic colors that envelop him as we hear the opening of Iron Butterfly's "In-A-Gadda-Da-Vida."

As previewed earlier, Spencer loves video games, and he winds up in a 2D sidescroller with 1991-era graphics. An 8-bit version of his father hits him with a tennis racket and bleats out "Be like me!" Back in the boiler room's security station, we see Freddy "playing" the video game on a tv. (Talk about slacking on the job). Freddy's having so much fun, he doesn't even mind when Spencer starts to "win" by beating his digital father

Let's hit the pause button for a second (or "Start" on the Nintendo controller). This is Freddy unlike we've seen him before. He's still sadistic, but he's enjoying his "soul food" much more. At this point in the series timeline, Freddy has killed every minor in Springwood. Since the souls of his victims give him power, he's effectively become a trickster God who can manipulate the waking world to a degree. Curiously, his power is limited within the physical borders of the town of Springwood. Freddy doesn't kill anyone right away because he knows for a fact that he will get them eventually. This seems on paper like it would be paradise, but he clearly has a bigger plan at play.

Tracy brings Maggie and John back to the house, which Maggie realizes is the same one from her dream. Spencer's missing until John "finds" him when he flies through the wall. Freddy is kicking his ass in the video game, and the effects are showing all over the house as Spencer's body crashes into walls with cartoon sound effects. Maggie can only watch on helplessly, unable to rouse him. (And why is Freddy trashing his own home?)

Convinced he's Freddy's son and thus not in danger, John decides to go in and help Spencer. Tracy is reluctant to help him, as she mentioned Doc showed her a better way. John doesn't have time for exposition, so he slaps her to provoke her to knock him unconscious. She obliges and pummels him onto the nearby table. John phases through it just like Nancy in *Dream Warriors* and Mark in *Dream Child*. (It's great to see that special effect one last time.)

Like Carlos, John falls into the boiler room, right outside Freddy's office/gaming lounge. Tracy appears beside him in a cascade of light, her "better way" to quickly fall asleep. Now, Tracy, John, and Spencer are in the same dream. (Is this a massive breach of continuity, or is it a possibility since Alice isn't guarding her gate anymore? Maybe Freddy's so powerful that all dreams in Springwood are his dreams. That's a terrifying prospect.) Tracy grabs Freddy's controller, seemingly ending his torment of Spencer, but he turns his razor hand into the "Power Glove" and locks them out of his office.

Now that Freddy's back controlling Spencer, he knocks him around a bit more, until the floor opens up and sends Spencer tumbling down the "Freddy hole" from part five. Only instead of feeding Jacob, it's delivering Spencer's soul right to Freddy. The television Spencer was watching fills up with blood, as Freddy enjoys his latest kill right in front of Tracy and John. At this point, Tracy has *had it*. As if accessing her dream power immediately, she vaults over to Freddy and kicks him right in the crotch (it truly was the beginning of the 90's). Though she's motivated by rage, it's refreshing to see someone who doesn't know who Freddy is jump right into the fray, but Maggie wakes her before he can kill her with a swipe of the claw. John's still asleep, so they drag him to the van and flee the town.

John wakes up in his bed. Again. But he's not taking the bait, declaring "Nothing is gonna make me get off this bed." And then it catches fire. He jumps out the window with a sigh, plummeting to the ground once again. This time, he sees a tag on his shirt. He pulls it, turning his shirt into a giant parachute. (Thanks, Freddy…?) In a bit of shared dream/reality physics, when he opens the parachute, the force sucks him through the van ceiling. Maggie stops the van and they run out to get him.

Freddy appears to John within the parachute. Father and son are finally face to face, except "John" isn't K. Krueger after all. As the last surviving teenager of Springwood, in a town full of delusional adults, Freddy needed John to leave Springwood to act as bait in order to bring back his daughter. His *daughter*? Before we can get answers, Freddy cuts John's parachute and he plummets to the ground, landing on a bed of spikes Freddy placed (while huffing, puffing, and breaking the fourth wall to point out his annoyance). John dies in Maggie's arms while large spiked holes in his chest bleed out. The effect looks great, and reminiscent of the puffs in a pool raft. He tries to warn her "it's not a b-" before his soul enters Freddy. We never even knew his real name.

Just like we saw the souls of his victims enter his body, Freddy becomes a flash of ghostly light himself, which enters Maggie's mind. Tracy can't see it happen, though she's been pleading with her to get back in the van. They burn rubber and cross the town line, shattering an invisible barrier. Goodbye, Springwood. Hello…*world*?

Back at the shelter, Tracy and Maggie take a second to let the past day sink in. Maggie absentmindedly runs four fingers on the condensation build-up on her window. Tracy, always of few words, tells her it's not her fault as she gets out of the van. They both later discover that nobody else in the shelter remembers Carlos, John or Spencer. Strangely, some of the other kids dream about Carlos. Only Maggie, Tracy and Doc remember them. Doc says Freddy must have "*erased*" them from the collective consciousness. (It's a little too convenient and based on the lax attitude of local law enforcement, they could just make up a story that they ran away. Personally, I like that it makes the case for Freddy's near omnipotence at this point. "Pride goeth," as they say…)

Maggie cries as she considers John's final words "It's not a boy." On instinct, she visits her mother. Or rather her *adopted* mother. Maggie discovers adoption documents, much to her mother, Mrs. Burroughs' surprise. That night, more of Maggie's recurring dream is revealed. The pigtail girl with the red ribbons finally learns what's upsetting her mother in the basement of her suburban house. She discovers a hidden lair with several other Freddy-like gloves. This is Freddy's house and the pigtail girl is Katherine Krueger, later adopted into the Burroughs family and given the name "Maggie" to protect her identity.

We'll still call her "Maggie" because, as she tells Freddy, she knows who she is. Even after she appears in the dream looking like an adult "pigtail girl." She's afraid of him, and the truth, but she gets in his face, defiant. Freddy explains that she's "his blood" and he needed her to return to Springwood to bring him out. He also implies that killing the local children was revenge for taking her away from him after his arrest (though let's be real, he was already well into his killing spree by then). Freddy's ready to let bygones be bygones, since his plan is finally revealed. He tells Maggie an infamous line that had to have appeared in many a New Line Cinema marketing meeting: "Every town has an Elm Street." That's why he didn't care that Spencer wrecked the house. Springwood's in his rearview. Maggie wakes up, but Freddy's on his way to stretch his post-Springwood legs.

Tracy dreams that she exits the shelter's bathroom and finds herself in a decrepit house. Not Freddy's, but rather her own home, complete with her disgusting, abusive father. She shows some rare vulnerability as the source of her anger appears before her, ready to molest her, yet again. It's exceptionally icky. Before it can go further, she says her dad is dead and she furiously beats him with a tea kettle, pulverizing his face. Sure enough, it's Freddy, but Doc's teachings have emboldened her to stand tall in her own dreams. Tracy gets pissed when he shows off Carlos's earpiece, but she survives their brief fight before waking herself up on the flames of the kitchen stove (damn, this girl is a natural dream warrior). She wakes up screaming, but Maggie's there to bring her to Doc for the final confrontation.

Doc hears Tracy calling in the shelter gym, but it's just Freddy's mimicry. Freddy appears to the dream doctor and proceeds to cut off his fingers to prove his immortality. He even counts them off: burning, burying, and holy water, his personal favorite (and a lot of ours', too). But the fingers appear whole momentarily. He gloats about how dream demons "gave [him] this job" before he goes in for the kill. Thinking fast, Doc rips off a piece of his sweater and wakes himself up as Tracy and Maggie rush into his office. He has an idea. It's time to fulfill the promise of the original film and pull Freddy into our world to die.

Doc hooks Maggie up to a sleep machine so he can pull her out based on the intensity of the readings. He and Tracy keep watch, though Tracy wants to go in with her. Maggie says it has to be "him and me." Doc gives her a pair of 3D glasses to act as a totem that can help her in the dreamscape. (There's been so much talk of bringing objects "out" of the dream, but not much about bringing them in. Alice brought in Sheila's bug zapper, but that's really it. It's a nice reversal.) Maggie falls asleep and enters the negative gate, bypassing the three dream demons in Doc's poster.

(One more note: *Freddy's Dead* came to theaters with a 3D finale almost twenty years before the resurgence of 3D with James Cameron's *Avatar*. Everyone who saw the film on TV or home video missed the 3D aspects, which were mostly easy to ignore when you don't have the capabilities at home. They're inconsequential to the plot, but a noble, if unsuccessful attempt to add something to the grand finale.)

After years of violating the mental landscapes of his victims and exposing their inner fears and desires, Freddy's daughter turns it around on him. She enters his mind and finds herself in what looks like a subway station with several doors and electrical currents (possibly his synapses). She enters one door and sees Freddy as a child, killing the class hamster offscreen as the rest of the kids make fun of him. Door number two jumps a few years later to teenage Freddy masochistically cutting himself. His foster father (another cameo, this time from Alice Cooper) tries to beat him, but Freddy's learned to enjoy it. He kills him offscreen with a razor. Door number three takes us to the night Freddy was killed by the parents of Springwood. The dream demons offer him immortality before he can burn to death, and he takes it. (The demons are actually all CGI, a rarity for the films of 1991, but a preview of what was about to happen to the industry as a whole.)

Finally, Maggie sees the entirety of her lifelong, recurring dream. Her parents were Fred and Loretta Krueger. When Loretta discovered his lair of evil and weaponry in the basement of their quaint, suburban house, she flipped out in front of their daughter. Fred, in turn, strangled his wife on the spot. When he realized little Katherine saw the lair, too, he decided not to kill her, but made her keep it a secret… only she didn't. Katherine told and he was caught. Freddy finds her, and with a great deal of effort, she pulls him out of the dream as Doc wakes her up. But he's not there. Time to tool up.

Doc, Maggie, and Tracy go to the shelter basement, where confiscated items are stored. The contraband included bats, several edged weapons, and even a pipe bomb Spencer made (A round of applause for the cops who were too lazy to collect these). Maggie is drawn to a makeshift pen in the basement, cut off by a door and a fence. She finds Freddy there, bleeding but alive. His burnt visage is gone, and he looks like his human self. It's a ruse to elicit sympathy, and God bless Robert Englund for selling it for a hot second. Of course, we all know it's a trick, so she knocks his glove off with a baseball bat. He might be mortal, but Freddy's dream powers are still intact. He locks Doc and Tracy out of the pen so he can fight Maggie to the death. (Snitches get four vertical stitches, even if they're your daughter.)

Maggie cuts him with his glove and they fight for a while. He climbs on the ceiling in a last bit of reverence for the original *Nightmare*, then she breaks his fingers. He gets the glove back, but before he can put it on, she pins him to a load-bearing column with the sharp objects she took from the locker. She then stabs him with the glove, and shoves Spencer's now-lit pipe bomb in his wound. Freddy *explodes*, now dead. We see the dream demons fly away, still at large. Now let's all enjoy a montage of the films up to this point.

## NIGHTMARE AUTOPSIS

It's time to address the red-and-green striped elephant in the room. Yes, *Freddy's Dead: The Final Nightmare* is incredibly strange and proudly goofy. Aside from Sam Raimi's *The Evil Dead* or Joe Dante's segment in *Twilight Zone: the Movie*, it feels like the only other horror film from the time period inspired by *Looney Tunes*. All three of the death scenes have an elasticity to their methods of torment: the chalkboard, the sound effects as the house gets destroyed, and Freddy breaking the fourth wall to wordlessly gripe about planting a death trap worthy of Wile E. Coyote. (Mr. Coyote could not be reached for comment, as he is currently embroiled in a lawsuit of his own.)

In addition to the popularity of the Power Glove, 1990 saw David Lynch create *Twin Peaks*, one of the biggest cult shows in television history. It was also profoundly and unapologetically weird. Combine its ascendancy with Talalay's previous role as a producer on a cameo-filled comedy from John Waters, and it goes a long way towards explaining the decisions made to finish the franchise in this way.

You may not agree with everything that Rachel Talalay did for Freddy's swan song. but you can't deny it was done by someone who'd seen it all. After the rushed productions and dearth of story in *Dream Master* and *Dream Child*, she wanted a meatier tale to build up the mythology before putting a cap on everything. It was even her idea to call it *Freddy's Dead: The Final Nightmare*, instead of *A Nightmare on Elm Street 6*. And boy, does it earn that feeling of finality, not just because this the first *Nightmare* film without a sequel tag. Talalay made sure the sixth entry in the *Nightmare on Elm Street* films was wildly different from any other entry, while also making it the sum total of all the films that came before it. Even Springwood feels like an empty shell of itself. A tumbleweed in the empty Ohio fields, almost like one of the dried-out towns from *The Grapes of Wrath*. *Freddy's Dead* enhances the legend, while making it feel definitive.

The *Nightmare on Elm Street* films are a series about how children pay for the sins of their dangerously flawed elders. Talalay makes the story of Freddy Krueger come full-circle by revealing the self-mutilating, physics-defying, gleefully sadistic dream demon was revealed to be... a parent, himself. Thematically, the rules apply to him, too, and he must face the same judgment he was doling out. Some people aren't a fan of this retcon, but to me, it absolutely fits in with the franchise. The idea that Freddy was one of "them" is both insidious and enticing. How could a child murderer live amongst his victims while being a parent himself? We've certainly seen real-life examples with the BTK Killer and John Wayne Gacy, not to mention Wes Craven's own *The People Under the Stairs* (released the same year as *Freddy's Dead*) By the end of the 1980's, it was possible to believe evil was living right next door, over the shared picket fence and dueling manicured lawns.

There are plenty of questions this brings up. Did the Kruegers know the Thompsons or any of the families of the kids he killed? Did he target Katherine's friends and classmates? Also, was 1428 Elm Street the Krueger residence *before* the Thompsons lived there? I couldn't imagine Marge and Don, having just murdered a man in cold blood thinking "Hey, let's remodel the murder room," and if so, it absolutely would have been part of the story Marge told Nancy. I don't believe they moved into Freddy's house, but I do think he used the Elm Street house we've seen to stir Maggie's memories. So score one sensibility point for the Thompson family.

We also have a soundtrack again! *The Dream Child* had an odd mix of hip-hop and hair metal, but the genres didn't speak to each other the way later soundtracks would (including *Judgement Night*, a subsequent film by *Dream Child* director Stephen Hopkins. Maybe he learned a lesson?). In addition to an orchestral score by Brian May that evokes "Flight of the Bumblebee," we also have some grunge for the first time. Before they blew up a few years later, The Goo Goo Dolls contributed several songs to the soundtrack, including the title sequence song, "I'm Awake Now" and "You Know What I Mean" when the van looks for an exit from Springwood. Years before Iron Butterfly was mined for a classic episode on *The Simpsons* (oddly enough about losing your soul), we heard it here as Spencer is sucked into the broken tv. And who can forget Iggy Pop's raucous metal riff over the end credit montage? Lisa Zane even contributes a song.

For perhaps the first time in the series, Freddy Krueger doesn't really try to be scary. Make no mistake, he's still a threat and Englund sells the menace, but as Freddy brushes with omnipotence, his hubris brings about his downfall. He's the hare and the world is his tortoise. Fear has always been his battery, but when you've consumed all of your resources, gaining the power to alter reality, where do you go? Why put on a scary face when you're having the time of your life clowning around, sipping souls by the furnace?

I've repeatedly taken umbrage at the idea that Freddy became a stand-up comic instead of the fierce killer he started out as. He was always a killer first and a jokester second. That's not a microphone, folks. That's a razor sharp hand coming to kill you and swallow your soul. However, it should be noted that *Freddy's Dead* is the first entry where he doesn't kill anyone with his claw. Not for a lack of trying, of course. Freddy's makeup in this entry is also an improvement on his worn, weathered look from *The Dream Child*. The makeup allows Englund to be the most expressive version of Freddy, and possibly the most human. It fits well for the story being told.

Talalay claimed she always tried to keep what worked about *Dream Warriors*, one of the high-water marks of the series, and roll it over to the subsequent films in the franchise. The paradigm is in place once again as we follow troubled teens and a faulty, but well-meaning institution. Instead of a mental hospital for suburban youths, we're in a shelter for runaway and at-risk teens in an undisclosed urban area. These new teens aren't just living in the shadow of their parents' lies. Carlos and Tracy bear signs of physical abuse.

Spencer may come from money, but he's in such a terrible spot with his father, he's committing arson. Neil Gordon would have his work cut out for him.

Maggie does what she can in the face of institutional decay, which is another aspect of the franchise Talalay and DeLuca focus on. Besides the crumbling infrastructure of the shelter, which appears to be under construction in several inconvenient places, the police we see in the film are worthless. They dump John at the shelter so they don't have to fill out paperwork, they let Tracy beat someone up (who maybe deserved it, but still), and they leave dangerous items where kids have access to them. The basement locker that doubles as an arsenal is supposed to be emptied out by local law enforcement. Maggie asks why the cops haven't picked it up yet and her supervisor, Kelly laments "The police are supposed to do a *lot* of things." Another supposed force for good that's failing the youth of America.

It's implied that Carlos is the glue of the group, as Spencer and Tracy don't seem to have much in common. In fact, they're borderline hostile to each other. Tracy is one of the angriest characters in the series, even before she meets Freddy. It takes him a while to finally get to her via the illusion of her father, but the fact that she sees through him and won't back down is another indicator that this would be the last film in the series. Debbie talked a good game in *The Dream Master*, but she still fell for Freddy's tricks. Tracy fights him, almost from the start. It's not hard to imagine her sharing a cot with Taryn as they protect each other from predators on the streets.

We're also leaving the version of Springwood we know behind and entering an urban atmosphere. It's not exactly *Freddy Takes Cleveland*, but there's more grit in the shelter than previous locales in the series. New Line Cinema would expand its slate to release films like *House Party* and *Menace II Society* to a broader, more diverse audience than ever before. It also continued its tradition of having strong Black actors go up against Freddy. Whereas before we had Kincaid, Sheila, and Yvonne as teens, we have Yaphet Kotto's Doc as the best shrink in the house and the smartest character in the film.

Yet another irony is that these films are full of children who are ignored by adults. We're told Freddy was finally arrested because his daughter was listened to when she revealed her father's crimes to the world. Maggie's arc is to regain her memory and identity and come to terms with a past she doesn't remember. Unlike Alice or Nancy coming of age in their youth, Maggie is an adult coming into her own, by reckoning with her missing pieces. Perhaps it's fitting that an adult, not a teenager, is the one to finally send Freddy to hell. The films are about teenage empowerment, but shouldn't that be the adult's role in society? To protect the children from evil? Surely the parents of Springwood thought they were doing that when they lit Freddy on fire, but Maggie fulfills that promise with the help of a teenager (Tracy) and a positive institutional force (Doc).

In *Never Sleep Again*, Robert Englund described *Freddy's Dead* as a time to "deconstruct and self-destruct." This couldn't be more apt. The music, the pop culture references, and 3D finale all come together to turn the film into the ultimate sendoff. Despite the later entries, it was truly intended to be the end. For some people, it might not go down smooth, but like the best characters in these films, it goes down swinging

## THE SHOOTING SCRIPT

The film's shooting script contains a few deleted scenes, which sometimes show up in TV versions and also in a workprint found on YouTube. Per this script, we don't meet Maggie at the shelter, but rather in her apartment as her (adopted) mother appears with a birthday cake. She's turning twenty-eight, which helps solidify the timeline more. Did Freddy wait for his daughter's birthday to enact his plan? Twenty-eight seems like a random age.

When we learn about the dream demons in Doc's office, he tells Maggie their ultimate goal is to permanently blend reality with nightmares. When Tracy later spars with Doc, he introduces the "concentration, meditation" phrase that Tracy repeats when she enters the dream world. In fact, Doc mentions if she tries hard enough, she can go into *anyone's* dream. This might seem like a massive retcon, but isn't that a version of what Kristen and Alice have already done? It's absolutely one of Freddy's abilities. It also fills the aforementioned plot hole when Tracy arrives next to John in the boiler room while slightly expanding the mythology.

Another standout implication is that the Springwood adults are afraid of John. When Tom Arnold's character ushers his wife away, he originally told John "You said you were getting out, but you brought back more!" That speaks to a backstory we never see, but remains fascinating. John also mentions the air in town makes you sleepy. It's not logical, but neither is the idea of a town stuck in a pocket dimension by a vengeful demon. When John and Maggie see the big chalk drawing of Freddy, a woman comes out to try and wash it away, to no avail. There's also graffiti near the high school that says "Glen loves Nancy." It's unnecessary, but a nice easter egg. When they arrive at the high school, we meet Sykes, a former teacher who has stapled his eyes open so he can't fall asleep. Blech. Later at the house, Maggie finds Freddy's lair before we see it in her dream. Wouldn't all that have been confiscated as evidence? Or maybe Freddy is just reforming reality to show it to her.

Back at the shelter, Tracy mentions the kids are dreaming of Carlos and Spencer, but Maggie's boss, Kelly, is dreaming of them, too. Tracy ponders the idea that they're all just Freddy's dream, which is too awful to dwell on, but a curious thought. The chalk drawing of Freddy later bubbles up on the street. A local child sees it and gets frightened. As the script says, children always know. When Maggie drives to the shelter for the final fight, homeless people stare at her as she drives like something from John Carpenter's *Prince of Darkness*. Also, Tracy doesn't spar with Freddy in her nightmare, which would have been a missed opportunity. (No "kung fu this, bitch?" Denied.)

After he dies, the big Freddy chalk drawing disappears. This shooting script ends with an epilogue where a little boy is being abused by his mother and we hear the whispering of the dream demons as they choose him to be their next avatar. Evil never dies, right?

## A NIGHTMARE ON ELM STREET 6

Freddy's final outing originally began as an outline by Rachel Talalay, which she then handed off to indie filmmaker Michael Almereyda (*Marjorie Prime, Tesla*) to flesh out into a full screenplay. With only a couple of produced scripts under his belt, Almereyda was widely viewed as a rising talent within the industry. Unfortunately, his *Nightmare 6* screenplay was very poorly received at New Line Cinema. ("Hate" is a strong word, but it's also the one Talalay uses to describe Almereyda's draft.) At this point, Talalay turned to executive producer and franchise veteran Michael De Luca for a fresh script based on her outline. This marked De

Luca's first proper feature writing credit, though he'd already cut his screenwriting teeth doing uncredited polishes on earlier *Nightmare* scripts and also on seven episodes of *Freddy's Nightmares*. While most of Almereyda's work was jettisoned, a few elements from his script carried over to the final film, prompting him to lobby the WGA to award him co-writing credit, which they denied.

Oddly enough, it was the Almereyda script that New Line chose to release in 1999 as a DVD-ROM feature on their *Nightmare on Elm Street Collection* boxset, which might've been an error on the studio's part. (No other *Nightmare* had an alternate draft included in this set, only their shooting scripts.) This alternate version of *Freddy's Dead* constitutes a fascinating "What if?" with a vastly different tone and much stronger continuity ties to earlier entries. Let's dig in.

Instead of "John Doe," we open on a now-teenage Jacob Johnson asleep on the airplane. He wakes up in time for another plane to collide with his. Wouldn't you know it, his plane is painted red and green. He narrowly misses getting decapitated by the other plane's wing, and instead falls out of the sky, still buckled in. During the fall, he sees the corpses of his fellow travelers right behind, er, above him. These include the jump rope kids, who sing the rhyme as the wind rips off their skin, and they become winged skeletons. They fly upwards, just as Jacob's shirt becomes a parachute. He breathes a sigh of relief, until realizing the wind current is taking him into the path of the skeleton kids, who cut his parachute. He plummets to the Earth, landing in his bedroom, where he wakes up. Well, that's a relief.

Alice pokes her head in to gently remind her son he'll be late for school. He opens the window and realizes the whole house is falling out of the sky, The skeleton kids return to taunt him as the house crashes in the ground, leaving a crater. Jacob emerges unscathed, but he notices a "darkness" forming. The script describes it as a growing shroud that passes over everything in sight, turning people into monsters, not that they even notice. He runs over the town line and sees Springwood covered in the inexplicable gloom.

Freddy emerges from the road and "inhales" the town gloom. Once he's finished, all that's left of Springwood is a giant vacant lot. Lifting his sweater, Freddy's stomach reveals swirling images of the town and its inhabitants. He then yanks Alice out of the ground and kills her with his blades right in front of her son. Despite ascending to the near godhood of the finished film, he still needs Jacob to give him "a ride." Before he can explain what that means, three Robocops appear out of nowhere.

(*Just kidding.* New Line never owned Robocop, but by the looks of this trio, Robocop would own *them* in court.) Clad in metallic black, dark visors, and heavy boots, these three enforcers are "the dream police." The reveal of their identities is saved for later, but it's initially obvious from the descriptions that they're Kincaid (Power Cop), Taryn (Blade Cop), and Joey (Sound Cop), the latter of whom wakes Jacob up with a supersonic scream. Just like John in the final film, Jacob wakes up in the middle of the deserted road. At least he has Alice's bracelet to remember her by. But wait a minute, did Freddy just *kill* Springwood?

Jacob hitchhikes to the nearby town of Rosedale and finds a halfway house in the middle of a neighborhood. Yes, a converted two-story suburban house that appears more respectable than the run-down shelter of *Freddy's Dead*. Jacob meets Karen, a teenager and resident there, and helps her carry in groceries in the face of local protesters. This angry mob doesn't want "dope fiends" and "pushers" near their kids, not that any of the residents have done anything like that. The house is run by David and Mary Ross, a couple who've never heard of Springwood, causing David to be suspicious of him.

In addition to Karen and now Jacob, the other teenage residents are Wesley, whose parents used to put cigarettes out on him, Gina, whose mother was a hooker who forced her into the trade, and Scott, a too-cool-for-school type who killed his abusive father in self-defense. (Yikes. This is low-hanging trauma fruit, even for Freddy Krueger.) As part of their agreement to live in the house, the kids do community service. During an outing, Jacob falls asleep and sees visions of a dark, demonic Springwood. That night, he further dreams of Freddy spitting hundreds of bugs out of his mouth. Jacob calls the other teens to a meeting where he lays out the truth about Freddy. He also theorizes that he's a "carrier," and that when he falls asleep, Freddy strikes. They don't believe him, so he plans to run away before Karen stops him. Jacob dreams of Alice's death again, causing him to have an epileptic seizure, which is mistaken for an overdose. An ambulance arrives and he's sedated just as he hears Freddy cackle "Every town has an Elm Street." A crooked Elm Street sign bursts from the ground, just like in the eventual film.

Now that Jacob's been asleep long enough, Freddy is free. The dream police show up and fight Freddy but fail to prevent his escape. How does he escape, you ask? He changes his clothes to an old-timey black-and-white convict outfit and jumps on a rope that falls through a hole in the ceiling. (Even this darker version of *Freddy's Dead* has a *Looney Tunes* influence!) The dream police confirm that Freddy has ripped a hole between dreams and reality. Jacob is still confused by the fan service, but it's honestly great to see Kincaid, Taryn, and Joey again, especially with amplified powers. Before they can get too far into expositional weeds, they confirm that they're still dead before Jacob wakes up in the hospital.

Back at the foster home, Wesley watches an old movie, which the script indicates features a cigarette-smoking makeup-free Robert Englund. He falls asleep and imagines "not-Freddy" talking to him through the screen, as the walls close in on him and his white blanket tightens around him. In a kill that echoes Debbie's death from *The Dream Master*, Wesley turns into a cigarette in a box that Freddy removes and smokes. Yes, he smokes him, lighting him on fire using a match shaped like Wesley's abusive father. When he's found, his body is burnt and charred, except for his head. There's a darkly funny moment when the coroner argues with his assistant, who can't believe he's "seen worse."

The neighbors are pissed and the other kids are distraught. Jacob surmises that Freddy's victims are giving him the power to swallow another town. Everyone balks when he mentions the dream police (understandably). Later, Karen tells Jacob how she dreams of her father killing her mother. They discuss dreaming, which Jacob claims they're already doing. The pair then enter a forest where Karen shapeshifts for fun. It's very romantic until she discovers a door and impulsively enters it.

Karen finds herself in her childhood home, where she hears the sound of her father beating her mother. She investigates only to find Freddy hitting a plastic blow-up punching doll version of her mother. Jacob appears behind her and tells her to wake up so they can escape. The dream police show up for another fight as Freddy turns into a punching doll (why?), and Karen wakes up with Jacob. He reveals he took a picture of her out of the dream, which he says Alice taught him how to do, but when did she ever learn to do that? The next morning, Karen tries to convince Gina and Scott that Freddy is real, but they still won't believe it. David warns Jacob he's about to be kicked out for the "trouble" he's caused.

Gina, the girl who doesn't want to be touched, dreams of arms ripping through almost every surface of her bedroom to grab and grope her. She runs through a door that leads to an elevator where Freddy waits. Echoing Carlos' last appearance in the "Freddy's Dead," he lets in a mob of zombies, including Wesley, who crowd the elevator so much she can't scream. They empty out when the elevator hits the "morgue" floor, but he's not done with Gina yet. The poor girl winds up in the "honeymoon suite," presumably the room where her mother made her turn tricks. She's trapped on the bed when a fat man walks in, only for Freddy to rip himself out of his body (maybe they wanted to keep the "birthing" effect from the first *Dream Child* draft). Despite the icky scene, there's a funny moment where Freddy is confused when "room service" is waiting outside. It's Jacob, who hits him with a cart as the dream police show up for another fight.

With Freddy distracted, Jacob attempts an escape with Gina, who overcomes her worst fear and lets Jacob usher her away. Freddy escapes the fight and grabs her on the way out, however. The dream police tell a frustrated Jacob he needs to dream of Springwood and bring Scott and Karen with him so they have a better chance of beating Freddy. Elsewhere, Freddy kills Gina by elongating his arms and "hugging" her entire body.

Now viewed as troublemaking addicts, Karen, Scott, and Jacob are taken to juvie to wait until they can be reassigned to a new foster home. Jacob is ready to give up, but Karen inspires him by bringing up Alice. After convincing Scott, the three of them fall asleep and enter "Nightmare Springwood," a dark, desolate place where the local populace have turned into mutants. They meet with the dream police, but are immediately separated from them by a massive brick wall. Karen and Jacob are then transported to the "nightmare" version of his old home.

Scott is alternately sent to a bar full of mutants where Freddy is waiting to… make him a deal? The pitch: give him Jacob and Scott can have Karen. I'm not sure how that works, but Scott decides to call on the dream police just before he's impaled on Freddy's blades. This last fight is an all-out brawl. Freddy takes them on one-by-one, allowing them to show off the range of their powers. He defeats them all eventually, seemingly dying in the process, but the dream police don't (can't?) die, nor can they kill Freddy.

The noise of the battle is so loud, it attracts Jacob. The dream police tell him in order for Freddy to die, he has to find the original source of his rage. Luckily "Nightmare Springwood" contains all the collective evil in the town's history, so a solution is nearby. Jacob runs off, thinking he knows where and what it is, while he tells them to find Karen.

Standing in front of the Elm Street house, Karen considers the mailbox where past tenants have put their name plates. Tenants like the "Thompsons" and the "Kruegers." (I guess Don and Marge *did* buy the house of the man they killed in this version. Weird.) Karen ransacks the place, eventually finding Freddy's childhood room full of broken toys, dirty clothes, and crude drawings revealing his abuse. Jacob arrives as Karen deduces that Freddy's abusive foster childhood was the source of his rage, and thus the way to kill him. Taryn shows up without the other dream cops, but it's a trick by Freddy, who stabs Jacob in the gut.

Freddy is about to sexually assault Karen, taking the form of her father, when she summons her mother to fight him. He turns back to Freddy and fights her off as Jacob saves Karen one last time before dying from his injury. Karen disappears, but Mr. Underwood, Freddy's own abusive foster father, shows up, frightening and beating the hell out of him while the dream police help. Mr. Underwood literally *rips* the souls of Freddy's latest victims out of him as he starts to melt and "Mr. Underwood" reveals himself to be Karen.

Freddy dies as the dream police grab her and run out of the Elm Street house. It explodes as a white mist overcomes the area. The dream police walk away with a fourth figure, possibly Jacob, joining them. Karen falls asleep and wakes up in the normal version of Springwood. The mutants are people again, and she finds herself wearing a gold bracelet with Jacob's name. The end.

## SCRIPT AUTOPSIS

Were Ken Sagoes, Jennifer Rubin, or Rodney Eastman ever asked to come back? We know Jennifer didn't know about it and Ken found out later. Talalay clearly knew that the dream warriors were one of the best parts of one of the best sequels, so it absolutely makes sense that she would try to have them return in some capacity. Still, it's a little sad that instead of being at peace, they're civil servants in the dreamscape. (What is this, *Beetlejuice*? Actually, throw in the mutated populace of "Nightmare Springwood" and it's very much like *Beetlejuice*.) It definitely doesn't evoke *Twin Peaks* as *Freddy's Dead* tried to. This version is much closer to *Eraserhead*.

Like the characters in the first *Dream Child* draft, it's easy to see early versions of the *Freddy's Dead* ensemble in this script. Wesley became Carlos, a victim of physical abuse, and Gina became Tracy, who was sexually abused, and it's possible that Scott became Spencer, who "faced his father" like Maggie told Spencer he had to do. These early versions are much different and less edgy than the ones in the final film. Tracy is far angrier than Gina and Scott's just an asshole.

The elements that carried over include telltale children's drawings, a doomed town, Freddy shapeshifting into a sexually abusive father (not to mention the other abusive parents), and the appearance of Freddy's own foster father. This begs the question, would we have seen Alice Cooper killing Freddy on screen or would they have gone with an actor or stuntman? Is it too much to imagine a makeup-free Kane Hodder beating Freddy Krueger to death? It's clear that *Freddy's Dead* was also a streamlining of this script, possibly to its detriment. How do we never find out who John Doe was when his identity is at the forefront of this draft? And having Freddy's own nightmare kill him is arguably more poetic than removing him from the dream realm and killing him in ours, though the film's ending does have appropriate symmetry with Wes Craven's original film.

While *Freddy's Dead* later featured the Recovery House Youth Center, this original *Nightmare 6* script alternately had the Rosedale Foster Home as a central locale. The two facilities had little in common, however, apart from housing vulnerable youth. The final film's Recovery House was located inside a repurposed industrial building in nearby Central City and had mental health professionals on staff. The Rosedale Foster Home operated from a repurposed residence in nearby Rosedale, a community roughly half the size of Springwood, and was run by only two people.

# INTERVIEW

## CLAY McLEOD CHAPMAN

### AUTHOR

ghost ..... **WAKE UP AND**
  eaters **OPEN YOUR EYES**

**So, you re-watched *Freddy's Dead* for this? Was it your gateway drug for the films, like it was for me?**

It was my first experience watching a *Nightmare on Elm Street* film in the theater, for better or worse. I was twelve, maybe thirteen when it came out. It's almost like you, as an audience member, can't choose which *Nightmare* you enter into if you're a child. I know I have my 3D glasses somewhere.

**Do you recall when you first encountered *Nightmare on Elm Street*?**

I can't give an exact age, but I can give a specific trauma.

**Perfect.**

(laughs) It's from the first film, and it had less to do with Freddy than with Tina. I have a phobia of clear plastic tarps, and there was something about her transparent body bag. It makes no logical sense to my moviegoing mind, which thinks body bags are black, but Tina's wasn't. She's inside the body bag and you see her face through this milky veil. Then her body is dragged by an invisible force. My imagination wants to think it was something intestinal or internal, but her bloody hand slides down the inside of the bag. That truly seared its way into my subconscious, to the extent when I was writing *Ghost Eaters*, that's what I was thinking of. I wanted to emulate that scene over and over. (laughs)

I was born in the '70s, raised in the '80s, and like a preteen-to-teen in the '90s. I became aware of Freddy Krueger when he was already ubiquitous. DJ Jazzy Jeff and the Fresh Prince were singing about him. There were 1-900 numbers on TV and he was on MTV. He was everywhere.

**Was *Nightmare on Elm Street* still frightening to you despite his overexposure?**

It's funny. His oversaturation made it easier to be frightened of him. It added to his mystique. I was always rationalizing my fears as a kid. If I was afraid of Jason, I could say "Well, it's not Friday and I'm not a camp counselor, so I have nothing to worry about. With Freddy, I didn't live on Elm Street. Then when I was twelve, I saw *Freddy's Dead* and he said "Every town has an Elm Street." As a twelve year old, wrapping my head around that concept that this evil entity had broken free of containment was horrifying to me. I was really taken by that notion that you can't compartmentalize or silo the notion of Freddy to one medium. He's franchising, baby! (laughs)

**I'm fully aware *Freddy's Dead* is far from the most beloved film in the series, but since you were kind enough to go back and watch it, let's talk about what it does well.**

Okay.

**I discuss the circular nature of the theme of parental retribution when it's revealed Freddy has a child.**

Yup.

**There's also a reason why Freddy's funnier in this entry. He's transcended his previous role as a trickster demon once he achieves his goal of killing all the kids in Springwood. Now he's a mad king in a vacuum who's trying to break out. Not to put too fine a point on it, but It's almost Shakespearean. He's like Alexander the Great. There are no more streets to conquer, so he's stuck in this bubble of a town where he has to listen to the sound of his own voice.**

**That would make me crazy.**

I would concur. You can take the first three movies as their own unit, then the next three as their own storytelling cycle. *New Nightmare* feels like an addendum to me. Watching *Freddy's Dead* again, I was struck by a part of the film that isn't really resonating. It's sort of mind-blowing how it starts off posting itself as apocalyptic. Like ten years from now, all the kids are dead and the parents are experiencing mass psychosis. The loftiness of this film is almost compelling, and I feel kind of saddened by the fact that it didn't follow that notion of "Look what they reaped."

Parents shouldn't bury their kids. Kids should bury their parents. This whole series, and this entry in particular, kind of shows what happens when the boogeyman wins. It becomes this negative space of grief. To your point, I find it compelling that Freddy has accomplished his mission.

You mentioned Shakespeare, but I was thinking *Richard III*. There's a conniving character who wants to usurp the kingdom, but when it happens, it's that famous line "My kingdom for a horse!" Except it's "My kingdom for a child!" So, he literally has to franchise. He has to expand his operation beyond the scope of this one town. I just find that to be a great story that the film itself has very little interest in telling. (laughs) We essentially get echoes of parts four and five, which are echoes of part three, where it's struggling to break out of that *Dream Warriors* mold where kids get powers and band together.

**That's very astute.**

Freddy even quotes Shakespeare! "Carlos, lend me your ear." It's baked in there, whether they admit it or not. We know. (laughs)

**Last time we talked, you mentioned your admiration for parts four and five. What is it about those entries, in particular?**

I love the focus on the mythology of Freddy, particularly in part five. What's compelling about his expansion through the series is that they keep having to introduce new backstory. In part one, he's a child-killing pedophile, and that's bad enough, but then later there's the whole "son of a hundred maniacs" notion.

I loved that! I've always been a fan of Stephen Hopkins. I love his style on *Judgement Night* and *The Ghost and the Darkness*. He and Renny Harlin excel at taking that MTV style and applying it to feature films, which is something I noticed in four and five. I thought Stephen Hopkins did that more succinctly. He's kind of like the poor man's Nicolas Roeg.

**Parts four and five definitely feel like a piece.**

Yes, they feel like they could have been filmed back-to-back, almost by the same person, even though I know they're not. The story they're telling seems to be continuous, whereas parts one through three feel isolated. They almost feel like a "part one" and "part two" to me. And which one has the dog urinating fire?

**Part four. That's Renny Harlin all the way.**

That's such a beautifully vulgar moment. As far as rebirths go, it rings true. (laughs)

**It's so crude, but it feels like they're trying to tie it to mythology, which I think Wes Craven would appreciate. Even though it's totally nuts.**

After part three, you really get a sense of Freddy doing a vaudeville act, but I really feel he becomes that Shakespearean trickster. In *Freddy's Dead*, there are at least two instances where he mugs to the camera. The first time is when he's jumping around Carlos after making him deaf. He looks at the camera and goes "Shhhhh." There's a complicity there that makes you go "Oh, this is for us." The second is when he rolls the bed of spikes onto the road. He looks straight to the camera! All pretense of empathizing for the victims is gone.

**People forget *Freddy's Dead* was really supposed to be the last one, so there's a strong sense of "This is it, smoke 'em if you got 'em. Let's go nuts." Do you have any particular favorites in the series?**

Part one is the classic, foundational text, but of course, I have a soft spot for part three. The problem I have with *Nightmare on Elm Street* is also what makes it terrifying. The notion of this Jungian monster invading your dreams, and there's no hope to it. There's no switch. I've always been more of a Jason man, myself.

**You and Grady Hendrix.**

I feel like I have no agency in these films. I'm screwed. We all have to sleep at some point. At the end of the day, to me, dreams defy a certain kind of logic. It's hard to engage, so by the time he's mugging and quipping, I kind of understood him. Maybe that takes his teeth away, or his claws. But him being more puckish felt compelling. Parts one and two are all dour and grim, even if he's starting to quip a bit. He just needed to find himself. (laughs)

The thing about part six is that it's a family affair, more than any other entry, except maybe parts three or seven. Rachel Talalay was a part of the New Line family for a while. Robert Shaye has a cameo. It's by far my least favorite entry of the series, but it feels as if it was made with love. I don't know if you can say that about parts four and five, which I enjoy more, but I don't think they have the same kind of heart.

**Definitely. Most of these films were made by directors who wanted to leave a mark and move on, but having Rachel Talalay make her directorial debut was like a homecoming.**

And she did *Tank Girl*! She's doing alright. The idea that this entire town is childless makes it like the *Children of Men* of the series. (laughs)

**Have the films influenced your books at all? Certainly *Nightmare* shares some DNA with your book *Whisper Down the Lane*, since both were inspired by the McMartin trial.**

The concept of Freddy is terrifying, but I think the thing that gets glazed over the most is that you're dealing with a man who has these compulsions towards kids. It's morally repugnant, but in later films, we're celebrating him. Except for the remake, which made the subtext like ubertext. It was way too much. Like if I was a victim of child abuse and I was watching *Freddy's Dead* when we got to Tracy's dream of her father, there's no catharsis. It gets to the cult of personality like with real life serial killers. Take away the supernatural and it feels like true crime before there was true crime.

I think what Craven did by integrating genre with a certain philosophical bent, set himself aside from what was out there. The level of thought that went into the first film, and how it plays out in each subsequent film just adds to the tragedy. I always think of Wes Craven having a tragic air to him because his highs are so high and his lows are so low. The sheer design of Freddy is immense. There was a complexity to Freddy that the other slashers didn't have.

# INTERVIEW

## MIKE WILLIAMSON
### DIRECTOR / EDITOR

MR. STATIC GREMLINS SECRETS OF THE MOGWAI

**This may be hard to believe, but my love of movies started with *Freddy's Dead: The Final Nightmare*.**

Oh, good. I like to hear that!

**I remember when you went on the *Killer P.O.V.* podcast for their infamous "drunken debates" episode and you defended it vigorously. I think it was a decade ago, but I always remembered when someone went to bat for *Nightmare on Elm Street*. Even, well...**

The most maligned one? (laughs)

**You know, sometimes I think we're the only two people on Earth who like this movie.**

I don't just like it. I love it.

**I'm assuming you're a fan of the other films as well?**

So *Nightmare on Elm Street* is my favorite film series, hands down. It's not *Lord of the Rings*. It's *Nightmare on Elm Street*.

**Same here. I call it my *Star Wars*.**

But it's not a guilty pleasure. I honestly think the creative standards set by the series, from film to film, are kind of unmatched, at least in the horror genre. The amount of talent behind the camera is insane. It blows away other series. Obviously, you've got Craven, you've got Renny Harlin, you've got Chuck Russell, you've got Frank Darabont. You've got all of these heavy hitters and it shows. Every movie is so smart, so clever, and so well-shot. The production design is [fantastic]. I love the series, like you said, as a movie fan, not just as a horror fan. There's a high standard of quality across every film, and they're not all the same. You feel the different filmmakers behind these movies.

**Do you remember when you first saw *Freddy's Dead*?**

Oh yeah, I was in high school. I was already a big fan of the series, but it was the first one I was able to see in the theater, and I went multiple times. It was a big deal! The 3D glasses had ads for *Suburban Commando* and *House Party 3* on the sides of them. It was like my event movie for the year. I remember having to negotiate with my mother, who was very religious and overprotective, even though I was like a sophomore in high school. My dad's name was Fred, and he had died, so she had a real problem with me going to see a movie called *Freddy's Dead*. (laughs)

**That's... unfortunate.**

I cut out a full-page *Fangoria* ad for *Freddy's Dead* that was my Trapper Keeper cover. I had the advanced one sheet and the standard one sheet on the walls of my room. The first CDs I ever bought were the *Freddy's Dead* soundtrack, the one with all the bands on it, not the score, and the John Williams and Steven Spielberg collection. (laughs)

**What do you think of the comedic direction Freddy took? I always posited that his jokes only meant he was enjoying killing his victims.**

I love the tone of the film. The unknown is what's frightening, but I think any time you're five sequels deep into a horror series, you can't really do that anymore. You know [Freddy], so I think it's wise to switch it up. I was thinking about this earlier today, but I'm a huge fan of HBO's *Tales from the Crypt*. I'm also a big fan of *Demon Knight*, though it doesn't really reflect what I like about *Tales from the Crypt*.

**I agree. I love *Demon Knight* as its own entity, but it was a script purchased by *Tales from the Crypt* to be its first theatrical film, and you can tell.**

I love it too, but if it didn't have the Crypt Keeper's opening and closing [scenes], it's not *Tales from the Crypt*. It's not a black comedy, morality play kind of thing.

**Completely. It doesn't fit with the tone of the series. It's like *Assault on Precinct 13* being bought by *The Twilight Zone*.**

That 1972 *Tales from the Crypt* movie is incredible, but it's a whole other thing. My first exposure to *Tales from the Crypt* was the HBO series, which is funny and dark. To me, *Freddy's Dead* is a better representation of that tone than any of the *Tales from the Crypt* movies. The tone of those is not what I loved about the series, even though I might love those movies. *Freddy's Dead* really nails Freddy Krueger as the Crypt Keeper in a way that's wicked, but witty. The umbrella that the whole film operates under is this sort of black comedy with stakes, like you said. It's still violent and he's still a threat, but for those of us with dark senses of humor, it really exploits that sort of gag that *Tales from the Crypt* was doing on HBO. He was getting funnier, but there was never anything like him doing a *Wizard of Oz* parody in the previous movies. It was so overtly camp. For fans that react to that negatively, who wanted him to be just a threat, like I said, five sequels in, I'm totally down for Freddy becoming the Crypt Keeper. It's legitimately funny. It's legitimately clever. It's not like they're attempting to make it more lighthearted. The jokes are landing. It's funny shit, you know what I mean?

**Yeah, when he's jumping around Carlos and making noise we can't hear, and especially when he breaks the fourth wall with the bed of spikes. It's full *Looney Tunes* at that point.**

I'm a huge Joe Dante fan. I love that kind of horror filmmaking. The sort of satirical takes on macabre subject matter. I think it's so much fun to do that, and this is the one where they went all out. For me, it hits like every time. It's really funny and really satisfying. I still think it's a thrilling movie, too.

**Even the basic setup is so different from the other films.**

It's a mystery that's got this, like *Nancy Drew*, *Hardy Boys* thing going on. As a fan of the series, it's fun to watch it unfold, because you're right. [Consider] the other movies. What's part three about? Oh, that's the one in the mental hospital. What's part four about? It's kind of more about where they're set. There's not much solving of anything other than making new characters have to figure it out. But we already know it. *Freddy's Dead* is the first film since the original where there's a mystery that's being solved. And who doesn't love a good mystery?

**Everything that's different about it works on the film's own terms. It also comes full circle when it's revealed Freddy is a parent, and thus subject to the same punishment he's been dealing out.**

That's true. At this point in the series, when you're revealing characters that are related to other characters, it's all, to be frank, bullshit. (laughs) You know, they're just making shit up, but it totally works, and you totally buy it. It's rewarding enough that you don't feel like…well, sort of like *Halloween II*, where you're like "Oh, she's his sister? That wasn't established at all!" But with this film, you sort of buy it. Like, why would I have known that? It's not about that, so by this point, you're like, "Oh, that's a cool little layer. I'll buy that he had a kid."

**Yes, it adds, but it doesn't change anything from earlier films. It's not like you suddenly sympathize with Freddy. You don't watch the other films imagining he was thinking of getting his daughter back the whole time. If anything, that's where he got the idea to take the kids from their parents.**

And that's not an unheard-of scenario for a killer to have a family, so it works.

**So, you liked the twist of Maggie being his daughter from the start?**

Oh yeah, I love it. All of the dots connected for me. I didn't feel like anything was outlandish, which is ridiculous to say in a movie series that is so outlandish. (laughs) It makes sense to me and she was a good character. It was a good performance [from Lisa Zane]. Nothing bumped for me at all when I was watching it. And it was surprising. It wasn't the kind of thing where I had pegged it early on that she was going to be his daughter. The reveal worked for me.

**I think this film, in the strictest definition, maybe not in terms of quality, is Shakespearean. At the start, Freddy has basically won by killing all the kids in Springwood, but he's trapped. He's been listening to the sound of his own voice for however long.**

(laughs) Yeah, Shakespearean in the sense of, it's like, familial drama…

**He's like a mad god facing the irony of having all this power, but nowhere to go until he connects with his progeny, who can free him.**

Yeah, I mean, I wouldn't say the plot in *Freddy's Dead* is the reason I love it, but it works for me. What I love is the tone. I love the style of filmmaking and the pace of it. I think it's cut really well. The tempo of the thing is really breathless. When I sit down to watch it, I'm always amazed how quickly it goes by, for me. It feels like a half hour long. It's the one entry that's kind of joyous. It's bubbly and frothy like a witch's cauldron, but it's so swift and smart and fun, that for me, it's the easiest watch out of all of them. I could put it on anytime and watch it from front to back, no matter what.

**It goes down smooth.**

It cuts to the chase and it stays in the chase, and the whole ride is super fun. So that's what I love about *Freddy's Dead*. Sometimes horror comedies don't work because comedy is hard, right? It's hard to be witty. Anyone can tell a joke, but that doesn't mean it's funny. But this is a legitimately smart, witty film made by clearly talented filmmakers. It has a great cast, great effects, and the icing on top is they gave us a 3D finale! You said you love movies, and *Freddy's Dead* exploits all different kinds of filmmaking techniques, you know what I mean? It's a murder mystery, it's got family drama, killer practical effects, killer visual effects, and it's got 3D. So, if you love movies, you get all this cinematic stuff for ninety minutes. I can't say that about the *Friday the 13th* series. It's fun, but to me, it's primarily dumb fun. The whole *Nightmare* series is actually cinematic. The artfulness that went into all of these movies is head and shoulders above really any other horror franchise. And *Freddy's Dead* is no exception. It has a different feel from the other movies, but it's still really smart filmmaking.

**Let's talk about the rest of the franchise. What are your favorites besides *Freddy's Dead*?**

I mean, I love part one. Everything is on the shoulders of part one, right? Like you can't not appreciate the genius concept of the first movie. The first movie is scary and inventive, and the cast is good. All of that said, I can't deny the feeling that…if you put this in your book, I'm gonna get hate mail…

**Hit me.**

The first movie ends on a lower note than it starts for me. It starts to get clunky and falls apart for me in the third act.

**Can you pinpoint when, exactly? I admit I'm not a fan of the compromised epilogue.**

I don't mind the epilogue. I fucking love a fakeout *Carrie* ending. I feel like it gets a little unintentionally goofy. The booby traps in the house and shit like that, is a little goofy to me. The movie starts off very threatening and sinister, and it ends, tonally, in a way where my heart isn't racing in the third act, the way it was in the first and second acts. That said, it's a fucking killer movie. It started this whole franchise.

Part four is probably my other favorite along with parts one and six. So, I love it, but of those three, it's the film that's tonally inconsistent for me. The script for part four isn't as smart as part one. Clearly. It's primarily a vehicle for special effects set pieces. That said, it plays better for me than the first one. There aren't sections that I'm bumping on in the fourth one like I am in the first, even though the first is like a work of genius. You know what I mean? So, one, four, and six are my favorites. Part two is my least favorite in the series. That's the one I feel like…

**They just wanted to get a movie going, but it's still unique.**

Yeah, they strayed from the concept, which can be kind of a fanboy way to criticize something. I am for artists taking a concept and doing their own thing with it. That's cool, but [part two] has a lot of unintentionally funny stuff in it that really just takes the whole the piss out of itself. Like exploding parakeets, you know? You can see what their intent was, but I don't feel like they're hitting the mark for me. When you see it in a theater now, it plays like gangbusters, but I think that's more because of the unintentional humor in it. Part two is the only one that I think really stumbles along the way.

Part three is killer, but for whatever reason, I've always preferred part four, which was a little slicker to me, and I liked that. But they're all fucking great. I was still in high school when I saw *New Nightmare* theatrically. I actually wrote a paper on it for my English class because I was so affected by it. Obviously, it stands on its own, but it's such a brave postmodern piece of art that somehow got funded. (laughs) It's crazy that it exists.

**There's no other movie like it. Not *Last Action Hero* or *The Purple Rose of Cairo*. It's singular.**

Yeah, because it deconstructs cinematic myth in a way that is so dead serious. Those other movies you mentioned, *Last Action Hero* and *The Purple Rose of Cairo* deal with cinema as escapism. They sort of poke fun at the culture of movies. *New Nightmare* treats movies, not just as art, but art that influences humanity. It really opened my mind in high school. I was shook by its bravery and how much it was saying. It's nearly impossible to make a movie where so much of it is commenting on theories of storytelling and gods and monsters, and to also still have it work as a movie that you enjoy, in and of itself. It's still exciting. It's not just intellectual, because it could have just been really talky, you know? It's still a visceral experience, but it's one that really makes you contemplate what art means to the world at large, and what stories mean to people, and why. So, I straight up wrote a fucking thesis paper on it in English class about about how *New Nightmare* was an important piece of art!

**Funny you should mention that. I went to SUNY Purchase for Dramatic Writing, and we had to take film classes for our BFA. I'll never forget one of our teachers was this brilliant Yugoslavian named Pavlé, who loved horror movies. We could pick a topic for the final paper for the year, so I wrote about parts one, three, and *Freddy's Dead*. I got a B+. Do you still have your paper anywhere?**

(laughs) I wish I did. It's in some landfill in Texas.

**Since we're rounding the bases, tell me your thoughts on *The Dream Child* and *Freddy vs Jason*.**

I love part five. Again, we have Stephen Hopkins, another really talented filmmaker. They're still pushing the envelope as far as cinema. There's that whole black and white scene, which they filmed in color, but painted everything gray. Just from a filmmaking perspective, I can imagine the production meeting about this where someone said, "Why don't we just take the color out in post or film it on black and white stock?" But the fact that it's so clear they're filming it in color, and have painted everything gray, including people? That's the level of sort of artistic integrity and insanity that this whole series has. Four sequels deep by then, and they're still pushing themselves to do things that are new and difficult and hopefully rewarding, cinematically. That's a really interesting way to do something cinematic, because your eyes are telling you something's off. That's why they did it, to give you this sense of unease as you're watching it. It's black and white, but it's not. It's just an insane concept. I don't know that many people would even think to do something like that. (laughs) It's such an off-the-wall idea. Part five is filled with so many cool ideas, and it's also a pretty sinister movie.

**It feels mean.**

The whole "son of 100 maniacs scene," I mean this is dark stuff. It's back-to-back with part six, and they couldn't be more different, tonally. That's what I love about the series. Like I said, it's different filmmakers doing their own thing. Even with part two, which doesn't really work for me, it's clearly a filmmaker's vision that's different from Wes Craven. [Jack Sholder] is doing his own thing with it. I respect them all, even though I like certain ones better than others. As a whole, I pretty much love all of them for different reasons,

**This has gotten me in trouble, but I've always said that even the worst *Nightmare on Elm Street* film is better than the best *Friday the 13th* film.**

Oh, I agree.

**I love the *Friday the 13th* films, but there's inherently more imagination and creativity, even in the lower ranks. Except for the remake.**

No, no. That's a very wrong-headed [film]. He's not a child murderer. They turn him into a child molester, and it's like, why does he fucking have knives on his hands? (laughs) That's the whole thing! It's a very difficult thing to molest someone while you're wearing that glove. (laughs)

**It's an empty film made by nobody, for nobody. It's numbers on a spreadsheet.**

Yeah, and like I said, *Freddy's Dead* feels so joyous, while the remake feels joyless. It's just this depressing IP regurgitation.

**And what about *Freddy vs Jason*?**

That's not one I revisit much. I don't dislike it, but it is what it is, you know what I mean? It's also IP circle jerking. There's no reason for that to exist at all. That said, it's done with enough humor and energy that I think it's an enjoyable watch. For fans of the *Nightmare* series like you and I, it certainly feels more like a *Nightmare* movie than a *Friday* movie.

**Absolutely. I'd recommend a rewatch, because it's thoroughly a *Nightmare on Elm Street* movie that just happens to have Jason in it.**

I don't dislike it, but for me, it's certainly not in the same league as the original series. But I certainly prefer it to the remake, by God. (laughs)

**Is there anything about *Nightmare on Elm Street* that you feel isn't talked about enough, or at all?**

That would only be the quality of *Freddy's Dead*. There are some movies I like that the majority of other people don't like. I get why most people don't like them. When I watch *Freddy's Dead*, I'm so happy. It just brings me so much joy, that when it's over and I hear someone shit on it, I'm just befuddled. (laughs) I don't understand how you can't have fun with this movie that is so bubbly and joyous, and still wicked and thrilling. It's like I'm speaking a different language when people tell me that it's the worst in the series or they don't like it at all.

I understand if you went into *Freddy's Dead* in the nineties expecting something really scary and were disappointed. I just wish people would judge *Freddy's Dead* on its own terms and by its own intentions, because to me, it hits its mark. You can tell what it's setting out to do and it fucking nails it. It's fun, it's funny, it's wicked, and it's cinematic. And I don't know what else I could ask for from a movie.

**Even now, I still can't help but smile when the ominous scales of the Goo Goo Dolls shift seemingly out of nowhere to full-on rock.**

The soundtrack is killer! Seriously, you see the New Line logo [with that music], and it's like my blood is pumping. (laughs) *Nightmare* is my favorite film series, and it always will be. It's a very active part of my life. It was so important to me as a middle schooler, sneaking videotapes into my friend's house to watch them, because my mom would never let me do that. To having to convince my mom I could see a movie called *Freddy's Dead* to writing a thesis paper on part seven. The whole series was really intertwined with key moments of me growing up and becoming a filmmaker. Watching the series as a film fan, and trying to figure out how they did things, and all this kind of stuff. It's a real gift for fans of movies.

# WES CRAVEN'S
# NEW NIGHTMARE

Freddy Krueger may have been gone, but he was not even remotely forgotten. The tenth anniversary of the original *Nightmare on Elm Street* was fast approaching, though it seemed New Line Cinema was moving on to other things, not the least of which was revitalizing the *Friday the 13th* franchise, which they'd recently acquired from Paramount Pictures. Still, Bob Shaye couldn't shake the thought of one more *Nightmare*. He called up Wes Craven in an attempt to heal their long-simmering rift, which was both creative and financial in nature. Their eventual meeting led to Craven deciding to add a new wing to "The House That Freddy Built," a notion that New Line was more than receptive to backing. The creator was returning, canon be damned.

Craven admittedly hadn't seen most of the sequels, but when he did finally watch all six films to that point, he couldn't follow the story, much less find a way to continue it. Given this, the director decided to go into an entirely new direction, one divorced from the continuity he'd established a decade prior. Little did he know how crucially it would shape the next phase of his career.

This new direction was, if nothing else, quite novel. What if a series of popular horror films unleashed a dark force on the world? What if the story of those films needed another entry in order to keep the demon at bay? And why do we, as a culture, even tell these stories in the first place? After writing about myths his entire career, Craven himself would become part of the myth in *Wes Craven's New Nightmare*.

# DREAM SCENARIO

We begin with what appears to be a then-modern remake of *A Nightmare on Elm Street*. The opening scene of the original film is reconstructed, but instead of a glove, someone is building a metal hand with long blades at the end of each fingertip. It looks like something out of *The Terminator* (released in 1984, the same year as the original film). An unseen man in a red and green sweater cuts his own hand off, intending to replace it with his creation, when Wes Craven yells "More blood!"

Are we still in the psychedelic drug sequence from *Freddy's Dead*? No, we're watching a film within a film. More specifically, we're on a film set watching a crew work tirelessly to make a new *Nightmare on Elm Street* movie. Wes Craven plays himself, as does Heather Langenkamp. Heather's husband, Chase (David Newsom) is the main special effects artist on the film, and father to their six-year-old son Dylan (Miko Hughes). Heather tries to hide Dylan's eyes for the blood splatter as she doesn't think it's appropriate for him to see. (Why is he there in the first place?) She is actually uncomfortable about all of this, especially the new razor hand. Chase tells her there's nothing to worry about. We can see they're on a set, and hey, this is how they make their living.

Over in the effects shop, the hand suddenly twitches, nicking Chase. Chuck and Terry, the other effects guys, look to see if maybe it's a short circuit, but the prop comes alive and kills them both. Like an evil version of Thing from *The Addams Family*, the deadly hand scurries about. Wes yells to "cut the effects," but these are no special effects. This is evil coming alive before the eyes of those who made it. Heather screams for Dylan as the blades of the hand make a familiar screeching sound on a metal pole. (Isn't it crazy that the *Nightmare on Elm Street* films have a recognizable *sound effect*? What other series of films has that besides *The Texas Chain Saw Massacre*?). She sees Dylan disappear across the set just as she wakes up in her own bed.

It was all a dream, but the earthquake currently shaking the house is very much real. Chase and Heather rush into Dylan's room and hold him until it's over. It happens all the time in California. What doesn't happen often is when someone wakes up with the exact same cut on their finger as it appeared in a dream. His wife's dream, no less. But Chase shrugs it off. Objects often fall during a quake. Chase leaves for a business trip to shoot a commercial and Heather has a talk show appearance to make. Nobody really focuses on the four nearly-parallel slits in the wall, seemingly caused by an aftershock.

Dylan's entranced by the original *Nightmare on Elm Street* playing on the living room television. When Heather turns it off, the boy inexplicably starts screaming. Just in time, Dylan's babysitter Julie (Tracy Middendorf) arrives. She's a confidant for Heather and seems to really care for Dylan, so as painful as it is for Heather to leave, she knows her son is in good hands.

Heather is interviewed by local celebrity Sam Rubin (playing himself), about the tenth anniversary of *A Nightmare on Elm Street*. He briefly brings up Dylan to ask if her child has seen it. She's taken aback, remembering earlier that morning, when he asks what we're all thinking: "Is Freddy really dead?" She knows she's not expected to give a real answer. Heather was just an actress who acted opposite Robert Englund. Speak of the devil...

*And here he is!* Robert Englund appears in full Freddy makeup to an adoring studio audience. Heather didn't know he was going to be there, but laughs as he cracks jokes and hams it up with the crowd to an upbeat remix of the original *Nightmare* theme music. (He even declares "You're all my children now" in a clear nod to *Freddy's Revenge*, surprising given Craven's vocal dislike of that sequel.) This is Freddy after ten years in the zeitgeist. Safe, friendly, sanitized. Your friendly neighborhood child murderer. But Heather sees something ominous in the way he interacts with the crowd. Not Robert, but Freddy. His silhouette is off-putting.

Before Heather and Robert leave the set, Robert has to provide autographs for all the kids. Sadly, nobody wants Heather's autograph. (The real Heather claimed this mirrored real life in *I Am Nancy*, but I'd be proud to have her John Hancock and I'm not the only one.) She then receives a call from Sara Risher (also playing herself), a New Line executive and a producer on all the *Elm Street* films along with Bob Shaye. She asks Heather to come to the New Line offices right away. They haven't called her in a long while, so the timing is fortuitous. Though we can't help but wonder why.

Sara greets Heather in the lobby and takes her to Bob Shaye's office. (Yes, Shaye plays himself, and looks like he's having a ball, even if he's not the best actor. Sorry Bob. But thanks for everything). He says Wes is writing a new film, "the definitive *Nightmare*," as he puts it. He wants Heather to come back and star in it. This should be a dream come true, but she's hesitant. Bob reveals that Chase has been secretly working on a new glove for the movie, which scares her since she had no idea. (Well, with last night's dream, she had some idea, but he never told her.)

Heather arrives back home to chaos. Julie's trying to soothe Dylan, who's having a fit after a nap. When Heather goes to hug him, he looks in her eyes and growls "Never sleep again." When Dylan finally stabilizes, Heather sees that Rex, his stuffed dinosaur plushie, has four parallel slashes in its side. The boy claims that Rex "saved" him, but how? And from what? Heather's worried, so she calls Chase on location and asks him to come home. This is when we see the new glove. Or hand, rather. A large monstrosity that's different from the Terminator hand we saw in the beginning, but is sharp and deadly, nonetheless. When Chase leaves the set, the hand mysteriously disappears.

While Heather waits for Chase to come home, she reads *Hansel & Gretel* to Dylan for his bedtime story. Everyone knows the story, but in this instance, Heather thinks it's too violent to read the ending to her son. He asks her to go on, but she hesitates just before the witch's grisly death. It's not a problem as Dylan has it memorized. He finishes it for his mom and says it's important to get to the happy ending. (Pretty insightful for a little boy.) Under his covers, the stitched-up Rex is a guard of sorts. Dylan tells his mother she needs a guard, too.

On his way home, Chase starts to fall asleep at the wheel, a common fear for anyone who's had to take a long road trip at night. As he nods off, the missing razor hand he was working on pokes through his seat, right in front of his crotch. Instead of tearing the seat, it ripples, much like Nancy's bathwater when she falls asleep in the tub in the original *Nightmare* (a Bob Shaye suggestion, which is actually very evocative). Nancy got away, but the threat of that scene is fulfilled here as the claw shoots out of the seat and rips Chase open as his truck crashes.

Soon after, the police pay Heather a visit and, judging by the dolly zoom on Heather when she opens the door, she already knows that Chase is dead. She visits the morgue to identify his body and sees the four long slash marks on his chest. Even though they look even and deliberate, the scars are attributed to the crash.

At Chase's funeral, we have a mini reunion of *Nightmare on Elm Street* cast members as Jsu Garcia, Tuesday Knight, Robert Englund, and John Saxon all play themselves. It's already a tragic moment when another earthquake hits. As everyone scrambles, Heather sees Dylan pulled into the casket by Freddy, who shows his face briefly. He looks different, but before his face can even register, she dives in after them. The interior of the coffin is a seemingly endless passage. Heather grabs Dylan as the claw that killed her husband slinks away into the dark recesses below. As they exit the coffin, Chase's corpse comes alive and beckons to Heather. She screams... then wakes up. The earthquake was real, but she has hit her head on the side of the grave. She didn't even jump in. There was no talking corpse, no coffin tunnel, and Robert Englund only as himself, paying respects.

That night, Dylan sleepwalks while the original *Nightmare* plays on TV once again. He sings the jump rope rhyme, which Heather assumes he heard in the movie. Dylan instead claims he heard it under the covers of his bed. "Kids singing, way down there with the man. The *mean* man," he emphasizes by slowly clawing the air with his fingers. He wants to get up "into our world," the boy further reveals. This barely has time to register before Dylan's nose starts to bleed. Perhaps worse, the TV isn't even plugged in.

Heather brings Dylan to her bed and tries to answer his questions about God. Can you talk to God? Why does God let bad things happen? God can't answer at the moment, but he knows Dylan needs a break, so Heather takes him to a playground the next day. John Saxon meets her there and they watch Dylan try to be a normal kid. She explains that Dylan's never been like this before, confessing she's at a loss. Though John only played her father on film, he's close with her in a way that the real *Elm Street* casts purport to be. He says Dylan should see a doctor, though his behavior isn't entirely out of the ordinary considering the past few days. Having turned their focus away from Dylan, he dangerously ascends a tall rocket ship structure on the playground and raises his hands to the sky. The child falls, but Heather manages to catch him. Why would he do something so dangerous? "God wouldn't take me."

Back at home, Heather receives a letter in the mail from an unknown sender. Literally, a letter from the alphabet on what appears to be burnt paper. She puts it in a drawer with the other letters she's accumulated the same way, but never wanted to arrange. Earlier, it was revealed that she has a stalker who sends the letters and calls her to sing the Freddy rhyme in order to scare her. Could this person be the one behind everything?

She calls Robert Englund to talk about what's happening and he listens to her while vigorously painting something in his home studio. He says Wes is still writing the new script and he's up to the part with "Dylan trying to reach God, whatever that means." When they hang up, it's revealed that Robert is painting a picture of Freddy, but not the one we know. A different Freddy we've only barely glimpsed when he grabbed Dylan at the funeral. Something much darker than what we've seen so far.

That night, Heather's sleeping in her bed when we see the Freddy hand rip through her sheet. It rises high above her to strike, but she wakes just in time. She walks downstairs to find Dylan singing the jump rope rhyme in a daze. He then lunges at her, revealing he's taped kitchen knives to his hands. Heather wakes up from *that* dream to discover Dylan has taken out the individual letters she's received and arranged them on the kitchen floor. They ominously spell out "ANSWER THE PHONE." It promptly rings and when she answers, we get another callback to the first *Nightmare* with Freddy saying "I touched him." He then licks Heather through the phone and she shrieks. Dylan suddenly vomits and drops hysterically to the floor while saliva leaks from the phone's receiver.

Unable to put it off anymore, Heather takes a near-catatonic Dylan to the hospital. She tries to reach him by telling him to get better and come home. Lin Shaye appears, playing neither herself nor reprising her role of the teacher in the first *Nightmare*. Rather, she's a nurse who gives Dylan sleeping pills, which he pretends to take. (He really *has* been paying attention to the *Nightmare* films). As Heather drives home, she passes actual earthquake devastation, which is also mentioned on the news. (The Northridge earthquake of 1994 happened after they filmed the earthquake scenes, so Wes had the aftermath filmed to include in the movie.) Speaking of Wes, it's time to pay him a visit.

Heather heads to Wes's cliffside mansion where he sheds some light on her predicament. Freddy Krueger isn't after her because he isn't real. She and the filmmakers behind the *Nightmare* films are being hunted by an ageless entity that's chosen Freddy as its current form. (Yes, demons can cosplay too and they don't abide by convention rules). This demon is on the loose because the franchise's storytellers held it prisoner in tales that were popularized over the years. The story dies when it becomes diluted, which is a not-so-subtle dig at New Line Cinema, but it rings true. The world now needs to be reminded that Freddy Krueger is frightening again, and this demon is ready to enter our world and show us how. The many earthquakes are an indication of just how close it's getting to the surface.

But how do you stop a very real evil like that? Wes tells Heather that she can stop it by playing Nancy once more. Her character was the first to defeat him, to "humiliate" her enemy, who is fueled by fear. Heather gave Nancy her strength and that strength can be used to defeat him by continuing the story with one more film. Wes is racing to finish the script and the scene we just saw is already written on his computer screen.

After Heather returns home alone, the local news reports the deaths of Chuck and Terry (whom we saw murdered by the claw in the opening scene) and also that the updated Freddy glove has been reported missing from the set. As if on cue, another earthquake hits the house. Nancy checks her closet and out pops Freddy! (While Wes had established it's actually a demon in disguise and we never know its true name, we'll stick to calling him Freddy for our purposes.) They fight on Heather's bed and Freddy sizes her up as if making sure this is the true nemesis he's been waiting for. He cuts her arm, echoing the Katja Institute scene from the original film and she wakes up.

Now convinced this is all really happening, Heather rushes back to the hospital to see her son. Julie is already there, having had a nightmare about Dylan and just wanting to make sure he's okay. The nurses notice Heather's concerning arm wound, which she blames on the earthquake like Chase did earlier. Dr. Heffner (Fran Bennett), Dylan's doctor, says there was no recent quake.

Later on, Dylan is asleep in an oxygen tent, seemingly safe. Until he wakes up, vomits, and growls "almost there." Dr. Heffner rushes into the room with a makeshift Freddy glove and is about to slash the child when Heather wakes up again to find Dylan missing. She runs down the hallway, but a nurse tells her she needs a pass. Heather gives her the Nancy response ("Screw your pass!") and finds Julie watching Dylan in an examination room. The cops want to question Heather, so she tells Julie to keep him awake. ("Don't fall asleep" makes a return as well, followed by Heather's wound bleeding afresh, just like the end of the original film).

While tending to Heather's wound, Dr. Heffner begins asking questions about her family history. Could she be abusing Dylan? The doctor suggests he might spend some time in foster care, angering Heather. (Just like in *The Dream Child*, parental rights are at stake, along with the lives of the protagonists.) Back in the exam room, Julie fails to stop the nurses from sedating Dylan. She tries to keep him awake, but Freddy appears behind her. He kills her brutally, mimicking Tina's death by dragging her up the walls and ceiling. It's bloody and awful. The nurses run to see what all the screaming is about, but they don't see what's killing her. Julie calls out to Dylan before she dies, just as Tina called out to Rod. As her lifeless body falls to the floor, Dylan yells for Rex. In the ensuing chaos of an onsite murder, Dylan sleepwalks out of the hospital. Heather knows he's going home, just like she previously told him to do. (Not literally. Damn, Dylan) She calls John Saxon for help as she rushes out of the hospital.

Time for one of the biggest sequences in the franchise. Heather chases Dylan across several lanes of the Los Angeles freeway, during which they're almost run over multiple times, and Heather is almost done in by an oil tanker. During all this, a giant Freddy materializes in the night sky above. His massive claw plucks Dylan up only to dangle him over the speeding cars. The boy breaks free, but an army of Freddy clones chase him off the road. Despite being hit by a car, Heather follows after.

Upon arriving home, she finds Dylan waiting, safe for now. Also, John has shown up to make sure everything's okay. He's concerned for both of them, but nobody hears Dylan's bed shake upstairs. Smoke begins to rise from his covers as we cut back and forth between his bed sheets rising, as if stretched by something underneath (part one, yet again), and Heather telling John "Fred Krueger did it." It's at this moment that something in John Saxon shifts. Heather follows outside to his car, and his wardrobe suddenly changes. He now calls her "Nancy" and wonders why she's calling him "John." She gets her answer when she sees his police badge. He's Donald Thompson. She's Nancy Thompson. And Freddy has fully emerged from Dylan's bed. He stares ahead, right into the camera, waiting for something.

Bidding him goodbye, Heather says "I love you too…Daddy," finally assuming her mantle. That's Freddy's cue. He moves through the house, casting a Nosferatu-esque silhouette. Heather turns back to her house, but it's no longer her house. It's the Elm Street house from the original *Nightmare* and she's now wearing Nancy's pajamas. It's *on*. Moving through the house, Heather grabs a knife. The unplugged television is playing yet another scene from the original, the scene where Nancy tells Donald, "Fred Krueger did it, Daddy."

A trail of sleeping pills (his version of breadcrumbs from *Hansel & Gretel*) leads Heather to Dylan's bed where Rex lies on the floor, slashed to pieces. Realizing Freddy has dragged Dylan down below, she swallows several pills before crawling under his sheets. Just like with Chase's coffin, she finds herself sliding down a long, enclosed space, which functions like a waterslide into hell. Freddy hell.

Heather exits the slide into Freddy's realm via a waterfall. But this is no mere boiler room she's now standing in. This is an ancient Greco-Roman ruin made of stone and littered with puddles of water. An ancient, fiery furnace burns as a pterodactyl flies overhead. The walls all have stone murals reflecting different eras of mankind, as if the creature that dwells here is older than humanity itself.

She finds a script on the ground and quickly reads it, revealing what has just happened to her. Freddy appears and they fight. He goes for Dylan, who runs into the furnace, which is barely functioning, so it's still a safe haven for the time being. Freddy extends his arm (like in the opening scene of part one) to grab the child, then unhinges his jaw as if to eat him like the witch in *Hansel & Gretel*. Nancy races to his rescue and, after getting stuck in the sentient mud of the realm (again with the part one!), she stabs Freddy. Dylan runs past his attacker to get out of the furnace and now Freddy's the one inside. He "shoots" is tongue at Heather (*so* much part one) and it wraps around her face, almost suffocating her. Dylan grabs the knife and stabs the end of his tongue as the score echoes *Psycho* for a few bars.

Howling in pain, Freddy retracts his now-forked tongue as Heather and Dylan lock the furnace door. They burn him to death, his true demonic form revealed as he dies amid the flames. Mother and son escape from the primordial realm as it explodes around them and a triumphant score blares.

Emerging from his bed sheets, they arrive back in Dylan's bedroom. Heather recites the happy ending of Hansel & Gretel, to Dylan's delight. She finds a copy of Wes's finished script on the floor with a thank you note from him. Dylan asks if it's a story she can read to him. Finally understanding the power of storytelling that Wes was talking about, Heather starts to read him the script as we pan out.

## NIGHTMARE AUTOPSIS

Two years before Wes Craven changed horror for the third time in as many decades, he released this master class in metatextual horror filmmaking. There absolutely is no *Scream* without *New Nightmare* setting the stage. There aren't even titles of any kind until the end credits, disorienting the audience into wondering what we're watching. And it was incredibly disorienting. *New Nightmare* was the first horror film I saw in theaters (not counting five years earlier when my dad took me to see *Ghostbusters 2*. I had to leave when the slime came through the tub, because I was five years old and my dad grossly miscalculated). I didn't hate it, but as a kid, I was confused by what I was watching. It was strange seeing a film that blurred the line between fantasy and reality when my basis for enjoying these movies was that I understood the difference between the two at an early age (okay, *after Ghostbusters 2*, but I got there). It's since grown on me to such an extent that I believe it's one of the best horror films of its era. There truly is no other film like it. You can bring up *The Purple Rose of Cairo* or *Last Action Hero* all you want, but neither one reaches the artistic heights of *New Nightmare*.

Earlier in the book, I mentioned that *Freddy's Revenge* was the series outlier, though a strong argument can be made for *New Nightmare*. Part two still *feels* like a *Nightmare on Elm Street* film, but *New Nightmare* has other fish to fry. It more closely resembles the story of *Ringu* and its American remake *The Ring* than a slasher film. Craven is also explicitly telling a story about and for adults instead of teens. Perhaps this is why the film wasn't a major commercial success, but *New Nightmare*'s legacy speaks for itself.

NEW LINE CINEMA

WES CRAVEN'S NEW NIGHTMARE

a filmscript
by
Wes Craven

HEATHER —
THANKS FOR HAVING THE GUTS
TO PLAY NANCY ONE LAST TIME.
AT LAST FREDDY'S BACK
WHERE HE BELONGS

REGARDS,
WES

Dylan's presence signifies a new element added to the franchise. We've previously seen kids in these films as background elements (the jump rope kids, who are absent here), used for sight gags (Angela, Jesse's endangered sister from *Freddy's Revenge*) or as key plot elements (Jacob, the titular *Dream Child* and young Maggie from *Freddy's Dead*.) But we've never seen a child be co-lead or utilized for the central theme. Craven juxtaposes Dylan against a group of adults who make horror for a living. We first see him on set watching a hand get cut off as blood spurts. It's all fake, of course. Until it's not. Until it is, again. Craven's working with layers upon layers.

Craven utilizes Dylan to somehow subvert and reinforce the parental dynamics of the original film. In *A Nightmare on Elm Street*, our protagonist is Nancy, the child who was more in tune to reality than her parents. In *New Nightmare*, Dylan is now the child who is more aware of the truth than Heather or Chase. However, unlike Marge and Donald Thompson, Heather learns the truth and saves both her and Dylan by playing her part. The parental figure is the one who realizes the truth and saves the child, which was nearly impossible in previous entries.

We've become accustomed to seeing parents refusing to believe their teens, but now Heather is in a position to be disbelieved by her peers. Her paranoia would be alarming if it wasn't so warranted. Craven was inspired by Roman Polanski's *Repulsion*, a film about psychosis, which includes a scene where walls crack open like the scene with the aftershocks. The character of Dr. Heffner was named after Richard Heffner, former head of the MPAA. Craven took his umbrage about being judged (unfairly, in his view) and turned it into a story of a mother who might lose her child to either an institution or an overwhelming evil. (Though I would wager Craven would call the MPAA one and the same.)

As a then fifty-five-year-old divorced father of two adult children, Wes deserves credit for so authentically crafting the character of a twenty-nine-year-old wife and mother. Of course, he couldn't do that without the real Heather Langenkamp. In real life, she's married to special effects artist David Anderson and is a mother as well. Wes wrote "Heather" based on her life, including the fact that she had a stalker after the original *Nightmare* was released. Perhaps wisely, Craven doesn't go for a cinema verité approach. He effectively turns real people into believable characters. As a result, there are people who cosplay *as* "Heather Langenkamp," as well as Nancy Thompson.

The redesign of Freddy Krueger here is something to behold. Craven wanted this iteration of Freddy to be scarier with a larger stature and muscles. The slasher's classic design is boldly updated, while forging an identity of its own. His pale, yellow eyes are a reminder that it's not even really Freddy, but rather a demon taking on a familiar form. He's taller, with split skin instead of burns. The sweater is now a turtleneck, which he covers with a trenchcoat, adding to his bulk. His hat is the same green as his sweater. The most significant change comes in the form of his new right hand, which adds the finishing touch (no pun intended) to his primal overhaul.

Freddy's new weapon doesn't qualify as a glove because it's organic. It's part of him and bigger than the gloves we've seen before with exposed bone and wire-like veins, which lead to fingers with larger, curvier blades, along with a new fifth blade on the thumb. While the glove we all know and love is iconic, this version works so well with Wes's concept that it makes you wonder if the hand-made glove is the jerry-rigged tribute to this original monstrosity. Almost as if the fictional character of Freddy Krueger worshiped the entity that takes the same form in *New Nightmare*.

Notably, this is the first feature for editor Patrick Lussier, who had a great run with Craven over the years, moving with him onto the *Scream* franchise and eventually directing films of his own like the *My Bloody Valentine* remake and *Drive Angry*. He shows off his chops cross-cutting between scenes with significant rising tension. Heather's hospital interrogation blends with Julie's death in a way that gives heart palpitations. But who could forget John Saxon's last scene in the film where Freddy rises from Dylan's bed and waits until he knows Heather has become Nancy once more? Is there a scarier scene than a monster just waiting for something offscreen to happen? It works so well as J. Peter Robinson' loud, orchestral score kicks in. While synthesizers appear at certain points, mostly to reference the original's Charles Bernstein score, Robinson's score is persistent and percussive, unlike many of the other scores of the series.

If you couldn't tell, *New Nightmare* references Craven's original like an urtext. The script for *A Nightmare on Elm Street* specifies the location as the San

Fernando Valley in Southern California, but despite the presence of *way* too many palm trees, the finished film never gave away its location. Craven solidifies *New Nightmare* as a Californian horror film, through and through. Where else could it take place besides Hollywood? The natural occurrence of earthquakes is actually worked into the script. Craven utilizes visual trickery in several scenes, including when Freddy's claws come out of Nancy's bed. At the start of the scene, we see the lamp next to the bed begin to unexpectedly tilt. Craven put the set on gimbals to make it look subtly disorienting

Craven also shifts away from looking at teenage friendships to examining parental figures. Heather and John aren't related, and he's disbelieving like the other adults in Heather's orbit, but he's sympathetic and ironically paternal in a way Donald Thompson never was. It's pretty easy to imagine John as Dylan's grandfather. There's also two key scenes between Dylan and Heather that explore this dynamic. The first comes when Heather tries to answer his questions about God after the death of Chase. Waxing philosophically with a six-year-old son after a beloved family member dies isn't a common scene in most horror films, but Wes Craven's films aren't most horror films. As much as some of them try to be.

The other scene is when Heather reads him *Hansel & Gretel*. On the film's commentary track, Craven claims he always wanted to explore the "magical world" that a child has under their covers. It's one of the only places that belongs just to children. A place that may seem bare, but it lets the imagination run wild. There's something great about a little boy explaining to his mother that she needs a guard like his stuffed dinosaur.

Craven returns to fable territory here and essentially retells the Grimm fairy tale through the lens of *Nightmare on Elm Street*. Heather and Dylan try to get back to their lives before they were haunted by this malevolent force. The film's thesis can be found in Heather's refusal to finish the story of *Hansel & Gretel* due its violence. But as her child knows, you can't just stop the story. For all we know, it can lead to a happy ending that we're being denied. Earlier, when Heather turns off the tv before Dylan can finish watching the first *Nightmare*, he begins screaming. This isn't Craven advocating that children should watch horror movies. The movie, or "tale" is being interrupted, so the entity just grows stronger.

After he lost the battle to preserve his ending on the original *Nightmare*, Wes Craven ends *New Nightmare* with one of the best final scenes in any horror film. It's not scary, nor is it meant to be. However, it's Craven's philosophy distilled to its essence: A mother tells her child a story that he will hopefully remember and possibly pass down, keeping the essence alive. The camera pans out and we see "Written and Directed by Wes Craven," confirming, as if we couldn't figure it out, that we just watched a film. And yes, the subsequent story Heather reads is inappropriate for a six-year-old, but he's just been to hell and back, literally.

Robert Englund has claimed *New Nightmare* as his favorite *Nightmare on Elm Street* film, and it's easy to see why. It's the scariest since the original and the only entry helmed by a returning director, now an elder statesman, rather than a mid-career journeyman. To be honest, towards the end of the above synopsis, I keep almost writing Nancy instead of "Heather." Wes would be smiling, wherever he is.

## FIRST DRAFT: A NIGHTMARE ON ELM STREET 7

We know of at least three drafts that Wes Craven wrote for *New Nightmare*, the first of which was in July 1993 and simply titled *A Nightmare on Elm Street 7*. While there are some deviations from the finished film, the structure and characters are broadly identical across the board. This first draft featured two distinct changes from what follows, and they're pretty wild. First, a paranoid "Wes Craven" is driven around in a van by actor Michael Berryman (of *The Hills Have Eyes* fame) as he struggles to finish the new *Elm Street* script. He even cuts off his own eyelids so he won't fall asleep, because he's waited seven years and four sequels for some eyelid slicing. It doesn't make it in the final film because, understandably, he'd rather talk to Heather in his mansion.

The other major change involves the role of Julie, the babysitter. Before she was the only other adult who listened to Heather, she was in league with the entity and even donned Freddy's glove and sweater at one point. How that would have further played out is anyone's guess, but one can imagine Julie pulling off a Ghostface mask and explaining her evil plan. It's completely unnecessary here, but all the more fascinating since *New Nightmare* was a dry run for *Scream*.

# SECOND DRAFT: FREDDY UNBOUND

Arriving three months later, the project's second draft gained a subtitle: *Freddy Unbound*. While it's much closer to the finished film, there are a slew of changes and variations, which we'll plumb through now. While Chase is still present in the opening nightmare, Terry is given the lines about their work "putting food on the table." When the claws comes alive, they go for Chuck's face and Terry's eyes instead of Chuck's throat and Terry's heart. It's a negligible change, but dead is dead. Also, Chuck is described as a big, burly man, unlike the wiry actor Matt Winston, who portrayed him in the film. Perhaps Craven wanted this small role to be a tribute to the effects technicians you'd see on film sets, or maybe he had a special effects artist in mind for a cameo. (Ironically, Matt Winston is the son of the late, great Stan Winston, the special effects maestro behind *The Terminator*, *Aliens*, and so much more. Everyone relax, we're still meta.)

After waking up during the earthquake, Heather notices Dylan's pajama pant leg is shredded "as if cut by sharp knives." She later tells Chase her dream was about Freddy instead of "some movie" and realizes, based on background noise, that her stalker was calling from "a boiler room."

In this draft, Craven has Heather say she never lets Dylan watch horror films, which is also true of *New Nightmare*, but here she doesn't find him watching the first *Nightmare* on TV. Instead, in a sly bit of commentary, he's watching a news report from the Bosnian War, a real life horror, and then-current political flashpoint. Heather also calls her agent to cancel her talk show appearance and he berates her. We never see "Jerry," but after she rebuffs his suggestion that she buy a gun, he jokes Dylan probably already has one.

When Heather arrives at New Line, we get a blink-and-you'll miss it cameo from Mike De Luca, who actually shot his scene but asked that it be cut over his own performance concerns. But don't worry, we've got more Bob Shaye. His scene is mostly similar, though he reveals that the earlier talk show appearance was a "trial balloon" for new, er, *Nightmare*. Also, the phone call he gets at the end of the meeting was a report that the glove for the new film has gone missing, along with Terry and Chuck.

Heather returns home to witness Dylan's seizure, but he growls "You are all my children now" instead of "Never sleep again." While this line is a direct callback to the talk show scene where Robert Englund's Freddy says it, it's also a curious nod to *Freddy's Revenge*. Either way, Heather and Julie rush him to the E.R. where we first meet Dr. Heffner among a tableau of post-earthquake carnage. She gives Heather sleeping pills for Dylan and tells her to keep him away from TV and video games. Instead, just "tell him a nice story." It's the best advice we'll hear her give.

When Dylan begs his mom to finish *Hansel & Gretel*, he begs her twice: first when Heather hesitates with the witch's death, then afterwards, when they return to their father. It wasn't enough for evil to be vanquished. We needed to see the story through until the end. Also, this is where Dylan first mentions Rex. Heather makes him take a sleeping pill, which he later hides under his pillow, just like how he does in the hospital in the finished film, and again later in the script. Little man's a pro.

The structure of Chase's death is slightly different in this draft. As he nods off, he notices a torn piece of seat upholstery from the claw's first attempt to push through. The claw doesn't just burst from the seat, but rises up, just below his field of vision, until he falls asleep. (And for those wondering, yes, Johnny Depp was written in as a cameo at the funeral, but never actually asked to appear.)

Instead of "Answer the Phone," the message from the mailed letters spells out "The Movie is Over. Freddy is Unbound." It's more cumbersome, but brevity returns when the entity calls Heather and says "I'm loose," instead of "I touched him." The latter is much creepier and appropriately profane for a Wes Craven script.

Speaking of profane, we get a whole new scene where Heather drives a convulsing Dylan to the hospital. On the way, she receives a second call from Sara Risher, who tells her that Chuck and Terry were found murdered, so the movie is cancelled. As the news sinks in, we see Dylan grinning in the backseat. He eventually moons a nearby car. Heather pulls over and grabs Dylan as his face contorts. "It's almost there, Heather. Almost there." Cue the black vomit, earlier than usual, now with "insects, worms, and worse."

At Casa de Craven, Wes elaborates on the entity, calling it "the forces of tooth and claw against the child." A fitting description, considering it's what made him want to give Freddy a glove in the first film. He also tells Heather "your spirit was the source of Nancy's strength… if he can get through the love you have around you, he'll be into this world. And then… then it would be total darkness." Not only is it more dynamic motivation than what's in the finished film, it also hints at an apocalypse of some kind. There's no elaboration on that idea, but it's understandable. This is just a theory, but it's entirely possible Wes bit off more than he could chew when writing himself as a character, especially in terms of dialogue. Still, it's fascinating to learn more about this primal force that takes the form of his deadliest creation. The scene ends when Wes makes her agree to "stay alive and make the movie." Then they "shake hands like warriors on the brink of battle." Ever the Dream Warriors.

When Heather calls Robert in this draft, we don't initially see what he is painting, but it's later revealed when she calls back and talks to his wife "Patrice." (In real life, Robert's wife is Nancy Booth, but it's understandable that Wes didn't want to confuse 1994 audiences with two Nancys in one movie.). Patrice nervously says she and Robert are heading out of town for the time being, and that they're out of the film.

There's no news report about Chucky and Terry's deaths before Freddy attacks as that's already been established by Sara Risher's voice-over. Instead, Heather witnesses a bulging shape move across her wall, which draws her to her closet, much like when Freddy pushed his face through Tina's wall to catch a glimpse of Nancy. (Even picturing it now, I know it would have been more effective than the CGI attempt to reference that scene in the *Nightmare* remake.)

Instead of merely sporting a claw, Dr. Heffner more fully turns into Freddy in Heather's hospital dream, echoing a deleted bit from the original film at the Katja Institute. On his third and final go-round in the franchise, I think it's safe to say Craven was a little wary of doctors, or at least the institutions they come from.

Julie still appears at the hospital, though it's now after she's seen Dylan rather than running into Heather beforehand. Her death also unfolds a little differently. Instead of a full-bodied look at Freddy, you only see his claw appear before Julie's killed by an invisible force. There's also no cross-cutting of Julie's death with Heather's interrogation by Dr. Heffner. When they find Julie's body, Dr. Heffner is the one who tells the nurse he sleepwalks instead of Heather. Another echo of part one is when the script refers to Dylan as a "lamb" when he crosses the freeway. He also sees a "Claw Mobile" on the road, which is essentially a Freddy-ized car. (Maybe it's for the best this wasn't used, as it feels like something out of *The Dream Child*.) There's also no zoom in on John/Don's police badge, or cross-cutting as Freddy emerges from the bed to get Dylan, which is one of the most iconic scenes in the series. (Man, editing is really important, but Patrick Lussier will tell us all about that in his interview. Does this aside count as meta? Does *that* one?)

As Heather takes the sleeping pills to go after Dylan, she utters the line "[the sleeping pills] are the only way I can join him," which is extraneous at this point. Heather doesn't fall out of the mouth of a Freddy statue when entering "Freddy Hell," but there's so much more to observe. The description of his domain is meant to be enormous and seemingly infinite. As she runs through it, the script notes she encounters Elizabethan and Babylonian architecture, providing visual hints that the realm is older than civilization itself.

## THIRD DRAFT: THE ASCENSION

The script for *A Nightmare on Elm Street 7: The Ascension* hews even closer to *New Nightmare*, though it does share some similarities with *Freddy Unbound*. There is a subtle, but significant change between scripts that's worth nothing. In *Freddy Unbound*, the entity is referred to as "the true, ultimate FREDDY SPIRIT." Yet in *The Ascension*, it's simply referred to as "the true Freddy."

Both drafts share similar deficits, as well. They feature less of Freddy's physical presence, and aside from a glance at his glove before killing Julie, we don't see Robert Englund in full Freddy regalia as he kills her. There's no "skin the cat," and curiously, no "Miss me?" when he pops out of the closet. (Maybe it was an on-set improv by Englund?) Neither draft contains the elongated tongue sequence at the end, which seems strange for such an involved special effect.

Crucially, Heather doesn't read the script to Dylan at the end. There's no note or voice-over from Craven, and the titles on the script turn to credits. It's understandable if Craven streamlined his ideas as principal photography inched closer, but we should be grateful for what, or whoever caused him to make those changes.

# INTERVIEW
## PATRICK LUSSIER
### EDITOR

WES CRAVEN'S
NEW NIGHTMARE **SCREAM**

**How did you get involved with Wes Craven?**

I was very lucky to meet Wes on [tv show] *Nightmare Cafe* in the fall of 1991. He asked me to edit his next feature, which was originally going to be *Village of the Damned*. When they couldn't get Linda Hamilton, that version sort of slid away as he got the idea for *New Nightmare*.

**I still can't believe *New Nightmare* was your first feature. I know you were working in television for a few years before that, but what do you think Wes saw in your work that made him call you to the majors, so to speak?**

That's a really good question. I did half the pilot of *Nightmare Cafe* and three more episodes. We really hit it off in the cutting room. I'd ask him tons of questions about why and how he would do things. I could cut very fast, so I could try things for him. The first cut I would show him would have all sorts of music and sound effects, which I knew he appreciated. It was a time where people were transitioning from cutting on film, which is a little harder to do than cutting electronically. I think that had a big influence on his choice, because he could see things quicker. Beyond that, we just hit it off really well. People could be intimidated or stand-offish with him, but I was, well-

**Canadian?**

Well, Canadian, but young enough to realize, in my mid-twenties, that he was a fount of experience and knowledge that I was fascinated by. (laughs) I would constantly ask him stuff while we were putting things together.

**You'd obviously seen *A Nightmare on Elm Street* before working on *New Nightmare*.**

I saw it on opening day in Vancouver. I was a fan of his work. *The Serpent and the Rainbow* was an amazing film. I remember seeing *The Hills Have Eyes* and thinking it was crazy, and I loved his sort of Rube Goldberg ending. It was one of the things we bonded over. We talked about that and the sledgehammer from the original *Nightmare on Elm Street*, which he had in his house. He rigged it up in his office and you'd see it as you walked in, thankfully not ready to hit you. That was a running thing he liked. Everyone loves a good trap. He thought the audience would like them, too. The whole *Saw* franchise is a confirmation of that.

**Wes loved his booby traps.**

Yeah, it was definitely one of his interests. I think it stemmed from his fantasy life as a child.

**New Nightmare was considered a homecoming for Wes, Heather, and many key figures in the franchise. How did it feel to be the "new guy" surrounded by returners?**

I was probably a little naive at the time. I remember Wes telling me how the project was going to work and asking me to edit it. I was in the process of immigrating from Vancouver, Canada to the United States. Wes sponsored me and helped me and my family move down.

They were already in conversations with New Line. I was someone with no credits and I think New Line would have been fine if someone else did it. (laughs) Someone who had credits they recognized, instead of a few seasons of *MacGyver*. Wes fought for me to do that. I met Bob Shaye before the movie started at a party at Wes' house and I chatted with him a little. To me, he felt a little suspicious of my talents (laughs), whether I was going to be worthy to join "the House that Freddy built." That was Wes's choice and I'm incredibly grateful for that.

Wes's concept for the film was so unique and ahead of its time, that they weren't quite sure what to do with it. But they knew having Wes back was something they could sell. After *Freddy's Dead*, I knew the chance to continue the series in an unexpected way was exciting, but [I think] they were mildly suspicious in their own right, because how is it going to work? We shot for a few days at the New Line offices with Bob Shaye, Sara Risher, and Mike De Luca, who we ultimately cut out. I spoke to him about that and he was quite grateful we cut him out. (laughs) But I think Mike De Luca was the best advocate for Wes in both production, and certainly post-production. He was the "young turk" at New Line, and now he runs Warner Brothers and oversees New Line. He could see what Wes was doing, and I think that advocacy went a long way to getting the support at New Line through to the completion of the version of the film Wes wanted.

**If I can get meta for a second, and I will, since we're discussing *New Nightmare*, my book discusses parts of the script that didn't make it to the screen. However, for this entry, there's not much that didn't make it in from *Nightmare on Elm Street 7: The Ascension*. I know Michael Berryman played himself at one point, driving Wes around in a van.**

Yeah, that was an early draft. It was pretty close to what Wes had in mind. The film had a great trailer, which was an extension of the concept of the movie itself. It had Wes and the filmmakers talking about having nightmares and making another film.

There were elements with the opening sequence that I remember Wes told me he dreamed of the night before they shot it. They made changes on set to accommodate his nocturnal psychic adventures. (laughs)

**I truly don't think there is another film like *New Nightmare*.**

Yeah, I'd agree with that.

**It's wholly unique. You're also editing performances from non-actors. Was that a challenge when you're editing, say, Bob Shaye's multiple takes?**

That was never a discussion. I think one of the things that attracted Wes to my editing style early on, was that I was always careful to make sure the best performances were chosen. Performance dictated everything. For each line of dialogue, I cut every reading back to back, so you could pick the one where [the actor] is the most believable. I've done that for every film I cut. You get to the cream of the performances very quickly, so there's never "Try and make him look good." It's like, this is the best he can look in the footage we have, the nuance and the details. Those scenes changed very little. I think the biggest angst over those scenes were from [cinematographer] Mark Irwin when the dailies were shown to New Line. He was very nervous about what they would think, seeing themselves projected on a big screen. (laughs) But everyone was happy with it. Sometimes there's resistance when you have an actor who is desperate to go to the cutting room to dictate how they're presented, but I never got that from Bob Shaye or Sara Risher.

Heather had a really interesting role because she's playing a dramatic version of herself, and Nancy by the end of the film. Same with Robert. I think they both really got what Wes was trying to do and had total faith in him. They trusted his unique genius/madness.

***New Nightmare* isn't really one of the films I go to when I'm in the mood to see a *Nightmare on Elm Street* film. It feels more like a prestige horror film that stands outside of any series.**

I think Wes set out to do that. Frankly, he was not a fan of *Nightmare 2*. Joel Soisson, who produced it, is a friend of mine and he's totally aware of it. (laughs) The schtick that became more present in the later entries really diminished what Freddy Krueger was in Wes's imagination. I think [he appreciated] a chance to revisit Freddy in a way that was no longer beholden to the continued success of each sequel. He was very anxious to make something less of a circus, and more terrifying and elevated beyond the constraints of the franchise. That's why *New Nightmare* stands apart, even from the first film. It's a film about wrestling with all the good and bad of the monster you created.

**There's an argument to be made that *New Nightmare* is Wes Craven's best film. I'm not positive I'd agree, but there's definitely a consensus out there, and I'd love to hear the case for it.**

Of the many films I've cut with Wes, it's my favorite film I've edited. I love *Scream 1-3*, *Red Eye*, *Music of the Heart*, and the sort-of tragedy of *Vampire in Brooklyn*, but there's something uniquely special and powerful about *New Nightmare*. I think Wes's writing was never as good as it was on that film, before or after. It was the pinnacle. Wes had something to prove to himself, to the audience, and to New Line. I think that played a huge part in that.

**What was it like watching Robert Englund's performance as you edit?**

Robert presents as Freddy in *Nightmare on Elm Street* pretty amazingly. I remember when we showed Wes the first cut of Freddy's talk show appearance and he said "Throw a net on that man." (laughs) He was having such a good time.

**You edited the aptly titled *Cursed* with Wes years after the *Scream* films. I always wondered why Wes went back to make *Scream 4* after the disaster of that film, on and off screen.**

There's a really simple explanation. It's "If this is the last movie I direct, I want it to be successful." It's that simple. I remember talking to [Director] John Frankenheimer about that exact thing on *Reindeer Games* a few years before he died. He was the original director of the *Exorcist* prequel and he was talking about chasing one more hit. I think he would have been better served if he had finished [directing at] *Ronin*, which is an amazing film. You're chasing it, like "I at least need the last thing to be something." The audience didn't get *My Soul to Take*, so he needed to make something that they'd understand him doing. As hard as it was going to be.

The editing in *New Nightmare* is superb, and there are at least three sequences of cross cutting that stand out. One of my favorite shots in the whole series is when the camera zooms in on John Saxon/Don Thompson's badge and you realize reality has shifted. But there's something I didn't pick up on until my last watch: Freddy emerges from the bed as this scene is happening, and he looks at the camera. But he doesn't move until Heather says "I love you, daddy," thus taking up the mantle of Nancy. That and the playground scene were fantastic.

The playground scene was shot early on. It bought me all the goodwill. I cut it and sent it to Wes, and he showed it to everyone on set. I went to the set that evening and people were looking at me. The DP said to me, "That's like Hitchcock-level construction." It was so tense, like putting a bomb under the table. I was like "Well, the way it was shot, I thought that's how it goes together." (laughs)

**Good answer!**

How else would you do it? I felt that during several scenes. Like you were saying about Freddy coming through the bed and waiting, that was written as two separate beats that weren't intercut. Weirdly enough, it was Bob Shaye who suggested they be intercut. I remember looking at him like "That's an interesting idea." Wes said "Well, we can try it." We also discovered that great moment where she says "daddy" and he rips the sheet like "Okay, game on!" It became so powerful. That's a truly collaborative moment between the filmmakers, the studio, and existing material. Everyone was trying to find the best moment out of it. It was one of my favorite moments [working] on the film.

**Wes was always an "idea man." He was a professor who references literature and philosophy, which came up during the writing of the script and the shoot, but did any of that come into the editing bay?**

Absolutely. There were all sorts of references. He was classically educated. His whole approach to the story was that Heather had to surrender to the myth, or she couldn't face it. Then you have the "inferno" ending, the breadcrumbs, and the *Hansel & Gretel* of it all. Those are all components. The film that it might remind you of most is a protracted version of *The Wizard of Oz*, which Wes loved as a kid. When Dororthy wakes up, she sees the farmworkers are the Tin Man, Scarecrow, and the Cowardly Lion. *New Nightmare* was really a culmination of so much of his life experience, both personally and professionally. I think there was an earlier draft where Julie (Tracy Middendorf) was an agent of Freddy. She had sort of a Freddy mask on. I'm not sure you saw that draft.

**No, I've only heard of that draft.**

Yeah, there was a version of it. He has Julie look suspicious as Heather gets these phone calls. Wes had [the actors] do takes as if they're the ones behind it, like the chauffeur in the beginning. You can see those elements in *Scream*. The reason "Everyone's a suspect" was because the actors were all told to have moments where they could be the killer. Even Henry Winkler, when he touches Neve Campbell's face, or how he comes at the two boys with the scissors.

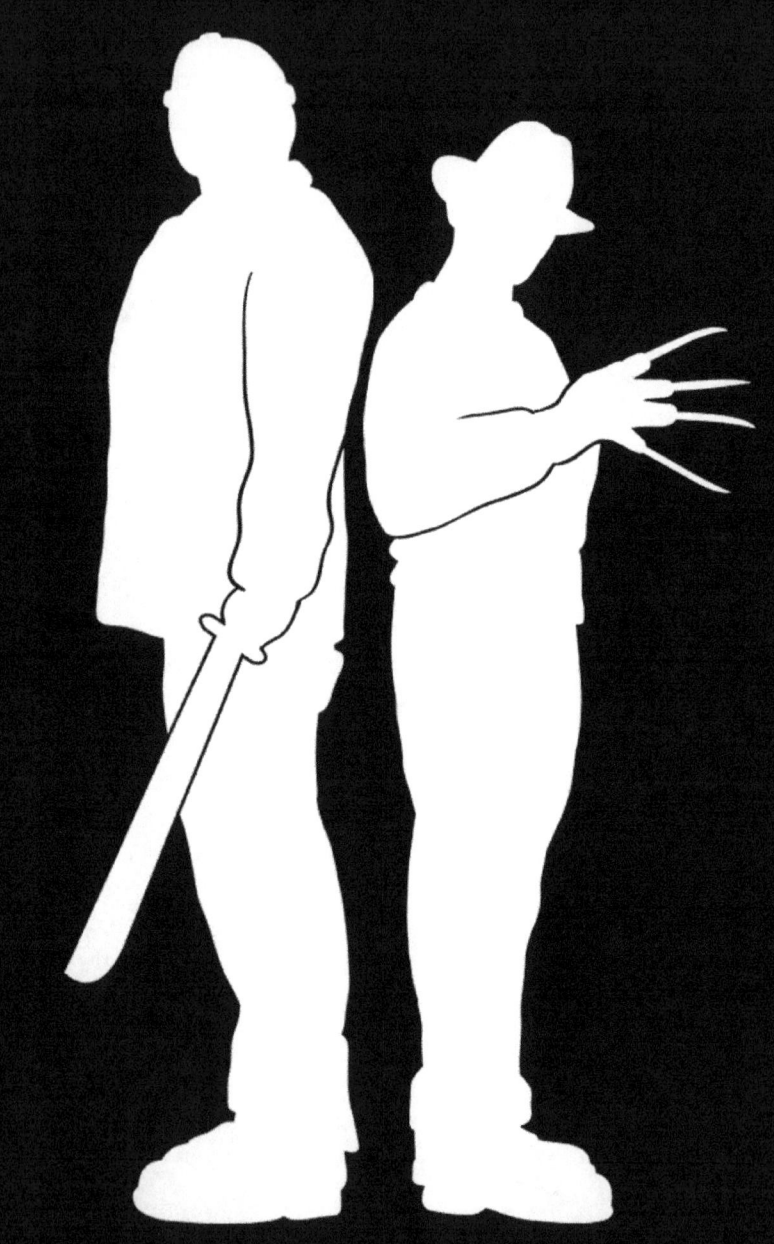

# FREDDY VS. JASON

Freddy Krueger was truly dead this time. It had been nine years since *New Nightmare* and seven since Wes Craven teamed with screenwriter Kevin Williamson to unleash his *other* meta horror masterpiece, *Scream*. He understandably had no interest in returning to his creation. Robert Englund kept working and New Line Cinema was riding higher than ever, thanks to the success of franchises like *Blade, Austin Powers*, and *The Lord of the Rings*. They'd even reached major critical acclaim with Paul Thomas Anderson's Oscar-nominated *Boogie Nights* in 1997. All major parties were satisfied by all accounts. So why on earth would anyone want another *Nightmare on Elm Street* film? The answer was simple: the fans. But they didn't just want more Freddy. They wanted a fight.

For as long as they've been around, horror fans have been playing the "What if" game with their favorite horror villains. What if Michael Myers from *Halloween* fought Pinhead from *Hellraiser*? Would Chucky from *Child's Play* win in a fight against the *Candyman*? But the most debated of all, was the question of who would win in a fight: Freddy Krueger or Jason Voorhees from *Friday the 13th*?

Most of you will be familiar with Jason Voorhees, but for the purposes of this chapter, a quick primer is in order. Jason was a physically and mentally deformed boy who drowned at Camp Crystal Lake, the summer camp where his mother, Pamela, worked as a cook. The counselors who were supposed to be watching him happily went off to have sex instead of doing their jobs. Pamela went on a killing spree to avenge her son, dying herself in the process. Jason came back to life (or was never dead, depending on who you ask) to kill anyone he crossed paths with at Crystal Lake. Eventually donning his infamous hockey mask, he slaughtered dozens of people over twelve films with various sharp implements, as well as his bare hands.

If there was a horror villain more popular than Freddy, it was surely Jason. Fans had wanted to see him and Freddy fight to the death for almost twenty years, despite the massive leaps in logic one would have to take. (Freddy kills in dreams, but Jason doesn't. Jason mostly kills around Crystal Lake whereas Freddy stays in suburban Springwood, etc.) But New Line Cinema was more than happy to figure those details out. They bought the rights to Jason and made *Jason Goes to Hell: The Final Friday*, a sendoff similar to *Freddy's Dead: The Final Nightmare*. The final scene featured Freddy Krueger's glove bursting through the ground to drag the defeated Jason's hockey mask down to the hell they conceivably shared. But why?

The question lingered on for a decade, during which time various writers would hand in many different drafts. Some kept continuity with previous films, some didn't even try. I can't possibly go over them all here. (Pick up the fantastic book *Slash of the Titans: The Road to Freddy vs Jason* for the full story on the years-long development process.) Eventually, the writing duo of Damian Shannon and Mark Swift wrote a version that became *Freddy vs Jason* as we know it today, a film that exists entirely due to the demand of a hungry audience.

## DREAM SCENARIO

The New Line Cinema logo appears with recognizable music cues from both Charles Bernstein's *A Nightmare on Elm Street* score and Harry Manfredini's *Friday the 13th* score. We're then launched into an effective prologue that's meant to catch us up to speed, while providing backstory for people who may have never heard of either character's bloody exploits.

Robert Englund enters as a then-human Freddy Krueger in his boiler room. He throws a doll into a furnace (apt metaphor) before sharpening a blade on his glove to kill a little girl offscreen. He puts a photograph of the child in a scrapbook, slowly licking the back of it, because yes, folks, he was a child predator in every way. He talks in voiceover about his exploits as the "Springwood Slasher" before an angry mob of parents arrives and burns him to death.

As if that wasn't enough to define the character of Freddy (and man, is it effective) we're treated to a montage from the first six films in the *Nightmare on Elm Street* series. *New Nightmare* is outside the standard canon, so Freddy has been narrating from "the bowels of hell," where he's been ever since Maggie sent him there. Since he's fueled by fear, he can't come back to life unless people remember him. ("Being dead wasn't a problem, but being forgotten? Now that's a bitch!") What's a demon to do?

We transition to a scene that would fit comfortably in any *Friday the 13th* film, even the one where Jason goes to outer space. (Don't ask) A camp counselor goes skinny dipping at night, only to wind up on the business end of Jason Voorhees's machete. Seemingly dead, the counselor morphs into several other slain counselors, insisting they "deserved to be punished." Jason is confused, but he sees his mother tell him he's special and that he has a mission: go to Springwood to "punish" the teens there. Lo and behold, "Pamela" is actually Freddy in disguise. He resurrects Jason in his stead to make the residents of Springwood think he's back.

As arguably the most anticipated horror film of all time, *Freddy vs Jason's* opening titles are intended to communicate that yes, this is what you've been waiting for. CGI flesh is quickly sliced, revealing "New Line Cinema presents" in blood. Freddy's cackle is heard as the text liquifies before splashing onto a hot surface, revealing the crossover's title. The nü metal band Spineshank can be heard as Jason's shadow is seen stalking Elm Street on a dark and stormy night.

The old Thompson house, 1428 Elm Street, is now inhabited by Lori Campbell (Monica Keena) and her father, a local doctor. Since dad's at work, she's having some friends over. They include Kia (Kelly Rowland), her best friend who tries to hide her vulnerability behind bravado, and Gibb (Katharine Isabelle), a combination tomboy and party girl, sporting a red baseball cap in tribute to P.J. Soles' character from *Carrie*. She's awaiting the arrival of her asshole boyfriend Trey (Jesse Hutch) and his friend Blake (David Kopp). Kia intends to set Lori up with Blake, because she's still pining for her ex-boyfriend

Will. Considering that Will moved away when they were fourteen, Kia insists she needs to move on.

This is easier said than done, especially when the Springwood dating pool includes the hapless moron Blake and Trey, the biggest douchebag we've ever seen in a *Nightmare* film. (Though to be fair, he'd fit right in at Camp Crystal Lake. The *Friday the 13th* films are known for having characters so thin and/or wretched, you can't wait to see them get eviscerated. That's never been the M.O. of *Nightmare on Elm Street*, but the presence of Jason means we're going to see some victims we won't care about. It's just priced in.) Lucky for us, all Trey does is treat Gibb like garbage. They sleep together in an upstairs bedroom. While Gibb showers, Jason enters, surprising Trey. He proceeds to stab him with his machete multiple times, then grabs both ends of the bed and folds it in half, along with Trey. Just an incredible kill.

Since Trey died horribly in a bed at 1428 Elm Street, the Springwood police department naturally assumes he was killed by Freddy. Yes, they've gotten wise to his machinations over the years, and understand that speaking Freddy's name out loud gives him power. It appears they've learned from their mistakes, at least until the sheriff (Gary Chalk) threatens to send one of his officers to Westin Hills if he doesn't keep his mouth shut. (Excuse me?)

The teens are separated at the police station so they can't share theories. Lori remembers hearing a cop say "Freddy," which doesn't ring a bell to Deputy Stubbs (Lochlyn Munro), who's new in town. Exhausted, she falls asleep and dreams of the little girl we saw in the opening scene, only now, it appears her eyes have been cut out. She tells Lori to "warn your friends. Warn everyone." Lori is suddenly transported to her front lawn, which has turned into a graveyard. The jump rope kids return, singing their song as blood cascades down her door. Freddy jumps into frame just as Lori wakes up to go home.

Later that night, Blake is admonished by his father for not watching his sister, a major sin in the *Friday the 13th* series, but he tells his dad to go away while sipping from a flask on his front porch. (Great.) He falls asleep and dreams of a lamb. (Remember that?) Blake is almost killed by Freddy, but he's not powerful enough yet. Instead, Jason is waiting for him when he wakes up and kills both Blake and his dad with a flick of the machete.

We next return to another familiar location in the *Nightmare* series: Westin Hills, now with more patients than ever before. Except they're all wearing the same bland clothes like inmates. Lori's ex Will (Jason Ritter) and his friend Mark (Brendan Fletcher) are among the patients lined up to get their meds, which happens to be, you guessed it, Hypnocil, now the preferred drug of Springwood. As lucid youths, both Mark and Will seem out of place in the psych ward, but Will becomes animated when he sees a news report on TV about a death at Lori's house. (At least station KRGR isn't in the pocket of Springwood PD.)

It's then revealed why Will is institutionalized: he claims to have seen Lori's dad kill her mom. Having lost his own brother to an apparent suicide, Mark sympathizes with Will and agrees to help break them both out so they can check on Lori. This involves Mark causing a raucous distraction in order to steal a key card. (Both Max and Dr. Gordon are long-gone, so it makes sense that there's nobody truly minding the store.) The next morning, Lori's dad tries to surreptitiously drug her juice with Hypnocil. She nods off and imagines Freddy morphing into her father. (It's 2003 and we love our 2003 CGI.) She then wakes up and leaves for school. The sheriff drops by to tell Dr. Campbell that Mark and Will escaped Westin Hills the night before.

Good ol' Springwood High School. Lori meets up with Kia and Gibb, who learn about Blake and his dad. Everyone at school seems to know what happened at Lori's house, including Linderman (Chris Rodriguez Marquette), a nerd with a not-so-secret crush on Lori. Kia tells him to fuck off. Besides, there's a rave at the local cornfield tonight. A traumatized Gibb is convinced to attend by the rave promoters, a portly jock Shack (Chris Gauthier) and a character named Freeburg (Kyle Labine), a fairly obvious knockoff of Jay from the View Askewniverse. (One can argue that it pays tribute to Kevin Smith and Jason Mewes' character, but it seems lazy in retrospect. Still, it's nice to see a former indie studio like New Line give a shout-out to the next generation of indie filmmakers. Plus, Freeburg is funny in a very Kevin Smith way, beyond the obvious aesthetics.)

Lori talks about her nightmare at school, inadvertently spreading the legend of Freddy. When she starts to recall the rhyme from her dream, Mark shows up to finish it as a warning. (It's a reversal of Nancy's first appearance in *Dream Warriors*). Will appears a moment later, asking him to stop scaring her and the rest of the student body. (This includes Evangeline Lilly as an unnamed extra.) Frightened and overwhelmed, Lori can't handle any more, so she faints right there in the hallway. Will and Mark run away as "Principal Shaye" arrives on the scene. (Robert Shaye in his sixth *Nightmare* appearance, seventh if you count *Freddy's Nightmares*.)

Kia reads a magazine in the nurse's office while she waits for Lori to wake up. She's considering getting a nose job when the magazine starts to read like a grossly realistic medical journal. Then Freddy's glove emerges from its pages and cuts off her nose. But Freddy is *still* not strong enough, so she just wakes up in a frenzy, no harm done. He doesn't even enter Lori's dreams beyond appearing as a silhouette behind a window.

Meanwhile, Will and Mark head to the library to do research. (Ah, 2003.) The local obituaries they search through are all blacked out, including the one for Mark's brother. There's also nothing in the town archives about Freddy, which they find even more suspicious. Given this, Mark asserts that his late brother's suicide was, in fact, a homicide as he dreamt of Freddy before his untimely death. Mark further recalls his brother saying that Freddy was powered by fear, which the Westin escapees unwittingly spread at Springwood High earlier that day. Realizing their dangerous gaffe, Will rushes to find Lori before she falls asleep while Mark holes up at his family home, where his parents are somehow absent.

Anyway, it's time to go to a rave in the cornfield! Kia, Lori, and Gibb arrive at a clearing amongst the stalks where glowsticks move in slow motion, beer flows, and techno blasts from a DJ's speakers. Linderman arrives and is promptly forced to do a beer funnel by Shack and his fellow jocks. He jokes about it with Lori, but Kia still tells him to get lost. The ordinarily meek Linderman sticks up for himself by calling Kia out on how her low self-esteem makes her a bully. Even Lori is shocked, but Kia kind of likes him for it. So, she asks him to dance. Will soon arrives at the rave to see Lori. He reveals he never moved away, but rather that he's been committed to Westin Hills for the past four years. Out in the field, Jason lurks and grabs a metal pole from an unused silo.

Gibb hears Freeburg gossiping at the rave about Trey and Blake's deaths, helping empower Freddy even more. It's kind of a dick move on his part, but this rave is full of potential Jason victims aka oblivious party animals. (I suppose Lisa had a pool party after Schneider died in *Freddy's Revenge*, but he was a scumbag and… well, yes, Trey was too.) Proving scummy even in death, Trey's twisted body appears to Gibb in the cornfield, insulting her for partying. In a drunken daze, she follows him to a distant silo. Inside the structure, however, it's an industrial boiler room with no exit. Freddy presses his face through the wall just like he did to Nancy in the original film. In reality, Gibb is passed out in the cornfield while a raver covered in glowsticks attempts to sexually assault her. (Gross, but how can nobody notice this? He's lit up like a neon Christmas tree.)

In a scene that should be familiar by now, Freddy toys with Gibb as she makes her way through the boiler room. When he finally goes in for the kill, blood explodes from her chest and she disappears. Back in reality, Jason has impaled both Gibb and her would-be rapist with his newfound metal pole. He's stolen Freddy's kill while also tossing the raver into the air. Freddy is *pissed*.

Undeterred, Jason encounters Shack and another jock who are drinking everclear and smoking weed. He kills the unnamed friend, and in desperation, Shack splashes Jason with the booze and lights him on fire with a tiki torch. Pretty savage for a high schooler, but it doesn't stop the masked maniac. In fact, Shack runs back to the rave, arriving just in time to get a flaming machete through the chest. Jason proceeds to cut through the wasted ravers (pun sort of intended) as Will, Kia, Linderman, Lori, and Freeburg leave together in Mark's van. Despite the shocking discovery of Gibb's corpse, Freeburg lights up a joint and passes it to a scared Linderman. ("*Dude*, that goalie was pissed about something").

Will takes Lori home where he makes a stunning revelation before she gets out of the van: that he saw her father kill her mother. She can't believe it as her father said she died in a car accident. Dr. Campbell shows up and forces Lori out of the vehicle. At this point, she knows he's lying, so she runs back to Will. Realizing they can only trust their peers, they go back to Mark's house for triage. They don't yet know that Mark has fallen asleep waiting for Will to return. He sees his dead brother Bobby (Zack Ward) in the bloody bathtub where he "killed himself." Of course, it's Freddy in disguise and he kills Mark by lighting him on fire and slashing his face just as Lori and Will arrive at his house.

Springwood is officially in lockdown. The Sheriff ponders the way forward now that it appears Freddy is back. Deputy Stubbs is still trying to help. He thinks they're too similar to the killings at Crystal Lake, but his boss shuts him down. Dismayed and confused, Stubbs discovers our remaining teens meeting in Freeburg's basement.

We then get an exposition dump about Jason and Freddy that allows the kids to realize Jason, though dangerous, is functioning as Freddy's pawn. Lori, who's been resting on the couch, away from the group, points out Freddy was killed by fire and Jason by water. (It's clumsy, and not what the screenwriters intended since Freddy just lit Mark on fire and Jason drowned in a lake.) Neither killer is scared by either element, but the teens don't listen to Lori. Instead, they turn on her just as her father appears in her face, trying to kiss her. It's so disgusting, but it's also very much a Freddy moment. When he reveals himself, she grabs his ear and rips it off before her screaming causes the group to wake her up. To her shock, she's still holding Freddy's deformed ear, re-establishing the lore of being able to take things out of dreams. The ear turns to maggots when she drops it on the floor. The plan is to immediately block everyone's dreams while they figure this out. Since Will and Mark never dreamed in Westin Hills, they google Hypnocil (which is *still* not FDA-approved, by the way) and realize it's their short-term answer.

Upon breaking into the hospital, they're able to walk around freely as Jason, hot on their trail, has already killed the security guard. The group split up and Will, Kia, and Lori discover a room full of young patients who've been rendered comatose due to excessive Hypnocil use. As bad as Freddy and Jason are, this is a pretty horrifying site. Is it possible their dreams were so vivid that they were pumped full of Hypnocil by Lori's father? That's right. Dr. Campbell's name is found on the hospital charts. Even all these years later, you still can't trust the parents of Springwood, even if they say they're working in your best interests.

Juxtaposed with this horrific scene is Freeburg smoking a joint apart from the group. He's just shameless. The weed puts him to sleep, just like with Spencer. Freeburg imagines that a giant caterpillar with a hookah sneaks into the room, one that looks suspiciously like Freddy in demonic stripes of red and green. Freeburg is amused, until the caterpillar shotguns the smoke from his hookah right into his mouth, causing him to wander in to see the coma patients, now devoid of the other characters. The patients sit up and point at him, despite having cotton taped over their eyes. The "Freddypillar" jumps into Freeburg's mouth, possessing him, somewhat differently than Jesse in Freddy's Revenge, though the specifics don't matter in this case. The possessed Freeburg flushes all the Hypnocil he can find down the drain.

Of course, Jason appears and finds the teens. He slashes a security console with his machete, electrocuting him, which is only a momentary hurdle. He grabs electrified hold of Stubbs, acting as a conduit to kill the deputy. This sends Lori, Will, Linderman, and Kia fleeing the hospital corridor. They pass "Freeburg," who won't move. "Freeburg" hides two giant tranquilizers behind his back, and when Jason approaches him with his machete, he fully injects both into his undead neck. This doesn't stop Jacon from bisecting him with the machete, but he then faints on the spot, entering the dream realm.

Round one of the titular fight begins in Freddy's boiler room where he berates Jason as Pamela. When Freddy reveals his true form to Jason for the first time, an enraged Jason cuts off Freddy's arms. You'd think that was the end of it, but they grow back (another part one reference). The fight now begins in earnest. It doesn't quite resemble kung fu, but it's still a battle to behold. Freddy isn't at the height of his powers, but you can tell he's getting stronger. Still, he's exasperated at this silent brute who refuses to die. It's not until a burst pipe stops Jason in his tracks that Freddy remembers to do what he does best.

It's been established that Jason is afraid of drowning, but let's suspend disbelief for a second to pretend he's scared of bad plumbing. It's rather dumb, especially for a film that keeps continuity with the previous sequels, but this script was heavily rewritten to include a few regrettable moments. Still, we won't throw Jason out with the pipe water. Freddy taunts him as his fear causes him to revert back to a scared, deformed child. He holds up Pamela's severed head while poking around in Jason's brain. Really, he sticks a finger blade in the side of his head to enter into his mind, poor kid. And yes, I just sympathized with Jason Voorhees, mass murderer. This is absolutely intentional on the part of the filmmakers.

Back in the "real world," the kids drive the van, containing a sleeping Jason and as much tranquilizer liquid as they could take from Westin Hills. The new plan is for Lori to fall asleep and bring Freddy out into the real world so Jason can kill him. They're driving to Camp Crystal Lake so Jason doesn't try to follow them anymore. "At least [he] has home field advantage." One gets the sense that they know it's not the best idea, but it's the one they've got.

Lori sets the alarm on her watch (just like part one), falls asleep, and immediately dreams of Camp Crystal Lake. She witnesses young Jason being bullied and pushed into the lake by the other kids. Lori tries to get the nearby counselors to help, but they're too busy… having sex outside of a cabin. If you think that can't get more sickening, the male counselor turns into Freddy and the female counselor is a corpse (which on repeat viewing, feels like a joke someone would tell in *Wet Hot American Summer*). Lori tries to save Jason from drowning, but Freddy breaks the surface of the lake to pull him under.

Back in the van, Jason appears to be drowning in his dream. This would only solve half the problem, so somebody has to pull back his mask and give him CPR. Linderman has asthma, Will's driving, and Lori's asleep, so the task falls to a reluctant Kia. It's a terrifying prospect, but Rowland and Ritter mine some humor out of it ("Kia, he has asthma!"). Before she can try, Jason bolts upright in the van, causing it to crash.

When Jason vanishes from the dream, an angry Freddy sets his sights on Lori and his facial features contort into something more demonic. Her alarm watch goes off, so she screams and rushes Freddy… but she's still asleep! Freddy has disappeared and she's suddenly back on the nightmare version of her front lawn. Lori wanders into the house, calling for her friends to wake her up. She sees her father approach her mother with a knife. Could Will have been right all along? No, it's just Freddy, straddling Lori's sleeping mother, just before he kills her with his blades. ("I've always had a thing for the whores that live in this house.")

Luckily for our heroes, nobody was hurt too bad in the crash, which happened just outside Camp Crystal Lake. They drag the sleeping Lori to a cabin where they try to wake her up to no avail. Jason follows them inside and a fire breaks out as Lori's friends attempt to defend her. Jason fatally throws Linderman into a wall mount, so Kia helps him outside. In the dream, Freddy's about to kill Lori when the cabin fire reaches her hand. Instinctively, she grabs Freddy and they take a trip back to the real world where Jason is waiting.

Round two begins in the waking world, where Freddy is vulnerable. As they continue to beat each other to bloody bits, Linderman sadly dies from his injury. Kia runs for help, but winds up intersecting Freddy before he can kill Lori and Will. She teases him with some bad improv, including a gay slur that was absolutely not in the script (I said we'll get there). She's too busy making fun of him to notice Jason come up behind her and whack her with the machete so hard that she flies into a nearby tree. Time in, guys!

As they go back at it, Will tries to commandeer a motorboat, but Lori won't leave. She needs revenge for what Freddy has done to their lives. That will have to wait, since Freddy and Jason are now battling using tanks of compressed air and construction equipment. The fight moves to the dock, which Will and Lori have doused with gasoline. Freddy cuts off Jason's fingers, causing him to drop the machete, which Freddy grabs mid-air. Now dual-wielding, he hits Jason with his own weapon, then stabs his eyes with his claw blades. Lori torches the deck as Jason rips Freddy's claw hand (and arm) off. The two of them are *drenched* in blood and gore, when the dock blows. The explosion lights them both up before knocking them into the lake.

From the shore, Will and Lori survey the fiery damage. Just when you thought it was safe to go back to Crystal Lake, a figure silently approaches brandishing a machete. It's Freddy, still barely alive, and focused on his victims instead of one-liners. Before he can land the killing blow to the couple, a badly injured Jason jumps out of the lake to impale Freddy with his own claw. He falls back in as a surprised Freddy drops the machete. Lori picks it up and decapitates him. She makes eye contact with Jason before he too dies in the lake. Injured but still alive, Will and Lori leave, triumphant.

An epilogue shows Jason rising from a mysterious body of water with Freddy's head as a trophy. It might be the same location, but the surrounding area feels less like Crystal Lake and more like the smokey void of his mindscape. However, since every iteration of the script ended with them in hell, it's safe to assume they're both back in the underworld, where they belong. As a final goodbye, Freddy's head winks at the camera. (A Bob Shaye note. Just like with the original film, he had to be involved with the finale.) Thus ends the original *Nightmare on Elm Street* cycle. Thanks for coming out.

# NIGHTMARE AUTOPSIS

*Freddy vs Jason* is distinct for many reasons, chief among them that it's the first film in the *Nightmare on Elm Street* series written by fans. Beyond the studio mandates given to other writers, Damian Shannon and Mark Swift collaborated on a script that contained what they wanted to see in a film where Jason and Freddy duke it out. Earlier screenwriters took liberties with the origins and backstories of the killers, but it was important to Shannon and Swift that their continuities remained intact. They also had the best idea out of all the scripts out there (and there were many). Having the two slashers fighting over victims is darkly hilarious. Mark Swift admitted their guiding questions while writing the script were "What would the fans think?" and "What would Wes Craven think?" While it's admirable to want to please the man who brought us *A Nightmare on Elm Street*, it's no surprise that Craven wasn't a fan of the crossover. Who could blame him? A film where his creation fights a monster from an entirely different film series was never something that interested him, despite the historical precedent set by Dracula, Frankenstein, and so many other classic monsters who appeared alongside each other as they grew in popularity. Craven never wanted a spectacle, but action director Ronny Yu was happy to make the film so many have been waiting for.

*Dream Master* director Renny Harlin was inspired by Hong Kong action films during the production of his *Nightmare*, but Hong Kong-born Ronny Yu was already a veteran of martial arts cinema when he took the job to direct *Freddy vs Jason*. His action fantasy *The Bride with White Hair* was well regarded and led to him directing the American *Ninja Turtles* riff, *Warriors of Virtue*. Despite his admitted aversion to the horror genre, Yu pivoted towards it with *Bride of Chucky*, another franchise sequel with blood, laughs, and complicated special effects. (*Bride of Chucky* also coincidentally featured John Ritter, father of this film's Jason Ritter.)

It's no surprise that *Freddy vs Jason* shares some DNA with *The Dream Master* given its use of Dutch angles and stylized fight choreography. Yu and Cinematographer Fred Murphy dramatically incorporate lots of blue light into the "real world" while drenching the nightmare world in reds and greens. There's also accelerated camera motion in several spots, along with more CGI than ever before.

The score references the original Bernstein theme in a few places, but it's not woven into Graeme Revell's score. Likewise with Harry Manfredini's *Friday the 13th* theme. Revell puts his orchestra to work, bringing a sense of terror and grandeur along with some tribal drum motifs. It compliments the film very well, while the nü metal soundtrack dates it. Yes, we have a soundtrack again, but it contains mostly forgettable bands. (That Spineshank song in the intro works gangbusters, though.)

There has been much speculation as to why Kane Hodder, the actor who'd been portraying Jason for over a decade, was recast in the film. Stuntman Ken Kirzinger was hired in his place, this despite the fact that Hodder had been vocal about wanting to return. Why mess with what had been working so well? It's a question fans have been pondering for twenty years, as Hodder himself was never given an explanation. I believe I have an answer, though like the end of the film itself, it might not be satisfactory for anyone.

Hodder's Jason was a hulking monster behind the hockey mask. He brought a physicality and brutality to the character that was unseen in the previous entries, and in many filmgoers minds, kept the *Friday the 13th* franchise going past its prime. For some, Hodder is as iconic as Englund's Freddy. The script was even written with him specifically in mind. However, based on Kirzinger's performance, one can discern that the powers that be clearly wanted someone else to play the masked butcher. Someone who, for better or worse, could appear more sympathetic. A Jason Voorhees you could root *for*? That had never been done. Sure, Jason kills indiscriminately in some vicious moments, but he doesn't seem to enjoy it, per se. He's back to killing because his "mother" wants him to (just another image of a bad parent in these films). We even see close-ups of his very human-looking eyes, reacting to various plot points, and even saving Lori and Will's lives at the end, even indirectly. A sympathetic Jason Voorhees was a new concept, even with his tragic backstory, and one that was completely different from the juggernaut Hodder was used to playing. Kenzinger did a great job in the role, but who's to say Hodder couldn't have pulled off the softer side of Jason? We'll never know, but it's clear he deserved his chance.

Apologies to fans of Jason Voorhees, but *Freddy vs Jason* is, first and foremost, a *Nightmare on Elm Street* film. Sure, Jason does the majority of the killing in set pieces that would be at home in a *Friday the 13th*, but Freddy is the true antagonist of the story. He sets everything in motion and Springwood is the primary locale for most of the film. If anything, Ronny Yu toys with making Jason a hero. In *Never Sleep Again*, he compares Jason to a samurai. The attempts to contrast him with the child-murdering Freddy are rampant throughout the film.

Visually, Freddy's look feels like a "greatest hits" pastiche. He's scary again with rotten teeth that age him without losing his menace. While his later demon form is unnecessary and redundant, he has the best-looking claw in the series besides *New Nightmare*. The blades are huge, and they curve at the tip, making him look deadlier than ever.

As we continue discussing the cast, we have to address the fundamental differences between the characters of *Nightmare on Elm Street* and *Friday the 13th*. Shannon and Swift intentionally created characters who would be at home in both franchises. The characters from *Nightmare on Elm Street* tend to be more emotional, introspective, and headstrong like Lori, Will and Mark. The characters from *Friday the 13th* lean towards hapless party animals, who distract themselves easily with drugs and sex like Gibb and Freeburg. Also, some of them are outright assholes like Trey and Shack.

Again, I have to apologize to fans of *Friday the 13th*. I enjoy those films very much as the fun, meat-and-potatoes slasher films they are. But their paucity of good characters is a function of the series. You expect a high body count and you don't reach it by spending time with people you like. Several of the films in the series make you root for certain characters to die. If you find yourself drawn toward any particular person, it's a happy bonus. That's not to say there aren't lesser characters in the *Nightmare* films or that every hapless counselor who faces off with Jason is disposable. But caring about the plight of the characters in the Nightmare films is practically priced in, whereas it's mostly an afterthought in the *Friday* films.

The outlier is Linderman, the nerd who has a lot of dialogue that evokes the postmodern horror films that came out in the wake of *Scream*. Kevin Williamson's script was hip and self-referential, so the teen-centric films that followed tried to copy it as best they could (meaning not at all). By 2003, the trend had mostly subsided, but there's still a hint of it when Linderman is doused with beer and says he was "penalized for my ability to read above a fourth-grade level." It's not as obnoxious as other films that tried to eat Williamson's lunch, but just because every town had an Elm Street, doesn't mean it also has a *Dawson's Creek*.

Since this is the first *Elm Street* film produced in Canada, a good portion of the actors are Canucks like Isabelle, Fletcher, and Munro, to name a few. Zack Ward (*A Christmas Story*) appears briefly, but he brings some gusto to the few lines of exposition he gives as Freddy/Mark. Mark is actually the only character that Freddy kills in the movie, not counting Lori's mom in a flashback. He may be the primary antagonist, but it's disappointing that we don't see more of the fantastical, fear-based death scenes we've grown accustomed to. Don't get me wrong, the bed folding scene is an all-timer and the finale delivers, but Englund's swan song deserved more hallmarks of the series we've come to love.

The film's first half is an interesting reversal of the established formula: the adults know about the danger, but the teens are oblivious. The kids who might know the truth are locked away in Westin Hills, now a makeshift prison instead of a therapeutic hospital. While there is a mention of group therapy, it seems like lip service to cover up the fact that the real reason the "patients" are there is to keep the legend of Freddy off the lips of the next generation. The doctors and local authorities have no compunction about doping them all up with Hypnocil, either. (Dr. Simms owes Nancy an apology.) Like the original film, the father of the final girl still represents institutional decline, but as a doctor instead of a police officer. Don't get me wrong, Springwood PD is more corrupt than ever, but this is the first time we've seen a medical professional in the franchise with genuine malicious intent. The only truly benevolent adult in the film is Deputy Stubbs, which is a change from the dynamics we've seen previously in the series, but of course, he has to die at some point so the teens fight for their lives on their own.

Another fascinating aspect to the story is that it takes the "sins of the parents" angle to a very dark conclusion. Not the wacky, Lynchian psychosis of *Freddy's Dead* where adults have basically dissociated from reality, but a deeply paranoid carceral state. The actions of the original parents who burned Freddy Krueger to death created a ripple effect that ended not just with the murder, but the forced imprisonment of anyone who utters the name "Freddy Krueger." The current parents of Springwood are aware that every "undesirable" is thrown in

Westin Hills to keep a tenuous peace. This conspiratorial nature borders on folk horror, which is a subgenre that hasn't been explored here before. Even if Freddy never came back to life, the film posits that he still "won" by corrupting the souls of the town. Granted, the youths of Springwood are blissfully unaware before the start of the film, so it's not entirely dystopian. Thanks to their rebellion, the main characters don't just send Freddy back to hell, they bring an end to the town's newly-implemented police state. Maybe now the parents of Springwood can finally be honest with their children.

To this day, *Freddy vs Jason* remains the highest grossing film from either franchise. Audiences still argue the impossible question set by the ending: who won, Freddy or Jason? The teenagers won. That's what makes this film part of the *Nightmare on Elm Street* canon.

## THE ORIGINAL SCRIPT

As mentioned previously, there were so many official scripts written for *Freddy vs Jason* that an entire book chronicles them all. For this book, we're going to look at the original draft of Shannon and Swift's *Freddy vs Jason* before it was rewritten for a shorter running time. Of all the sections in this book that focus on script changes, this one is by far the longest, as their original vision was more fleshed-out and coherent. It was also devoid of the infamous "f word" in the finished film.

An *Elm Street* tradition, the script opens with a quote from *Paradise Lost*. The screenwriters are clearly fans, but most of their fanservice works without calling too much attention to itself. The montage of scenes from previous *Elm Street* films has less voiceover, and we get a re-staging of the end of *Jason Goes to Hell* with Freddy grabbing Jason's mask. Jason's dream also starts with the unnamed counselor he kills being a jerk to a little kid. The kid gives her the finger when she runs from Jason, which is a cute representation of his subconscious. Before appearing as Pamela Voorhees, Freddy mocks him by reciting the "Ki, ki, ki, ma, ma, ma" theme. As Pamela, Freddy specifically orders him to kill *once*, then disappear. And Jason doesn't just resurrect. He comes out of the ground and steals a machete from a local store at Crystal Lake.

At Lori's house, her friends realize her father set up a nanny cam in his absence. (So we're also in a surveillance state. Great.) The official word on Lori's mom is that she abandoned her family instead of dying in a car accident. (That seems much crueler than at least admitting she's dead. Don't give the girl hope). After Trey's death, the teens are made to stay in the house instead of going to the station. Lori still dreams of the eyeless little girl, but she also sees a vision of a bloody Tina from part one. (Presumably not played by the considerably older Amanda Wyss.) Tina takes the second half of the little girl's dialogue in the finished film ("Warn your friends"). Blake's dad only appears to tell him he's a shitty babysitter, then exits the movie. Jason still kills Blake by throttling him with his porch swing.

In Westin Hills, Will has been convinced by the doctor that Lori's mom left and he didn't actually see anything. Mark is now named "Carlos," but we'll still call him Mark for our purposes. It's great they wanted to add more diversity to the series, but Carlos is already a character in *Freddy's Dead*, in case you haven't heard. (Get it? Never mind). Mark mentions the "quiet room" and Dr. Simms before bribing a guard with a comic book to let him and Will escape. When they get to Mark's house, his mother is home, a sad woman who's glad to see him. Mark tells Will that they no longer use the bathroom where his brother (now named Miguel) died.

Also a deleted scene on the home release, Lori exits her house in the morning and recalls something from her nightmare. She approaches her yellow front door with her key and scrapes off a section of yellow paint, revealing the house's familiar (to us) red paint. At school, we meet Freeburg's stoner friend, Scott, who was combined with Freeburg into one character since he has no discernable personality. (Also, to pad Jason's body count.) His character might be extraneous, but there are some excised moments that could have remained. For example, Kia's nose bleeds when she wakes up in the nurse's office. Will and Mark are run out of the school by Principal Shaye. (They promoted the teacher from *Dream Master*? Good thing he can finally quit his bartending gig.) On the way out, they encounter Gibb, who tells them Lori will be at the rave. A nice character bit happens when Will shows up at the rave, Kia gives him a beer, which the script indicates is his first.

In lieu of a flaming machete, Shack dies when Jason crushes his head in the midst of doing a beer bong. This is what puts out the fire that engulfed Jason. There's also a character dubbed "Trippy Dude" who's seeing color trails on psychedelics before Jason kills him with a machete. The rave massacre commences, but just before Jason can kill Linderman, Will hits him with Mark's van. Mark also dies before Will drops Lori off at home. His mother discovers the body and screams. (This would've seemed *especially* unfair to that poor parent having already lost a child to Freddy.)

When Lori finally goes home, she doesn't run away after confronting her father. She finds her mother's belongings in the basement (proof that she didn't run away), as well as the nanny cam inside "Mr. Nuzzles," a Furby lawsuit waiting to happen. She checks the camera and sees Jason in her house. Finally, she finds her father's security badge. It turns out he works for The Katja Institute! Previously, there was mention of his colleague, Dr. Simms, and since Priscilla Pointer was eighty-three in 2003, it's entirely possible she could've made a cameo. Instead of running to Will, he later visits her in the backyard, while noting his dad got rid of the rose trellis. These are some great easter eggs that don't distract from the film and would have been great additions.

We get a brief montage of scenes around town. It should be noted the success of this film led to Shannon and Swift getting the job to write the *Friday the 13th* remake, which also featured a brief montage towards the end of the film that was cut. Here's hoping they finally get that montage someday. The script here shows us the aftermath of the cornfield slaughter, Mark's parents in mourning, and finally we end at the police station. A determined Stubbs tells the sheriff about "reports on Voorhees as far away as Manhattan." Stubbs never makes it to Freeburg's place, but we see him later.

Over in Freeburg's basement, Lori dreams of a scene out of *The Fly*, which she was watching on tv earlier. She winds up in a giant web as a Freddy-like spider tries to kill her, followed by a giant version of her father. ("I won't let him get you.") It functions as a reference to Debbie's death in *The Dream Master*, as well as a metaphor for what Springwood is doing to its children. Lori pulls an ear *and* a tooth out of her dream, freaking everyone out. Linderman, in particular, who is more of a joke in this draft. ("Wesleyan was my safety school. WESLEYAN!") Lori appears to take control of the scared group, becoming the de facto leader, just like an *Elm Street* heroine.

Instead of going back to Westin Hills, the group breaks into The Katja Institute, but the scene is structurally the same as the finished film. The coma patients include a guy who was transferred from Westin Hills when he "cut off his own eyelids to stay awake." Dr. Gordon referenced someone doing the same thing prior to the events of *Dream Warriors*. Some fans believe this unnamed patient was Jesse Walsh, but this can't be the same guy from sixteen years ago, right? Another improvement on the finished film is that Freeburg wants to smoke weed in the midst of their mission, more to calm his frayed nerves than just because he wants to get stoned. Jason electrocutes Scott (oh yeah, he's here, too) just like Stubbs in the finished film.

During the boiler room fight, only one of Freddy's arms gets cut off. The script indicates Freddy's face was meant to convey "Why won't you die?" instead of him saying the line in the film. Also, the water pipe doesn't burst as a result of the fight. Freddy realizes he has to scare him. Jason doesn't appear as his younger self. The inside of his mind is more vivid with corpse trees, skull rocks, and the water of the lake is blood.

Back in the van, Will comments on how crazy it is to drive Jason back to Crystal Lake, possibly as an attempt to get in front of the audience. Linderman apologies to Kia, endearing him further. Better late than never, Deputy Stubbs appears at a roadblock, but he lets them go when he sees the comatose Jason. He radios Crystal Lake, and by the time they get there, a local cop interrupts the group in the cabin. Jason barges in with an ax he found, and his machete is a backup. When Freddy comes out and faces Jason, Will says "Place your bets." (Lori takes the line in the film's trailer, which is absent from the final film.)

Instead of some terrible improv, Kia finds herself running from Jason, then stopping when she realizes he'll stop if she's not afraid of him. She closes her eyes and intones "Jason is nothing" repeatedly to herself. She opens her eyes to Freddy grinning as Jason brings the machete down. ("Wrong one, bitch.") Kia died because she got her killers mixed up, which is not only really funny, it also signals to audience members who may be unfamiliar with the monsters that it's okay to just have fun with it. (But no, let's go with "How sweet, dark meat.")

Did you ever wonder why there was a construction site at Camp Crystal Lake in the finished film? The answer comes in the form of another set of iconic 80's villains, greedy real estate developers. Yes, the original script saw real estate developers arguing in a nearby office trailer, but rest assured, Freddy and Jason make quick work of them. One is named Phil, possibly a reference to Phil Scuderi, one of the investors on the original *Friday the 13th*. Before they're turned into human shields by the maniacs, we hear them complaining about a Crystal Lake local who wants to halt the redevelopment, some guy named Tommy Jarvis. Fans of the *Friday the 13th* series would recognize him as Jason's nemesis over the course of several films.

Another funny, almost Raimi-esque moment happens when Lori throws Jason's machete at Freddy, but misses and hits Jason's leg. Freddy mocks her aim, but Jason takes the machete right out of his leg and keeps fighting. Freddy eventually begs for mercy and tries to appeal to Jason that they should be a team. "I got the brains, you got the brawn" he says, referring back to *Freddy's Revenge*. It's fruitless, of course.

The fight also ends in a much more spectacular fashion. Jason accidentally kicks Freddy's severed hand, with the glove, into the lake. Freddy reaches in and tears his heart out. The explosion still sends them flying into the water, but a hole opens up at the bottom of the lake. Jason grabs Freddy as they fall into the mysterious void, along with the water, leaving a dry lakebed. That was definitely not in the budget.

Deputy Stubbs shows up with an apologetic Dr. Campbell and a wounded Linderman. The survivors debate who won when they find Freddy's glove. Dr. Campbell talks about destroying it when Freddy's arm shoots out of the ground, grabs his leg, and pulls him into the earth as Lori screams. Cut to Freddy, putting his glove back on to fight Jason in a hellish pit surrounded by demons and tortured souls. The end. Forever.

As far as we know, there were two other endings considered. In the one on the DVD, Lori is about to finally lose her virginity to Will when he sprouts finger knives and kills her. This was added by another writer and shut down (thankfully) by frustrated and confused test audiences, bless their hearts. Another ending had Freddy and Jason landing in hell, represented by a black void. They're about to resume their fight, when chains shoot out of nowhere to restrain them. A figure emerges between them, revealed to be Pinhead from the *Hellraiser* films, asking "Gentlemen, what seems to be the problem?" The rights to the character belonged to Miramax, so that was a non-starter.

## END OF AN ERA

*Freddy vs. Jason* was released in North America on August 15, 2003, the day after the Northeast blackout. For just over twenty-four hours, the Northeast section of the country was without power, to say nothing of the ability to go to the movie theater. I have vivid memories of waiting to see if traffic lights were working so I could safely drive to see it. (Plus, if the traffic lights were working, so would movie theaters, right...?) When it was safe, I arrived at the UA Westbury 12 to a packed house. It was no outlier. *Freddy vs. Jason* grossed a jaw-dropping $36,400,00 on opening weekend alone. It topped off domestically at $82,622,655, leading to a worldwide total of $116,632,628. Not bad for a film that languished in development hell for over a decade, and absolutely phenomenal for a slasher film. It was one hell of a swan song.

# INTERVIEW
## STOKELY CHAFFIN
### EXECUTIVE PRODUCER
#### FREDDY VS. JASON

**You were already producing hits like *I Know What You Did Last Summer* and *Sweet Home Alabama* during the famously-long gestation period of *Freddy vs. Jason*. When did you board the project?**

I came in when it was dormant. I had worked with [Producer] Neal Moritz for many years and eventually I was hired by Toby Emmerich to come to New Line. I was glancing through their projects and when I saw *Freddy vs. Jason*, I said "Absolutely! Why hasn't this been made already?" Nobody else wanted it for some crazy reason, and they were happy to give it to me. I got my hands on the script, which was written by good writers, Mark Swift and Damian Shannon, but it was extremely convoluted and confusing. Fortunately, I started dating David Goyer at the time. He knew I wanted to get the movie made, so he read the script and said, "I know exactly how to fix this." He was the *Blade* guy, so New Line hired him happily.

**I read that original draft. It was over 120 pages, which would have made the film over two hours long.**

A dense 120 pages. It was good writing, but there was too much story, too much plot, too much going on. It was like a closet with too much stuff in it. You have to take everything out and put back what you really need. If it's confusing on paper,

I can't imagine how it would've translated on screen. I thought David did a great job of filling in the connective tissue and making sense of it.

**With all the scripts floating around, as a producer, how did you know this was the best script to produce?**

I had a lot of faith in David and his other work. He had such a strong sense of story and causality. I hate being confused in movies. When you're crystal clear about what's going on, it's a gift to the viewer, I think. It also helped the acting because everyone knew what they were doing.

**Having worked on film sets, I know credits can sometimes be nebulous, despite the amount of work everyone does. You're credited as "Executive Producer," but can you break down what that entailed for this film?**

I do get asked this all the time because being a producer is such an amorphous thing. You can go about it in so many different ways, whether you're the one who finds the material, develops the material, pays for the production. There are so many different ways to get involved with film because it takes such a village, right? It takes so many contributions, so you have to have humility about producer titles. In any producing job, there's jobs I could do and jobs I couldn't do, like the line producer, who's on set and has a whole range of skills that boggle my mind.

In this case, I was the one who found it on the development pile. Like, "Guys, what are we doing?" That and *Iron Man*. I was over the moon about them both. "Guys, we have *Iron Man*! Why aren't we doing this?" I was a new hire and they were looking for you to come in and find projects for you to be excited about and champion. I worked for Neal Moritz, who is also a genre filmmaker who has transcended genre filmmaking in every way. At the time, when you're an up-and-coming producer, you get made what you can. I must have had twenty projects set up around town, but you don't control what gets made. It's the people at the studio, who have the money who decide. You just hope you have enough irons in the fire to get a movie made every year or so. You're still selling. You have to get the heads of distribution and marketing on your team. I can't say I was particularly great at that, to tell you the truth. I had to put together packages that were so unbelievably good that they couldn't say no. That's why I left.

**But you did give us *Snakes on a Plane,* which my friends and I were there for opening night. We were those people.**

Well, thank you. We [originally] had Ronny Yu [as the director] and Toby had developed like nine scripts. Like come on, guys. It's snakes! On a plane! It doesn't have to be Shakespearean-level writing. Anyone who wants to see it is because of the title. But we kept rewriting it so many times that Ronny Yu had to leave. By the way, Ronny is a genius. He has so much integrity as a filmmaker and he's a great guy, but he walked. We got David Ellis to direct it, who I really liked, and he did a great job on *Final Destination 2,* but Ronny really got it fundamentally.

**You can tell with *Freddy vs. Jason* he brought a style that built off the previous films, but was his own. I still think he was a great choice to direct.**

We got so lucky. He was so good and so great with the actors. Jason Ritter was an absolute sweetheart. It was his first big break, which was also lucky for us. Ronny was known as a very artistic horror director and a real talent. I think he was disgusted with Hollywood. I can't say I blame him at all with the development hell on *Snakes on a Plane.* You know, you're not gonna win a Golden Globe for *Snakes on a Plane.* I hope it gets remade one day and it's terrifying. That would make me happy.

**What was Bob Shaye's reaction to resurrecting *Freddy vs. Jason*?**

He was so thrilled that a senior executive was so passionate about it and wanted to get involved. He loved it and loved me, I think, because I made horror movies. That's why I went there in the first place. Bob was excited that I liked genre filmmaking. The stars aligned, but I cared about those things. As a "baby producer," genre is the first thing you do because the audience will show up on Friday night in a group or on dates. Horror is the most exciting, fun movie experience there is. It's visceral. You're all physically in it together.

Neal hadn't made horror before *I Know What You Did Last Summer,* which was my find. He wanted to cater to a youth market. Mrs. Lamont was my fifth grade librarian at Verner Elementary in Tuscaloosa, Alabama. She said "Stokely, I know you're a huge reader, so try Lois Duncan." So, I read everything! I went through her books like a forest fire. *I Know What You Did Last Summer* was the one that chilled me to my soul.

**Did Bob have any mandates? Aside from his cameo, of course.**

You know, I think they'd run into a wall with development. That happens sometimes, where you think you've taken a project as far as you can. Like you're out of ideas. Sometimes it's about getting the best writer you can, and David was able to solve those problems brilliantly. They liked the basic idea of Shannon and Swift's script, and David found the throughline. Along with that cast, there was no stopping it. We were lucky, honestly.

**Were you worried that the blackout of August 2003 would hurt the box office?**

Oh, we thought we were sunk! We thought we'd open to $800,000 around the country, but it turned out New York City was our best place. People were hot and the only place that still had air conditioning was the movie theaters. It's just one of those things you never know. I thought the movie theaters would go dark, but it became known quickly in New York City that they were open. We did huge there.

**This was one of those films that horror fans never thought they'd ever see. I still think it's the best version of *Freddy vs. Jason* that was possible.**

Well, thank you. Honestly, I believe genre material should be the best quality it can be. To a point, you know, you have to go, "Okay, this isn't *American Beauty,* so let's make the idea we have." You still demand causality and clarity. It took years for the right story to come along, but you know a powerful story when you hear it. I just came in in the eighth inning.

**Even though it's called *Freddy vs. Jason*, I always looked at the film as primarily a *Nightmare on Elm Street* film, as opposed to a *Friday the 13th* film.**

I'm glad. I thought that's what we needed to do, especially coming from the studio that birthed *Nightmare on Elm Street*. It made sense for it to be a little biased. Let me ask, do you think [Freddy] won at the end?

**While I love the ambiguity of the last scene where you, the viewer, get to decide, my honest interpretation is that it ends with them back in hell. Since they're back where they belong, it's kind of narratively irrelevant. Really, the audience is the winner. I always appreciated that while the film is a fun slasher movie that ends with the promised battle royale, there was a real attempt to tell a story that furthered Wes Craven's themes that were present throughout the franchise.**

Thank you for saying that. I agree with your philosophy. You need to serve some meat and potatoes. Everyone who buys a ticket deserves to be told a compelling, intelligent story. It's so funny, my kid is thirteen now and he goes "That's just lazy writing, Mom." Like he can identify it all the time. It's probably from growing up with me as an armchair critic.

**Is there anything else you'd like to bring up about the film or New Line that isn't discussed enough?**

I'm just grateful to Sara Risher and Bob Shaye, who built the legacy and foundation of New Line. And a huge thank you to the fans, most importantly! They kept coming back and giving another chance to some dicey movies that didn't always honor what I've just been saying. I really appreciate how they showed up for us.

(Photo courtesy Charles Mineo's Ultimate *Freddy vs Jason* Archive)

# discussions with charter members of the
# DREAM WARRIORS

**Stephen Graham Jones**
**Grady Hendrix**
**Clarke Wolfe**
**Adam Cesare**
**Phil Nobile Jr.**
**Diandra Lazor**

# INTERVIEW
# STEPHEN GRAHAM JONES
## AUTHOR

MY HEART
IS A CHAINSAW

THE ONLY
GOOD INDIANS

**After writing several books about the subject, including the *Indian Lake* trilogy, I have to ask if you're sick of talking about slashers at this point.**

Never.

**Great to hear. Do you recall the first time you saw *Nightmare on Elm Street*?**

I saw it on VHS in eighth grade. My "love affair" with slashers is intimately wrapped up with Freddy, specifically. My friends and I would watch *Friday the 13th, Halloween,* and *Nightmare on Elm Street* in my friend's garage, which was separate from his house. His dad had a Freddy glove, since Freddy was big enough to merchandise, and he'd scratch it down the garage door, terrifying us. It was wonderful. I know Freddy gets a lot of grief these days for being too quippy, but let me tell you, back then he was the funniest thing in the world. He could be funny and scary in the same moment. People forget that. They may see him make a joke out of context and it may land flat, but in the context of its original housing, they tend to work.

**Even as he's joking, he's still going to kill you. There's sort of a horizon he crosses in part 6, where it's just not scary to the audience, but none of his victims suddenly think they're safe.**

For sure. I was doing an event in Connecticut a while back, and someone asked if I could be killed by any slasher, who would it be? I chose Freddy, because of the manner in which he kills you. For instance, if you were afraid of roaches, he turned you into a roach. Therefore, at the moment of your death, you get confirmation that your fears are legitimate. When Jason hits you with a machete or folds you in half in bed, you might not see it coming or even know what's happening. Freddy's pleasure comes from making the death poetic, like turning into a television set or whatever it is.

**You've written your share of imaginative scenes in your bibliography. Where does *Nightmare on Elm Street* fit into your work?**

The wonderful thing about the franchise is the dream logic. If I could boil *Nightmare on Elm Street* down into a single image, it would be the "oatmeal stairs" from part one. To me, that's so specifically dreamlike and perfect for the moment, that I think it's been hugely influential on me. Also, I know people are saying we should make movies sexier, but I kind of like Wes Craven's impulse was not to show a lot of skin. I respected that he did that a lot. He was really the only one doing it, too.

**The franchise is mostly free of gratuitous nudity, which was definitely an outlier of the time.**

I agree. All the other slasher [films] had that gratuitous nudity, and you feel kind of dirty. You know they didn't want to do it, and they felt they were in a position where they had no choice, and you become part of that process. It's weird and yucky, you know?

**Do you always go back to the original or do you consider the sequels as well?**

I think *The Dream Master* might be my second favorite, now that I think of it. That gear-up montage Alice has was hugely influential to me. Sometimes, I wonder if all my little versions of gear-up moments are my own versions of that. It felt like "Oh, I should've seen this coming the whole time," which is how those moments should feel. I love four and *Dream Warriors*, of course. I guess *Freddy's*

*Dead* is the weakest because I think [the humor] goes further than that horizon you're talking about. But to tell you the truth, when you get that deep into a continuous slasher franchise that isn't resetting, you kind of have to go over the line into the ridiculous. The trajectory is that if you're not getting ridiculous, you're not pushing it hard enough.

**Talk to me about final girls. I posit that Nancy is maybe the best final girl of all time.**

I agree. She's my favorite final girl. When she finally confronts Freddy at the end, she uses her brains instead of her muscles. That's how you win the battle. If the slasher has reduced you to adopting their methods to beat them, muscles, machetes, chainsaws, whatever it is, then you're cashing in a bit of your identity to do it. Nancy stays who she is and wins. I think that's such a better victory.

**I see plenty of Nancy and Alice in Jade Daniels from your *Indian Lake* trilogy. Can you think of how their DNA is entwined?**

That's a good question. Nancy reads a book about booby traps and figures out she has to turn her back on Freddy. Jade is doing a version of that by weaponizing her knowledge of slasher movies. The reason she's doing a version of it is because I can't just write Nancy fan fiction [Laughs]. I have to come up with something new.

I think most slashers are coming-of-age rituals, because it's mostly late-highschoolers who are going through this meat grinder. Over the course of the story, Nancy has to come to terms with her parents not being these bright, shining people. Her dad doesn't help her when she calls and her mom's always drinking. They both circumvented the law to do this horrible thing. Not to say Freddy didn't deserve it in some sense, but if you start to allow mob justice, the world goes crazy. They didn't go through the right channels, and that's what juiced Freddy up, in my opinion. I think Nancy has grown up by understanding her parents are flawed people. She has a wider conception of the world.

**The slasher trope of "the event/accident in the past that led to the killing spree" is different in these films, not least because Freddy is taking revenge on the kids of Elm Street, instead of the parents who killed him.**

Yeah, Jade calls it "second-removed slashing." Freddy could just as easily come for the parents, but he knows it will hurt them worse if he comes for their children. The problem with that is he's outside of his purview. He's basically stepped outside the lines of causality. The kids haven't done anything to him, which gives them the ability to push back, which Nancy finally exhibits.

**Is there anything about *Nightmare on Elm Street* you wish people would talk about more?**

You know, people always talk about how Debra Hill brought authentic teenagers to the screen. John Carpenter brought the scares for *Halloween*, but she gave the characters lines that teenagers would say. I feel like the first *Nightmare* has a whole lot of that, too. They're all older, but it feels like they're talking like teens talk. It feels authentic to high school, like the way Glen has the sound effect tape he plays on the boombox to lie to his mom. That was instrumental to getting *Nightmare on Elm Street* to catch on for a whole generation. It was about us.

# INTERVIEW
# GRADY HENDRIX
### AUTHOR

**THE FINAL GIRL**    **My Best Friend's**
**SUPPORT GROUP**    **EXORCISM**

**Do you recall how *A Nightmare on Elm Street* entered your life?**

I didn't see the first two films until years after [they were released]. I snuck into part three with my friend and we went bananas for it. It's like the *X-Men* of the franchise, you know what I mean? When Heather Langenkamp came back as the counselor for the kids, it blew my mind. Like, "Oh, a final girl can come back and help another final girl in another movie."

That was one of the seeds that stuck with me as I wrote my book *The Final Girl Support Group*. I wasn't allowed to see *Friday the 13th Part 2*, but I read in *Fangoria* that Adrienne King, the final girl from part one, returned only to be killed immediately. I didn't even know who she was, but I knew she deserved better. I actually didn't see another film in the series until *New Nightmare*. I didn't like it at the time, but I saw it about two years ago and I loved it. It's so smart. I think the only flaw with *New Nightmare* is that Wes Craven is bad at acting as "Wes Craven." (laughs) But, I was really blown away at how good it was, and I was really unimpressed with myself that its virtues flew over my head when I first saw it.

**I think that happened for a lot of people. I completely agree that *Dream Warriors* is the *Nightmare X-Men*, especially about how these misfit kids can only rely on each other and become a team. Your books reflect that theme,**

**not just with *The Final Girl Support Group*, but also, and especially *My Best Friend's Exorcism* and *The Southern Book Club's Guide to Slaying Vampires*. Did *Dream Warriors* inspire you?**

It wasn't anything overt that I was aware of, but I think that's why I responded to *Dream Warriors* and the *Nightmare* movies in general. I really liked the idea of friends helping each other in these movies. They're more social than some other slasher films. It's also one of the reasons I like the *Scream* franchise. So much of [those films] is unlikely people coming together to fight Ghostface.

It's also why I feel like parts four and five are kind of undervalued. Alice Johnson has a great backstory as the final girl. [Part four] has the best "tooling-up" scene of any '80s action movie and the dojo fight's a classic. But also, there's a real empathy and sympathy between the characters. They're sort of helping each other fight Freddy. A *Friday the 13th* movie is more about chopping the cast down until there's one person left, and the *Halloween* films were similar. The *Nightmare on Elm Street* movies seemed to be about groups of people, even the first one. Johnny Depp is terrible at fighting Freddy, but he does his best.

**I love the characters in these films, but especially in four and five. They have such great chemistry.**

I just think as a final girl, Alice's arc is right there in the movie. It's not like she goes from a possible victim to a fighter. She's got this alcoholic dad, just like Nancy's alcoholic mom from part one. I guess there's a lot of alcoholism running through [the series].

It's interesting. The *Friday the 13th* movies have always been my sweet spot. Jason Voorhees enjoys what he does and puts a flourish on things, but he doesn't take it too far. I enjoy the *Halloween* movies for what they are, though they're very grim and humorless. Freddy has always been in the other direction. Of all the franchise slashers, he's the one who touches you the most. He's the most sexualized. Michael Myers and Jason are very asexual. In *Nightmare*, the phone is licking Heather Langenkamp and Freddy's coming up between her legs. Part two has so much sexual subtext. Freddy even has a baby in one entry, and he's a pedophile! There's always been this really creepy sexual aspect to him. Freddy's a little like the musical theatre major you hang out with who's always "on." They're like, "Let me sing 'Happy Birthday' with perfect pitch." No one wants that. (laughs)

**He always wants to remind you he knows the choreo, even when you go to Applebee's after the show.**

I re-watched *Nightmare* and *Nightmare 2* over the holidays, along with bits of parts four and five because I was writing something about slashers. It made me want to rewatch all the films in a row, because I do think it's the most interesting slasher franchise. The kills are super-creative, and because Freddy lives in dreams, which is already really appalling, there's a meta level to the films. The thing that struck me while re-watching them was that nobody believes the kids. In the *Halloween* movies, there's no issue about what's happening, even though Loomis is running around saying Michael is evil. In the *Friday the 13th* movies, the kids don't believe the camp is cursed like the legend says. In the *Nightmare* movies, it's always about the kids having to stick together, because nobody believes them. That's something that's been in a lot of my books, and I wouldn't be surprised if I picked it up from them. I forgot how horrible and useless the adult characters were. They would rather think their kid is crazy than admit they did this horrible thing in their pasts, which is biting their kids in the ass. That's how adults appear when you're a kid. They don't believe you, they won't be honest with you, and they'll do anything but admit they're wrong. That's unique to the *Nightmare* franchise.


**Let's talk about final girls. Your book *The Final Girl Support Group* features original characters based on popular final girls, who are being murdered. "Heather," based on Nancy Thompson, is characterized as the wild card. She is basically a homeless addict who cracks jokes, and most horror fans would expect her to lead the group to victory like Nancy. How did you decide her role in the narrative?**

I needed five characters. An odd number always works better. I wanted to hit the iconic franchises, and I had to include *Nightmare*. Something that really struck me when considering those franchises is that actresses like Heather Langenkamp and Adrienne King (Alice Hardy from *Friday the 13th*) were young when they appeared in their respective films. Unbeknownst to them, they'll have a relationship with this monster for the rest of their lives. They will have to make their peace with these franchises in their own ways. In taking "Heather" seriously, I noticed there's something traumatic with the *Nightmare* franchise that's unlike the others. A killer who enters your dreams is a violation on so many levels. Watching a bystander watch their sleeping friend get killed, when they're safe and awake but helpless to do anything to stop it, is so horrifying in a way a lot of slashers aren't. Thinking through it, I realized nobody was going to believe "Heather," even after the killings are over and she's killed "The Dream King," [the Freddy counterpart in the book]. They'll be seen as suicides and the studio that picks this story up to make it would be a fly-by-night company that will probably rip her off. She became the character my heart went out to the most, and the most fun to write, even more than the main character. It's always fun to write the wild card. They could just flip the table at any moment.

In the book, Heather is so crazy and selfish, but on the other hand, she turns out to be right about the Dream King, and saves the day by being who she is. So, I loved giving her that hero moment, because I thought going through the events of a *Nightmare* movie would leave you a psychological trainwreck. Look at all the kids in the *Nightmare* movies, and they're taking drugs to stay awake. I don't think you turn that off when the credits roll. I had to use her judiciously, because I didn't want to give away that she'd be the one who kicked ass. She's the least likely to, but also having seen Heather Langenkamp kick ass in part three. She comes back in that film to help save the kids.

**Is there anything else you'd like to add about the *Nightmare* films that people wouldn't immediately realize or consider?**

Wes Craven is really undervalued as a director. I think he just wanted to work, and he had gaps in his career, where he just couldn't get a job. But you look at his filmography and it's *Last House on the Left*, *Nightmare on Elm Street*, and *Scream*. Even after those stone cold, zeitgeist-changing classics, he has five or six movies that are really good. It's an amazing batting average, and I think he still gets dismissed as a journeyman. He doesn't have the easily-identifiable style of John Carpenter or Dario Argento, but you look at stuff he did in *Nightmare* and *Scream*, you can see he was really ambitious. It's like how Steven Spielberg was initially dismissed as a schlockmaster. Now he's considered a genius, and I think people will feel that way when Wes Craven is re-evaluated. He knew what he was doing in a sort of Howard Hawks, unflashy way.

**You're absolutely right. I've always thought of Wes Craven as an "ideas man," as opposed to a visual stylist. He seemed interested in the text and subtext of his films, not that they didn't look fantastic.**

Well, there are two scenes in *Scream* where [Sidney and Tatum] go to the high school and learn about the killings. They're both minute-plus, one-takes with characters entering and exiting the frame, camera movements and lens flares. That's not easy. It's very ambitious. When you look at the dream sequence in *Nightmare* where Tina is killed, it's shot amazingly well. It's full of sleight-of-hand gags and visual effects that left me kind of stunned. Like when Freddy jumps out from behind the tree that's too skinny. They just did an optical and it looks great!

**It costs a dollar and works like a million.**

I think there's something interesting about the *Nightmare* films. All franchises go in different directions after their first films. In some sense, *Halloween* is about babysitting and *Friday the 13th* is all about camping. There's something appealingly lonely about the *Nightmare* movies. They're built around characters doing the loneliest activity we do: sleeping. You're isolated and at your most vulnerable when you're asleep. More than any other franchise, it's about kids teaming up to help each other out because the adults don't believe them. They lock them away, dismiss them, and sacrifice them for their cover-up. That's what I really responded to in those movies. The only people who could help you are the people around you. Your friends, who are just as lonely, vulnerable, and isolated as you are, but together, you stand a fighting chance. That always really resonated with me. You can see it a bit in my book *My Best Friend's Exorcism*. Even though I'm more of a *Friday the 13th* guy, that core is the reason why I always loved the *Nightmare* films.

# INTERVIEW
# CLARKE WOLFE
## ACTRESS / FILMMAKER

**MALUM** **A SHINING EXAMPLE**

**Do you remember the first time you saw *A Nightmare on Elm Street*?**

Yes. When I was a kid, I wasn't allowed to watch rated R movies, but of course, my younger brother was. He actually had the big boxed set of *Nightmare on Elm Street* films that came out before *Freddy vs. Jason*. I remember he had it on during the scene when Freddy appears in front of Tina with the long arms, and I thought, "Huh. This is so goofy, isn't it?" Later, I got more into film. *Scream* came out when I was in high school and I was like, "Whoa, I'm really into this." So, I sat down and watched *A Nightmare on Elm Street* start to finish and said, "I totally get it now."

**You've been a known horror aficionado for years. Do you think the public perception of these movies have changed over time?**

That's a really interesting question. There are legal reasons why we haven't gotten another *Friday the 13th* movie since 2009. We've gotten two new forays into *Halloween* from Rob Zombie and David Gordon Green. I feel like Freddy is remembered, but I don't know how much we talk about *Nightmare on Elm Street* like those other two series. I think part of it is that Jamie Lee Curtis is a wonderful mouthpiece for *Halloween*. She's very active on social media, and always out there reminiscing, and Jason fans are clamoring for a new movie, but I don't feel the same way about the *Nightmare* films. I think they get left out, which is silly, because for my money, it's the best of the slasher franchises that we think of.

**I couldn't have put it better, but I hope I did, or this book won't sell.**

(laughs) Great minds…

**Do you have any favorite entries in the series besides the original?**

I like the original a lot, but I love *New Nightmare*. It's so well done. Freddy is scary and I like the makeup design. And I will say, wholeheartedly, that I unironically love *Freddy vs. Jason*. It's so fun, so good, and there are sequences and images in it that are actually scary. It felt like they pulled some of the best mythology out of both franchises and it worked together seamlessly. And, of course, I love *Dream Warriors*. Who doesn't?

**Let's talk about Nancy. The concept of the final girl has been around for a while, but it really permeated the culture in recent years. Speaking of being left out, Nancy Thompson is a popular final girl among fans, but mainstream audiences might not be familiar with her.**

I'm a huge Wes Craven fan. He's my favorite of all the horror auteurs. I really respect and love so much of his work. I admire him. He was responsible and intentional when it came to the onscreen violence in his films. To me, the "Wes Craven heroine" is usually the most thought-out, nuanced, and complicated, because I think that was important to Wes, as a creator.

Now, I don't want to fault any final girl that came before or after, but I absolutely respond to Nancy, because that's the type of character I can connect to. I love Jamie Lee Curtis's performance in *Halloween*, but I don't really relate to Laurie Strode.

**To me, there really is a "before Nancy" and "after Nancy" because we'd never seen a final girl like her before. Wes is rightfully credited for bringing so much to the table, but I always felt the character of Nancy was never recognized.**

Like a lot of his horror contemporaries, I think he never got the opportunity to branch out. If a director makes a successful horror film today, they get a superhero franchise. The industry has changed to be so money focused. Like, "Hey, your movie made ten times its budget, so we're moving you more money and a bigger franchise, and we don't care if you came from horror movies." Wes was never able to do that, and I know that was something that weighed heavily on him. As a fan, I think that's unfortunate.

**The 1980's codified the idea of the "final girl" as the one person who could defeat the killer because they were virginal and innocent. There's certainly an innocence about Nancy, but I personally don't think Wes cared at all if she was a virgin, not least because her boyfriend is played by Johnny Depp. Plus, he knows his way around a rose trellis.**

I think Wes wanted her to look like the girl next door, but Nancy was very self-actualized for a teenage girl. That said, she's not puritanical. Obviously, Tina is sexualized and she dies early on, but I don't think Nancy survives because of any sort of morality. She survives because she's intellectual and proactive. Also, knowing what I know about Wes Craven, he was very anti-puritan. (laughs)

**Absolutely.**

I think there was an opportunity in *Scream* to recreate the bedroom scene from part one with Neve Campbell and Skeet Ulrich. They even look like [Heather Langenkamp and Johnny Depp]. I agree with you. I don't think Nancy needs to be this pure, perfect soul in any way.

**I see the DNA of the *Nightmare on Elm Street* films in so many horror films today, especially in films like *It* and *Smile*. What do you think is the legacy of the *Nightmare* films?**

The mythology of *Nightmare on Elm Street* is really thought-out and the higher concept was ahead of its time, for its time. Now, horror fans expect rules. They know the formula, and the success of *Nightmare on Elm Street* is a huge part of that. Obviously, John Carpenter and Debra Hill didn't know what they were getting into when they made their "little movie." (laughs) Sean Cunningham absolutely knew what he was getting into [with *Friday the 13th*]. With *Halloween* and *Friday*, you can't see the assailant. They're either a shape or a figure, not to disparage the work of those actors. I know Kane Hodder and the actors who played Jason took that role seriously. But having Robert Englund, a trained actor and cinephile working within the scope of cinema history, is what elevates the whole thing to be considered a game-changing moment in pop culture. It's really important for our villains to have a face.

Yes, there's always going to be a "guy in a mask" who stalks teens, but the rule-ified, game-ified films of today can be traced back to *A Nightmare on Elm Street*. I think it showed, on a mass scale, that you can trust the audience to be intelligent and follow you down this path, as opposed to just the feeling of being scared or titillated.

**Is there anything you want to bring up about the *Nightmare* films that you feel isn't discussed enough?**

Of all the old-school iconic slasher franchises that made, let's say, more than three entries, I think [*Nightmare*] is overwhelmingly the strongest. Like with any franchise, the quality fluctuates, but the movies are consistently cinematic throughout. Whereas the mandate for a while with the *Halloween* films was "Michael Myers terrorizes the town." You can never get beyond that, and I don't know if that necessarily attracts the best behind-the-scenes talent. Same with *Friday the 13th*. They're very simple, structural movies.

With *Nightmare on Elm Street*, look at Frank Darabont and Renny Harlin. Rachel Talalay has gone on to be an incredible director. She directed "Puppet Patrol," one of my favorite *Doom Patrol* episodes, and so on. That's important. We don't see that in franchises as much anymore. People were hired to do something interesting. Like, "play within these rules, but let's grow the universe," as opposed to "just do what we've been doing, but maybe cheaper or a little cleaner." The *Nightmare* franchise has that in spades. No other horror franchise, especially a slasher franchise has that.

# INTERVIEW
## ADAM CESARE
### AUTHOR
**CLOWN IN A CORNFIELD** **INFLUENCER**

**Based on your body of work, I'm assuming you're a big lover of horror films. Where does *A Nightmare on Elm Street* fit into your slasher canon?**

Here's a funny thing. I put it completely outside the canon. There are slasher-like elements in the first film, but I don't find it to be particularly slashery, even among the supernatural slashers. I'm weird in that I take [*Nightmare*] and *The Texas Chain Saw Massacre* out of what counts as a slasher to me.

I think the first film is perfect. It's one of the greatest movies ever made. I saw it on VHS when I was a kid, and I saw *New Nightmare* at the Islip Triplex. I was eight and I made it really far, but I ran out of the theater when Dylan ran across the freeway. I couldn't hack it. I was too young and it was too loud, too scary. Freddy came out of the sky to pick him up with his glove, and it was too much for me. But I begged my dad to go, because Freddy is such an interesting… slasher. We'll go by your definition. (laughs)

**Character or antagonist works, too.**

I do think there's a case to be made that [Freddy] doesn't fit so cleanly into the slasher boom and what those films were. We're around the same age. There was that sort of schoolyard boom about Freddy. Kids just talked about the one part of a Freddy movie they'd seen and spinning lore from that. *New Nightmare* came out when I was in elementary school and I had to see it on screen. It was an event.

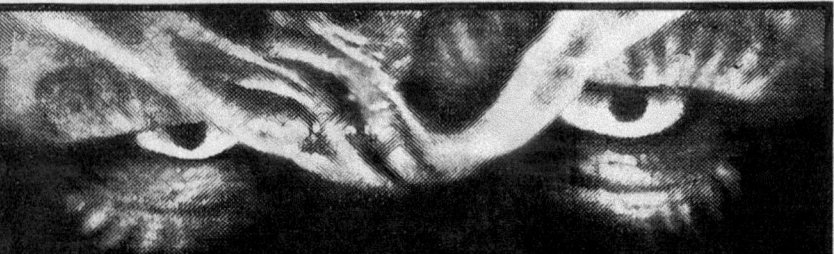
Exhibit A in the childhood traumatization of Adam Cesare.

**Same here. I was nine and it was the first horror film I saw in theaters.**

It loomed so large in my mind. If you look at the school of like, the "new horror," Wes Craven is probably the [director] I gravitate to most. Not just his films, but his general ethos. He was kind of like the professor of the bunch. The layers of meaning and the Freudian aspect is what separates him from the pack, and I'd say it's what separates the first film and *New Nightmare* from the other sequels. I'd view them as bookends. There's a little break between [*Freddy's Dead*] and *New Nightmare,* making it kind of a legacy sequel. I may be a little bit of a different fan. I like *Dream Warriors* just fine, and I love Chuck Russell's films, but to me it's the best of the middle sequels. The franchise is interesting to me because of its cultural impact, and what Freddy became later on, but the original is ride or die. Nothing touches it.

This doesn't happen so much with the *Nightmare* series, because new films aren't coming out, but every once in a while, people rank all the films. It seems psychopathic to me when I see rankings that have anything but the first one as the best. (laughs) I know taste is subjective, but I have a hard time even putting myself in other folks' shoes to be like, "How?" I just love it so much.

**Yeah, I don't see many rankings where they don't put the first entry.**

Recently, I've seen the remake ranked high, and it's usually because the person's twenty. (laughs) It's such an ageist thing for me to say, as the guy that wrote *Clown in a Cornfield*, but it's true. You start getting older and you're like "Oh, this is why people become curmudgeons!" You're just losing a certain amount of touch with what the kids are into, and how media is consumed.

I've tried to do a thought experiment: if I were a kid and I watched a double feature of the *Texas Chain Saw Massacre* remake and the original, which one would I like more? I don't even know. But that's not even to talk about the *Nightmare on Elm Street* remake, which is an affront to God. (laughs)

**My joke about the remake is that if you watch it, you can imagine guns pointed at the cast and crew, just off camera. Nobody wants to be there.**

After I saw the remake in college, my wife, then-girlfriend was like, "You've been in a foul mood all week." (laughs) She later revealed to me that the *Nightmare on Elm Street* remake made me so upset and unlivable for like, five of our dates, that since it was early in our relationship she almost broke up with me! If I'd have gone a little harder on hating that movie, I wouldn't have a child. Like, it almost cost me my family! Maybe don't put that in your book. (laughs)

**Oh, that one is staying close to my heart.**

You know what? Leave it in. So, Michael Bay's not going to call me? It's fine. (laughs)

**I'm sure everyone wants to forget about the remake by now.**

You know, I'd never seen any [repertory] screenings of the original until I went to LA to do a bunch of meetings. It was just before COVID, and Brian Collins put together a screening and did a Q&A with Heather Langenkamp and Amanda Wyss. I was sitting two seats over from them and I was like, "Wow, there's no better way to see this movie."

**You appeared on *The Scares That Shaped Us* podcast a few months back to talk about *New Nightmare*.**

Oh, yeah, so you've heard me wax poetic about *New Nightmare* for like, two hours. (laughs)

**One of the ways you described the film is that it's the "most Wes Craven film ever." Can you expand on that point? Personally, I always thought that description belonged to *The People Under the Stairs*.**

That's a good one, though!

**It's not even about quality, as much as I love *People Under the Stairs*, I just think it contains most, if not all of the hallmarks of his films. Not just booby traps, but a social message, messed up families, a major suburban secret…**

It has a lot of the same stuff. It has kids in danger, but so does *New Nightmare*. Maybe it doesn't have the social element that *People Under the Stairs* has, but it kinda does, in the sense of how disconnected these people are, like being in Hollywood and stuff. I think there's a case to be made for that.

**Can you expound on that a little, or should I just pull up the podcast?**

(laughs) I give you carte blanche to pull quotes from that episode, because I bet it was a lot fresher, and I bet I sound a lot smarter on that one. [Wes] literally shows up and starts talking about the psychoanalysis and the tulpa element of what Freddy Krueger is in that movie, how he dreamed him into existence. Besides that, there's the "kids in peril" stuff, which I think is very prevalent in *People Under the Stairs*, even going back all the way to *The Hills Have Eyes*.

**Even *The Last House on the Left*, to a degree.**

Yeah, but all the Hollywood stuff in *New Nightmare* I think, is so telling. I'm talking to a guy who's writing a book about it, but it's so interesting to watch him talk about that movie. A big part of why he made *New Nightmare* was because he made a deal with Bob Shaye to get points on the sequels. It's like quid pro quo, which, to me, is the recipe for a bad movie. Like, "Oh, he's gonna do this kind of thankless, hack job to get his rights back, or to get a piece of something that he should have had from the beginning." Then you look at it and it's such a smart Hollywood movie in my estimation.

The amount of real stuff that he puts in the "Heather" character that is from Heather Langenkamp's real life is fascinating to me. It's really incredible. I think that's another area of interest with him. He never made a documentary, but I could see him having a keen interest in making one. It's like he's working that kind of stuff out. It's so LA. You go from a suburban setting for these stories to [a place where] the freeway is a literal villain. Like, I find it so interesting. It's like his career trajectory. [Craven] is this guy who's traveled through literally every element of the film industry and has seen what a "machine" film is, and he's making a movie to parlay his way into, you know, ownership of something that he originally created. It's so fascinating! And I think you can see him having fun and making a meal out of it with the movie. Look at Freddy's hell. We're living in a post-*Hellbound: Hellraiser II* world when he's making *New Nightmare*.

**Right. Less industrial pipes, more elements. Stone, fire, water…**

For years, he externalized a lot of ideas about how Freudian and Jungian all this stuff is, then he brings you to the psychoanalyst hell that is Freddy's lair. It feels like he's saying, "If I had my druthers, I would have done this the first time." Freddy is also a lot scarier. He changes his look to more closely resemble the guy he saw outside his window when he was a kid. It feels personal, in a way that the seventh film in a franchise probably shouldn't, you know?

**That's true. Even though it's the seventh installment, it feels singular, even if it led to Craven's meta era.**

It's a dry run for *Scream*. I mentioned this in the podcast, but in some ways, it's better at what it does than *Scream*, which I know is controversial. When *New Nightmare* talks about movies, and what movies are and what movies do, it does a lot better than when *Scream* talks about movies and what movies and what movies are and what movies do, and how they relate to people

**Well, they're trying to do different things. *Scream* is from the fan point-of-view, whereas *New Nightmare* is the filmmakers' point of view.**

Exactly, but it becomes that later in the *Scream* franchise. They try to tackle those ideas later with Wes Craven involved, but I don't think they're as good as the way that those ideas are articulated in *New Nightmare*.

**Is there anything else that you want to say about the *Nightmare* films that people don't talk about enough?**

I try to separate Freddy Krueger in that first film from the Freddy Krueger that was a product of my childhood imagination. Like dressing in the sweater, getting toys and bubble gum, all that stuff. It's such a nostalgic thing for me. Here, let me show you what's hanging on my cork board…

*[Adam shows me an old, rubber action figure of Freddy from his childhood, which is still in it's packaging].*

I didn't buy this at a con. This isn't me trying to be retro. For whatever reason, I just bought this when I was a little kid at the 7-Eleven, probably right down the block from Blockbuster. It was probably before I'd even seen the first *Nightmare on Elm Street*. For a lot of folks in our era, Freddy predates their first interaction with him with the movies, which is such an interesting thing. You can't say that about a lot of characters. Maybe now you can, because there's so much merch and cosplay, but it's hard to reckon what a thing that was if you weren't around for it. Being interested in this Freddy Krueger character was integral to my love of horror. There were commercials with him and bumpers on VHS tapes. Just the myth of this.

It's easy now to go to a con and be like "Oh, everyone here is dressed as Art the clown." That's just a thing. It wasn't as prevalent then, and it was like the first kind of thing to do that. So that's what I think of when I think of *Nightmare on Elm Street*. I think of the outsized influence that Freddy, just as a tulpa, has had on me has had on my life and my interest in this stuff. Just seeing that image, that toy, and getting interested in it kind of set me on a weird path to, like, beg my dad to go see that movie before I could handle seeing it. All this stuff is because it was this cultural thing.

# INTERVIEW
# PHIL NOBILE JR.
## CURRENT EDITOR-IN-CHIEF

**FANGORIA**

**I refer to the *Nightmare* films as my *Star Wars* because, for many people, *Star Wars* was what got them into movies in the first place.**

So, which entry is your *Phantom Menace*?

**Well, it's funny, *Freddy's Dead* was the first horror film I saw when I was six, and I never looked back.**

It's an interesting point, though. The sequels kind of get the rough edges sanded off of them, but that makes them good gateway material for kids who are able to handle the gore, but maybe not something that feels super real or super serious. There's a campy level to the sequels, I think after part three, which make them accidental gateway movies. *Nightmare on Elm Street* is one of those franchises where the first one is so good, the sequels kind of cheapen the whole thing for me a little bit. (laughs) I enjoy them, I get it, but it's not my franchise like it's yours.

**You're not the only one I've spoken to who's said it's not "their franchise," which is very much a term for horror fans. Since you're the editor of *Fangoria*, I imagine you have a birds-eye-view of the horror landscape. I see the influence of the *Nightmare* films in horror today, especially in the *It* and *Smile* films, but they're not really talked about.**

Just now, I was like "Yeah, sure. I'm sort of monitoring where horror is in 2025," but my first thought was that there's not much of a Freddy footprint before you mentioned the comparison points. I think what *Nightmare* did in 1984 was throw away the rulebook. In theory, that meant they could do anything. Not budget-wise, but it freed [the filmmakers] up from what had been a very repetitive slasher formula up until that point. We're currently in the seventh year of a slasher renaissance if you count 2018's *Halloween* as the beginning. *Heart Eyes* came out today. But where's Freddy in the mix? It's an interesting question. Any time a slasher or horror film can pivot towards the fanciful or the campy, that's Freddy's work. His big contribution was that the killer didn't need to mindlessly hack up teens one at a time. He freed the genre, or subgenre if you will, in a way that still maybe hasn't been fully capitalized on.

Like you said, *It* happened, but [the *It* miniseries] happened in 1990, probably because of Freddy. I don't think it's a coincidence that they got a real actor like Tim Curry to play Pennywise, whereas so many of these movies were made with stuntmen in masks. Robert Englund brought performance to it in a way where suddenly a guy with a sack over his head isn't that interesting. That's how you get stuff like *Brainscan* or 1986's *Trick or Treat*.

### Also *Dr. Giggles.*

Yeah, I think Freddy was a bucket of technicolor paint dropped onto slashers, which at that point had only been a limited palette, in a way. As much as we love Jason in Crystal Lake and Michael Myers in Haddonfield, Freddy's canvas was so much bigger. That, in turn, let people open their minds to what a low budget horror movie could get away with. You saw it manifest across the decades in different ways. But today? I feel like we're sort of missing the mischievous fun that Freddy brought to horror. After the first two films, the kills were long jokes with punchlines. That's what you showed up for. You cared about Nancy and maybe Jesse in part two, but after that, you were there for Freddy. That was his other big contribution. Freddy became the killer you rooted for, and the other franchises leaned into that after the fact. I think that's a Freddy thing. I don't think you were supposed to root for Jason, but you definitely were in *Friday the 13th Part VI*. It's no coincidence that part six is the funniest *Friday the 13th*.

I think Freddy taught us not to take the slasher genre so seriously and to be in on the joke in a way. Frankly, you don't have *Scream* without Freddy. Then *Scream* influenced a whole other generation of self-aware horror. You may not think *I Know What You Did Last Summer* has anything to do with Freddy, but I think there's a line that goes from his pranksterism and playfulness morphing into a self-aware postmodern thing that happened after the fact.

One of the reasons the remake of *Nightmare* didn't land was because they wanted to go back to the darkness of the original. At that point, Freddy's footprint was such that not only did you need Robert Englund, but you needed the playfulness that the sequels brought, which changed the canon completely. It's all about the fun of it. I mean, they handed out 3D glasses in the theater for *Freddy's Dead*. It was very much like William Castle by then.

**You mentioned 2018's *Halloween* as the rebirth of the slasher revival. I'd also call it the "final girl" revival, with its major focus on Laurie Strode and her descendants. Now that horror fans know the term "final girl" as well as "slasher," where do you see Nancy in the canon?**

Yeah, there's a purity to Nancy as a final girl, because she is, to use the online parlance, "the best to ever do it." She's proactive in a way that a lot of final girls aren't. My [favorite] franchise is *The Texas Chain Saw Massacre*. I've made a point multiple times that [final girl] Sally Hardesty barely gets a closeup in the first hour of that movie. She's not the protagonist until she's the last one standing, but Nancy is your touchstone. She's on a journey that's richer than most final girls are afforded. You can argue Sydney Prescott from "Scream," but on the other hand, she lives in the shadow of Nancy because of Wes Craven. How could she not?

Nancy is so smart. She *feels*. Heather Langenkamp didn't play her as a novice actor running through beats and landing on marks. She brought an inner life to that performance that I think you're hard-pressed to find in most of the post-*Scream* slasher movies. I don't want to badmouth any contemporary slashers, but I have to watch a lot of them. We forgot how good the day-job actors were in, like *Friday the 13th Part 2*. You believe these people in a way that you don't believe in *Jason X*, where they're all kind of getting above it. But Heather is invested in that performance, which makes her special. Anytime someone sets traps in a home, they automatically think it's from *Home Alone*.

**She did it first.**

She did! *Straw Dogs* kind of did it, too, but Nancy's traps were the best. I think it's all down to Wes writing her as a person and Heather bringing a third dimension to that character that a lesser actor wouldn't have done. I know she revisited the role twice, but it didn't diminish the first film. And that can happen sometimes.

**Certainly not with Robert Englund. Many fans want to see him back as Freddy, myself included, but if he wants to retire, I say let him. It was his bar to set. Let it be someone else's attempt to clear.**

I think a big reason you haven't seen another *Elm Street* is that nobody has cracked the code of "What do you do without Robert Englund?" In 2025, there's two ways to go. Certainly, if we got Andy Serkis playing a photorealistic chimp who's taking over the planet, we can get enough of Robert Englund to do motion capture for Freddy in a meaningful way without relying on his seventy-seven-year-old body. I think we have the technology to do that, and it's one of the few instances where nobody would fault anyone for going that route. If you can do that, we're halfway there.

Alternately, you would need someone to reinvent it completely. There's that analogy about the beehive: Move it one foot away or ten miles away and the bees will find it. If you move it half a block away, they get confused and die. The *Elm Street* remake was half a block away. Its fatal flaw was that it wasn't close enough, nor was it different enough. They were trying to replicate something, but they didn't have an original idea to move away from it, and it wasn't close enough to the original thing.

I'd be curious to hear a take from Mike Flanagan or David Bruckner. *The Night House* has some of the best dream sequences I've ever seen in a movie, and I think that's the other secret sauce. We have to remember that these films need to have amazing dream sequence set pieces. You can only run through so many steaming boiler rooms. You have to come up with more cool shit that puts the viewer in the mind of a dream sequence. Just little things, like when Nancy is running up the stairs and they turn into marshmallow? I've had that dream. It was so simple, yet so authentic. Another remake would need authenticity about the dream state.

**There weren't many media outlets that celebrated the fortieth anniversary of *Nightmare on Elm Street*. I think it was just *Fangoria* and *Rue Morgue*. Can you tell me why you put Freddy on the cover?**

It was 100% about the fortieth anniversary. As Tony Timpone probably told you, any time Freddy was on the cover, they sold three times as many issues back in the day. We obviously weren't expecting that to happen, but if you look at my tenure at *Fangoria*, I've gotten the Shape, Chucky, and Leatherface on the cover so far. I wanted to do all the ones I grew up watching. The opportunity to put Freddy on the cover was too great to pass up. I went out to the artist Matt Ryan Tobin, and his pitch was too good. Then I chased the content. There are two pieces in that issue about the fortieth anniversary. New Line Cinema is called "the House That Freddy built," but *Fangoria* is the magazine that Freddy built. Sometimes he was on three covers in a row if there was a new *Elm Street* movie. So, we had to honor the anniversary, but if and when there's a new movie, I'll be the first one putting it on the cover. That's where he belongs.

**Is there anything else you want to add about the *Nightmare* films?**

I think in a weird way, beyond the movies, the other secret ingredient of Freddy's success was that he came up with MTV. He became this weird, campy, drag act for lack of a better term. It's an actor with a bunch of shit on him doing a persona and making campy jokes and one-liners. It's drag in a literal way. In the homophobic, AIDS-phobic 80's, Freddy was a drag act teenage boys were "allowed" to enjoy. I think that's worth digging into in a deeper way.

# INTERVIEW
## DIANDRA LAZOR
### aka "Sassy Sledgehammer"
### ACTRESS / PRODUCER

**Your story of getting into *Nightmare on Elm Street* was similar to mine in that you had to watch what was available, instead of watching them in order like the general public. Can you talk about how you experienced watching them?**

I've had obsessions with things since I was little, so I don't think I've had a love for anything with a particular order. I never really thought I should start from square one. Like we discussed, you kind of start with what was available at the video store. I honestly had no idea why *Freddy's Dead* was the first one I saw. Maybe it was just in stock at the time, but I'd go back and pick up random DVDs that were in stock. It wasn't until I watched all the films that I realized there was a cohesive story and maybe even a year into my fandom that I started to think of it as one complete piece, as a franchise. For the longest time, it was bits and pieces of this universe that I loved, but I never looked at it deeper than something I was fascinated with. I didn't really look at films that way at the time, based on what I could get my hands on.

I don't think my video store even had part three. I think the only way I even watched it was because I bought the DVD from Best Buy and popped it in at my aunt's house. I was like, "I heard Nancy dies in this one and I'm not happy about it." (laughs)

**Since you watched the sixth entry first, did you get the sense that it was the end of a larger story?**

No, it's like *New Nightmare*, when Heather says "Every kid knows who Freddy is. He's like Santa Claus." That was all I knew. He was a guy in a red and green sweater with a claw hand who haunts your dreams. That's it. Now, that's not to say I didn't see bits and pieces of other films. I remember being pretty terrified of Marge being burnt to a crisp and sinking into the fog in the bed in part one. For some reason, it was always on TV for me. I didn't know anything about it. I knew some of the imagery because it was so ingrained in pop culture. I had no idea there was a cohesive story or even that I should pay attention to more than just Freddy, because the villains were always so front-and-center. I didn't stop to think about the heroes until I watched the other movies and I started to connect with them.

**Your love of Nancy Thompson is well documented. Did you relate to any of those other heroes?**

I connected with Maggie [from *Freddy's Dead*, played by Lisa Zane] because that was the first [*Nightmare*] movie I watched and it was the one I kept watching. I thought she was such a smart character, kicking Freddy's butt. She was really tough and cool and I had never seen a character who was cool like that. I loved that she had this connection to Freddy as his daughter. It was very surface level, but I loved it. Outside of Heather Langenkamp, the person I got the most starstruck meeting was Lisa Zane because it took me back to the early days of my fandom. It was an incredible experience.

The other character I connected with was Alice. I always looked at Nancy as someone I felt like I was, but hadn't fully become yet. She was aspirational for me. I connected with Alice because I thought of myself as a timid person, even if I was a little goofy. Alice has this whole move at the end where she becomes a butt-kicker, not just with the karate, but the way she talks and how she is with her friends. She became a spitfire with a real attitude about her. I also loved the scene of her getting ready.

I was also a huge daydreamer like Alice. I was constantly living in my own little world. I think they finally gave it a name: "maladaptive daydreaming."

It sounds so stupid, but I was in dance at the time and I would picture myself on stage in a cool *Nightmare on Elm Street* number where I would pop out as Maggie and they'd go "Oh my god, it's Maggie!" Then I'd watch part four and I'd imagine popping out as Alice.

Overall, it was these strong female characters that made me go "Man, I love *her* and I love *her*." I only had two really cool reference points at that point in time, then it was just kind of Nancy and no turning back. I really connected with the women in *A Nightmare on Elm Street*.

**A core memory for me is seeing Nancy appear in *Dream Warriors*. My introduction to her as a character is when she helps Kristen. Do you have any moments in the series that take you back to where you were when you first saw them?**

That's tough. There are little feelings I get over the years. When I visit my parents in the summer, I stay in my old room and it still smells like it did when I was an early fan, and it transports me back to watching *Freddy's Dead*. Specifically *Freddy's Dead*. Even if I'm watching any of the other ones, *Freddy's Dead* conjures up that smell. I'm here, living in Southern California and I was on my way back from something the other day, and I played "I'm Awake Now" by the Goo Goo Dolls, and I still went back to that time. Feeling that same feeling, that excitement all over again. Just seeing that New Line logo and hearing the first notes of "I'm Awake Now." If that counts, that's without a doubt one of them.

**Oh, it counts. *Freddy's Dead* starts with a vibe that's trying to welcome you in. It's usually not one of the more celebrated entries, but there's still so much to love. I just rewatched *The Dream Child* and I never thought I'd have that much to say about it.**

*The Dream Child* is the one I've seen the least and I think I know the least about. The mix of goofy and dark doesn't quite sit well with me, but I love Alice in it. I love that she's a teen mom and I really admire her spirit all throughout as she's fighting for this child. One of my favorite things about the *Nightmare* franchise is that every movie has some fear or message or truth related back to things that real teenagers face. We might not have friends in our everyday life who are drug addicts, or going through teen pregnancy all at the same time, but they are things that happen to teenagers and I love that *Nightmare on Elm Street* addresses that.

I like the deeper elements of [*The Dream Child*], like the teen pregnancy and the fear of being a young mom or a single mom. I've come to really like the story of Amanda, mostly because of [Amanda Kruger actress] Beatrice Boepple. She wrote this book, *The Krueger Curse*, as a deep fan, but there are things in it she didn't even realize make sense. For example, she wrote that Amanda's family were German and they moved to Columbus, Ohio. I've lived there and I know there's a huge German population. I asked her if she knew that and she said, "Absolutely, I did not." I also love the character of Yvonne. The best thing about that movie is the cast of characters.

**They're one of the best casts in the series, and having met them, you can tell they're friends in real life.**

I was at an event last weekend with several cast members from the films. I have to see who said this, I think it was Brooke Thiess, but they said the *Nightmare* people are like a family. They're the closest casts out of any of the franchises they've seen. I think that comes through in their portrayals of the movies, which is why the casting is so spot on. Every single one of those actors is similar to those characters in a way. Those character friendships are very understandable and they exist within each of those actors, individually, which makes it feel authentic. It's one of the most powerful components of the franchise.

**I want to touch on *New Nightmare*. It's one of Wes Craven's best films, though it's strange because it feels less like *A Nightmare on Elm Street* and more like *The Ring*. It's one of your favorites in the series, correct?**

It's my favorite in the series and my favorite [film] of all time. I have come to love that movie because I love Wes Craven and it represents everything I love about Wes Craven. When I first saw it, I hated it.

## Really?

I was like, "This doesn't feel like a *Nightmare* movie. This isn't actually Freddy. This isn't actually Nancy. What are they doing?"

## "What's this kid doing here?"

Right! "Why does Freddy have a trench coat and leather pants?" I was a very good English student in high school, and I was always delving into the deeper meaning of things. I came to love doing that. The more I delved into the series and the more I learned about Wes and looked at the movies, the more I loved Wes's work. He was such a huge ambassador of that kind of storytelling. Everything always meant something deeper to Wes. It was like he said "Alright, we're not just gonna make a movie about a movie."

In my mind, it was like a professional fan film, the most official fan film you could ever have. Who's never once thought, "What if that character encountered the real people [behind them]?" What would they do? That's exactly what *New Nightmare* is. More than that, it's a deeper story about the monstrosity you create with a widely popular horror film. Horror is looked down upon, so what does it say when people resonate with it so hard that they just can't get over it? That they just can't let it go, or get away from it? Like "I want to be a regular actor or a regular director for all these things, but I just can't escape this nightmare." It's a horror film about those exact feelings and thoughts.

In its own way, it's a meta remake of the first movie. There are so many similarities with the first film. The acting and the music are terrific. The script is intriguing. Wes mentioned he put his nightmares into his movies, and that's in there. Even more than that, *New Nightmare* takes the idea that Freddy is the [result] of the sins of all your parents to an ancient level. He's not actually Freddy. He is just an entity that represents fear and evil, that loves the person so much, he adopted it. I look at that and see the core of "A Nightmare on Elm Street." "New Nightmare" isn't about the parents who created the monster. It's about the filmmakers who created the monster. So it parallels the core idea of the original "Nightmare" and what makes Wes so special. That's why I love it so much.

**I keep bringing this up, but the *Nightmare on Elm Street* franchise is so underserved.**

Yeah.

**Is there anything you'd like to bring up about the series, the films, or even individual characters that you think isn't discussed enough, or at all?**

Hmmm, I might go on a little bit of a rant here.

**This is absolutely the place for it.**

When I first became a fan, my entire goal was to find more fans of Nancy because everybody was so interested in Robert and Freddy. It was the norm for a long time, and it still is, overall. Everybody's talking about Michael Myers and Jason. Everyone wants to dress as them. You can put on a Jason costume and make TikTok videos where you dance as them and everyone will know who that character is. It's super popular, but if someone came out and did that with Nancy, they wouldn't know, because those characters aren't necessarily the main focus.

Everybody has some sort of connection to the evil [characters]. They crave it because they can't do it in their own lives. We look at Freddy, who's scary, and he helps us master that fear. It's also the thing that's poking at the rules and the people who say "Don't you want to have a wife and kids? Don't you want to get over that 'horror thing' and have a traditional life?" It's the thing that makes us want to go "No, dammit! I love it and I love doing all these things, and if I weird you out, good!" That laugh in the face of the status quo is why I think people embrace the monster. It lets us be a bit naughty, but it's all pretend.

The horror heroes are most like us in our normal lives, but when we really watch the movies, we identify with the heroes more than the monster. We don't want to grow up and become a child killer. We watch these movies and they help us overcome very real fears in our life. They help us to fight.

I think part of the reason *Nightmare on Elm Street* is falling behind is, while they have Johnny Depp, he hasn't really been involved in the franchise. Neither has Patricia Arquette or Laurence Fishburne, but Jamie Lee Curtis became heavily involved in *Halloween* after becoming a name outside of it. She's become popular and [her character] Laurie Strode has become popular. I think it would be similar if Kevin Bacon went back and went hard into *Friday the 13th*. When you have giant people involved, it keeps it going. Part of what *Nightmare* has working against it, is that we haven't had another movie or a video game or a new TV show or something like that. I've had people tell me it's falling down on their rosters because there's nothing to keep their interests. When you're a really big fan of something, you keep going hard for it, but most people who generally like horror aren't that into it because there's nothing really new. Also, the rights are pretty expensive.

I think it's a shame, because there are so many creative, cool things that can be done with *A Nightmare on Elm Street*. The cast and the fans, we're all doing our best to keep it alive in books, documentaries, games, TikTok, and whatever we can create. But we still want to see more and the franchise would be stronger if we got more. Even for the general public, it's on the backburner. Everyone knows who Freddy is, but Freddy's been on a vacation for a really long time. People have kind of forgotten about him.

**It's sad, but I like to think we're keeping the boiler burning a little bit.**

I think we do. We're the reason that *Nightmare* has a flame. It's not giant, but we're definitely keeping it in the conversation.

# AFTERWORD:
## KEEPING THE
## FURNACE LIT

What do we talk about when we talk about *A Nightmare on Elm Street*? Why are these films still with us? They've certainly earned their place in the horror canon, sitting comfortably next to the *Friday the 13th* and *Halloween* series in terms of scope and influence. Yet, they're constantly left out of the conversation.

The other two franchises have multiple documentaries, books, toys, Halloween costumes, and so much more to keep their names alive. To mark the fortieth anniversary of *Halloween*, Jamie Lee Curtis and award-winning filmmaker David Gordon Green made a new trilogy of films where Michael Myers faces off against his resourceful nemesis and former final girl Laurie Strode. There hasn't been a *Friday the 13th* film in over a decade due to an ongoing lawsuit, but during that time period, Jason Voorhees appeared in an incredibly popular online multiplayer video game while also popping up as a playable character in both *Mortal Kombat X* and *MultiVersus*. There is also a much-anticipated streaming series in the works from indie powerhouse A24. The respective cultural impacts of those masked maniacs are enormous. So, if Freddy's face is on the horror Mount Rushmore next to Jason and Michael's pasty white masks, where is the appreciation for *Nightmare*?

November 9th, 2024 marked forty years since the release of *A Nightmare on Elm Street*. (It was also my thirty-ninth birthday.) To commemorate the anniversary, Warner Brothers announced a release of the original film in 4K… and that's it. One disc of one film with no new supplemental features, no new plans to acknowledge the legacy of the rest of the films in the series and artwork recycled from a previous release. It's unbelievable and yet inevitable. A cycle of nine films, now four decades old, which has gone on to inspire generations of filmmakers and fans, to make hundreds of millions of dollars, which permeated the zeitgeist, was marked by the release of a single film. "But it's the best film," you might say. "It's the one that started it all!" Well, if you've gotten this far in the book, you must realize by now that the "all" matters.

In Mick Strawn's *Behind the Screams*, Rachel Talalay, now a successful director on such television shows as *Dr. Who* and *The Flash* laments that during the shooting of one episode, there was a budgetary issue she was able to solve because she learned how to improvise from working on the *Nightmare* films. The practical special effects and craftsmanship holds up remarkably well compared to other low-budget films of the 1980's. And make no mistake, despite their financial successes, the budget on the films was always low. *A Nightmare on Elm Street* is never talked about enough as a powerhouse of imagination and ingenuity.

One of the gravest sins in horror is how maligned the *Nightmare* saga has been in recent years. It has merely a fraction of the caché its peers enjoy and just about all of it revolves solely around the character of Freddy Krueger. Once again, I'm not taking anything away from the masterful Robert Englund, but the films have always been more than him and, to his credit, he knows it. The "Freddy" of it all has been foregrounded for so long, it's possible modern moviegoers see him more as a comedian than a boogeyman. One has to wonder: where is the representation for the other characters? Where are the dream warrior Halloween costumes or the latest-generation video game? And that's just merchandise! After the 2010 remake (justifiably) left a bad taste in audiences' mouths, talks of a follow-up ceased. For years, there have been rumblings about rights issues preventing a new film from being made, but how complicated must it be when the hunger for such things is already out there?

I've spent so much time talking about a group of people I'm proud to call myself part of. The ones who love these films. The fans or rather, the "Fredheads." That moniker, by the way, is taken from an unused script for *Freddy vs. Jason*, which involves a cult of people who worship Freddy Krueger. Such is the depths of our appreciation: we canonize material that was rejected. We make it available because there isn't much out there for us to grab onto beyond the films themselves. While there are few licensed toys and costumes, the best content is bespoke and handmade by the fans. Just like Nancy, we have to do everything ourselves. From documentaries like *Fredheads* and *Never Sleep Again* to this very book, the films are held aloft by a DIY ethos that has replaced the corporate fan service that other films enjoy.

Like myself and so many others, Diandra Lazor discovered the *Nightmare* films in a vacuum. When she was younger, her peers were confused by the Nancy Thompson Halloween costume she made herself. Yes, Nancy Thompson, *not* Freddy Krueger. Her father even dressed up as Don to take her trick-or-treating. Why dress in pajamas when you can be a witch or a superhero? She didn't find fellowship in her fandom until much later when she befriended fellow superfan, and *Fredheads* co-director Paige Troxell. The two of them understood that, to a degree, Nancy *was* a superhero. In *Fredheads*, Lazor discusses how "nobody ever talked about Nancy, except for Paige and I. So where are all the Nancy fans?" It might be hard to imagine a movie character that the general public is unfamiliar with to be a role model, but not for them. "To me and others, Nancy was the representation of hope," elaborates Lazor. "You don't need superpowers to kick ass. You could just be a regular person and have the strength and courage to stand up for what's right." Troxell idolizes Nancy for the same reasons, stating "all she had was herself and that was enough."

Writer, director, and prolific artist Nathan Thomas Milliner was being bullied when he discovered *A Nightmare on Elm Street*. In Freddy, he saw the ultimate bully, but he also saw hope. "There are two types of slasher fans: the type that identify with the killers (the aforementioned *Friday the 13th* and *Halloween*) and the type that identifies with the teenage heroes like in *Nightmare on Elm Street*." Milliner was definitely the latter. "I knew what I was getting when I went into a *Halloween* or *Friday the 13th* film, but I never knew what I was going to see when I went into a *Nightmare* film. They were so imaginative and creative. [*Dream Warriors*] was the first slasher film where the kids banded together to fight [Freddy] and the kids are iconic. You recognize Taryn or Kincaid just by their clothes or hair." One look at the posters he's made for most of the *Nightmare* films and see he includes the protagonists in every piece of art he does for the films. That's a rarity for artists trying to sell art based on the franchise, but he always does.

If there's anything people should take away from this book, it's the importance of the *Nightmare on Elm Street* films. My greatest wish is that when people talk about *Nightmare on Elm Street*, they talk about Wes Craven's groundbreaking concepts. About outcasts who found their power within themselves and stood up against a monster. About the craft of the filmmakers, the ever-evolving special effects and techniques that stand the test of time. About how, unlike other horror films, none of the films are ignored in the overall continuity. About how they all culminate in a complete story about parental failure. About how Nancy Thompson is the best final girl who ever did it, despite the fact that Jamie Lee Curtis is more of a movie star than Heather Langenkamp. About how Robert Englund used his classical training, body language, and twisted humor to define nightmares for a generation.

Over forty years ago, when Wes Craven created *A Nightmare on Elm Street*, he couldn't have imagined the impact that he, Freddy Krueger, and Nancy Thompson would have on the world. One that permeated our imaginations for decades, while scaring us senseless. Ten years later, he made *New Nightmare* to re-establish the paradigm and make sure the story stayed fresh. It's been fourteen years since the last *Nightmare on Elm Street* film, and it's clear, once again, that Craven was ahead of the curve. We have to talk about *Nightmare on Elm Street* to keep the dream alive.

Lowell Greenblatt
May 16, 2025

# Acknowledgements

This book would not have been possible with the support of so many people I have to thank. First off, my editor, Dustin McNeill, who took a chance on a first-time author. Seeing my name next to Harker Press silhouettes still hasn't driven home the fact that I'm in excellent company, but I'll get there someday.

My siblings Andrea, Larry and Robyn, for their lifelong love, support, and trips to various movie theaters and video stores.

Matthew Orozco, my friend, podcast co-host, and editor at *Macabre Daily* for your consistent support. I'm not just talking about the endless stickers. Also, I need more stickers…

My fellow authors Ariel Powers-Schaub and Scout Tafoya for fielding my myriad questions and inspiring me with their intrepid prose. I'm not sure I qualify as a peer, but together, I consider you my very own Lester Bangs. If he took the Substance. And Tony Todoroff for the simply fantastic cover art.

James Weiss, Jonathan Gray, and Hilary Cato Stabb Gray, for their lawyerly guidance and advice.

Stephanie Gajeski, Alexandria Imperato, Kimberly Leszak, Matthieu Dupee, Robert P. Ottone, Adam Green, and Felissa Rose for gassing me up. Chris and Bridget Douglas, for letting me crash at their lovely house between conventions.

The wonderful folks at the Brooklyn Horror Society, Necromantic Brew Co., The Twisted Spine bookstore, and Strange Love Parlor for fostering a horror community that enriched my writing.

Ron Demaio, founder of the Student Television Arts Company (STAC) of Herricks High School, for teaching me all about film: what it can do and what I could do with it. Rob Gioia for inviting me back to share it with the next generation. The kids are alright with you in charge.

Gina Rugolo Judd, Danny Hassel, Shannon Quinn, Michael Melamedoff, Lito Velasco, Karl Custer, Jr., Nathan Thomas Milliner, Shane Cappuccio, Amanda Taraska, Paul Tremblay, and every single person who was interviewed for this book.

To the other pillars of *Nightmare on Elm Street*: Rachel Talalay, Robert Englund, and Robert Shaye.

Finally, to Annette Benson, for her priceless contributions to this book and the films it covers.

# In Memoriam

The author wishes to acknowledge the following individuals for their contributions to the series. May we never forget those who gave us so much to remember through their art.

Wes Craven

C.J. Strawn

Jacques Haitkin

The author would also like to honor the memory of Hanna Pitter, who sparkled plenty.

# About the Author

Lowell Greenblatt was that kid at sleepovers who wanted you to rewind so he could see how the effects were accomplished. This has led to a fruitful career writing reviews and conducting interviews for *Macabre Daily*. Lowell is a human IMDB with a B.F.A. in Dramatic Writing from SUNY Purchase, who sustains himself on iced coffee and physical media. He resides in Queens, N.Y. with his wife Brittany, and their dogs, Merlin and Phantom.

# YOUR SOURCE FOR ALL THINGS SPOOKY!

# WWW.MACABREDAILY.COM

 @MACBAREDAILY    @MACBAREDAILYYT